KATHARINA VON WERZ

KATHARINA VON WERZ

Herausgeberin und Autorin
Editor and Author

Eva Karcher

DISTANZ

»Kreativität entsteht aus dem Machen, nicht aus dem Nichts.«

Katharina von Werz

Unzeitgemäß? Das 20. Jahrhundert gierte fortschrittsversessen nach Trends, neuen Stilen und Sensationen. Seit der Jahrtausendwende jedoch wird mit oder trotz der zunehmenden Allgegenwart des Internets als globalem Kommunikationsmittel eine Zäsur von elementar bewusstseinsverändernder Wirkung immer deutlicher.

Das Unzeitgemäße ist das neue Zeitgemäße. Denn alle kulturell-ästhetischen Wertmaßstäbe, durch die sich unsere Weltgesellschaft definiert, stehen gewissermaßen Kopf. Alter und Nachhaltigkeit gelten als neue Jugend, Handwerk und Tradition als neue Tugend – und Einzelkämpfer, Außenseiter, Solitäre als neue Leitfiguren.

Auch in der Kunst erhält heute die aufmerksamste Beachtung, wer sich über Jahrzehnte außerhalb der herrschenden Strömungen des Mainstreams zu behaupten wusste – allen voran Frauen, Pionierkünstlerinnen wie Maria Lassnig, Yayoi Kusama oder Yoko Ono, deren Werke nun endlich die ihnen gebührende Anerkennung erfahren.

Eine dieser Einzelgängerinnen ist die Malerin und Bildhauerin Katharina von Werz. Seit Anfang der 70er Jahre entwickelt und entfaltet sie eine faszinierend vielschichtige, unverwechselbare visuelle Formensprache. Naturbeobachtungen wie zahllose Wahrnehmungen von Sinneseindrücken sind Ausgangspunkt für einen kreativen Prozess, innerhalb dessen das jeweilige Motiv allmählich in ein »inneres Bild«, so die Künstlerin, transformiert wird.

Dieser experimentelle Prozess, in dessen Verlauf sich Formen und Farben ständig verwandeln, sich trennen und verbinden, aufeinanderprallen und miteinander verschmelzen, verschwinden und wieder entstehen, ist der Existenzkern der manchmal explosiv dynamischen, dann wieder sanft schwingenden Gemälde und Skulpturen: »Ich versuche, über den Gegenstand hinaus durch absichtslose Umwege – einen rissigen Farbauftrag, Spritzer, ein kritzeliges Liniengeflecht – eine aus dem gelenkt Zufälligen entstehende Bildwirklichkeit zu (er)finden.«

Was Katharina von Werz mit ihrer Kunst sichtbar macht, ist Bewegung als Idee und Lebensenergie, in die Vergänglichkeit eingeschlossen ist als Voraussetzung für Vitalität. Ewige Erneuerung in jedem Augenblick, Dauer in jeder Sekunde.

"Creativity arises from doing and making things, not from nothing."
Katharina von Werz

Anachronistic? Hell-bent on progress, the 20th century craves trends, new styles, and sensations. Since the start of the new millennium however, with (or perhaps in spite of) the increasing ubiquity of the Internet as a global communication tool, it has become increasingly clear that a radical break has occurred in the way we think of and perceive the world. The anachronistic has become the new new. All cultural and aesthetic norms by which our global society defines itself have been turned, to a certain extent, on their head. Age and longevity are seen as the new youth, craftwork and tradition the new virtues, and nonconformists, outsiders, individuals outside the mainstream the new heroes.

In art too, the highest regard is afforded to those figures who have managed to assert themselves outside the prevailing trends of their time, and have done so for decades and decades. This is particularly true of female artists, pioneers in their fields, the Maria Lassnigs, Yayoi Kusamas, and Yoko Onos of this world, whose works are now finally receiving the recognition they have long deserved.

One such individualist is the painter and sculptor Katharina von Werz. Since the early 1970s she has developed and evolved a fascinatingly diverse and unmistakable language of forms. Observations of nature, combined with sensory perception of every kind form the basis of a creative process, in which, in the words of the artist, the subject is gradually transformed into "an inner picture."

This experimental process sees forms and colors constantly mutate, fracture, and combine, collide with and melt into one another, disappear, and reemerge. It is this process that constitutes the vital spark inherent in the artist's paintings and sculptures which oscillate from being violently dynamic to gracefully fluid. "I try to create a visual reality that evolves through half-controlled chance and that starts with the object but then goes beyond it, by taking various random diversionary paths—chapped brushwork, a squirt of paint, a scrawled web of lines."

What Katharina von Werz makes visible with her art is movement as an idea and as a vital force that includes transience as a precondition for animation: eternal renewal in every moment, endurance in every second.

»Das Geheimnis ist, sich immer wieder selbst zu überraschen.«

Katharina von Werz, 2012

Es ist sieben Uhr dreißig. Wie fast jeden Tag öffnet eine Frau die Haustür einer Münchner Villa. In weinrotem Pullover und schwarzem Rock, an den Füßen flache Spangenschuhe, läuft sie federnd über einen schmalen Steinweg zur Eingangspforte. Die Kaffeetasse in der Hand, winkt sie einem Jungen strahlend zu, der auf der Straße auf sie zukommt. Er grinst: »Hallo, Boppi, muss mich beeilen.«

Katharina von Werz, von allen Boppi genannt, liebt solche kleinen Rituale. »Mein Enkel«, sagt sie, »ist mein Guten-Morgen-Bote. Danach fällt es mir leichter, an die Staffelei zu gehen«. Glockenhelles Lachen, schelmischer Blick. Die Künstlerin ist eine jener Frauen, die jugendlich, beinahe mädchenhaft wirken, alterslos charmant und seit ihren Dreißigern mit der gleichen zierlichen Figur. Im Erdgeschoss des vom Architekten Alois Ludwig 1910 gebauten Familienhauses liegt ihr Atelier, doch eigentlich dehnt es sich über zwei weitere, ineinander übergehende Räume bis in den Garten hin aus. Ganz hinten bewahrt sie in einem kleinen, von Grün umrankten Pavillon Werkzeuge, Ton und Gips auf, und manchmal formt sie hier auch ihre Skulpturen.

Als Bilderdepot für die eigenen Gemälde nutzt sie das Zimmer im linken Flügel. In Reihen stehen die Werke voreinander, werden Besuchern präsentiert und je nach Stimmung und Arbeitsphase immer wieder neu arrangiert. An einer rückwärtigen Glaswand reihen sich auf schmalen Simsen skurrile Fundstücke und Sammelobjekte aneinander, kleine afrikanische Figuren neben dem Backenzahn eines Mammuts, ein indischer Ganesha neben einem gestrickten Strumpf oder ein Mohammed aus Zucker – Andenken eines Fests in Marokko.

Der unwiderstehliche Boheme-Mix aus Kunst und Folklore, historischen Objekten, Souvenirs und Haushaltskram setzt sich auch im zentralen Salon mit seinen hohen, lichtdurchfluteten Erkerfenstern und einer filigranen Sitzgruppe des Wiener Werkstätten-Mitbegründers Josef Hoffmann fort. Hier mischen sich auf den Fensterbänken kleine Plastiken der Künstlerin mit Kakteen und anderen Topfpflanzen, hängen Werke von so unterschiedlichen Malern wie Jean Hélion, Rupprecht Geiger oder Richard Pousette-Dart an der Wand und maßgefertigte segelartige Leuchtschirme des befreundeten Lampendesigners Jan Roth von der Decke.

Den Übergang zum Atelier im rechten Flügel bewacht ein vom Bildhauer Franz Weickmann geschnitzter Löwe aus Holz. Hier, im Laboratorium der Künstlerin, türmen und stapeln sich rings um die Staffelei Bilder und Bücher, Notizblöcke und Skizzenmappen. In der hintersten linken Ecke sind über einem kleinen Schreibtisch Zeitungsausschnitte, Skizzen und Fotos an eine Wand gepinnt. Sie zeigen die Skyline von New York, fliegende Tauben und einen Filmkuss von Liz Taylor und Richard Burton: Animationssplitter, emotionale Bausteine eines sich immer wieder neu zusammenfügenden Mosaiks aus Leben und Kunst.

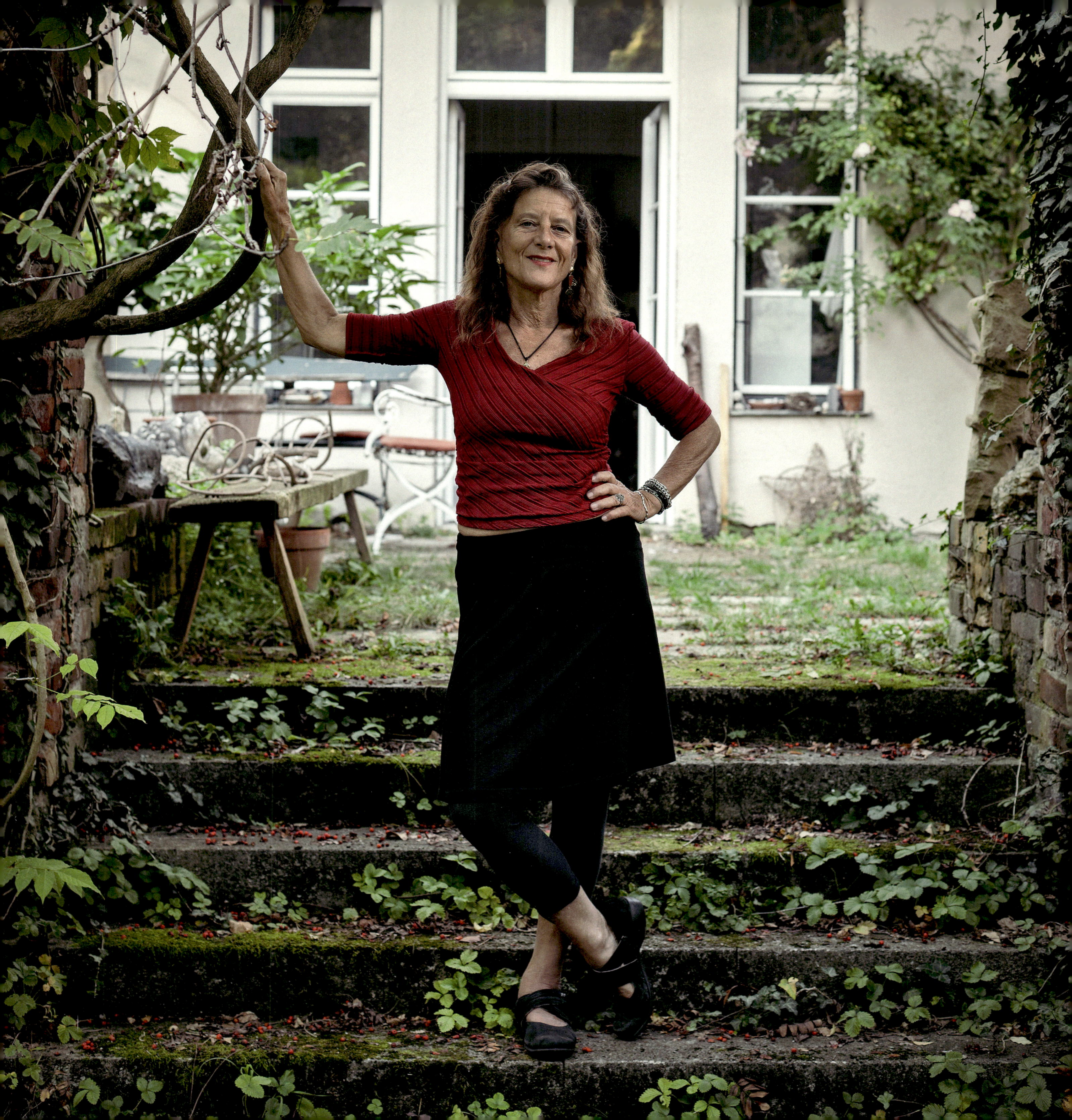

Katharina, brauchst Du das kreative Chaos im Atelier?

Es scheint so – hier ein angefangenes Bild, dort eine unfertige Tonfigur, da die Farbpalette, hinten auf einem Tisch die Pinsel und mitten im Raum die Staffelei. Dazwischen laufe ich hin und her. Es ist meine Art, mich zu stimulieren, wenn ich mich mit all diesen Utensilien, den unfertigen Arbeiten und früheren Studien umgebe. Kein Künstler beginnt ja bei Null. Jeder braucht seine Rituale.

Welche sind Deine?

Ich stehe um sieben, spätestens halb acht Uhr auf. Als erstes brauche ich einen Kaffee. Mit der Tasse gehe ich gegen halb neun in mein Studio und nähere mich den Arbeiten vom Vortag. Wenn der Funke nicht sofort zündet, krame ich in meinen Beständen, arrangiere die Farben neu oder blättere mich durch Bücher von Künstlern hindurch, die ich schätze – Alfred Kubin zum Beispiel, oder Tizian. Wenn auch das nicht hilft, gehe ich in die Küche, koche noch einmal Kaffee, trinke ihn langsam und sage mir dabei immer wieder leise vor: »Gleich geht's los.« Mein ultimativer Trick ist übrigens Abzeichnen. Aber der beste Rat bleibt der von Picasso: »Einfach anfangen.«

Wenn es so einfach wäre! Wann weißt Du, dass ein Gemälde gelungen ist?

Wenn ich merke, es folgt kein nächster Schritt mehr. Ich bin keine Konzeptmalerin, die eine Idee umsetzt. Bei mir geht es um den Prozess, um das Erleben der eigenen Sinne. Ich gehe von einer sehr ungefähren Vorstellung aus und versuche, mich diesem inneren Bild, das ich nur ahne, anzunähern. Wenn es gelingt, ist es wie ein Rausch. Und wenn dazu noch die Sonne scheint, wirkt es, als ob die Bilder doppelt aufgewacht sind. Dann begeistere ich mich an mir selbst, das ist das Allerbeste! Leider dauert so eine Euphorie immer nur Augenblicke.

Und dann?

Beginnt das Ringen von Neuem. Ich gerate ins Stocken oder lasse mich ablenken … Wenn ich überhaupt nicht weiterkomme, stelle ich das Bild weg und vergesse es. Zwei, drei Wochen später hole ich es dann wieder hervor, fange noch einmal von vorne an und male es bis zu dem Punkt, an dem ich aufgehört habe. Mit etwas Glück führt es mich dann ganz woanders hin. Es gibt viele Anfänge bei mir, die in die unerwartetsten Richtungen führen können. Selten passiert es allerdings, dass ich die ursprüngliche Inspiration überhaupt nicht mehr nachvollziehen kann. Dann habe ich das Werk verloren und vernichte es.

Ist das ein Grund für Dich, in ein Tief zu geraten?

Nein. Ich habe gelernt, Anfällen von Depression gegenzusteuern. Was mir dabei hilft, ist die Disziplin der Kreativität. Kreativität entsteht aus dem Tun, aus dem Machen, nicht aus dem Nichts. Seine Geistesblitze muss man lange umgarnen. Manchmal gerate ich in eine manische Phase, und alles wird für eine Zeitlang leicht und fließend. Das ist dann ein wunderbares Hochgefühl, das mich für flaue Zeiten entschädigt.

Was ist entscheidend bei Deinem Malprozess?

Am wichtigsten ist, dass das Bild stark genug ist, um mein Taktieren zu überleben. Es mag eigenartig klingen, aber es ist oft ein Kampf. Einerseits ist da ein Gegenstand, von dem ich ausgehe. Aber ich will ihn nicht

I

IN THE STUDIO

"The secret is to always surprise yourself."

It is seven-thirty. Just as on almost any day, a woman opens the door to a villa in Munich. In a burgundy pullover and black skirt and wearing flat-heeled Mary Jane shoes, she walks with a spring in her step down a narrow stone path to the gates. With a coffee cup in one hand, she waves with the other to a boy coming along the street, all the while smiling broadly. He smiles back and greets her: "Hello Boppi, got to hurry."

Katharina von Werz, known by nearly everyone as Boppi, loves life's little rituals such as this. "My grandson," she says, "is my 'good morning messenger.' Seeing him somehow makes it easier to face the easel." A peal of laughter and a mischievous look. The artist is one of those women who appear youthful, near girlish even, agelessly charming; one of those women who has managed to keep the same slight figure since her thirties. Officially, her studio takes up just one room situated on the ground floor of her family home, built in 1910 by the architect Alois Ludwig. But in reality her studio sprawls out into two other rooms that merge into each other, and as a result it extends all the way to the garden. At the end of the garden in a small pavilion covered in creeping plants, she keeps her tools, clay, and plaster, and it is here that she sometimes makes her sculptures.

The room in the left wing is used to store her own paintings. The works are stacked in rows and are shown to visitors here. They are pulled out and reshuffled again and again, depending on the mood or stage of work von Werz is currently in. On narrow ledges that run along a glass wall at the back are row upon row of strange and wonderful objects the artist came across in her travels, on display alongside other collector's items: miniature African figures beside the molar tooth of a woolly mammoth, an Indian figurine of Ganesha next to a knitted stocking and a figure of Mohammed in sugar—a souvenir from a celebration in Morocco.

The irresistible, bohemian mix of art and folklore, historical artifacts, souvenirs, and household objects is continued in the main lounge with its tall bay-windows awash in light and graceful table and chairs designed by Josef Hoffmann, co-founder of the Wiener Werkstätte. The window sills hold small sculptural pieces by the artist that stand beside cacti and other houseplants; on the walls hang works by such diverse artists as Jean Hélion, Rupprecht Geiger, and Richard Pousette-Dart, while custom-made, sail-like light fittings by the lamp designer Jan Roth—a personal friend—hang from the ceiling.

The passage to the studio in the house's right wing is guarded by a carved wooden lion, the work of sculptor Franz Weickmann. It is here, in the artist's "lab" where she experiments with ideas and techniques, that pictures and books, notebooks, and various portfolios of sketches are stacked high around the easels. In the left-hand corner scores of newspaper clippings, sketches, and photos are pinned to the wall above a small desk. They variously depict the New York skyline, flying pigeons, and a screen kiss of Elizabeth Taylor and Richard Burton: freeze-frame fragments, emotional building blocks that merge to form a constantly morphing mosaic of life and art.

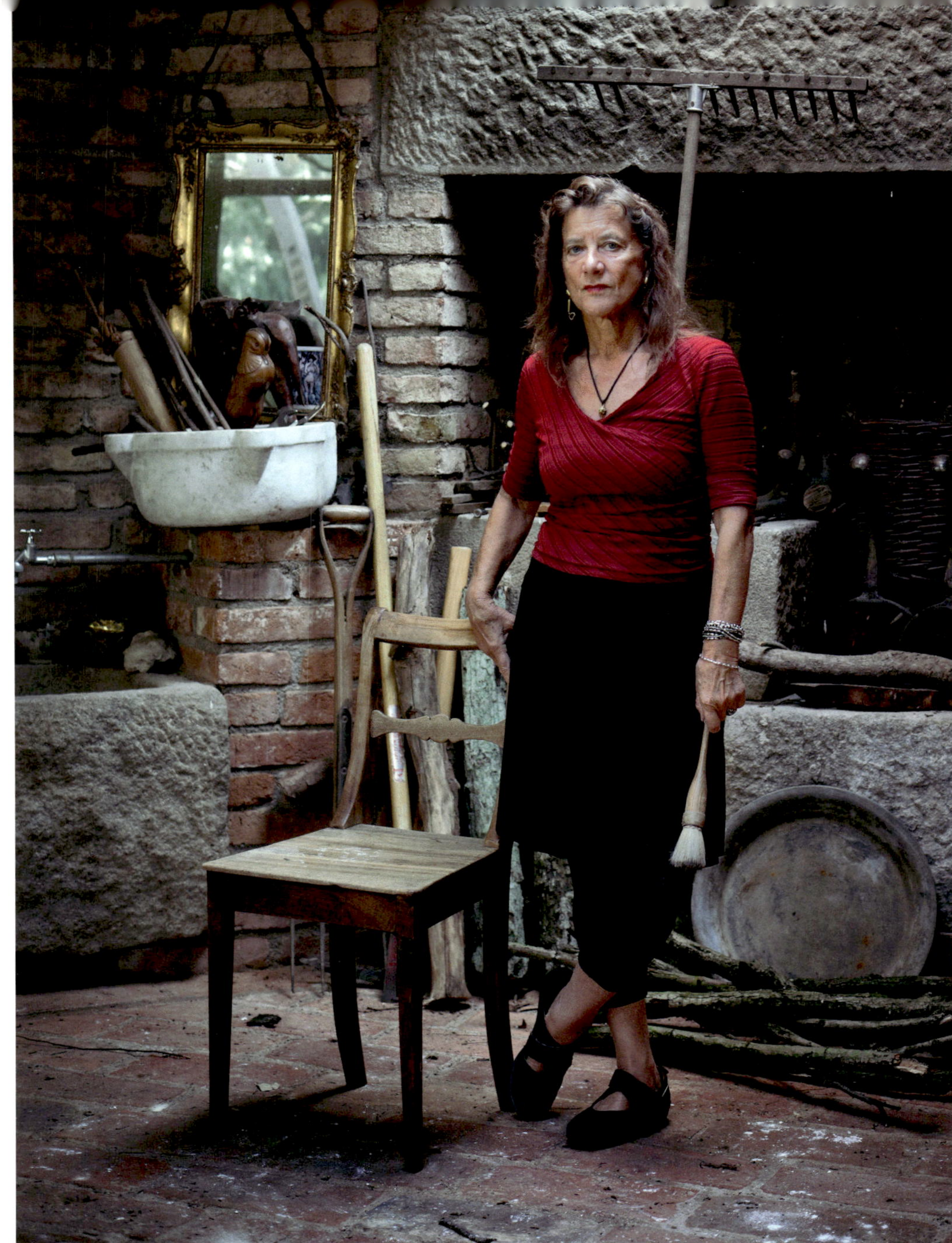

Katharina von Werz im Werkstatt-Atelier / in her studio

als solchen zeigen, sondern ihn transformieren. Wobei er sich aber auch nicht in Abstraktion auflösen darf. Sondern er muss dazwischen bleiben. Das Geheimnis ist, sich immer wieder selbst zu überraschen.

Am Anfang war es mein Garten. Mein Mann Franz und ich lassen ihn wachsen, wie er will. Alles wuchert wild – Bäume, Sträucher, Hecken, Blumen, Kräuter, Gräser. Manchmal komme ich mir in meinem Atelier vor wie im Aquarium, so, als ob ich unter Wasser malen würde. Es ist alles so grün! Inzwischen arbeite ich oft in der Natur, im Sommer am Meer auf Korsika und im Frühling am Chiemsee. Es gibt viele Landschaften in meinem Werk. Seit über zwanzig Jahren konzentriere ich mich jedoch auf Figuren. Früher waren sie verbannt, weil ich mich an sie nicht heranwagte.

Warum das?

An der Akademie in Genf habe ich zwar viel Akt gezeichnet ... Aber nach einem Modell zu porträtieren, dazu war und bin ich zu scheu. Es ist ja eine sehr intime Situation, weil das Innere mitmalt. Nie könnte ich wie Frank Auerbach, den ich verehre, jeden Tag einem Modell gegenübersitzen! Dabei fällt mir ein Foto ein, das vor einiger Zeit in der Süddeutschen Zeitung abgedruckt war. Es zeigt eine Äffin, ein Mandrillweibchen, das sich eine Hand vor die Augen hält – ganz klar eine Bitte-nicht-stören-Geste, wie der Evolutionsbiologe Mark Laidre herausfand. Wobei das raffinierte Tier die Augen nicht geschlossen hat, sondern ab und zu durch die leicht geöffneten Finger hindurchspäht, um herauszufinden, was sich um sie herum abspielt.

Klingt lustig!

Ist es auch. Als ich das Bild sah, dachte ich, genau das ist die Haltung, in der es mir selbst am ehesten gelingen würde, jemanden zu porträtieren. Indem ich so tue, als ob ich ihn nicht anschaue oder höchstens aus den Augenwinkeln ... Zum Lachen, oder? Finde ich auch. Aber eigentlich ist mein Interesse nicht das Porträt. Es geht mir um eine bestimmte Stimmung, die meine innere Wahrheit spiegelt.

Das Sujet als Vorwand?

In gewisser Weise, ja. Aus meiner Frühphase gibt es mehrere Selbstporträts, alle eher statisch, meine Versuche, mich an die Figur heranzutasten. Inzwischen experimentiere ich viel freier. Allmählich hat sich herauskristallisiert, dass ich zentral Bewegung darstellen will. Die Bewegung von Körpern. Körperlichkeit interessiert mich total, deshalb arbeite ich seit zehn Jahren auch plastisch.

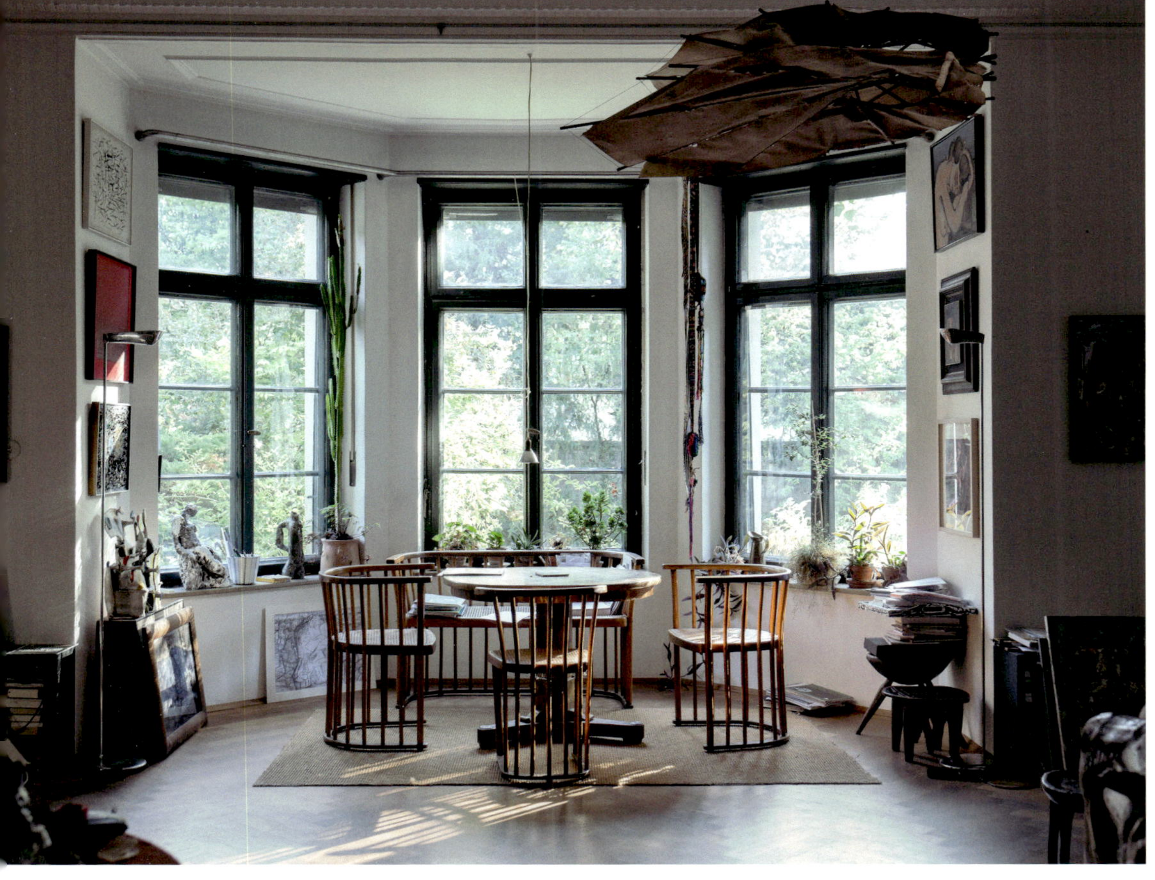

Salon mit Sitzgruppe von Josef Hoffmann und
einem Lampenschirm-Objekt von Jan Roth
Living room with table and chairs designed
by Josef Hoffmann and lampshade object by
Jan Roth

Katharina, would you say you need creative chaos in the studio?

It looks like it—over here's a canvas I've started on, over there an unfinished clay figure, over there the palette, on a table at the back the brushes, and in the middle of the room: the easel. And then there's me, walking back and forth in between it all. It's my way of stimulating myself, by surrounding myself with all these utensils, the unfinished works and earlier studies. No artist starts from scratch. Everyone needs their little rituals.

What are yours?

I get up at seven, by half-eight at the latest. The first thing I need is a coffee. I take the cup with me into my studio at around half-past eight and take a look at the work from the day before. If I don't feel a spark kindle straight away, then I start rummaging through the piles of studies and unfinished work, or I'll rearrange the colors or leaf through books by artists that I admire—Alfred Kubin for example or Titian. And if that doesn't help then I go into the kitchen, make myself another cup of coffee, drink it slowly and say to myself quietly again and again: "It'll happen in a second." Incidentally, for me the ultimate trick is to draw the outlines of something. But really Picasso had the best piece of advice: "Just start."

If only it was that easy! When do you know a painting's a success?

When I see there is nothing left to do on it, that there's no "next step." I am not a concept painter who translates an idea to the canvas. My work is all about the process, the experience of my own senses. I start off with just an inkling of an idea and then attempt to feel my way towards this inner image, of which I have only the vaguest sense. When I pull it off, it's intoxicating. And if on top of that the sun is shining, it's as if the images have come to life even more. When that happens I feel ecstatic about myself, nothing beats it. Sadly, such a sense of euphoria lasts just a matter of seconds.

And what happens then?

That's when the struggle starts over afresh. Everything comes to a standstill or I get distracted … If I end up not making any headway at all, I put the picture away and forget it. Two or three weeks later I pull it out again, start all over afresh and paint it up to the point where I left off. With a little luck, it'll take me off in a different direction completely this time. In my work I experience many starts that can end up leading me in the most unexpected directions. What seldom happens however, is that I lose sight of the original inspiration completely. If that happens then I give the work up as lost and destroy it.

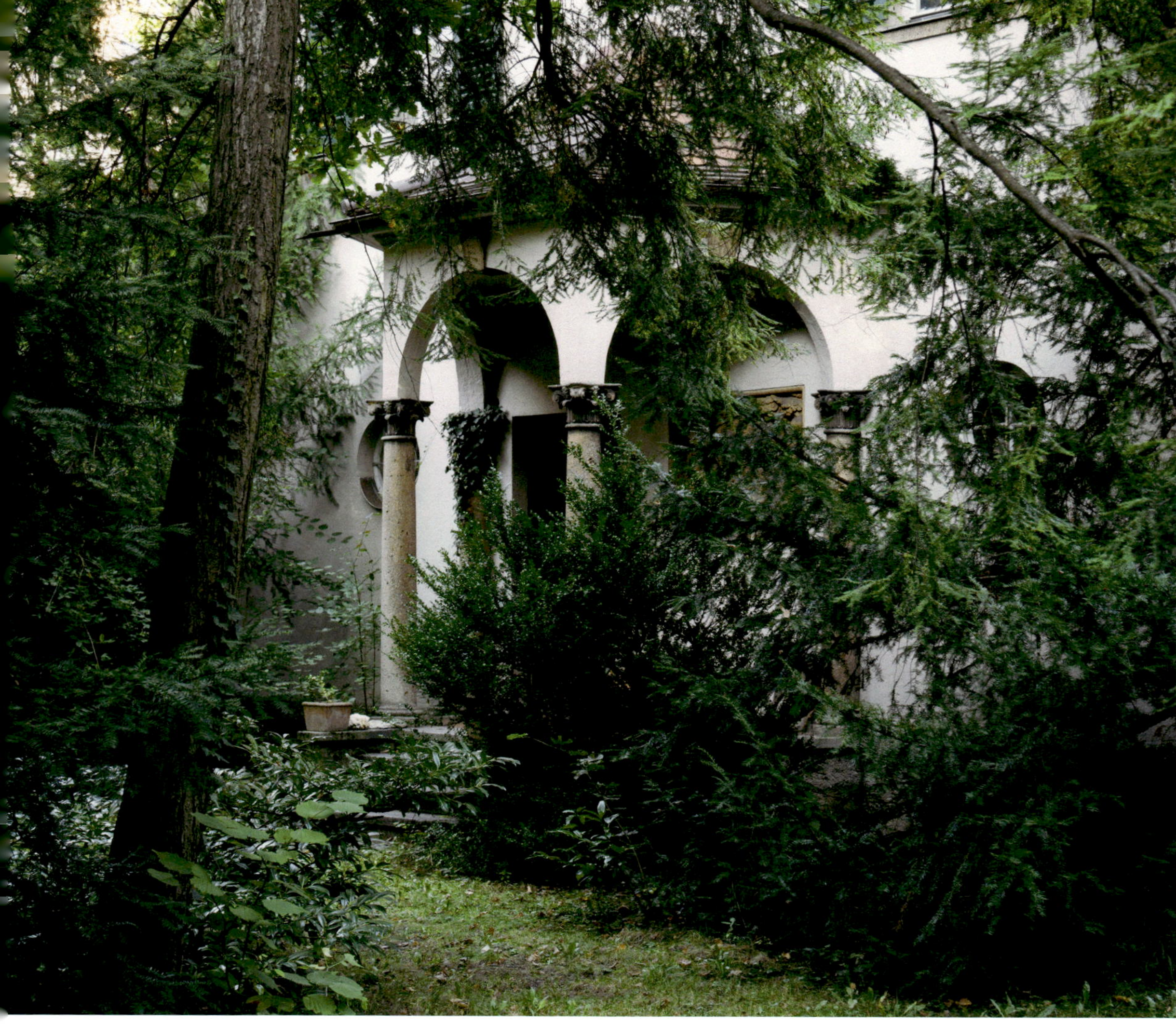

Die meisten aus Terrakotta, aus Ton. Es ist der ideale Stoff für mich, denn ich kann ihn formen und deformieren. Ton ermöglicht mir ein weiches Modellieren, vergleichbar mit dem Malen. Das Material spielen zu lassen und mit ihm zu spielen, ist sehr befriedigend. Die Reste verwende ich übrigens weiter. Ich bin fasziniert von diesen Klumpen, sie regen meine Vorstellungskraft an. Manche Figuren bleiben roh, manche besprenkle ich mit Farbe, mit pointillistischen Tupfern, und glasiere sie am Ende.

Oh ja, es gibt einige Künstler, auf die ich mich in meiner Arbeit beziehe. Auerbachs Freund Leon Kossoff ist einer von ihnen, auch Francis Bacon, der wie die beiden zur School of London der figurativen Maler nach dem Zweiten Weltkrieg zählt. Außerdem fühle ich mich Willem de Kooning, William Turner, Jan Vermeer, Eugène Leroy und Giorgio Morandi künstlerisch verwandt. Und Marc Chagall. Ich finde ihn sehr gut, er kann ja nichts dafür, dass seine Werke so oft auf Postkarten gedruckt wurden, bis man sie als Kitsch missverstand. Wenn ich darüber nachdenke, besitzen diese Künstler alle eine ähnliche Qualität: Sie schaffen entrückte, traumverlorene Räume, wie mit einem Schleier überhaucht ... Vielleicht auch ein wenig surreal und magisch. Das ist die Sphäre, die ich suche: in der Schwebe bleiben.

Nein, oder nur indirekt. Ein Beispiel ist das Genrebild *Die verkehrte Welt*, das der holländische Meister Jan Steen um 1663 malte. Es spielt in einem Bordell, die Sitten sind lose, aber das hat mich nicht vorrangig interessiert. Sondern die Dynamik zwischen der männlichen und der weiblichen Figur im Vordergrund. Wie er seinen Unterschenkel über ihr Knie streckt und sie sein Bein mit ihrer Hand berührt. Das Spannungsgeladene dieser Komposition. Oder *Venus und Adonis* von Tizian, ein Werk, das er um 1554 malte. Es ist so sinnlich! Die nackte Venus versucht ihren Geliebten Adonis davon abzuhalten, auf die Jagd zu gehen – vergeblich. Er wird dabei getötet. Wieder ist es die Interaktion dieses Paars, der ich nicht wiederstehen konnte. Es sind sehr oft die intimen Rhythmen zwischen Paaren, die ich in meinen Serien variiere. Der Tanz ihrer Körper.

Ja, auch. Was ist Erotik? Für mich ist sie vor allem mit Sehnsucht verbunden, einer Sehnsucht, die nicht unbedingt nach Verwirklichung strebt. Das Gegenteil jedenfalls von »I only shave my legs, if I'm going to have sex ...«, ein Satz, den ich in einem Restaurant am Nachbartisch aufgeschnappt habe – für mich das totale Gegenteil von Erotik!

Does that put you in a trough?

No. I have learned how to steer clear of succumbing to depressions. What helps me is the discipline of creativity. Creativity arises from doing and making things, not from nothing. You have to spend a long time teasing out its flashes of inspiration. Sometimes I find myself in a manic phase, and everything runs smoothly for a while. Those periods are wonderfully exhilarating, they make up for the sluggish times.

What is the decisive factor in your painterly process?

The most important thing is that the image is strong enough to survive my tinkering with it. It may sound a little strange, but it is often a struggle. On the one side there is an object, the thing I start with. But I don't want to present it as such, and instead my aim is to transform it. But at the same time it can't dissolve into abstraction. It has to remain somewhere in between. The secret is to always surprise yourself.

Which subjects recur frequently in your work?

In the beginning it was my garden. My husband Franz and I leave it to grow as it pleases. Everything grows wild—the trees, shrubs, hedges, flowers, herbs, grasses. There are times when I look out of my studio and feel like I'm in an aquarium, as if I were painting under water. Everything is so green! I now work in nature quite often, in summer on the coast of Corsica or in spring on the shores of Chiemsee. There are many landscapes in my work. For more than twenty years now, however, I have concentrated mostly on figures. When I first started off they were banished from my canvases because I lacked the courage to paint them.

Why's that?

At the academy in Geneva I did draw a lot of nudes ... But to portray a life model: I was always too shy for that, and I still am. It's a very intimate situation, because the inner you is also present in the act of painting. I could never sit opposite a model day in, day out, like Frank Auerbach, who I admire greatly! It reminds me of a photo that was printed a while ago in *Die Süddeutsche Zeitung*. It depicted a female monkey, a mandrill, holding one hand over its eyes—in a gesture that quite clearly said "please do not disturb," as the evolutionary biologist Mark Laidre established. The clever animal did not shut its eyes, but would peek every now and again through its lightly opened fingers to see what was going on around it.

Sounds funny!

It is. When I saw the picture, I thought that is precisely the position in which I would most likely be able to portray someone from life. If I were to act as though I wasn't looking at him, or at the most only out of the corner of my eye ... Ridiculous, isn't it? I certainly think so at any rate. But actually my interest lies somewhere other than the portrait. I am interested in a certain mood that reflects my inner reality.

The subject as a pretext?

To a certain extent, yes. There are several self-portraits from my early phase, all tend to be static: my attempts at approaching the figure. Nowadays I can experiment much more freely. Gradually over time the idea emerged that what I essentially want to depict is movement. The movement of bodies. I am totally interested in corporeality, which is why for about ten years now I have also been working in the plastic arts.

Indirekt, denn ich war sehr klein, als sie schon alt waren. Mein Großvater Max war ein sehr guter, kultivierter Maler, der aber Mühe hatte, den ganzen akademischen Kram über Bord zu werfen. Im Kern blieb er bürgerlich. Ein gediegener Salonkünstler, kein Erneuerer wie Franz Marc, mit dem er übrigens in derselben Malklasse war. Meine Großmutter Cateau stammte aus einer holländischen Familie, doch als sie Max heiratete, gab sie die Malerei bald auf.

Hmm … Im Vergleich zu meinem älteren Bruder Dieter, der als wissenschaftliches Genie galt, war mir tatsächlich die Rolle der Künstlerin zugeteilt. Aber ich hätte auch Tänzerin werden können oder Volksschauspielerin. Die Entscheidung für die Malerei habe ich nach der Schule getroffen. Immerhin bin ich mit Bildern aufgewachsen und wahrscheinlich hat sich allmählich doch irgendwie die familiäre Vorbelastung durchgesetzt, subversiv, aus dem Unterbewusstsein.

Für mich ist das Leben ein Ganzes. Ich hätte weder auf meine Familie noch auf meine Kunst verzichten können. Also versuchte ich, beides miteinander zu verbinden, und im Großen und Ganzen ist es mir gelungen.

Ja, vor allem wenn ich an unsere Maskenfeste denke. Karneval und Fasching sind seit Generationen sehr wichtig bei uns. Vor allem mein Vater, eigentlich Architekt, war ein Verkleidungsvirtuose. Sogar an unseren Geburtstagen verkleideten wir uns für unsere Freunde. Mein Vater trat dann gerne in den verrücktesten Kostümen auf, einmal zum Beispiel als russischer Lotse in einem alten Pelzmantel. Als er ihn öffnete, steckten in den Innentaschen lauter typische Souvenirs, diese Puppen, Matrjoschkas und anderes Spielzeug. Er hatte ein großartiges Talent für's Absurde!

Ja, und uns vor allem vermittelte, wie wichtig Humor ist. Ich glaube, ohne Humor könnte ich nicht überleben. Er demaskiert, schützt vor Selbstüberschätzung und lässt andere Haltungen und Meinungen gelten. Er macht durchlässig für das Schicksal anderer und fähig zur Anteilnahme. Für mich ist er ein unverzichtbares Element von Kreativität.

Auch. Aber in der Kunst geht es mir um Schönheit. Ich bin fest davon überzeugt, dass es eine Urbedürfnis bei uns allen gibt, sich die Welt schön zu gestalten. Ich male, weil ich eine Schönheit brauche, die mich trägt.

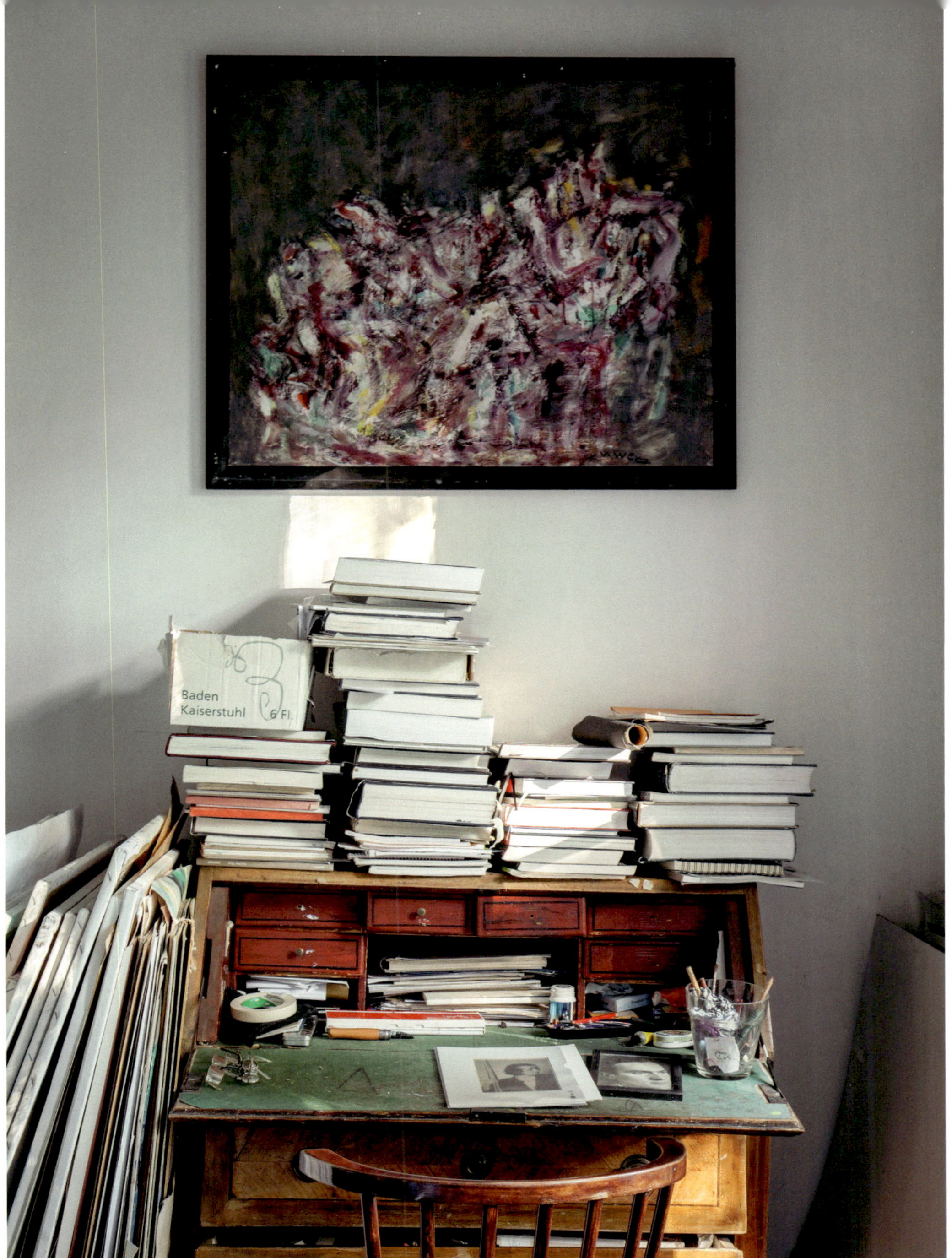

Sekretär im Atelier mit Arbeitsmaterial
und Gemälde der Künstlerin
Escritoire in artist's studio stacked with
material, painting by the artist

What materials do you use for your sculptures?

I use terracotta, clay, for the most of them. It really is the ideal material for me, as I can form and deform it. Clay allows me to model the figure softly, as compared to painting. The material plays with the form and I play with the material: it's very satisfying. Incidentally, I also use the left-over clay. I am fascinated by these lumps, they arouse my imagination. Some figures remain raw, while others I dot with paint, dabbing it on in a Pointillist manner, before finally glazing them.

You just mentioned Frank Auerbach as a role model you look up to. Are there any others?

Oh yes, there are several artists who I draw from in my work. Auerbach's friend Leon Kossoff is one of them, so too is Francis Bacon, who, like the other two, belonged to the London School of figurative painters after the Second World War. In addition to these painters, I feel an artistic affinity with Willem de Kooning, William Turner, Jan Vermeer, Eugène Leroy, and Giorgio Morandi. And Marc Chagall. I think he is really good; he can't help it if his works were reproduced on postcards so often that they became misunderstood as kitsch. Now that I come to think about it, these artists all possess a similar quality. They create abstracted, dream-like spaces that appear suspended beneath a veil … Perhaps they are also a little Surreal and magical. That is the realm I aim for in my pictures: maintaining a sense of suspension.

There are series of yours that make explicit reference to works by specific artists. You don't use them as a model though, do you?

No, or if so, then only indirectly. A good example is the genre painting, *Luxury Beware* by the Dutch master Jan Steen (painted around 1663). It is set in a brothel and is a depiction of lose morals, but that's not what interested me the most. What drew me to the painting was the dynamic between the male and female figures in the foreground. The way he stretches his thigh over her knee while she strokes his leg with her hand. This provides the suspense in this composition. Another example is *Venus and Adonis* by Titian (painted around 1554). It's just so sensual! The naked Venus tries to stop her lover Adonis from going to the hunt—in vain. He is slain during it. Again it was the interaction between this couple that I found absolutely irresistible. Very often my series are a variation on the intimate rhythms between couples. The dance of their bodies.

An erotic moment?

Yes, that too. But what is eroticism? For me it is most closely tied with longing, a longing that doesn't necessarily strive to be fulfilled. Whatever it is, it certainly isn't: "I only shave my legs if I know I'm going to have sex …" A remark that I overheard in a restaurant at a table beside mine—for me the exact opposite of eroticism!

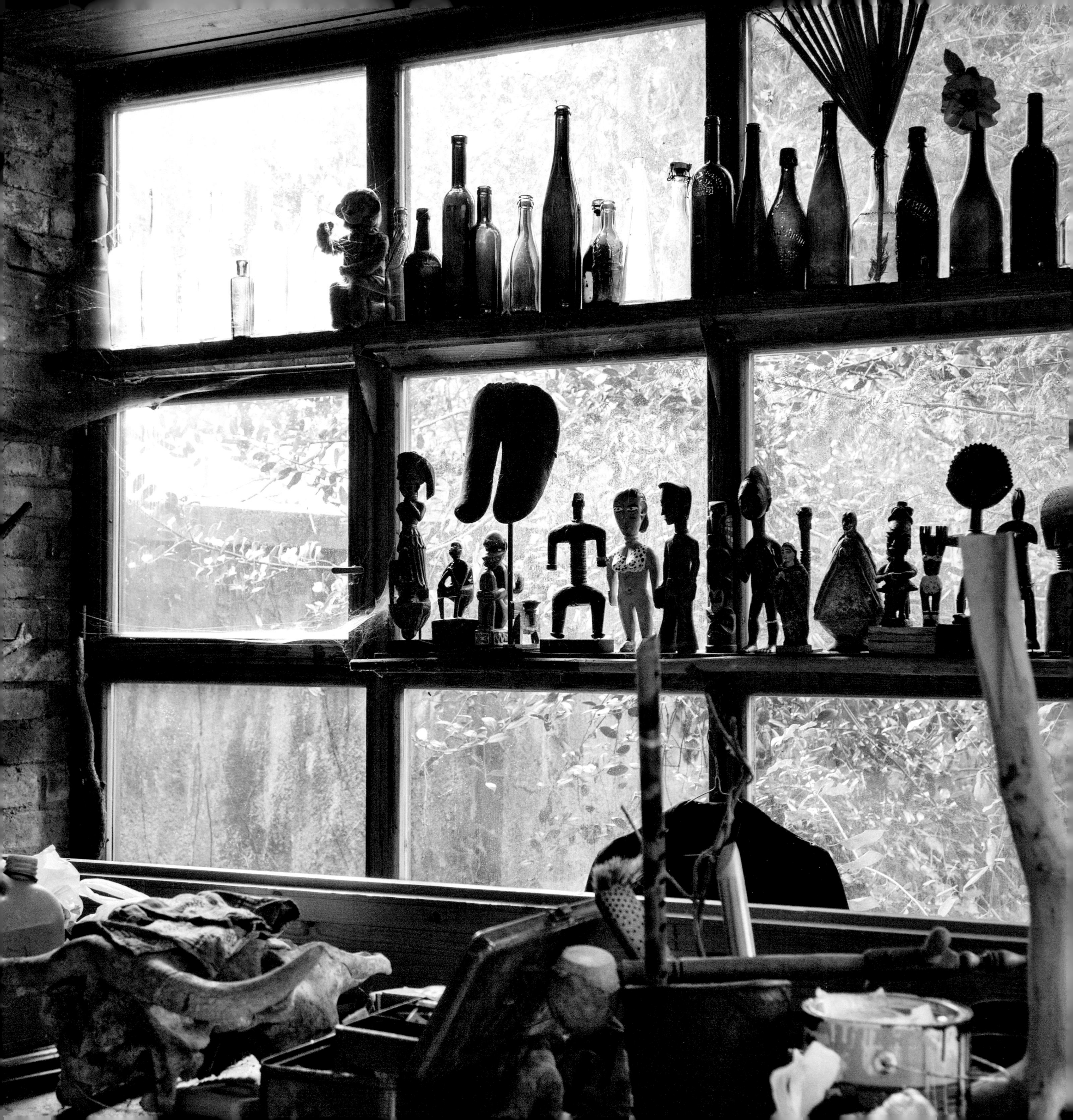

Both your grandmother and grandfather were painters. Have they influenced you in any way?

Indirectly, as they were already old when I was only very small. My grandfather, Max, was a very good, cultivated painter, but one who had difficulty throwing all the academic stuff overboard. When it came down to it, he was still quite bourgeois. A dignified salon artist, not an innovator like Franz Marc, who was in the same painting class as him by the way. My grandmother, Cateau, her family were Dutch originally. But she gave up painting soon after marrying Max.

When did you know that you wanted to become an artist?

Hmm … Compared to my older brother, Dieter, who everyone saw as a scientific genius, if the truth be told, I was assigned the role of artist. I could have also become a dancer or an actress. I decided to pursue painting after I had left school. That said, I grew up surrounded by pictures and this predisposition made itself felt eventually, subversively, through the subconscious.

Your studio is integrated into your house. How have you managed to combine family and painting, especially when your three children were infants?

For me life is a whole. I wouldn't have been able to sacrifice my family nor my art. Which is why I tried to combine the two, and overall I'd say I managed to pull it off.

The idea that life is a *Gesamtkunstwerk* was held by the bohemians of the turn of the last century. Artists who are currently enjoying something of a revival. Did the bohemian tradition also apply to you and your family?

Yes, especially when I think of our masquerades. Carnival has been very important to us for generations. My father especially was a master of disguise. He was an architect. We even got dressed up for our friends on our birthdays. My father loved appearing in the wildest costumes. Once for instance he dressed up as a Russian naval pilot, wearing an old fur coat. He opened it to reveal all the trappings associated with Russia, stuck in the inner pockets of the coat: dolls, matryoshkas, and other toys. He had such a great talent for the absurd!

Which he used to stimulate your imagination?

Yes, and which also gave us a sense of how important humor is. I don't think I would be able to live without humor. It unmasks, it protects us from hubris and gives space for other attitudes and opinions to coexist with ours. It makes us open to the fate of others and able to sympathize with them. For me it is an indispensable part of creativity.

And a part of your art?

That too. But what I really care about in art is beauty. I am convinced that there is a deep, instinctive need in all of us to make the world beautiful for ourselves. I paint because I need a form of beauty that can carry me.

»Ich bin sehr eingebettet in meine Familie. Mein Mann und
meine Kinder und deren Kinder beflügeln mein Dasein.«

Katharina von Werz in Saint-Tropez, 1980

Ihre erste Erinnerung? »Meine rosafarbenen und himmelblauen Farbstifte!« Katharina von Werz zögert
keine Sekunde. »Ich war ungefähr vier Jahre alt und habe diese Stifte gehütet wie einen Schatz. Ich nahm sie
überall hin mit, genauso wie einen weißen Muff aus Kaninchenfell, den mir meine Eltern damals zu Weihnach-
ten geschenkt hatten.« Die Zeiten waren karg, es herrschte Krieg. Um ihre kalten Füße aufzuwärmen, stapften
die Kinder im kalten Herbst manchmal sogar barfuß durch frische Kuhfladen.

Katharinas Mutter Fe, Ärztin, die in München bei Koryphäen wie Leo von Zumbusch studiert hatte,
dem Gründer der dermatologischen Klinik, war drei Jahre vor der Geburt der Tochter durch einen tragischen
Unfall ihres Mannes Günther Hepp Witwe geworden. Dieser, ein junger Chirurg mit glänzenden Karriereaus-
sichten, gehörte zu einer Gruppe prominenter Münchner Extrembergsteiger, deren Ehrgeiz es war, als erste
Alpinisten einen Achttausender zu bezwingen. Häufig im asiatischen Hochgebirge unterwegs, erfährt er wäh-
rend einer Expedition im Sikkim-Himalaya von der Geburt seines Sohnes Dieter, Katharinas vier Jahre älterem
Bruder. 1937 verunglückt Hepp zusammen mit sechs Freunden bei seiner bis dahin gefährlichsten Tour zum
Nanga Parbat durch eine Eislawine, die nachts ihr Höhenlager verschüttet.

Seine Witwe, die Hitlers NS-Regime verabscheut, überlegt kurz, mit ihrem Bruder Adi nach Amerika
auszuwandern, doch aus Rücksicht auf ihren Vater Max, der damals 71 Jahre alt ist, bleibt sie in München.
Hier lernt sie 1939 den Architekten Helmut von Werz kennen, ihren zweiten Mann, Katharinas Vater, der, 1912
im damals noch ungarischen, später rumänischen Siebenbürgen geboren, mit fünfzehn Jahren nach München
kam. »Deshalb hatte ich als Kind einen rumänischen Pass.« Ihr Vater, dessen Familie die siebenbürgischen
Papierfabriken in diesen Horrorjahren verliert, gründet 1946 ein Architekturbüro, das in den folgenden Jahr-
zehnten zahlreiche Aufträge in München plant und realisiert, so die Nazareth- und die Evangeliumskirche,
die Prähistorische Staatssammlung (seit 2000 Archäologische Staatssammlung) und das Hochhaus des Bayerischen Rundfunks.

»Doch eine besondere Begabung meines Vaters war eine theatralische«. Die Künstlerin blättert in
einem Fotoalbum. »Puschu, so nannten ihn alle, nutzte jede Gelegenheit, sich zu verkleiden. Je grotesker
die Kostüme und je surrealer die Rollen, desto mehr war er in seinem Element! Vielleicht habe ich sogar
ein bisschen von seinem Talent geerbt…« Sie lacht ihr hohes, vergnügt glucksendes Kichern. »Er war sehr
erfinderisch mit fantasievollen Kulissen, ob barock oder bäuerlich. Er liebte es, seine Frau und uns Kinder zu
verzaubern.«

Schon die Generation vor ihm hatte diese Neigung zur mehr oder weniger bizarren Performance
leidenschaftlich kultiviert, allen voran der Vater von Katharinas Mutter, ihr Großvater Max. 1866 als Sohn

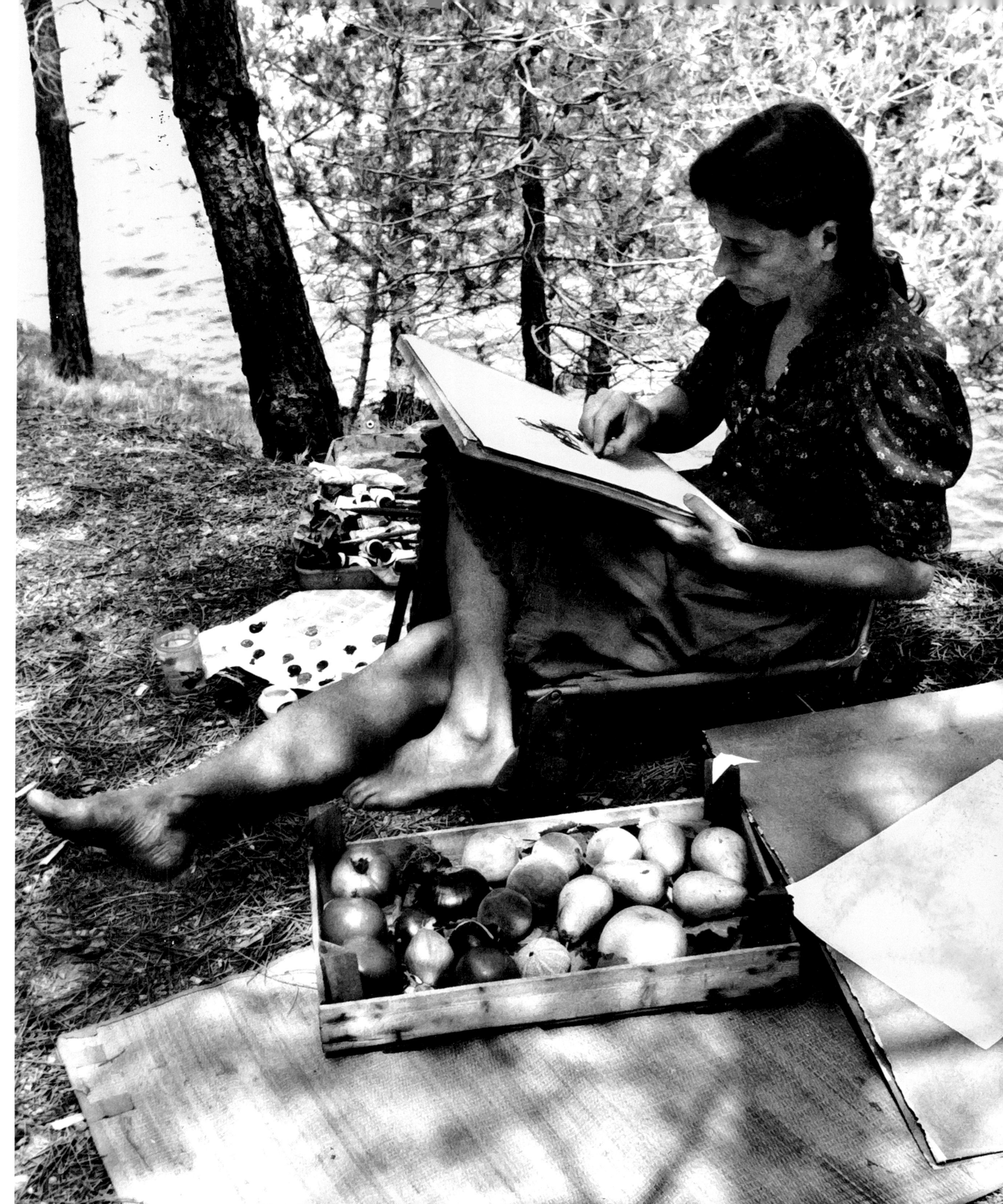

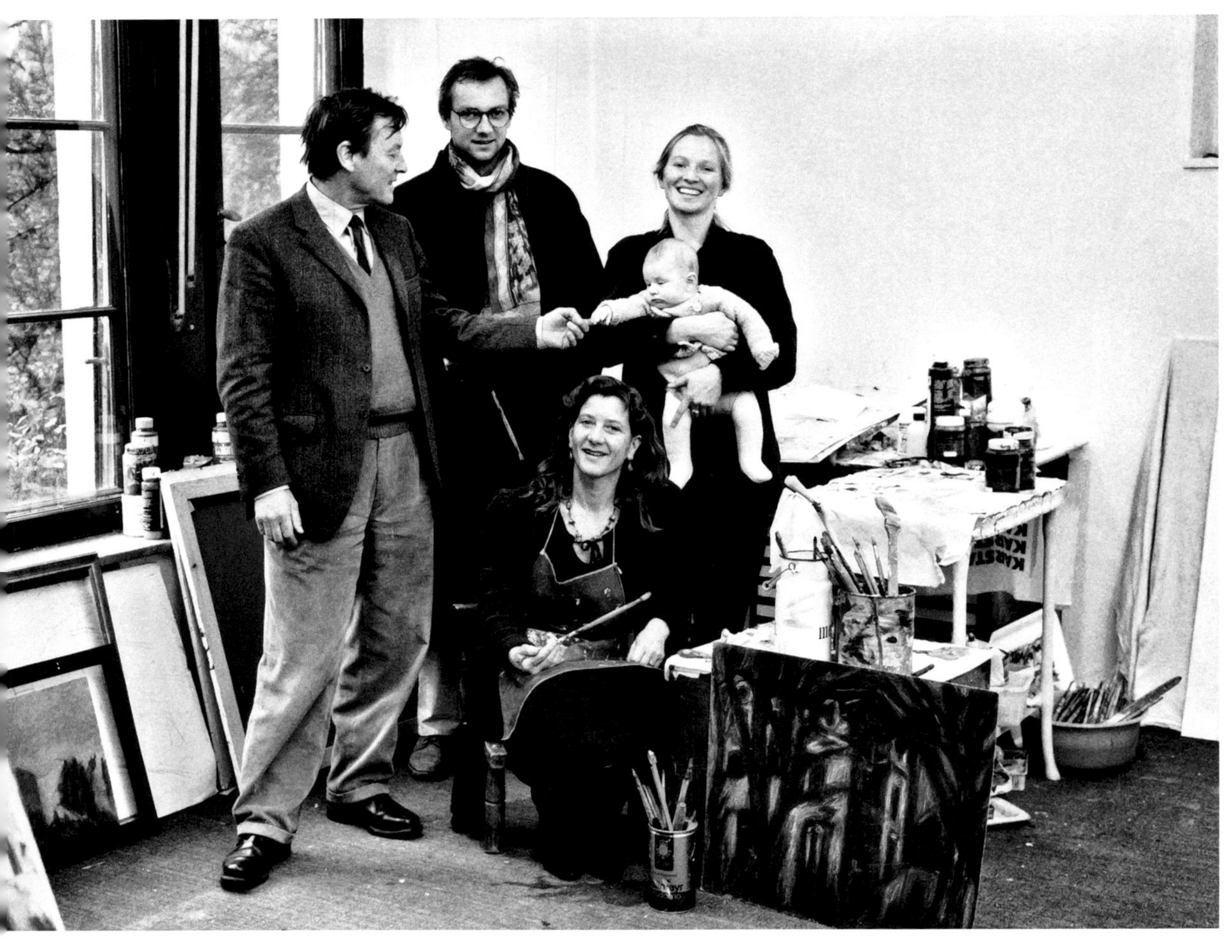

Franz Moll, Lorenz Moll, Anna von Zumbusch
mit/with Leni, Katharina von Werz, 1992

des Hoteliers Johann Samuel Obermayer geboren, dessen Schwiegervater August Schimon 1859 das erste Luxushotel Münchens »Zu den Vier Jahreszeiten« in der Maximilianstraße gebaut hatte, wuchs er, wie auch sein Bruder Adolf, in einer Zwischenetage des Hotels auf, das sein Vater führte. Noch mehr als heute war das prachtvolle Vier Jahreszeiten damals Münchens gesellschaftlicher und kultureller Mittelpunkt.

Max künstlerische Begabung schien zu einem Teil genetisch bedingt, waren doch zwei Brüder seines im ungarischen Pest geborenen Großvaters August Schimon selbst Maler. Der eine, Ferdinand Schimon, porträtierte Wiener Schauspieler und große Komponisten wie Ludwig van Beethoven oder Carl Maria von Weber und war mit Franz Schubert befreundet, von dem eine kleine, intime Gouache erhalten ist.

»Mein Großvater, der schon als Kind dauernd zeichnete, wusste spätestens nach seiner Militärzeit, dass er Maler werden wollte«, erzählt die Künstlerin. Seine Studienzeit, die 1886 begann, hielt Max allerdings für verschwendet. In seinen Erinnerungen beschreibt der Freigeist die Münchner Akademie als »blödsinnige und stumpfsinnige Malschule« und beklagt, wie schwer es ihm gefallen sei, sich von diesem »Akademismus« zu befreien. Nach der Jahrhundertwende wurde er dann mit Porträts bekannt, in der Spätphase außerdem mit Blumenstillleben und in seinen Anfängen mit Illustrationen für die Zeitschrift *Jugend*. Ein Porträt der Mutter Fe als kleines Mädchen war 1913 Titelbild einer Ausgabe: Im weißen Kleidchen sitzt das Covergirl mit Lockenhaar und einem Apfel in der Hand auf einem Tisch, eingerahmt von blauen Blüten.

1890 mietet Max, der nach dem Tod des Vaters weiterhin im Vier Jahreszeiten wohnt, wo er auch seine Pferde hält und dem jüngeren Bruder, der zum Direktor berufen worden ist, als Finanzchef beisteht, ein Atelier in der Georgenstraße 40. Hier lernt er in der Hofmannschen Malschule seine spätere Frau Cateau Kalff, Tochter aus einer holländischen Bankiers- und Sammlerfamilie kennen. Ihr Lehrer Jan Voerman stammt aus dem Umkreis von Piet Mondrian, doch Cateaus »klare Blumenstillleben orientierten sich eher an Van Gogh, den ihr Vater sammelte«, so Katharina von Werz. Nicht nur als Maler, sondern auch als Innenarchitekt war Max Obermayer gefragt. So gestaltete er die American Bar im Vier Jahreszeiten, später das Kurhaus in Davos und Villen in Hamburg wie im Rheinland. Oft arbeitet er mit seinem Schwager, dem Architekten Emanuel von Seidl und seinem Freund Richard Riemerschmid zusammen.

Maler und Architekten, dazu die Maskeradentradition der Münchner Boheme vor und nach der Jahrhundertwende, die schon Großvater Max als Kind erlebt, wie er in seinen Tagebüchern schildert. Diese Mischung aus großbürgerlicher und künstlerisch-liberaler Kultur prägt das Leben der Malerin und ihrer Familie bis heute. »Mein Mann Franz und ich haben seit den 70er Jahren zusammen mit närrischen Freunden und Gelegenheitsperformern immer wieder Kostümfeste inszeniert.« Ihre Stimme wird schwärmerisch: »Einmal schrieb der deutsche Schriftsteller Michael Ende dafür sogar ein groteskes Theaterstück. 1996 fand einer der letzten großen Faschingsbälle zum Thema Bayerisch-Arabisches Filmtreffen statt. Rund 600 Gäste kamen in den verrücktesten Verkleidungen und führten bizarre Sketche auf, für den besten verlieh eine Jury die Goldene Palme.«

"I am very grounded in my family life. My husband and
 my children and their children buoy up my existence."

Her first memory? "My pink and light blue color pencils!" Katharina von Werz answers immediately without even having to think. "I must've been about four years old and I guarded these pencils as if they were treasure. I took them everywhere I went, along with a white muff made of rabbit fur that my parents had given me for Christmas." Times were tough in those days, Germany was at war. To warm their feet in the cold autumn months, the children would even walk barefoot through fresh cowpats.

Katharina's mother Fe was a doctor who had studied in Munich under such luminaries in their field as Leo von Zumbusch, founder of the dermatological clinic. She was widowed by a tragic accident that killed her first husband, Günther Hepp, some three years before Katharina was born. Hepp, a young surgeon with a promising career laid out before him, belonged to a group of prominent, extreme mountain climbers from Munich. Their burning ambition was to be the first alpinists to conquer an eight-thousander. He had made frequent expeditions in the Asian mountain ranges where all fourteen eight-thousanders are found. He first heard of the birth of his son, Dieter, Katharina's older brother by four years, while on an expedition in the Sikkim Himalayas. In 1937 Hepp was killed along with six friends on what was then his most dangerous tour to date, scaling Nanga Parbat. The avalanche buried their camp during the night.

His widow, who detested Hitler's NS regime, considered emigrating to America with her brother Adi. What kept her from doing so was her father Max, 71 one at the time, and she stayed in Munich to be near him. And it was in Munich that she met the architect, Helmut von Werz, her second husband, in 1939. Von Werz had come to Munich at age fifteen and was originally from Transylvania. He was born a Hungarian citizen in 1912, before Transylvania changed hands and became part of Rumania. "That's why," Katharina von Werz explains, "I had a Rumanian passport as a child." Her father's family owned a series of Transylvanian paper mills and lost them in the terrible events of this period. In 1946 he founded an architectural office that went on to plan and realize numerous contracts in Munich over the following decades, including the Nazarethkirche, Evangeliumskirche, the State Prehistoric Collection (known since 2000 as the Archäologische Staatssammlung, or State Archaeological Collection), and the home of Bayerischer Rundfunk.

"But one of my father's talents was his flair for the theatrical," von Werz says. The artist leafs through a photo album. "Puschu—that's what everyone called him—used every opportunity to get dressed up in disguises. The more grotesque the costumes and the more surreal the roles, the more he felt in his element! Perhaps I've inherited a bit of his talent ..." She lets out a high, gleeful giggle before continuing: "He was extremely inventive when it came to scenery, whether Baroque or rustic, it was always imaginative. He loved to enthrall his wife and us children in this way."

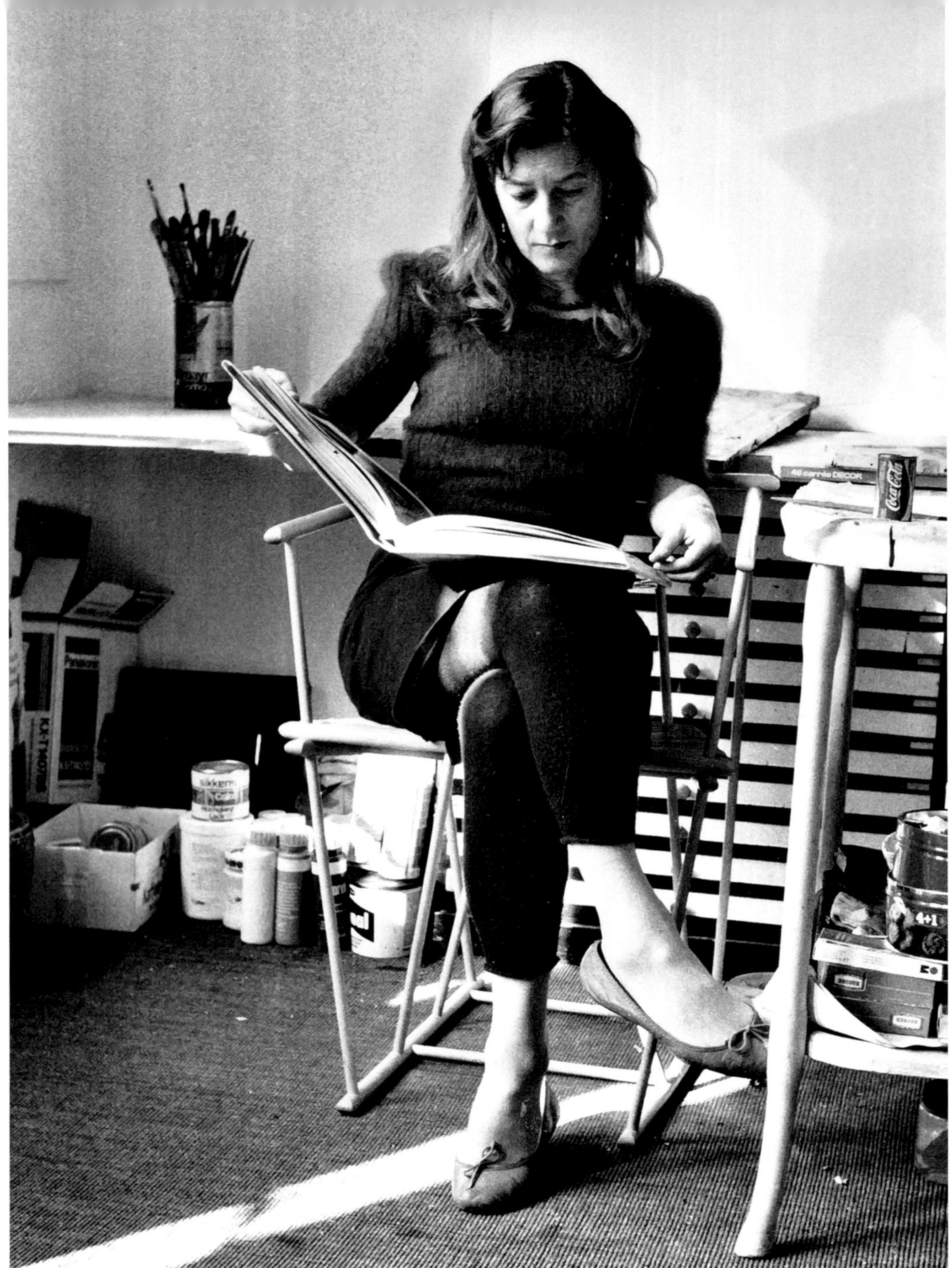

Heute widmet sich Franz Moll, Architekt und bis 1997 Geschäftsführer einer Münchner Baufirma, leidenschaftlich seiner »Franz-Moll-Stiftung für die kommenden Generationen«. Zusammen mit dem Journalisten und Anti-Atomkraft-Aktivisten Claus Biegert hat er 1998 den »Nuclear–Free Future Award« ins Leben gerufen, der mit Konferenzen rund um den Globus und prominenten Mitstreitern wie dem berühmten, 2008 leider verstorbenen, deutsch-amerikanischen Informatiker und Wissenschaftskritiker Joseph Weizenbaum oder Patti Smith, der Patin des Punk, für ein Ende des Atomzeitalters kämpft.

Den Kreativfaden, der sie mit ihren Vorfahren verbindet, behalten auch die drei Kinder des Paars in der Hand, Goldschmiedin Anna, Drehbuchautor und Schriftsteller Lorenz und der Architekt Xaver, alle inzwischen selbst Eltern und mit ihrem Anhang regelmäßig im Haus der Eltern. Katharina von Werz braucht dieses Clan-Gefühl für ihre Kunst: »Ich bin sehr eingebettet in meine Familie. Mein Mann und meine Kinder und deren Kinder beflügeln mein Dasein.«

Helmut or "Puschu" was not alone in this, in fact it seemed to run in the family, with previous generations on her mother's side also cultivating this proclivity toward various forms of bizarre performance, particularly Katharina's grandfather, Max. Max was born in 1866 to the hotel manager Johann Samuel Obermayer. His father-in-law, August Schimon, had built the first luxury hotel in Munich in 1859, the hotel "Zu den Vier Jahreszeiten", situated on Maximilianstraße. Max grew up with his brother Adolf on a mezzanine floor in the hotel run by his father. At the time, the splendid *Vier Jahreszeiten* hotel was a social and cultural meeting point in Munich life even more than it is today.

Max's artistic talent seemed to have been passed down to him, as two great-uncles on his mother's side had also been painters. One, Ferdinand Schimon, had made portraits of Viennese actors and famous composers such as Ludwig van Beethoven and Carl Maria von Weber, and was friends with Franz Schubert. He made a small, intimate gouache of Schubert that has survived.

"By the time he left the army, my grandfather, who apparently was forever drawing even as a child, knew for sure that he wanted to become a painter," Katharina says. However Max later looked back on his studies, which began in 1886, as a wasted opportunity. In his memoirs the freethinker describes the Munich academy as a "stupid and dull painting school" and complains of how difficult it subsequently became for him to liberate himself from this "academicism." From the early 20th century onward he became known for his portraits and illustrations for the magazine *Jugend*, and later on in his career for his still lifes of flowers. In one edition of the magazine from 1913, a portrait of Katharina's mother Fe as a little girl featured on the cover. She is seen wearing a white frock, her hair hangs down in curls as she holds an apple while resting her hand on a table, framed by blue blossoms.

After the death of his father, Max continued to live in the *Vier Jahreszeiten,* where he also kept his horses. His younger brother took over as company director, with Max serving as financial manager. In 1890 Max took out a lease on a studio at Georgenstraße 40. And it is here, at the adjoining Hoffmannsche Malschule, that he met the woman who later became his wife: Cateau Kalff, the daughter of a family of Dutch bankers and collectors. Her art teacher, Jan Voerman, was an acquaintance of Piet Mondrian. But Cateau's "clear still lifes of flowers are much closer to Van Gogh, an artist her father collected," says Katharina von Werz. Max Obermayer was successful not only as a painter, but also as an interior decorator. He designed the American bar in the *Vier Jahreszeiten,* and went on to complete designs for the spa resort in Davos and villas in Hamburg and the Rhineland. He often worked with his brother-in-law, the architect Emanuel von Seidl and his friend Richard Riemerschmid.

Painters and architects, the tradition of masquerade balls held in bohemian circles in Munich before and after the turn of the century, which Katharina's grandfather Max experienced at first hand as a child, as described in his diaries: this blend of bourgeois culture and artistic, liberal life informed the painter's life and that of her family, and its influence can still be felt today. "My husband Franz and I threw several costume parties in the seventies, eighties, and nineties. They were attended by some of our more quixotic of friends and occasional performers," she recalls fondly. "The German author Michael Ende once wrote a grotesque play for one of them. In 1996 we held the last big carnival ball; the theme was a meeting of Bavarian and Arab film. Around 600 guests turned up in the wildest costumes and presented bizarre sketches to the crowd. The best sketches were awarded a mock Palme d'Or by a jury."

Katharina's husband, Franz Moll, architect and until 1997 general manager of a Munich-based construction firm, now dedicates virtually all of his time to the "Franz Moll Foundation for the Coming Generations," his own brainchild. Together with the journalist and anti-nuclear activist, Claus Biegert, he set up the Nuclear–free Future Award in 1998, which campaigns for an end to the nuclear age by holding conferences around the globe featuring such famous campaigners as Joseph Weizenbaum, the German-American computer scientist and science critic, now deceased, and Patti Smith, icon of American punk.

The creative thread that links Katharina with her forefathers is also shared by her three children: Anna, a goldsmith, Lorenz, screenwriter and writer, and Xaver, architect. All of them are now parents themselves and they and their families are frequent visitors to their parents' home. Katharina von Werz says that this sense of belonging to a clan feeds into her art: "I am very grounded in my family life. My husband and my children and their children buoy up my existence."

»Mein Stil: Aus Nichts Etwas zu machen. Es soll möglichst
nicht luxuriös sein und auf keinen Fall eine Marke.
Die Wirkung soll auf meiner Zusammenstellung beruhen.«

Katharina von Werz als Ritter/
as knight Sonnenfeind, 1990

Zwar beschreibt Katharina von Werz mit diesen Worten ihre unnachahmlich eigenwillige Art von Mode,
doch gleichzeitig liefert sie auch eine treffsichere Definition der individualistischen Lebensweise der Boheme.
Bis heute fasziniert diese künstlerisch-intellektuelle Subkulturbewegung, die vor über 150 Jahren in den Groß-
städten Europas als Gegenentwurf zu angepasster Bürgerlichkeit entstand – zunächst in Paris und etwas später
um die Jahrhundertwende in Berlin und München. Freiwillige Aussteiger und Außenseiter der Gesellschaft,
benannten sich die Bohemiens nach den aus Böhmen stammenden Zigeunern, einer unfreiwillig in Elend und
Armut existierenden, von der Gesellschaft kriminalisierten und diskriminierten Randgruppe.

Bohemiens waren Künstler und Literaten, die eine kreative Existenz außerhalb der autoritätshörigen,
arbeitsamen bürgerlichen Mitte verklärten, deren scheinheilige Doppelmoral sie vor allem verachteten. Sie
trafen sich in Cafés und Kabaretten, wohnten in bestimmten Vierteln und Quartiers und kultivierten hier ihre
Anti-Uniformität. Fraglos waren sie der notwendige Gegenpol zu einer sie umgebenden Sphäre der Biederkeit,
Spießigkeit, Mittelmäßigkeit und Obrigkeitsergebenheit, die sich kurz vor und um 1900 verdichtete. »Der Erz-
typ der Bohème«, erkannte der Soziologe Theodor Geiger, »ist der Anarcho-Nihilist.«

Derart heftig wie damals sind Salon und Avantgarde, Bürgertum und Boheme wohl nie wieder aufeinander-
geprallt. Nicht als Konflikt, sondern als fruchtbare Spannung durchzieht dieses Nebeneinander der Gegensätze
die Familiengeschichte von Katharina von Werz. Künstler und Architekten auf der einen, Unternehmer und
Wissenschaftler auf der anderen Seite, prägen sie auf eine Weise, bei der sich liberale mit konservativen Werten
verbinden. Diese fruchtbare Synergie aus unternehmerischem und kreativem Talent zeigte sich bereits in der
Familie des Ururgroßvaters August Schimon, dessen beide Brüder Maler waren. Zwar reüssierte Schimon als
Weinhändler, Gastronom, Immobilieninvestor und Erbauer des Hotels »Zu den Vier Jahreszeiten«, das 1858
eröffnete. Doch fanden in seinen Weinwirtschaften Zur Goldenen Rose und Zum deutschen Ritter regelmäßig
Faschingsfeste statt, dekoriert von den bekanntesten Künstlern der Stadt – offensichtlich ein Tribut an die eigene
bohemieske Neigung.

Sich fantastisch bis grotesk für große Motti-Bälle zu kostümieren, hatte in den Jahren vor und nach
den beiden Weltkriegen einen völlig anderen Reiz und eine ungleich größere Bedeutung als heute, wo selbst
die exzentrischsten Outfits und Körperfetische zum gängigen Straßenbild gehören und jede Form von Underground sofort in Marketing verwandelt und in den medialen Mainstream endloser Entertainment-Bilder eingebettet wird.

So berichtet der Maler Max Obermayer, Großvater von Katharina von Werz, in seinen Erinnerungen von
der schier überwältigenden Feierlaune der Münchner in den Jahren bis zum Ausbruch des Ersten Weltkriegs:

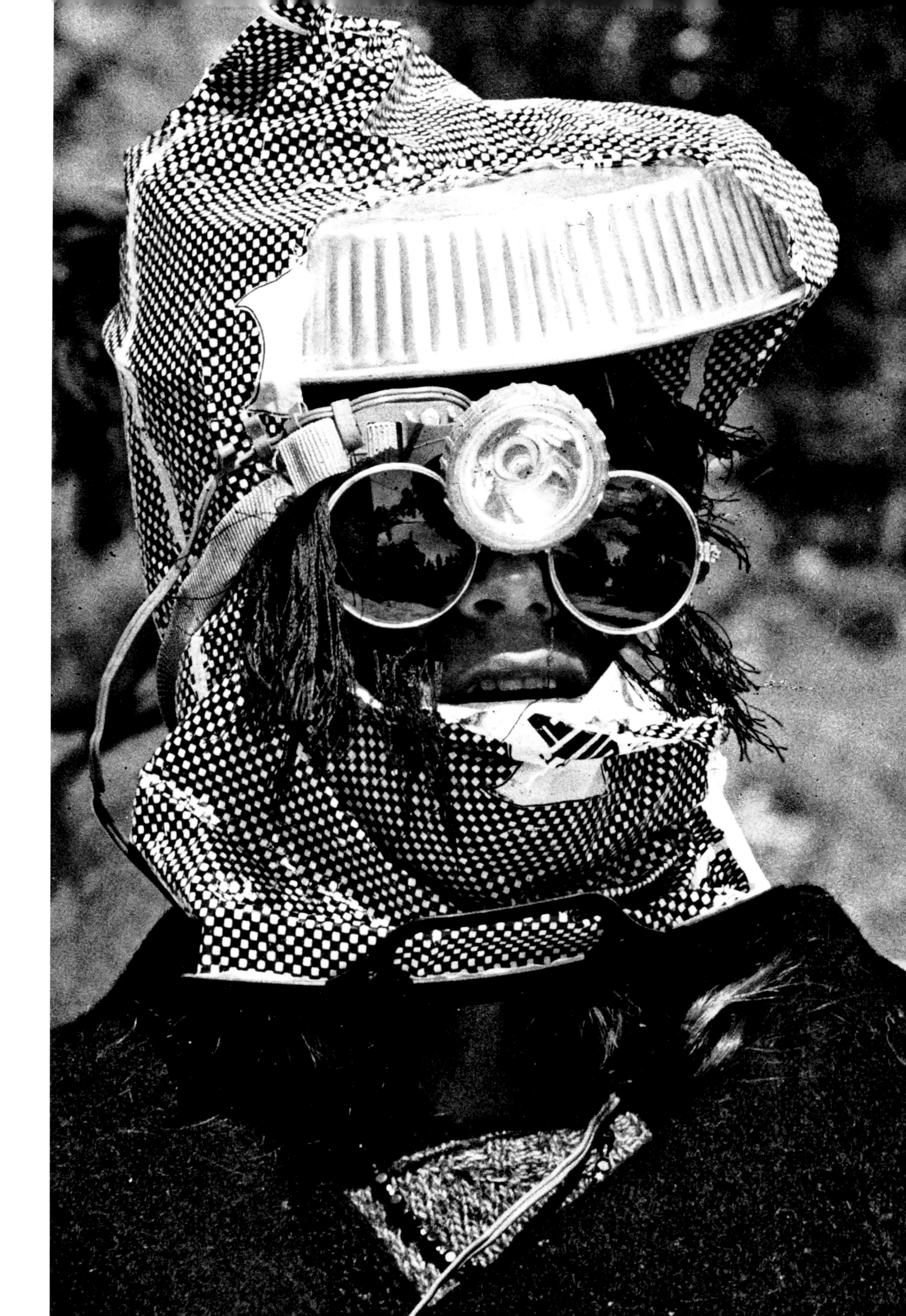

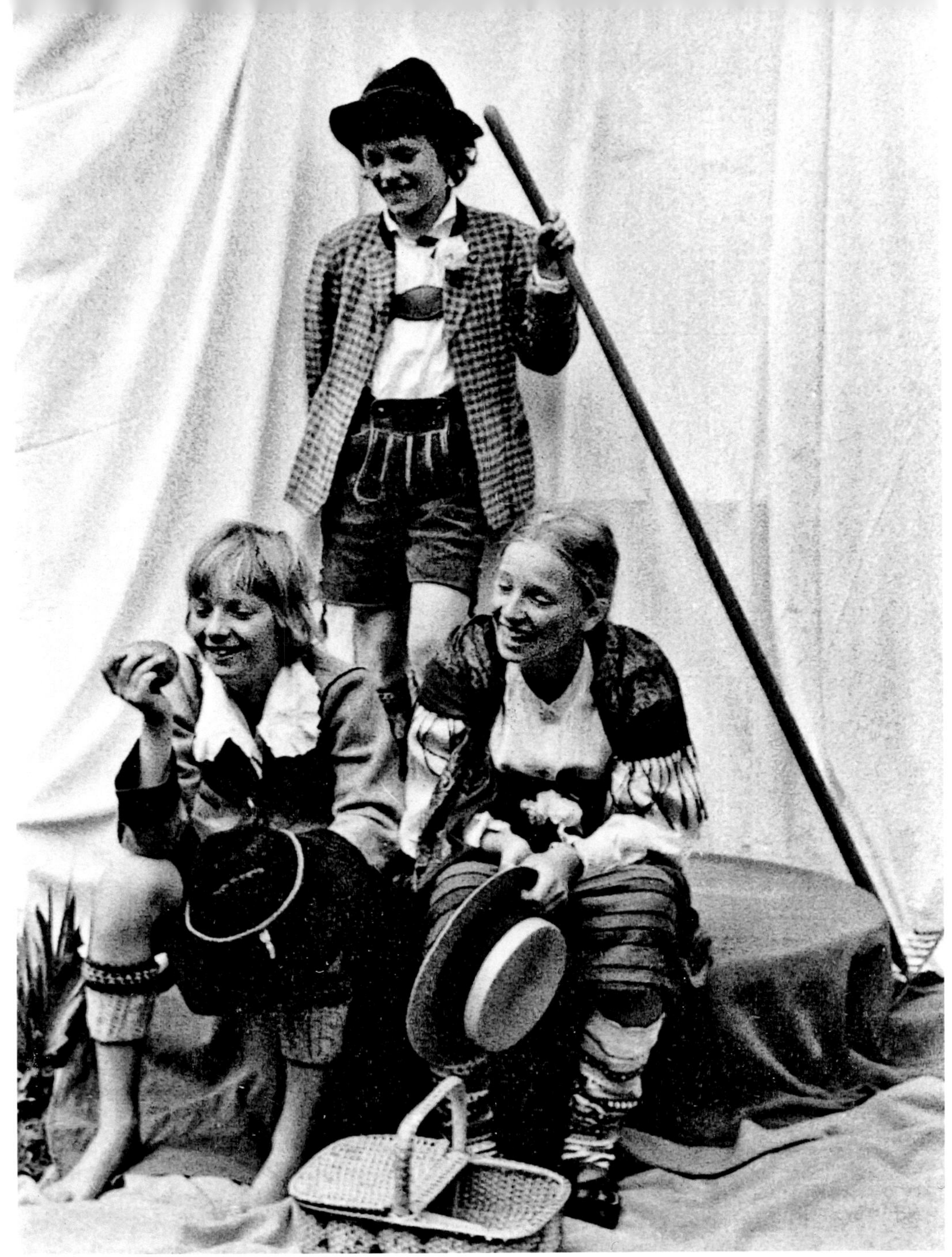

Die drei Kinder von Katharina von Werz
in bayerischer Tracht/Katharina von Werz's
three children in Bavarian costumes, 1975

»In jedem Lokal wurde an mehreren Abenden der Woche getanzt, in jeder Familie gab es ›Lämmerhüpfen‹ (Tänze für den noch ungeübten Nachwuchs; Anm. d. Autorin), die Atelierfeste schossen wie Pilze aus dem Boden, die Schulkinder warfen auf den Plätzen ihre Schulranzen auf einen Haufen und tanzten Ringelreihen. Es war, als ob die Menschheit ein Taumel ergriff (...) eine tolle Zeit, ein Jagen nach Vergnügen – und doch war sie innerlich unkünstlerisch, im Grunde ein Sich-selbst-Belügen. Kamst du von auswärts und fragtest den alten Dienstmann, der deine Koffer entgegen nahm: ›Na, wie geht's euch denn?‹ – dann konntest du zur Antwort bekommen: ›Lusti samma, lusti!.‹«

Lustig waren sie zweifellos, die Maskeraden, doch auch kritisch und satirisch wie die Kabaretts, die damals »wie Pilze aus dem Boden schossen«, so Obermayer, der um 1890 dem Künstler-Sänger-Verein beitrat, dessen Aufführungen beinahe ebenso beliebt waren wie die Balladen der Elf Scharfrichter, dem ersten politischen Kabarett Deutschlands in der Münchner Türkenstraße. »Es war wie eine Sucht, eine Krankheit, seine Kritik an den herrschenden Zuständen an den Mann zu bringen«, schreibt der Maler. »Es ist derselbe Geist, aus dem wenig später der ›Simplicissimus‹ geboren wurde.«

"My style: To make something out of nothing. No luxury if
at all possible and never brand names. The effect should
come from the overall look."

This quote from Katharina von Werz refers to her inimitable and unconventional fashion style, but it is
also an accurate description of the individualistic lifestyle of the bohemians. This artistic and intellectual underground movement still fascinates today, 150 years after it arose in the cities of Europe as a counterculture
to bourgeois conformity—first in Paris and sometime later, around the turn of the century, in Berlin and Munich.
The bohemians, a mix of voluntary dropouts and social misfits, named themselves after a marginalized group of
gypsies who were thought to come from the region of Bohemia (now in the Czech Republic) and lived—involun-
tarily—in abject poverty, criminalized and discriminated against by the rest of society.

The bohemians were artists and literati, who romanticized a creative existence away from the obedience
and hard-working ethos of the middle class, whose sanctimonious double standards they roundly condemned.
They met in cafes and cabarets, and lived in particular quarters of the city where they cultivated their stance
against uniformity. They were no doubt a necessary counterbalance to the all-pervading moral uprightness, nar-
row-mindedness, mediocrity, and deference to authority that surrounded them shortly before and around 1900.
"The archetypal Bohemian," claimed sociologist Theodor Geiger, "is the anarchic-nihilist."

Never again has the world of the salon and the avant-garde, the middle class and the bohemian clashed
to such a degree as at this time. This juxtaposition of opposing elements not only permeates the family history
of Katharina von Werz, but has created a productive tension rather than conflict. Artists and architects on one
side, entrepreneurs and scientists on the other, all have influenced her family in a way that has united liberal and
conservative values. This fertile synergy between entrepreneurial and creative talent was already evident in the
family of her great-great-grandfather August Shimon, whose brothers were both artists. Schimon was a successful wine merchant, restaurateur, property investor, and built the hotel Zu den Vier Jahreszeiten that was opened
in 1858. Yet, carnival parties were regularly held in his wine taverns Zur Goldenen Rose and Zum deutschen Ritter,
decorated by the best known artists in the city—obviously a tribute to his own bohemian leanings.

Dressing up in costumes that ranged from the fantastic to the grotesque for grand themed balls had a
completely different attraction and a much greater significance in the years before and after the two World Wars
than it does today, when even the most eccentric outfits and fetishes are part of the everyday street scene, and
every form of underground trend is immediately picked up by advertising and embedded in the endless stream of
pictures published for entertainment by the mainstream media.

The painter Max Obermayer, grandfather to Katharina von Werz, writes in his memoirs about the over-
whelming desire to party in Munich in the years leading up to the outbreak of the First World War: "Dances were
held several times a week in every local venue, and in every family there were *Lämmerhüpfen* [events organized

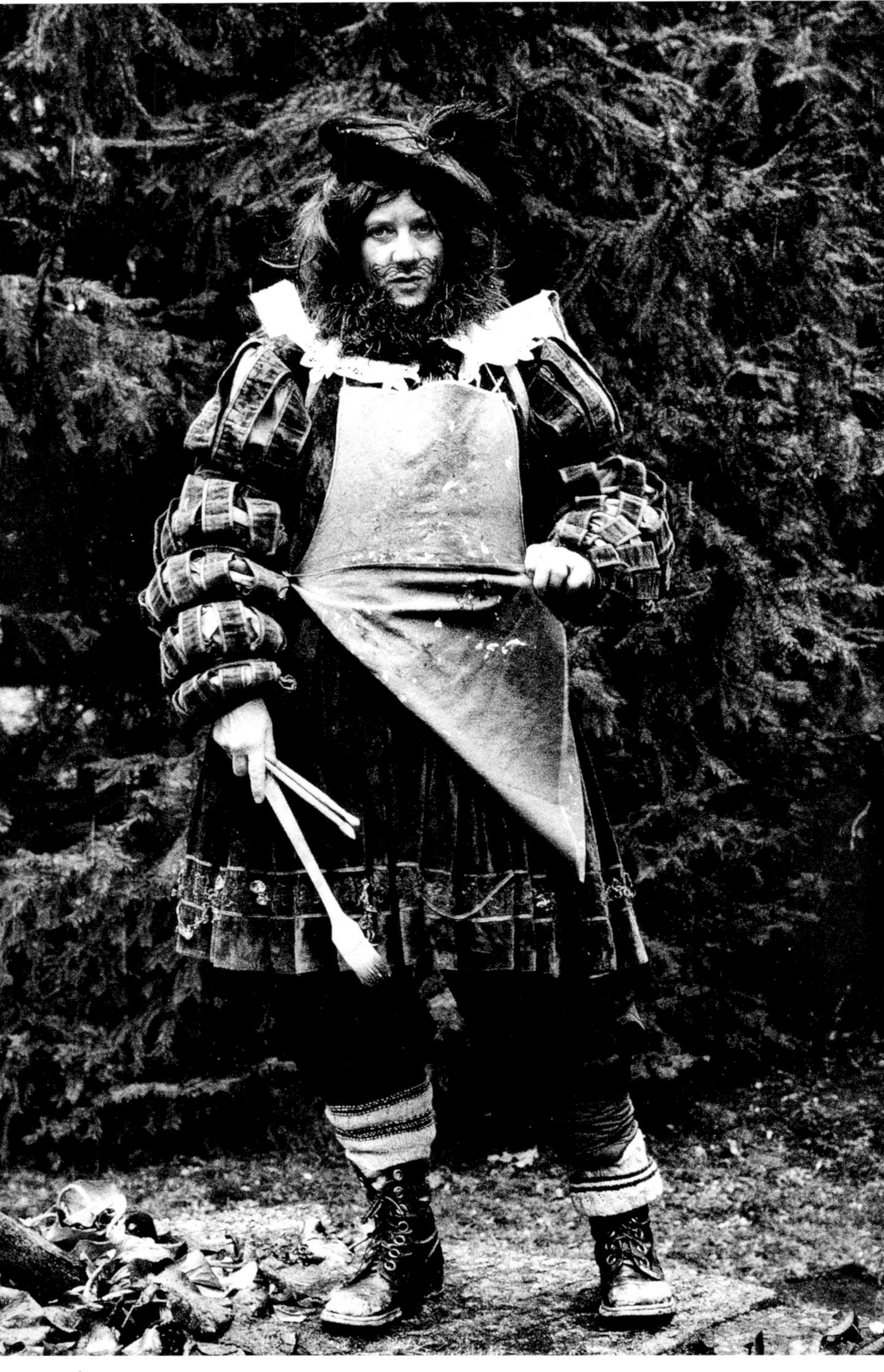

A

A
Katharina von Werz als Malerfürst/
as Prince of Painting, 1991

B
Katharina von Werz als Alpenkönig/
as King of the Alps, 1980

C
Puschu von Werz als/as Napoleon, 1960

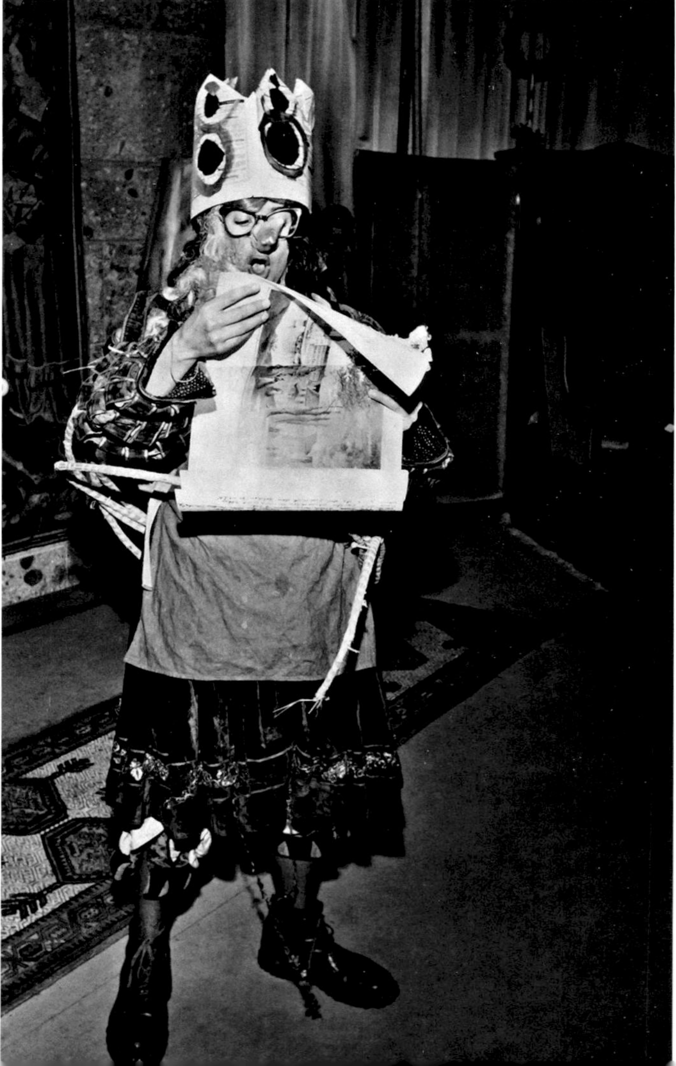

B

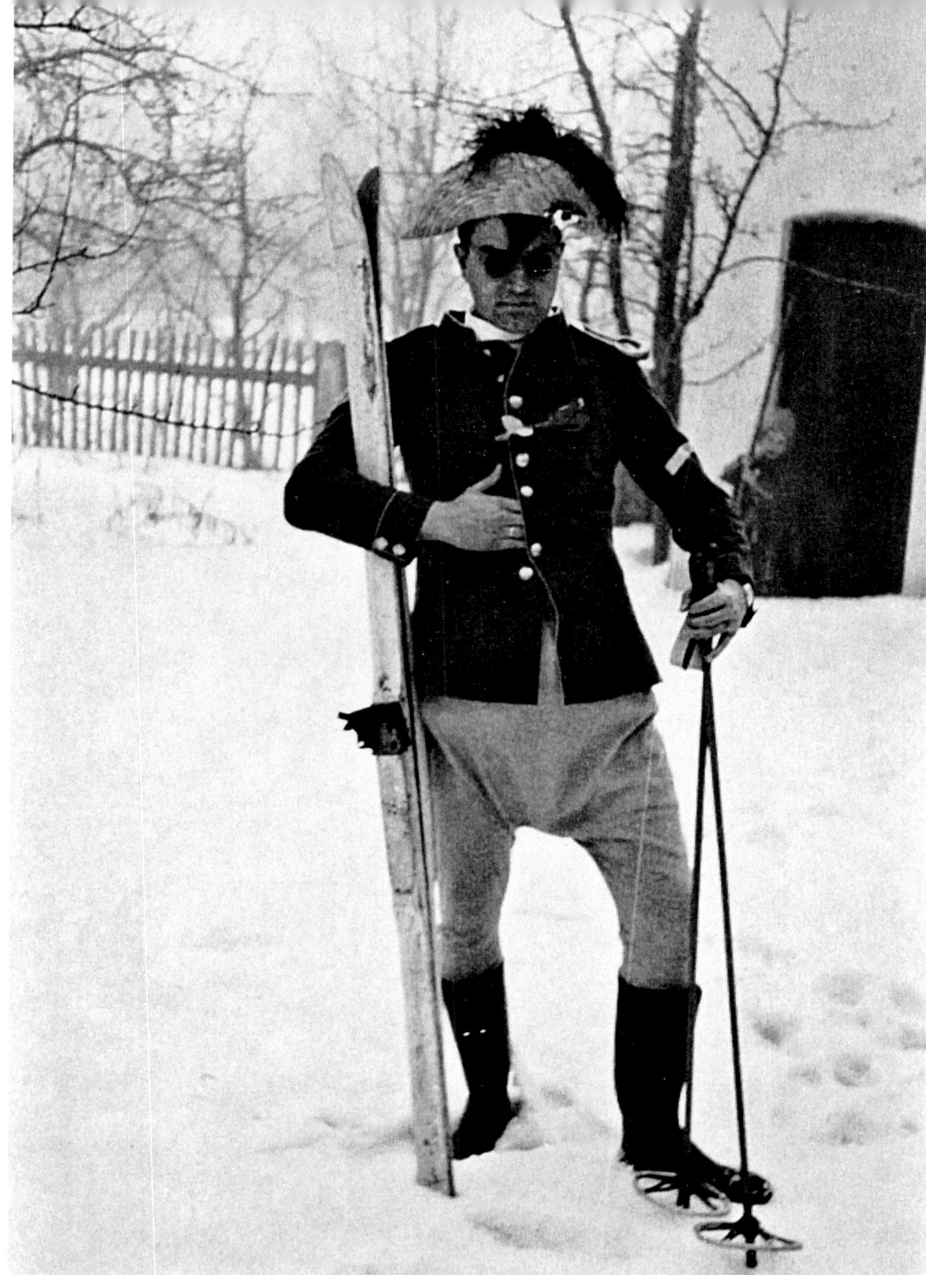

c

for young people who were still learning how to dance; note from the author], studio parties sprang up like mushrooms all over the place, school kids threw their schoolbags in a heap on the town squares and danced ring-a-ring-of-roses. It was as if humanity had been gripped by a frenzy (...) a wonderful time, chasing pleasure—and yet in its essence it was not artistic, basically a type of self-deception. If you arrived in the city and asked the old servant who was there to carry your suitcase, "So how are you?" you might well get the answer: "We're having a grand time, a grand time!"

Fun was without a doubt to be had at the masquerades, but this was also a time of critical satire, for instance, at the cabarets that "sprang up like mushrooms" at that time, according to Obermayer, who joined the Künstler-Sänger-Verein, a club for artists and singers, around 1890. Its performances were almost as popular as the ballads of the *Elf Scharfrichter*, the first political cabaret in Germany that was performed in Türkenstraße in Munich. "It was like an addiction, an illness, to openly criticize the prevailing conditions," the painter writes. "It was the same spirit that gave birth to 'Simplicissimus' a short time later."

The seamless transition from foolish transgressions to subversive rebellion not only affected the carnival and costume parties of these years but also influenced the events that Katharina von Werz and her family organized with a group of like-minded people between the seventies and nineties. The artist particularly remembers her "grandfather's masquerade chest, a huge box full to the brim with carnival costumes and props, including a Bosnian embroidered bolero, knight's armor, princesses' coronets, little skirts for horse riders in the circus, clowns' noses, and gaucho ponchos. Once, at the age of seven, I dressed up as a *Postillon d'Amour* with a small post horn and spurs on my boots while my brother was a Red Indian, and my grandfather describes how our eyes lit up."

While Max Obermayer once tattooed the décolleté and arms of his wife and an aunt by hand with purple Chinese dragons, his granddaughter also excelled in disguises, at times quite daring and bizarre. In 1989 at a friend's birthday party she arrived on the snowy ski slopes of Val Fex in Switzerland dressed as the knight *Ritter Sonnenfeind* (fig. p. 27), unrecognizable in her costume with a plastic bag that she had cut out and placed on her head as a helmet, a baking pan sticking out underneath as the brim, as well as a pair of glacier goggles and a night lamp, and sideburns made of bast fibers on her cheeks: an inscrutable heroine.

Similar to the costumes of her father, who once dressed up as Napoleon during his Russian campaign of 1812, those worn by Katharina von Werz are always self-ironic, mischievous, and have a touch of caricature to them. In 1991 she posed in a bold outfit, consisting of a beret, big, puffed sleeves, a spattered apron with palette, brushes, and the condescending look of genius, as the master painter Rembrandt (fig. p. 30)—an excellent parody that was captured in a series by photographer Stefan Moses.

A unique combination of performance and happening also marks the large carnival parties that Franz Moll and Katharina von Werz initiated together with fans for several hundred guests. Even the invitations, designed by the artist, were an event in themselves. While in 1968, under the spell of "Oriental" exoticism, sultans and belly dancers were invited to the opening of the "bazaar," a second "meeting of Bavarian and Arab film" in 1996 challenged its

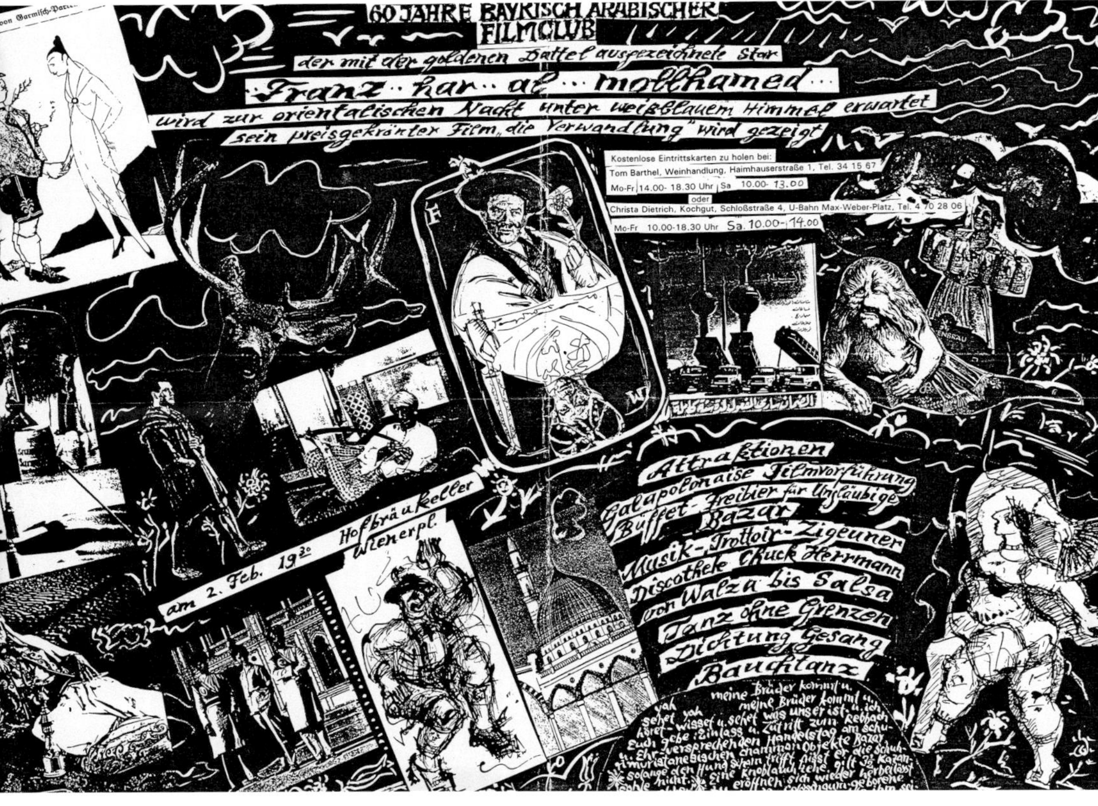

A

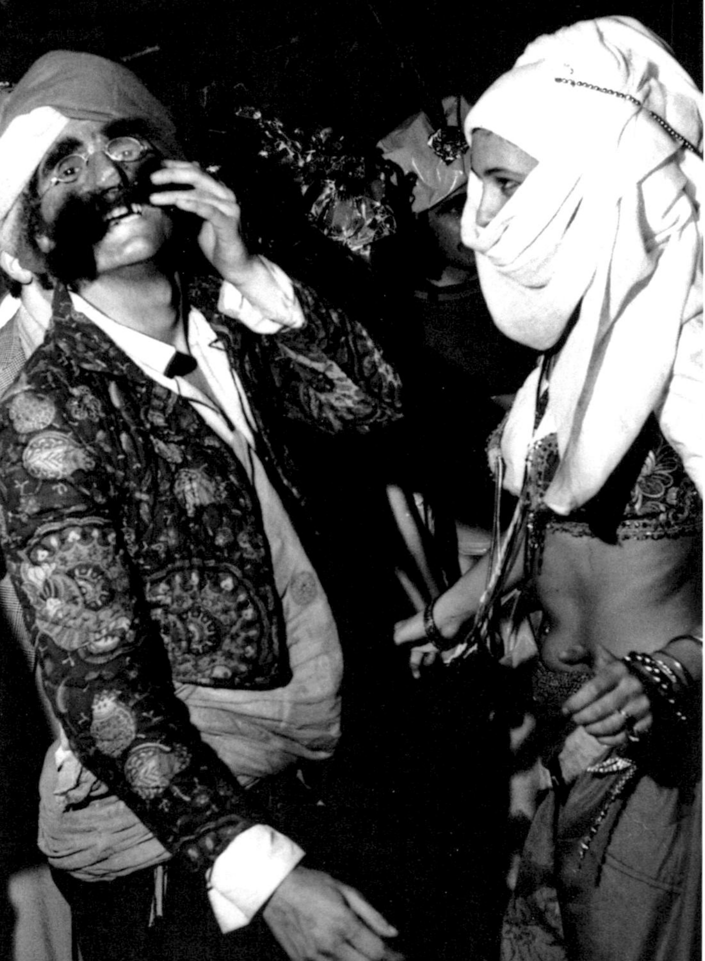

B

C

A
Einladung zum Bayerisch-Arabischen
Filmclub/Invitation to the Bavarian-
Arabian Film Club, 1996

B
Sultan mit Bauchtänzerin/Sultan with
belly dancer, 1996

C
Orientalischer Musiker/Oriental
musician, 1970

D
Franz Moll, Katharina von Werz,
Schlangenbeschwörung/snake
charming, 1978

E
Fakir auf dem Nagelbrett/on a bed
of nails, 1970

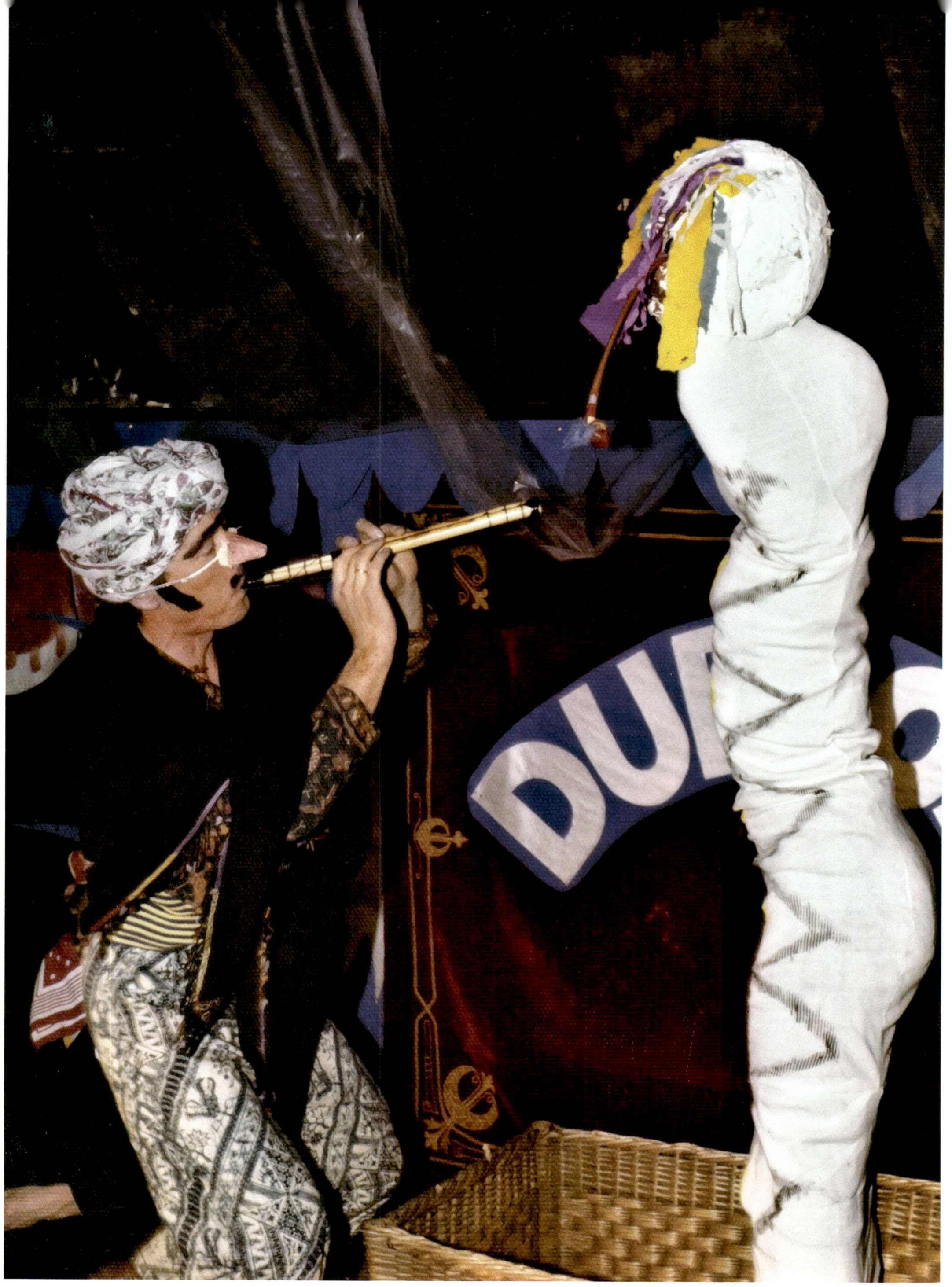

D

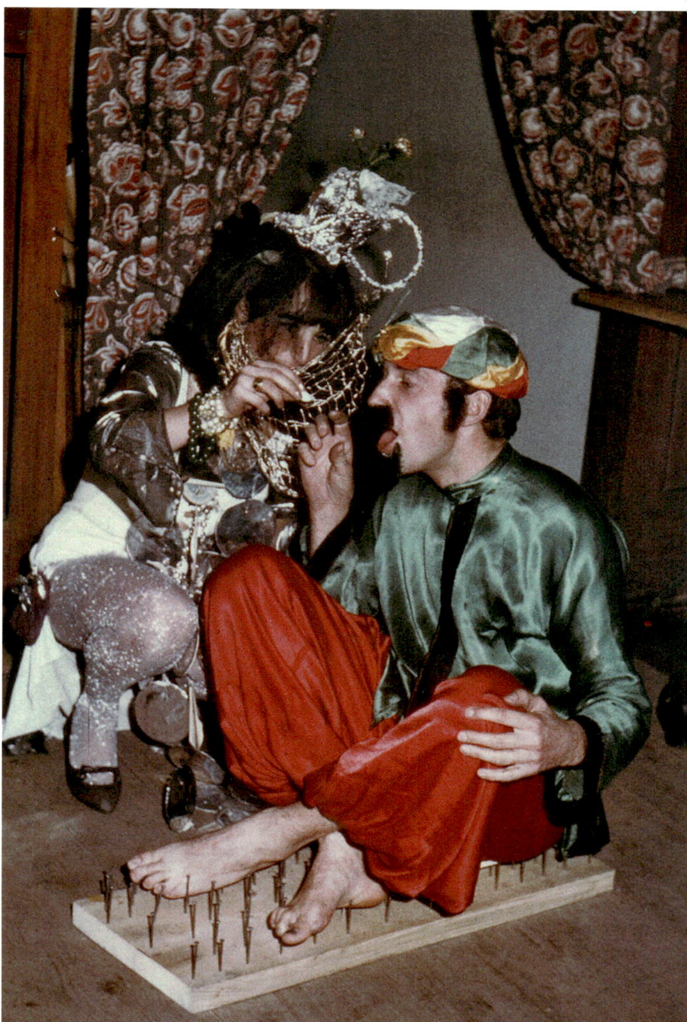

E

Die fließenden Übergänge des närrisch Grenzüberschreitenden zum subversiv Rebellischen prägen die Karnevals- und Kostümfeste nicht nur jener Jahre, sondern auch die Veranstaltungen, die Katharina von Werz und ihre Familie mit einer Gruppe Gleichgesinnter zwischen den 70er und 90er Jahren inszenierten. Genau erinnert sich die Künstlerin an »Großvaters Maskeradenschachtel, eine riesige Faschingskiste mit Unmengen von Requisiten, darunter bosnische gestickte Boleros, Ritterrüstungen, Prinzessinnenkrönchen, Zirkusreiterinnenröckchen, Clownsnasen und Gaucho-Ponchos. Einmal, mit gerade sieben Jahren, war ich ein Postillon d'Amour mit einem kleinen Posthorn und Sporen an den Stiefeln, und mein Bruder ein Indianer, und mein Großvater beschreibt, wie unsere Augen gestrahlt haben.«

Tätowierte Max Obermayer damals Dekolleté und Arme seiner Frau und einer Tante eigenhändig mit blauroten chinesischen Drachen, so brillierte seine Enkelin mit zum Teil wagemutig skurrilen Charaktermasken. 1989 ging sie anlässlich eines Geburtstags im Freundeskreis als Ritter Sonnenfeind (Abb. S. 27) auf die Schneepiste im Fextal, bis zur Unkenntlichkeit vermummt mit einer wie einen Helm über den Kopf gestülpten, aufgeschnittenen Plastiktüte, unter der ein Kuchenblech als Hutkrempe hervorragte, dazu eine Gletscherbrille und Nachtlampe auf der Nase und Haarfransen aus Bast um die Wangen: eine Heroine der abgründigen Art.

Wie die Kostümierungen ihres Vaters, der einmal als Napoleon beim Russlandfeldzug 1812 auftrat, sind auch die Verkleidungen von Katharina von Werz stets selbstironisch, schelmisch und eine Spur karikaturistisch. So posierte sie 1991 in einer verwegenen Montur aus Barett, wulstigen Puffärmeln, fleckiger Schürze mit Palette, Pinseln und herablassendem Genieblick als Malerfürst Rembrandt (Abb. S. 30) – eine großartige Persiflage, die der Fotograf Stefan Moses in einer Serie festhielt.

Ein einzigartiger Mix aus Performance und Happening zeichnet auch die großen Faschingsfeste aus, die Franz Moll und Katharina von Werz mit ihren Fans für mehrere Hundert Gäste initiierten. Schon die Einladungen, entworfen von der Künstlerin, waren Ereignisse. Wurden bereits 1968 im Bann orientalischer Exotik Sultane und Bauchtänzerinnen zur »Bazareröffnung« gebeten, so forderte 1996 ein zweites »Bayerisch-Arabisches Gipfeltreffen« eines imaginären Filmclubs zu noch tolleren Darbietungen und Vermummungen heraus. Auch eine Schlangenbeschwörung befand sich im unerschöpflich satirischen Repertoire, ebenso wie 1979 die Einladung des tanzverrannten Paars zum »Turnier um die Silberne Tanznadel« mit den »Dressler-Zwillingen« als Juroren und einem Conferencier, dessen Name »Horst Heinz Schmalzbach« allein schon genügte, um die anarchische Komik dieser Nächte zu veranschaulichen.

Doch die Krönung dieses komödiantischen Talents ist der Videofilm »Crocodilus und Persea oder der verzauberte Krebs«, den Katharina von Werz 1973 zusammen mit ihrem Mann und den Kindern drehte, wobei sie die Rollen mit den jeweiligen Familienmitgliedern besetzte. Das Stück des Zeichners, Schriftstellers und Musikers Franz Graf von Pocci (1807 – 1876), dessen Geschichten des Kasperl Larifari bis heute Kult sind, handelt, so die Künstlerin, »von einer Feenmutter, deren Tochter von ihrem Vater, dem Magier Crocodilus, in einen Krebs mit Scherenhänden verzaubert wird«. Am Ende bereut der Krokodil-Papa seine Tat, Kasperl schlägt einen Menageriebesitzer k.o., der ihn wieder in einen Käfig sperren will, und die Familie ist glücklich vereint.

In der letzten Einstellung skatet Kasperl, verkörpert von Sohn Lorenz, in schwungvollem Slalom eine Landstraße hinunter, und alle schmettern den Ohrwurm der unschlagbaren ersten Boygroup der Welt, der Comedian Harmonists, »Ein Freund, ein guter Freund ...«. Der surreale Sketch, für den Katharina von Werz die furiosen Szenen, darunter Salti ihrer Tochter Anna, in einzelnen Sequenzen filmte und später den Ton zu jeder Rolle nachsprach, besitzt jenen scharfzüngigen Witz, der Humor als eine philosophische Qualität begreift: »Der Humor ist ganz nah bei der Nächstenliebe. Er entkleidet, es bleibt nur die Essenz übrig, jenseits der Masken. Er erschafft Augenblicke der Wahrheit.«

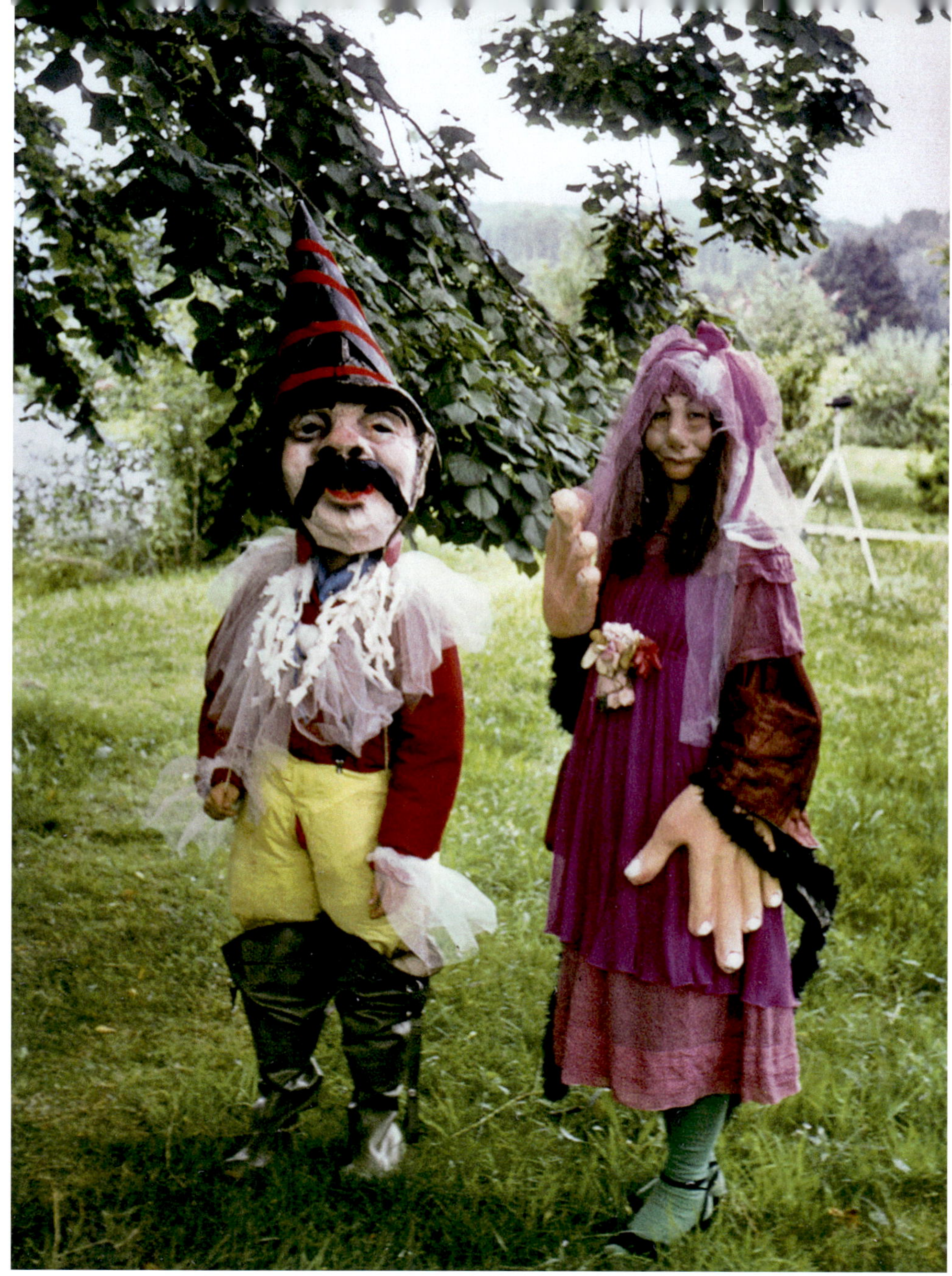

guests to come up with even greater shows and costumes. Snake charming was even included in the repertoire that was as always unfailingly satirical, just as the invitation from the ballroom dancing enthusiasts to the "Championship of the Silver Bar" with the Dressler twins as adjudicators and a *conferencier* or master of ceremonies whose name "Horst Heinz Schmalzbach" sufficed to illustrate the anarchistic humor of these evening events.

However, the climax of this comedic talent has to be the video *Crocodilus and Persea or The Enchanted Crab* that was filmed by Katharina von Werz in 1973 with her husband and children who she cast in different roles. The plot of the piece by draftsman, writer, and musician Franz Graf von Pocci (1807–1876), whose stories, the artist explains, center around Kasperl Larifari, are still cult today, and involve a "fairy, whose daughter is transformed into a crab with scissor hands by her father, the magician Crocodilus." In the end, the daddy crocodile regrets what he did, Kasperl knocks out a menagerie owner who wants to trap him in a cage again, and the family is joyfully reunited.

In the last shot, Kasperl, personified by her son Lorenz, skates down a country road and everyone belts out the catchy tune from the unbeatable first boy band in the world, the Comedian Harmonists, "Ein Freund, ein guter Freund ..." Katharina von Werz filmed the fast-paced scenes, including somersaults by her daughter Anna, in separate sequences, recording the soundtrack afterwards, and speaking all the parts herself. The surreal sketch is imbued with that sharp-tongued wit, which regards humor as a philosophical quality: "Humor is very close to altruistic love. It undresses, until only the essence remains, stripped of all masks. It creates moments of truth."

»Im Sommer male ich am Meer oder am See, und dann nehme
ich meine Modelle möglichst unauffällig ins Visier – ich denke,
sie merken nichts, aber das tun sie doch ... Meistens freuen sie
sich über die Skizzen, die ich von ihnen mache.«

Anna von Zumbusch mit/with Leni,
Katharina von Werz beim Zeichnen/drawing,
Lorenz Moll, Korsika/Corsica, 1992

Sie eine Nomadin zu nennen wäre übertrieben. Aber Katharina von Werz muss sich bewegen, geografisch
und physisch. Mit den ersten Besuchen bei den Verwandten ihrer Mutter Fe in Holland kam nicht nur die Neu-
gier auf, immer neue Orte zu entdecken, sondern auch die Lust darauf, sie sich mit dem Körper zu erobern, beim
Wandern, Skifahren, Schwimmen. »Alle in unserer Familie waren und sind sportlich«, sagt sie. »Ich brauche
den Sport nicht nur für Gelenkigkeit und Kraft, sondern auch für meine Stimmung.« Also joggt sie, radelt und
macht zweimal pro Woche Gymnastik in einem »Turnverein, der überhaupt nicht schick ist«, was ihrem Hang
zu schrägen Szenarien entgegenkommt, aber auch dem »Bedürfnis, ohne Vorschriften das zu trainieren, was mir
gerade wichtig ist«.

Da Sport und Reisen für die Künstlerin und ihre Familie traditionell zusammengehören, gibt es, den
Jahreszeiten folgend, Fixpunkte, an denen man sich trifft, oft auch mit Freunden. So bricht der Clan immer kurz
vor Ostern zu Langlauf und Bergtouren ins Engadin auf und mietet sich im Hotel Fex ein, unweit von Sils Maria
und St. Moritz. »Inzwischen verausgaben wir uns dabei nicht mehr, aber früher haben wir im Winter richtig
große, schweißtreibende Touren gemacht.«

Katharina von Werz erinnert sich zum Beispiel an einen Aufstieg mit ihrem Mann und Lorenz, dem Sohn
des Malers Rupprecht Geiger, 1966 zum italienischen Gran Paradiso, dem mit über 4000 Metern höchsten Berg
der Grajischen Alpen. »Es gab einen Sturm am Gipfel und unsere Hütte war so kalt, dass wir unsere Skischuhe
anbehielten, sogar während wir schliefen«. Vier Jahre später verlor Freund Lenz bei einer anderen Expedition
zum französischen Dôme de la Lauze im Écrins-Massiv in meterhohem Pulverschnee sogar seine Skier, »doch
irgendwie kamen wir am Ende alle heil wieder unten an«. In den 70er Jahren nahm sie sogar an mehreren
Skilanglauf-Marathons teil. Einer fand im tschechischen Isergebirge unweit der Stadt Liberec (dt. Reichenberg)
statt, ein anderer, der »Koiserlauf«, zwischen Kirchberg und St. Johann in den Kitzbüheler Alpen, »sehr anstren-
gend, aber es hat riesigen Spaß gemacht«.

Das Gegenprogramm zu den Winteraktivitäten ist Sartène, »die korsischste aller korsischen Städte«, wie
der französische Schriftsteller Prosper Mérimée den Ort beschrieb. Hier verbringt die Familie den August, und
für die Wochenenden gibt es ein Anwesen am Chiemsee in Pfifferloh.

»Jeder Ort hat seine ganz eigene Ausstrahlung und Natur.« Wenn sie skizziert, entdeckt die Künstlerin
»gerade im Vertrauten immer wieder Neues«. In Pfifferloh setzt sie sich zum Beispiel gerne an einen nahe-
gelegenen Weiher, die magische Bergkulisse vor Augen, und malt stundenlang, »beinahe wie in Trance«. Oder
sie fährt mit dem Auto durch die Landschaft, parkt irgendwo und verliert sich in ihre Zeichnungen. Manchmal
blicken ihr Spaziergänger über die Schultern, doch einmal stand plötzlich ein Polizist vor ihr. »Ich hatte auf

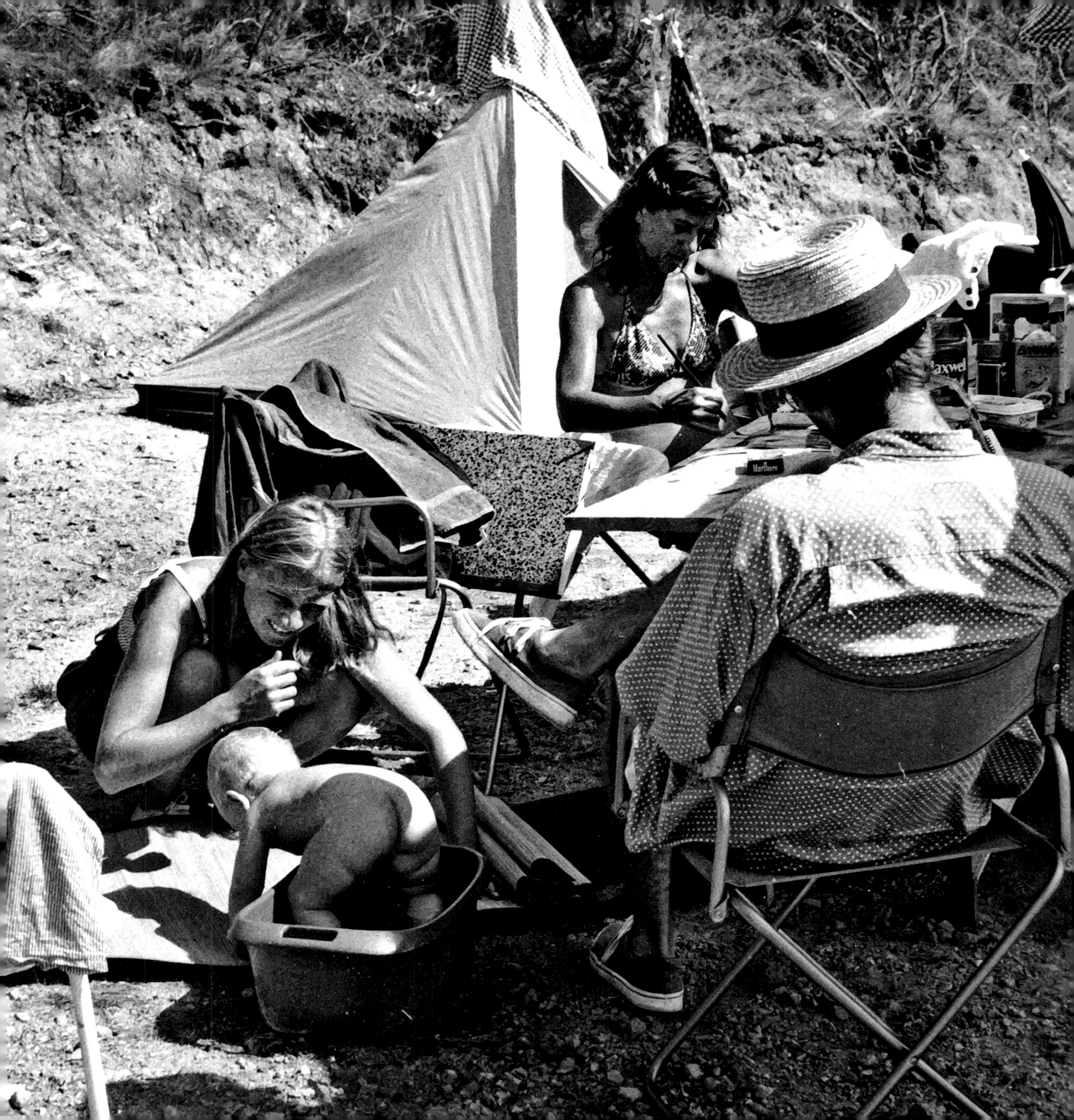

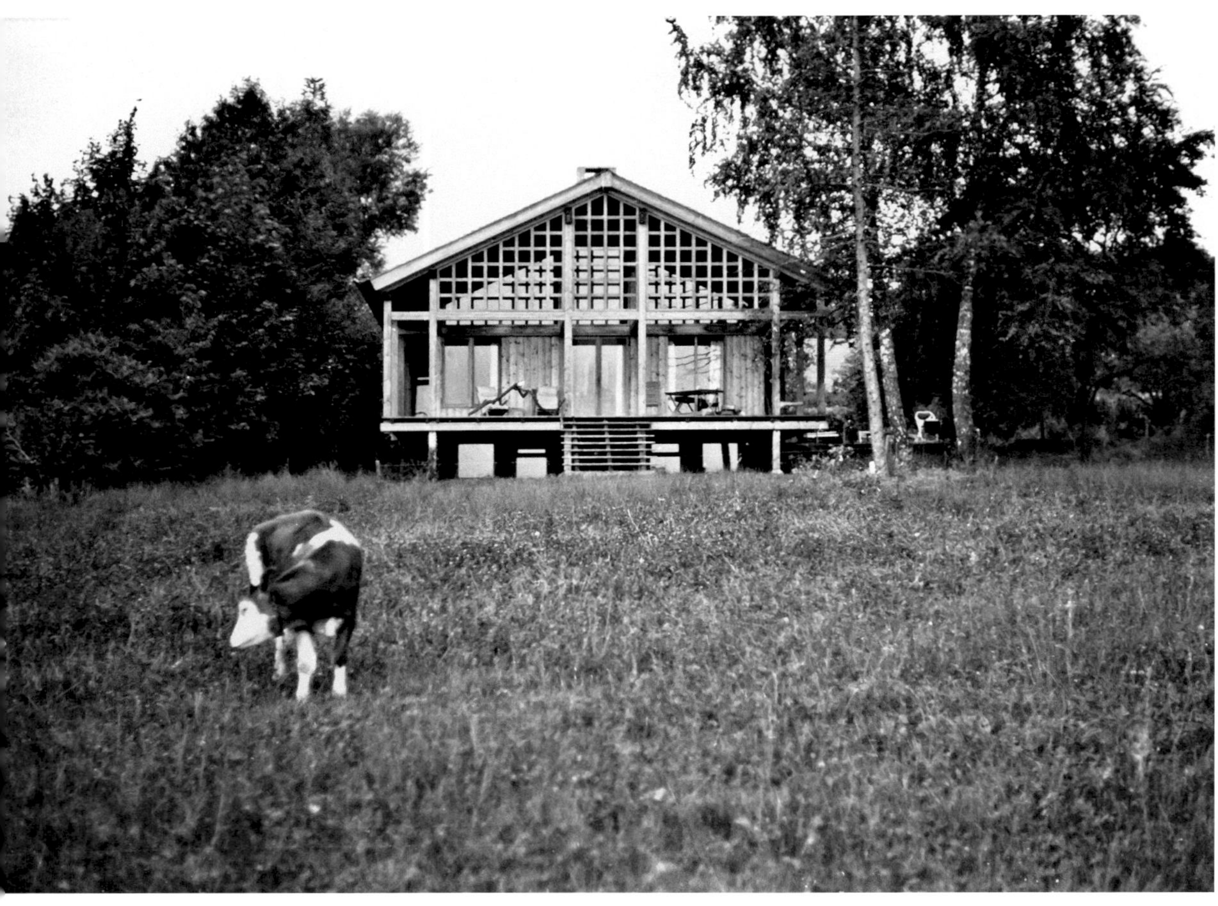

dem Grünstreifen vor einem Haus geparkt, und er wollte mir einen Strafzettel verpassen. Aber dann sah er meinen Block, grinste und rief einem Kollegen zu, der in ein paar Metern Abstand wartete: ›Des is ja a Hobbymalerin‹.« Diese Art von Situationskomik genießt Katharina von Werz – gut gemeinte Einschätzungen, die jedoch haarscharf daneben treffen. So fand sie es auch »lustig, dass ich in einem beeindruckenden Film der Regisseurin Gaby Imhof-Weber als Chiemseemalerin vorgestellt wurde«.

Korsika dagegen ist das Antiprogramm zur Chiemgau-Idylle, ungezähmt und nicht ganz ungefährlich. »Ende der 70er Jahre entdeckten wir Sartène, einen Ort oberhalb des Hafenstädtchens Propriano im Süden der Insel. Wir waren auf der Suche nach guten Plätzen zum Windsurfen, denn unsere Kinder wollten nicht nur am Feringasee surfen.« Das Meer dort gab den Ausschlag. Von nun an kam die Familie regelmäßig, zeltete jahrelang und behielt auch angesichts der Wasserflugzeuge, die über sie hinwegsegelten, um einen der häufigen Waldbrände zu löschen, die Ruhe.

Selbst als sie von den Blutrachefeldzügen der Mafia in der Gegend hörten, blieben sie furchtlos, obwohl diese nicht selten in unmittelbarer Nähe stattfanden. »Noch immer werden Menschen in Propriano am helllichten Tag erschossen«, berichtet Katharina von Werz, »von einigen kennen wir sogar die nächsten Verwandten. Aber wir haben diesen Ort mit seiner wilden Schönheit über die Jahre so ins Herz geschlossen, dass wir hier schließlich ein kleines, sehr einfaches Haus gebaut haben, Typ Bergerie.« Inzwischen ist die Künstlerin sogar mit einigen Einheimischen befreundet, darunter zwei Brüdern, »von denen der eine ein talentierter Kunstfälscher ist«. Was Gelegenheit »zu speziellen Fachgesprächen« bietet – wieder ist da ihr ansteckend vergnügtes Lachen.

Skurrile Typen und Geschichten, Abenteuerlust gemischt mit der Neigung für kuriose Ereignisse und Begegnungen charakterisieren auch die Reisen, die Katharina von Werz allein, mit Mann und oft mit Familie unternimmt. Eine ihrer frühesten führt die junge Künstlerin 1957 zur Avantgarde-Malerin Gabriele Münter nach Murnau, die sie bewundert. »Ich schenkte ihr ein kleines Bild, für das sie sich herzlich bedankte. Umgekehrt erhielt ich von ihr eine Zeichnung mit Widmung, was mich sehr rührte und stolz machte. Es war eine unvergessliche Begegnung.«

Unvergesslich war Jahre später auch ein ganz anderes Erlebnis, der »unfreiwillige Gewaltmarsch zum Apollontempel bei Bassae auf der griechischen Peloponnes. Mein Mann und ich waren vom Weg abgekommen und irrten eineinhalb Tage durch die Landschaft, bis wir das Heiligtum endlich vor uns aufragen sahen. Umso mehr haben wir das majestätische Bauwerk und die milde Abendsonne dort dann genossen.«

Es folgte die Eroberung weiter entfernter Kontinente, beginnend 1964 mit Indien. »Mit dem Schiff starteten wir in Venedig, legten in Beirut und Haifa an, fuhren anschließend durch den Suezkanal, wo wir in Massaua und Dschibouti Zwischenstopps machten, und dann cruisten wir durch das arabische Meer nach Bombay (heute Mumbai). Es war aufregend. Von hier aus ging es mit Zug und Bussen weiter nach Delhi, Rajasthan und nach Fatehpur Sikri. Hier in der Felswüste bei Agra besichtigten wir die feenhaften Sandsteinpaläste und Haremsanlagen des Großmoguls Akbar. Wir waren acht Wochen unterwegs – eine Traumreise, wie man sie heute nicht mehr machen kann!«

"In summer I paint at the seaside or beside the lake and then I try to scrutinize my models as inconspicuously as possible. I'd like to think they don't notice anything, but they do … They're usually happy with the sketches I make of them."

To call her a nomad would be an exaggeration. But if there is one thing Katharina von Werz must be able to do, it is move, geographically and mentally. The first few trips when she accompanied her mother Fe to visit relatives in Holland not only aroused her curiosity to discover new places but also the desire to conquer them through physical exercise, in short with her body, by hiking, skiing, and swimming. "Everyone in our family was sporty and the same goes for the children now," she says. "I need sport not only to remain strong and supple. I need it for my mood." As a result, Katharina von Werz goes jogging, cycles, and does gymnastics twice a week in "a sports club that is anything but stylish," which suits her fondness for the bizarre, as well as her "need to do the kind of exercises that I feel will do me good, regardless of what others are doing."

As sport and travel have always been interconnected in her family, there are several fixed points in her calendar, when the wider family get together, often with friends. With this purpose in mind, the von Werz clan always head off, a few days before Easter to the Engadine valley for some cross-country skiing and climbing. They stay at the Hotel Fex, not far from Sils Maria and St. Moritz. "We don't push ourselves quite as much as we used to. But we used to go on really long tours in winter, so strenuous we would all break out in a sweat."

Katharina von Werz remembers a climb she embarked on with her husband and Lorenz, son of the painter Rupprecht Geiger, in 1966 to the Italian Gran Paradiso: at over 4000 meters the highest mountain in the Graian Alps. "There was storm at the summit," she says, "and our hut was so cold that we kept our ski boots on at night." Four years later her friend Lenz even lost his skis in meter-deep powder snow during another expedition to the Dôme de la Lauze in the Massif des Écrins in France. "Somehow we all managed to come back down again in one piece." In the seventies von Werz even took part in several cross-country ski marathons. One such event was held in the Czech Jizera Mountains, not far from the city of Liberec, another between Kirchberg and St. Johann in the Tyrolean Kitzbühel Alps. By her own account it was "very exhausting, but a lot of fun."

The counterpoint to these winter activities comes in the form of Sartène, "that most Corsican of all Corsican towns," as the French writer Prosper Mérimée said. It is here that the family spend August. On the weekends they also have a house on Chiemsee in Pfifferloh.

"Every place has its own atmosphere, its own nature." When sketching, the artist always discovers "something new, especially in the familiar." In Pfifferloh von Werz likes to find a spot beside a near-by pond, and, with the magical mountain scenery in full view, will paint for hours on end, "almost as if in a trance." Alternatively she might take the car, drive through the countryside, park up somewhere and lose herself in her drawings. It is customary that people out walking look over her shoulder, but one day she realized a policeman was standing over her. "I had parked on the stretch of grass in front of a house," she explains, "and he was about to issue me

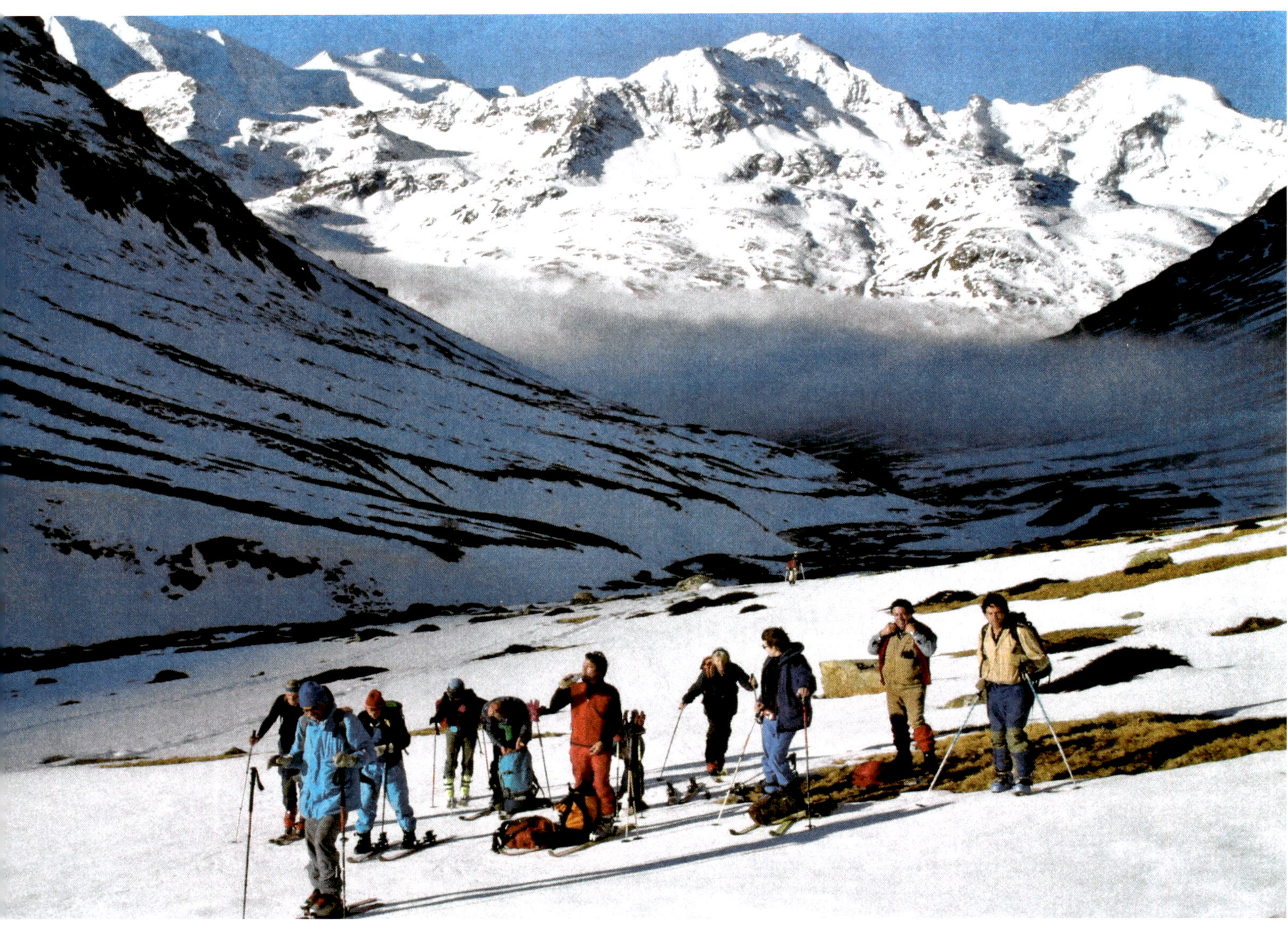

Katharina von Werz und Freunde/and
friends, Anstieg zum/ascending the
Piz Grevasalvas, 2002

Auch Marokko acht Jahre später hatte dieses Tausendundeine-Nacht-Flair. »In Marrakesch mieteten wir eine Ente, einen Citroën 2CV, und fuhren weiter nach Casablanca, Fez und über's Atlasgebirge bis nach Tafraoute, einen Ort mitten in der rosa granitenen Felslandschaft des Antiatlas.« Die Wüstendünen von Mhamid und das Berberdorf Imilchil im Atlasgebirge waren ebenfalls Teil der Tour, »bei der zwar irgendwann eine Autoscheibe in der Hitze zersprang, aber sonst alles ziemlich märchenhaft blieb«.

Eine Stadt besitzt für Katharina von Werz eine ganz persönliche Bedeutung: die Zarenmetropole St. Petersburg, wo sie 1995 zusammen mit Rudi Tröger eine viel beachtete Ausstellung in der Muchina-Akademie der Künste hatte. Nicht nur Sport, auch Kunst und Reisen gehören für sie untrennbar zusammen: »Reisen steigert die Kreativität, weil es das Erleben intensiviert.«

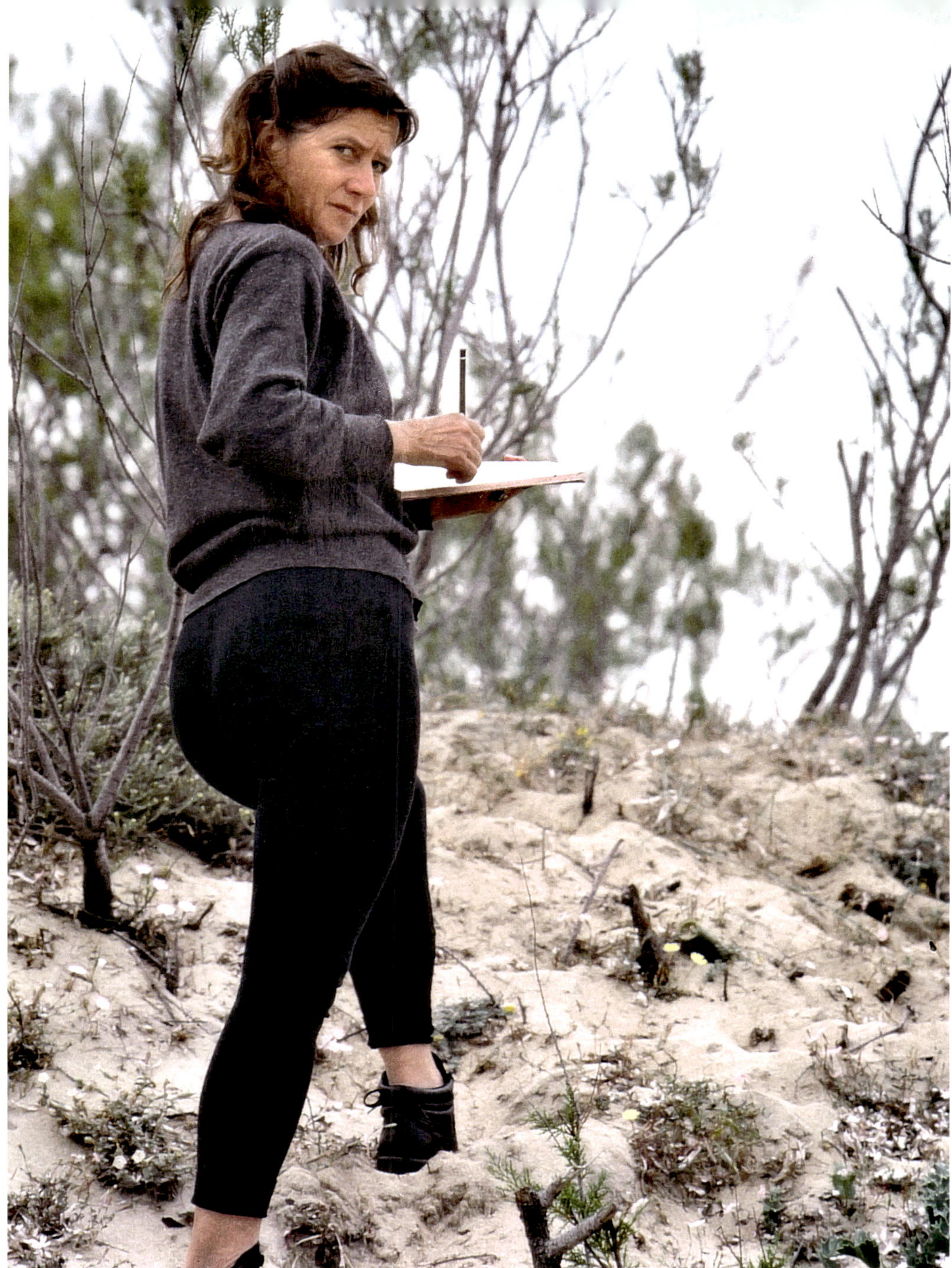

Katharina von Werz, Tralicetu,
Korsika/Corsica, 2008

with a ticket. But then he saw my pad, grinned, and called a colleague, who was waiting just a few meters away. He said: 'We've got an amateur painter here.' Katharina von Werz enjoys these moments of comedy—well intentioned guesses that somehow still get close to the truth. In the same vein, she also thought it was funny that in a film by the director Gaby Imhof-Weber she is introduced at one point as "one of those Chiemsee painters."

Corsica, by contrast, is the exact opposite to the Chiemsee idyll, untamed and not entirely without its dangers. "Sometime in the late seventies," she says, "we discovered Sartène, a place to the north of the port town of Propriano, on the island's southern shore. We were looking for good spots to go windsurfing, because our children didn't just want to go surfing on Feringasee" (in Bavaria). The sea there was what captivated them. From that point on the family kept coming back, for years sleeping in tents and remaining unfazed by the sight of sea planes as they soared over their heads on their way to put out the forest fires that regularly break out there.

They even remained undeterred when they heard about the bloody vendettas, campaigns of violence, carried out in the area by the mafia, despite the fact that such acts often occurred close by. "People are still shot dead in broad daylight in Propriano," says Katharina von Werz. "In some cases we've even known close relatives of the dead. But over the years we've grown so much to love this place, its wild beauty, that we decided to build a small, very simple house there, a kind of *bergerie*." The artist has now even made friends with some of the locals, among them two brothers, "one of whom is a forger of artworks, and a talented one at that." A friendship that leads to "expert talks between people of the same craft"—and once again, she breaks out in her infectious laughter.

Bizarre characters and stories, a taste for adventure mixed with a love of strange events and encounters also characterize Katharina von Werz's travels to exotic lands, embarked on either alone, or with her husband, and often with her children. One of her earliest travels in 1957 took the young artist to Murnau, to see the avante-garde painter Gabriele Münter, who she greatly admired. "I gave her a small picture I'd done; she was most appreciative. And in return I received a drawing from her, with an inscription that I found very moving and which made me proud. It was an unforgettable encounter."

Another unforgettable experience was the time she relates thus: "We were forced to march to the temple of Apollo near Bassae on the Peloponnese. My husband and I had lost the way and spent one-and-a-half days wandering through the country without any idea where we were, until we finally suddenly saw the temple towering above us. After what we'd just been through, we were able to savor the majestic structure and the gentle evening sun all the more."

And so starts her conquest of distant continents, starting in 1964 with India. "We set off from Venice by ship, docked in Beirut and Haifa, then sailed through the Suez Canal, where we stopped over at Massawa and Djibouti and then cruised across the Arabian Sea to Bombay (now Mumbai). It was so exciting. From there we took the train and bus on to Delhi, Rajasthan, and Fatehpur Sikri. It was there in the rocky dessert near Agra that we visited the fairy-tale-like sandstone palaces and harem complexes of the great Moghul emperor Akbar. We were on the road for eight weeks, it was a dream trip, of the kind you can no longer go on today!"

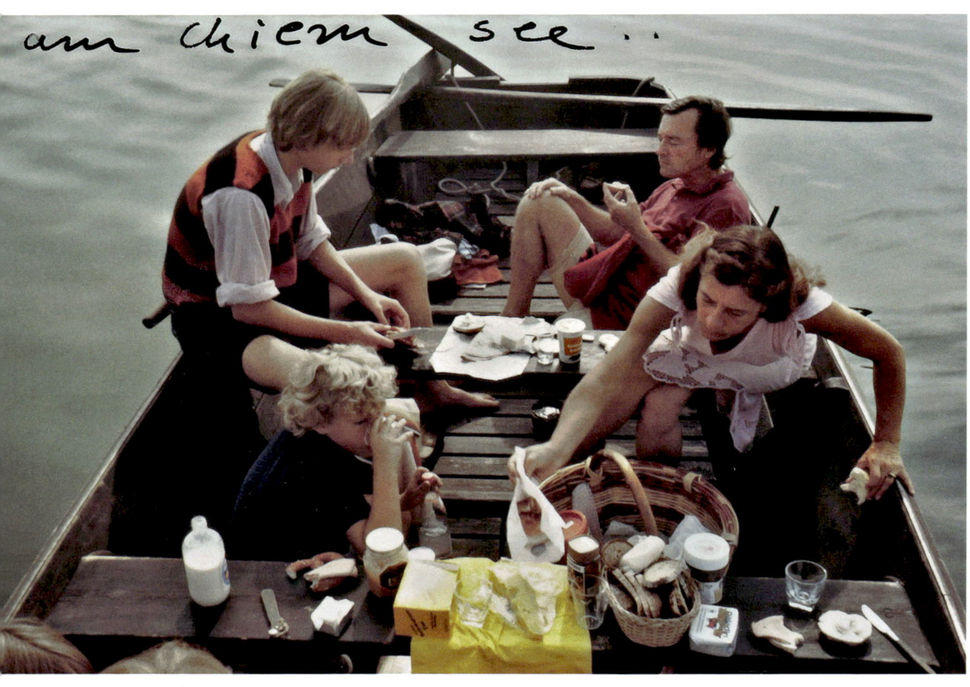

A

A
Robert, Lorenz, Franz und/and
Katharina von Werz, Frühstück im Boot/
breakfast in the boat, 1980

B
Alexej Talajik, Katharina von Werz,
Karl-Heinz Thalmann, Prof. Vasilij Kozyrev,
Museum für angewandte Kunst/Applied
Arts Museum (Muchina), St. Petersburg,
Russland/Russia, 1995

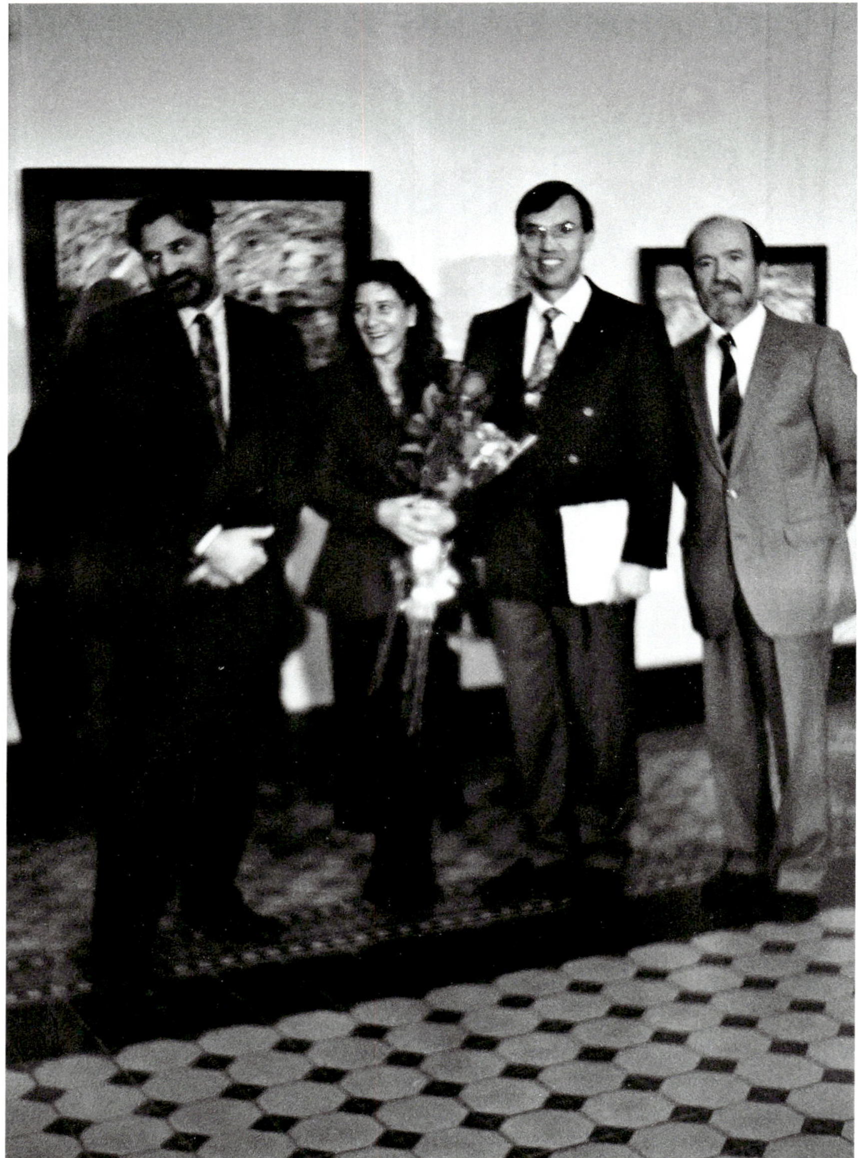
B

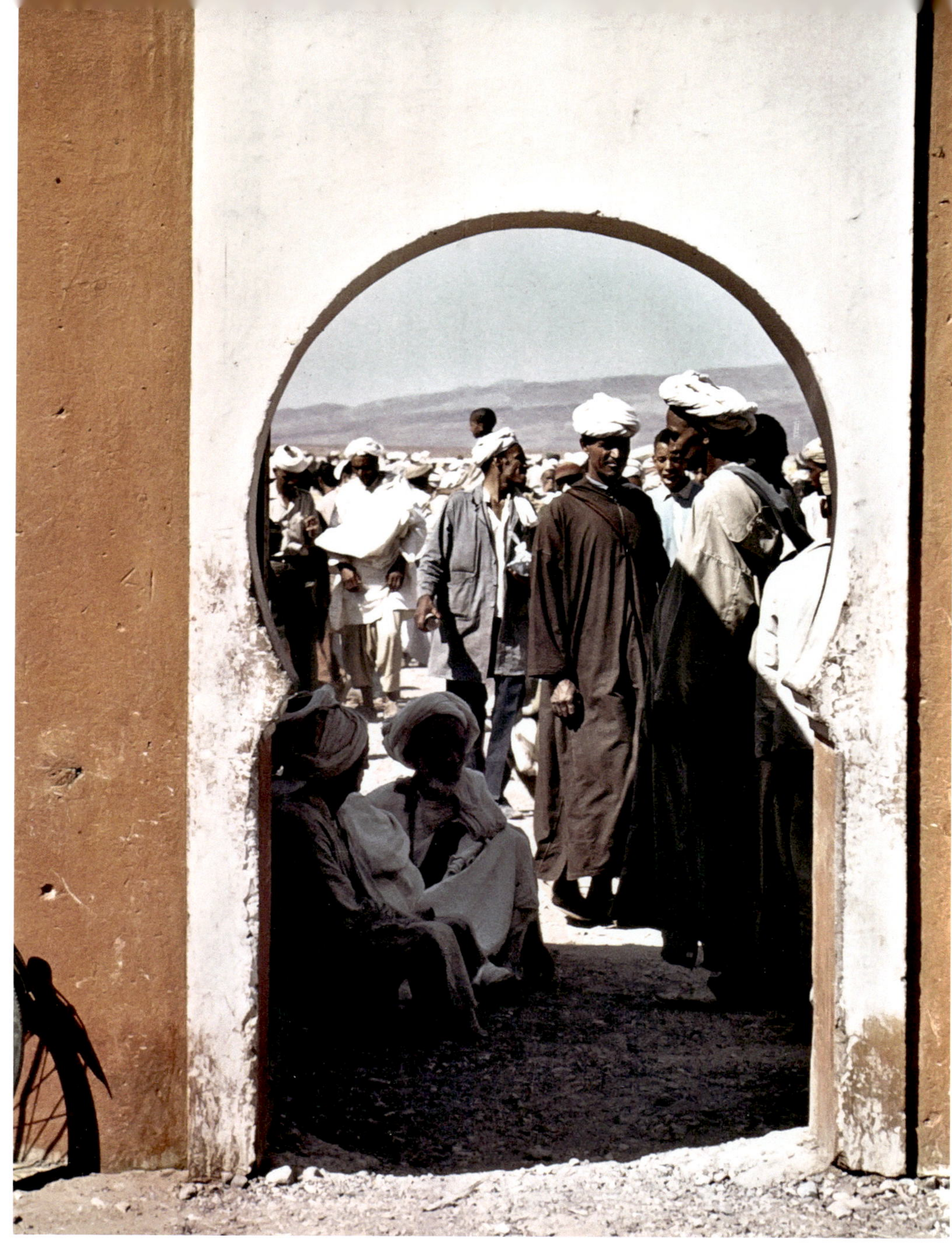

Marokko/Morocco, Ouarzazate, 1972

Morocco, visited some eight years later, also shared something of this *Arabian Nights* flair. "In Marrakesh we hired a 2CV and drove to Casablanca, Fez, over the Atlas Mountains to Tafraoute, a place in the middle of the pinkish granite rocky landscape of the Anti-Atlas." The dessert dunes of Mhamid and the Berber village of Imilchil in the Atlas Mountains were also on route during the tour, "during which a car window cracked in the heat, but which otherwise passed without incident and was like a living fairy-tale."

One city is of special importance for Katharina von Werz: St. Petersburg, where in 1995 she and Rudi Tröger had a widely admired, joint exhibition at the Saint Petersburg State Art and Industry Academy. Not only sport, but art too is inseparable from travel for her. In her own words: "Travel increases creativity, because it intensifies experience."

»Ohne den wohlwollenden Zuspruch von Künstlern, Galeristen und Kuratoren hätte ich mir vielleicht nicht direkt ein Ohr abgeschnitten. Aber meinem gestalterischen Tun wären sicherlich Grenzen gesetzt gewesen. Vielleicht hätte ich ohne jedwede Resonanz andere Ventile gesucht? So aber haben mich viele glückliche Zufälle weitergetragen, und einige ermutigende Begegnungen halfen mir, meinen Weg zu gehen.«

Katharina von Werz und/and Ellsworth Kelly
bei K. v. Werz in München/at K. v. Werz's in
Munich, 2000

Es sind wenige Tage, aber es gibt sie: Tage, an denen die Künstlerin ihre Arbeit unterbricht und sich ihrer Rolle als Gastgeberin widmet. Einer dieser Anlässe war 1995, als sich der große Pop-Art-Künstler Robert Rauschenberg wünschte, den Abend nach der Eröffnung seiner Ausstellung auf der Praterinsel »in lockerer, münchnerisch künstlerischer Atmosphäre zu verbringen«, wie Katharina von Werz erzählt.

Unvergesslich bleibt ihr auch der Besuch von Ellsworth Kelly im Frühjahr 2000. Freunde bringen den Star der amerikanischen Hard Edge-Malerei und -Skulptur anlässlich seiner Ausstellung in der Städtischen Galerie im Lenbachhaus mit. Bei selbstgemachten Salaten, Käse, Pasta und viel Wein diskutiert, plaudert und lacht man entspannt und angeregt – Sternstunden, an die sich die Familie gerne erinnert.

Katharina von Werz findet diese Begegnungen zwar »sehr inspirierend«, aber »meine Arbeit entfaltet sich in einem anderen Resonanzraum«, erklärt sie bestimmt: »Ohne den wohlwollenden Zuspruch von Künstlern, Galeristen und Kuratoren hätte ich mir vielleicht nicht direkt ein Ohr abgeschnitten. Aber meinem gestalterischen Tun wären sicherlich Grenzen gesetzt gewesen. Vielleicht hätte ich ohne jedwede Resonanz andere Ventile gesucht? So aber haben mich viele glückliche Zufälle weitergetragen, und einige ermutigende Begegnungen halfen mir, meinen Weg zu gehen.«

Mit allen Kommentaren zu ihrer Arbeit setzt sie sich intensiv auseinander. Besonders freut sie sich über spontane und persönliche Reaktionen wie den Brief des Malers Günther Förg, der ihr 2004 schreibt: »Ihre Bilder haben mir so gut gefallen, dass ich Sie fragen wollte, ob es einen Katalog dazu gibt.« Oder über die Kartengrüße des Fotografen Stefan Moses. Er hat sie und ihre Familie oft porträtiert und schickt nach jeder Ausstellung hinreißende Kitschmotive mit Schmusekätzchen und Blumensträußen per Post: »Du klügste, größte aller Malerinnen (...) deine starken, vollen Leinwände geben Kraft zum Überleben! (...) Es ist alles so gut!! Und die Raucherin!!! Und die Morgenfrauen! Die haben alle so einen großen Atem!«

Ihn bestätigen auch ihre Galeristen. So nennt Michael Hasenclever, der zwischen 1972 und 1984 fünf Ausstellungen mit ihr machte, ihre künstlerische Entwicklung erstaunlich: »Fand ich ihre Gemälde am Anfang eher introvertiert, so wurden sie im Lauf der Jahre bemerkenswert farbstark, dynamisch und weltzugewandt – ziemlich athletisch für ihre zierliche Statur.«

Fred Jahn, der seit der Jahrtausendwende drei Ausstellungen mit Gemälden und Skulpturen realisierte, stellt fest: »Jedes Mal war die Resonanz der Besucher stärker und meine Begeisterung größer. An ihrer Kunst imponiert mir, wie rhythmisch sowohl in der Form als auch in der Farbigkeit sie die heitere Stimmung der Motive in schwingende Malerei und Plastik übersetzt.«

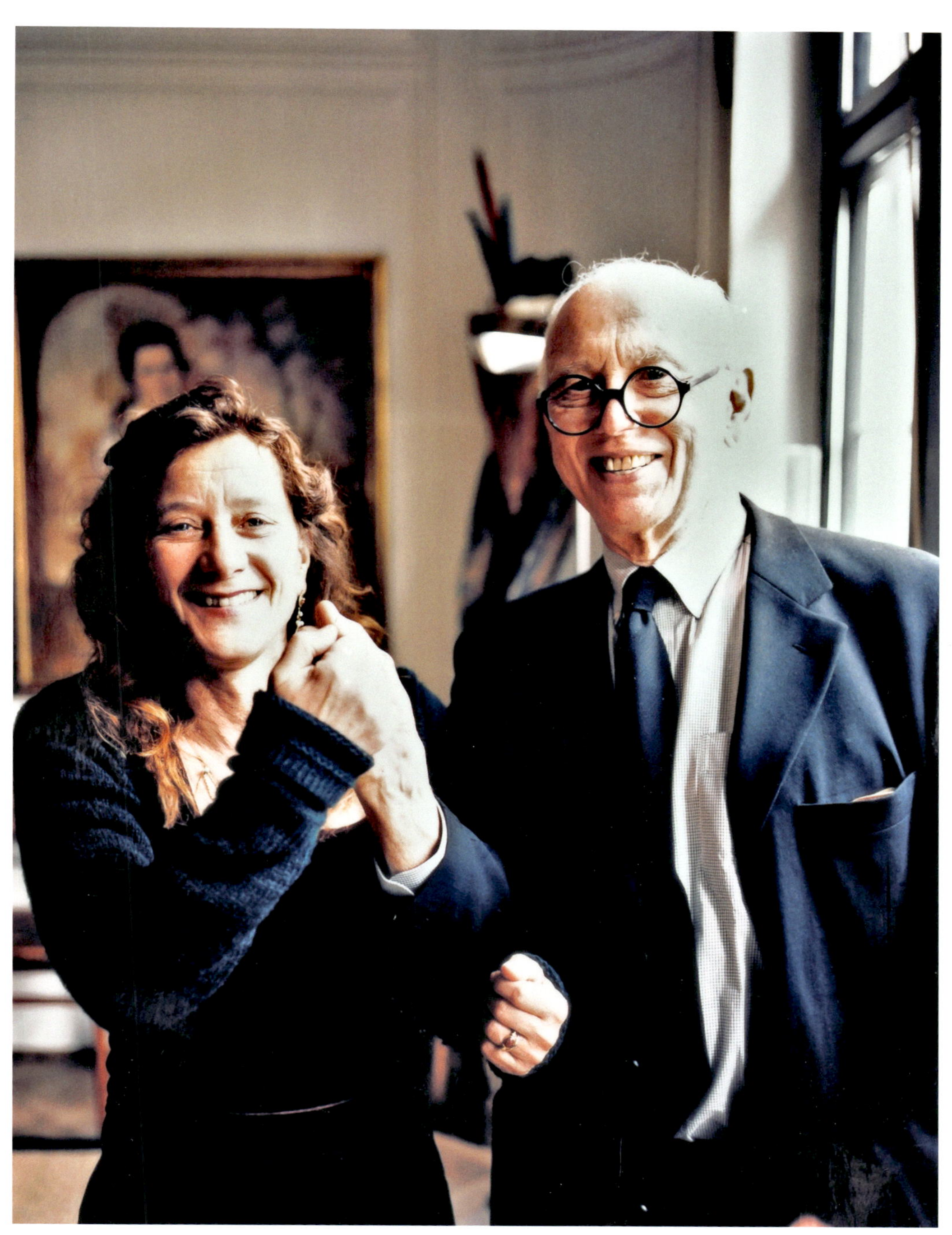

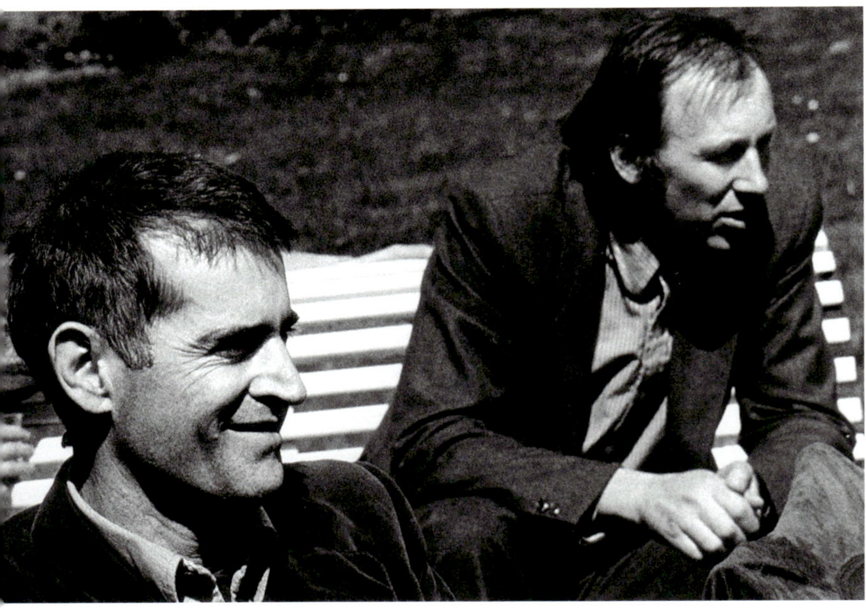

A

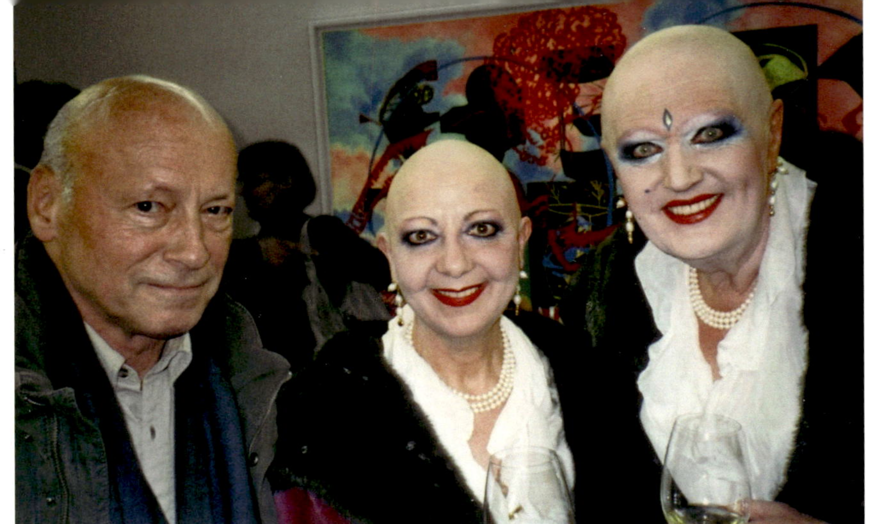

B

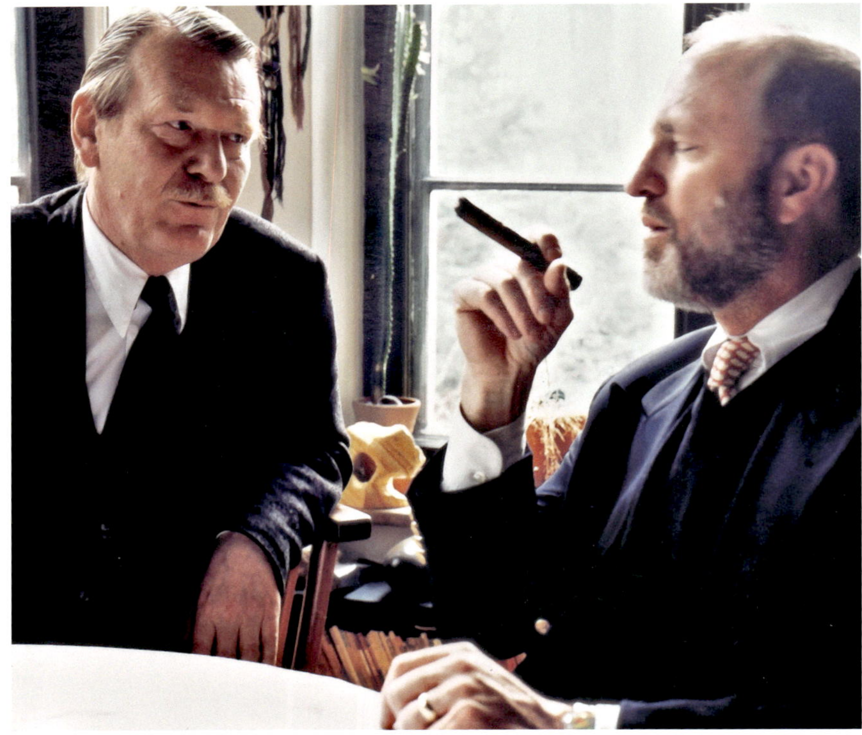

C

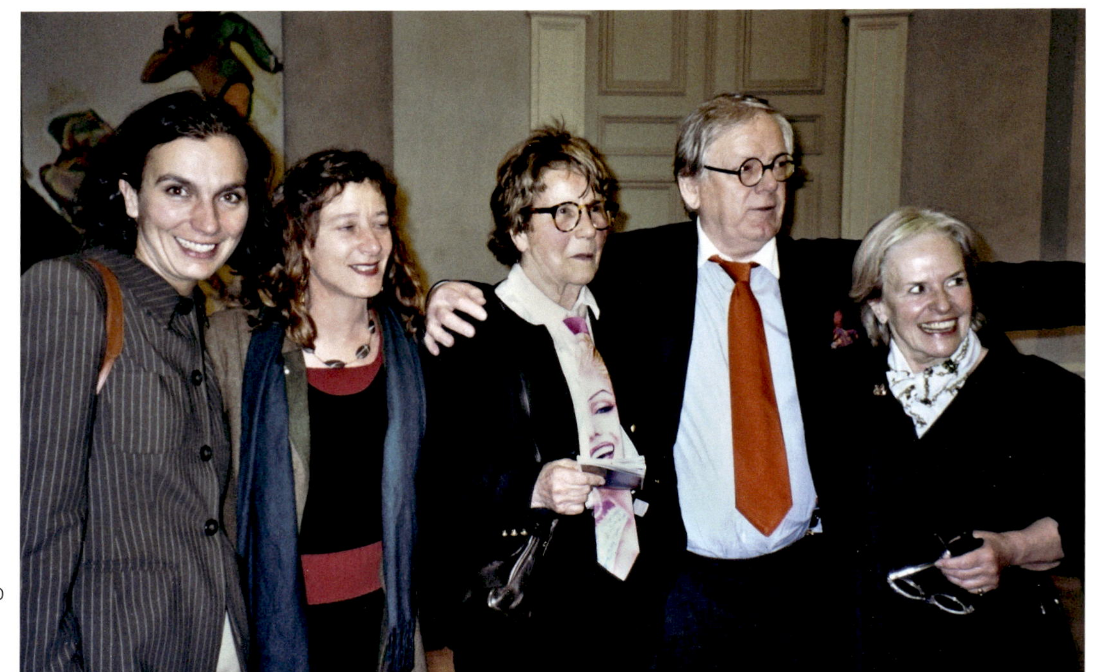

D

"If I had not been received favorably by artists, art dealers,
and curators, I don't think I would have cut my ear off. But my
creative work would definitely have been affected. Perhaps
I would have looked for other outlets if I had not got any
response? But as it is, many fortunate coincidences have
helped me continue and several positive encounters have
encouraged me to follow my own path."

A
Martial Raysse, Michael Hasenclever, 1979

B
Helmuth Klewan, Eva (rechts/right)
& Adele, Köln/Cologne, 2010

C
Fred Jahn, James Cuno, 2000

D
Christiane Lange, Katharina von Werz,
Maria Lassnig, Carl Haenlein, Marlies Biehler,
Bayerische Akademie der Schönen Künste,
München/Munich, 2003

They may be rare but every now and then there are days when the artist interrupts her work and dedicates herself to the role of hostess. One such occasion was in 1995 when the great Pop artist Robert Rauschenberg wanted to spend the evening after the opening of his exhibition on the Praterinsel "in the relaxed atmosphere of Munich's art world," says Katharina von Werz.

Another unforgettable moment was a visit from Ellsworth Kelly, who was in town for his exhibition at the Lenbachhaus in spring 2000. Friends brought the star of American Hard-Edge painting and sculpture along with them to dinner at Katharina von Werz's home. Over homemade salads, cheese, pasta, and much wine, the guests discussed ideas, chatted, and laughed at each other's stories in a convivial atmosphere—a highlight from that time which the family remembers fondly.

Katharina von Werz finds these encounters "very inspiring," but "my work," she asserts, "evolves in a different environment, a sounding box of a different kind. If I had not been received favorably by artists, art dealers and curators, I don't think I would have cut my ear off. But my creative work would definitely have been affected. Perhaps I would have looked for other outlets if I had not got any response? But as it is, many fortunate coincidences have helped me continue and several positive encounters have encouraged me to follow my own path."

She takes every comment about her work seriously. Particularly special to her are spontaneous and personal reactions like the letter from painter Günther Förg, who wrote to her in 2004: "I liked your pictures so much that I wanted to ask you if there's a catalogue of them." Or the greeting cards from photographer Stefan Moses. He has often photographed the artist and her family, and, after every exhibition, sends delightful kitschy motifs of cuddly kittens and bunches of flowers by mail: "you, the cleverest and greatest of all painters (…) your strong, full canvases give us the strength to live!(…) They are so good!! The woman smoking!!! The women in the morning! They're done with such verve."

His words are confirmed by her art dealers. Michael Hasenclever, who organized five exhibitions of her work between 1972 and 1984, describes her artistic development as astounding: "I found her early paintings quite introverted but over the years they've become notably more colorful, dynamic, and worldly—pretty athletic for a woman of her slight build."

Fred Jahn, who has realized three exhibitions of her paintings and sculptures since the beginning of the new millennium, says: "Each time, we got a greater response from visitors and my enthusiasm grew. What impresses me about her art is how rhythmically she recreates the lively mood of the motifs both in terms of form and color in her dynamic paintings and sculptures."

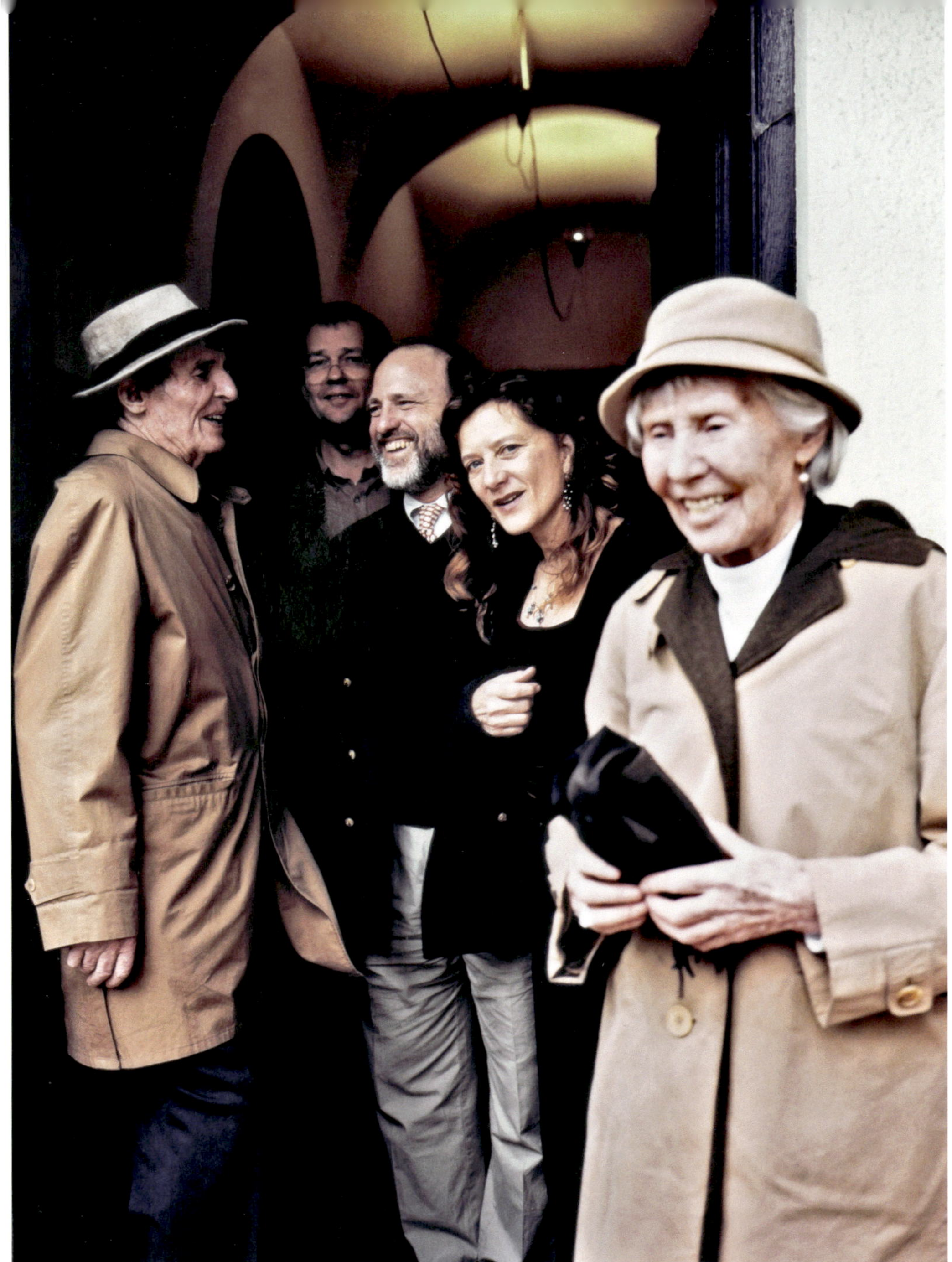

Rupprecht Geiger, James Cuno,
Katharina von Werz, Moni Geiger bei
K. v. Werz in München/at K. v. Werz's
in Munich, 2000

Ihr dritter Galerist Helmut Klewan schließlich, der ihre
Arbeiten zwei Mal zeigte, hält sie für »eine sehr intelligente
Malerin. Schon ihre frühen, mit diffusem Licht gemalten Bilder
sind souverän von westlicher Malkultur getragen. Bei den spä-
teren gefällt mir, wie raffiniert sie die Tradition der 40er und
50er Jahre fortsetzt. Ihre besten Bilder haben die Kraft eines
Willem de Kooning aus seiner stärksten Periode um 1950.«

Anerkennende Worte finden auch Museumsdirektoren
und Kuratoren, die Werke ankauften und ihre Arbeit über die
Jahre verfolgen. So beschreibt James Cuno, der Präsident und
Vorstandsvorsitzende des J. Paul Getty Trust die Künstlerin
als »seltenen kreativen Geist in einer Welt voller Konkurrenz-
denken und Kommerz. Sie ist eine Magierin – gleich, ob sie
zeichnet, malt oder bildhauert, mit Familie und Freunden theatralische Aufführungen in verschwenderischen Kostümen inszeniert oder ihr Haus für Freunde und Besucher öffnet, die sie mit
guten, selbstgemachten Köstlichkeiten und viel Wein verwöhnt.
Sie ist wie John Cage, sie findet in allen Bildern und Klängen
unserer Welt Schönheit und macht sie zu einem besseren Ort.«

Helmut Friedel, Direktor der Städtischen Galerie im
Lenbachhaus, wiederum betont den »ungebrochenen Aus-
druckswillen« ihrer Kunst, deren »innere Unruhe und Not-
wendigkeit, sich in farbigen Pinselkaskaden zu ergießen. Diese
Malerei gleicht mehr dem elementaren Sprudeln und Wirbeln
des Wassers, der Luft und des Feuers, als dass sie statuarische
Beständigkeit vermitteln würde.«

Carla Schulz-Hoffmann, ehemalige stellvertretende Generaldirektorin der Bayerischen Staatsgemäldesammlungen,
vertieft diese Analyse: »Katharina von Werz arbeitet in ihrem
Werk konsequent an der Neuformulierung einer eigenständi-
gen künstlerischen Haltung, die unterschiedliche Traditionen
der Moderne voraussetzt und selbstverständlich integriert. In
ihren lichten, scheinbar flüchtig hingeworfenen Bildwelten
geht es ihr um die Auslotung eines labilen Gleichgewichts zwischen Figuration und Abstraktion.«

Michael Semff, der Direktor der Staatlichen Graphischen Sammlung München, dagegen entdeckt in ihren Bildern und Skulpturen »einen genuin barocken Zug. Er offenbart sich im malerischen und plastischen Zugriff, in der vehementen Inbesitznahme der Leinwand und der Terrakotta. Aber ihre Farbigkeit meidet eher die
allzu warmen Töne. Der vorherrschende Klang der Bilder ist oft kühl, dramatisch. Weiß spielt eine prägende
Rolle. Ihre Werke strahlen Energie und Großzügigkeit aus, einen nicht selten chaotischen Bewegungsstrom. Es
sind keine Bilder von eingängiger Harmonie, aber ihre zunächst oft verstörend erscheinende Wildheit fügt sich
in ein übergeordnetes System, in dem alle widerstrebenden Kräfte zum Ausgleich kommen.«

Bernhart Schwenk, der Oberkonservator für Gegenwartskunst in der Pinakothek der Moderne, hebt
darüber hinaus die dialogische Qualität ihrer Kunst hervor: »Ihre Malerei versetzt die Welt in farbgetränkte
Schwingungen und beginnt – gewissermaßen tanzend – aufzulösen, was vorher Gewissheit schien. Sie entzieht
dem Betrachter die Kontrolle über eine einzig mögliche Sicht der Dinge, schafft vielmehr Felder möglicher Blick-
weisen. Auch wenn sich ein Gemälde wie *Dame mit Hündchen* (Abb. Cover und S. 64) einem traditionsreichen
Thema nähert, so geschieht dies mit rein malerischen Mitteln und einer spielerischen Freizügigkeit. Auf diese
Weise macht die Künstlerin die Betrachter ihrer Bilder – wie auch ihrer bildhauerischen Arbeiten – zu bewusst
Unwissenden, den freiesten aller Sehenden.«

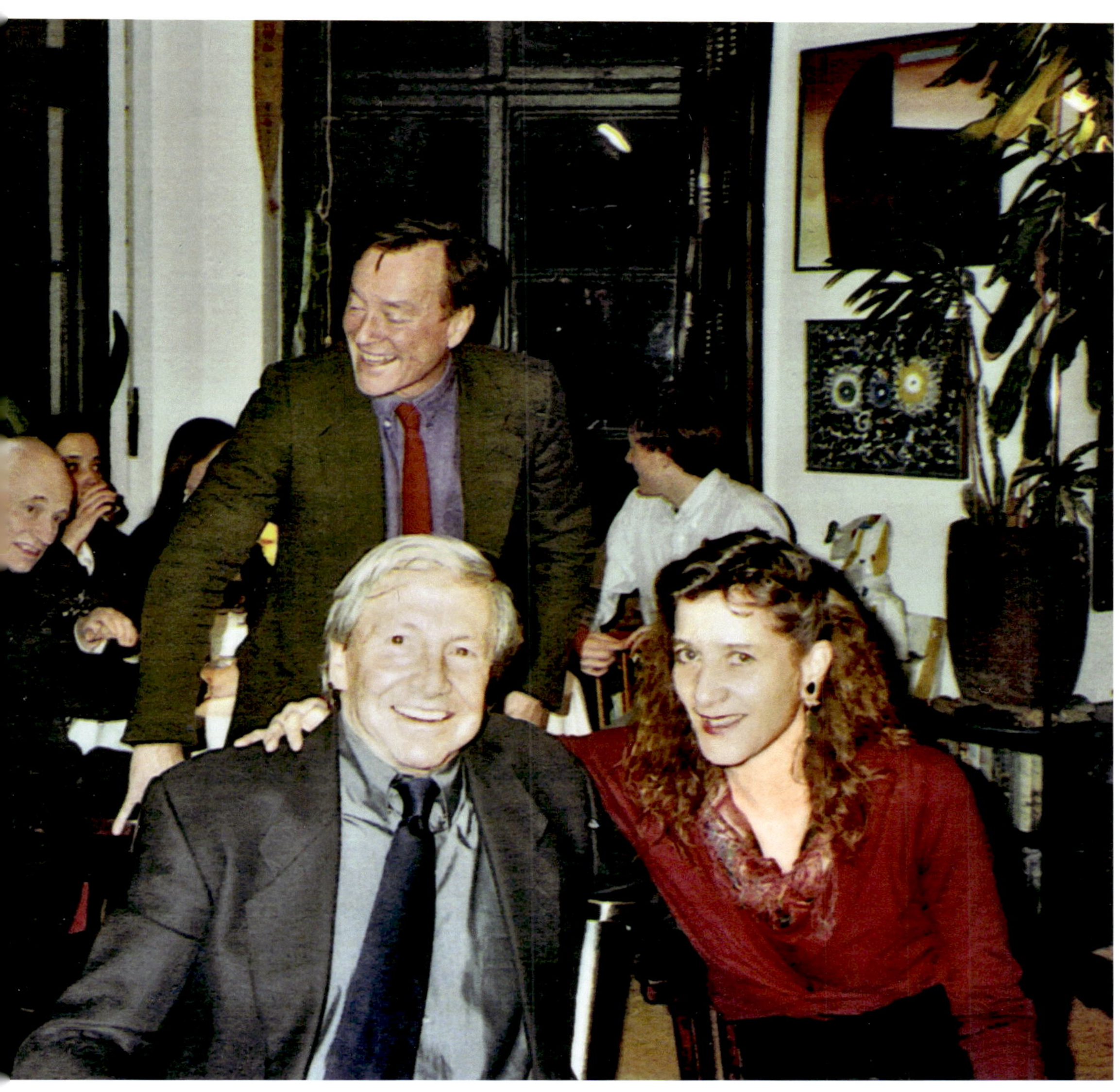

Her third art dealer, Helmut Klewan, who has exhibited her works on two occasions, considers her to be a "very intelligent painter. The earlier paintings with their diffused light masterfully incorporate Western painting traditions. I like her later works for the finesse with which she takes up the traditions of the forties and fifties. Her best pictures have the power of a Willem de Kooning at his peak around 1950."

Words of acknowledgment can also be heard from museum directors and curators who have bought works, and followed her career over the years. James Cuno, president and member of the board of directors of the J. Paul Getty Trust, describes the artist as a "rare creative spirit in a competitive and commercial world. She is a magician—whether she draws, paints, or sculpts, stages theatrical performances with friends and family in extravagant costumes, or opens her home to guests whom she indulges with good, homemade treats, and lots of wine. She is like John Cage, she finds beauty in all the images and sounds of our world and makes it a better place."

Helmut Friedel, director of the Städtische Galerie im Lenbachhaus, stresses the "unabated will to express" in her art, whose "inner unease and vital urgency flow into the cascading brushstrokes of color. This style of painting has more in common with the elementary bubbling and swirling of water, air, and fire than any attempt to communicate statuary permanence."

Carla Schulz-Hoffmann, former deputy director general of the Bayerische Staatsgemäldesammlungen, takes this analysis further: "Katharina von Werz works consistently in her art toward the formulation of a new, independent artistic approach that both presupposes and naturally integrates the various traditions of Modern art. In her lucid images that almost appear to have been quickly dashed off, she is concerned with the search for a delicate balance between figuration and abstraction."

Michael Semff, director of the Staatliche Graphische Sammlung in Munich, on the other hand, discovers in her pictures and sculptures "a genuine Baroque influence. It is evident in her approach to painting and sculpture, in the clear ability to take full possession of the canvas and the terracotta. But the coloring tends to avoid overly warm tones. The dominant tone of the images is mostly cool, dramatic. White plays a prominent role. Her works radiate energy and liberality, quite often a chaotic stream of movement. They are not pictures of easy harmony, but what at first appears as an almost unsettling wildness, fits into an overriding system in which all conflicting forces are reconciled."

Bernhart Schwenk, the chief conservator for contemporary art at the Pinakothek der Moderne, emphasizes the quality of dialogue in her artwork: "Her painting sets the world in motion with lavish color, and begins—almost as if dancing—to dissolve all that previously seemed to be certain. She takes away the viewer's control over one subjective perspective, creating instead multiple possible viewpoints. Even when a painting, like *Dame mit Hündchen* (fig. cover and p. 64), takes up a traditional theme, it happens—solely through her painting techniques and a playful sense of openness. In this way, the artist makes the viewers of her pictures and her sculptural works fully aware of what they do not know—the freest of all spectators."

»Ich malte die Frau in mir.«

Willem de Kooning

Der Satz des Radikalgenies des abstrakten amerikanischen Expressionismus gefällt Katharina von Werz. Wie alle Künstler bewegt auch sie sich innerhalb der Tradition der Kunstgeschichte und ihrer klassischen wie modernen Meister. Wahlverwandtschaften entdeckt sie vor allem bei Malern, die Gestalt und Körper dekonstruktivistisch erforschen, wobei sie sie in Bewegungsrhythmen zerlegen, dabei verwandeln und neu erfinden. Die Riege ihrer Heroen reicht von Giorgione, Tizian, Peter Paul Rubens und Eugène Delacroix bis zu Leon Kossoff und Alfred Kubin, doch de Kooning scheint ihr größtes Ideal. »Ich liebe diesen Maler und ganz besonders seine ›Woman-Serie‹«, sagt sie, »nicht nur, weil er, wie ich zu einem Teil, holländische Wurzeln hat. Sondern auch, weil ich die flüssigen Rhythmen seiner Pinselbewegungen einzigartig finde. Aus seiner gespeicherten Malerfahrung, seinem außerordentlichen Können speist sich sein immer wieder geübtes, anteilnehmendes Sehen.«

Auch Katharina von Werz vertraut ihrem »Grundstock an künstlerischem Training«, den sie aus dem Unbewussten abrufe. De Koonings »wunderbare Freiheit, die sich an nichts mehr anlehnt«, zu erreichen, mag ihr manchmal wie ein Sehnsuchtsziel erscheinen, doch gelingt es ihr immer wieder mühelos, in Serien wie *Schöne Frauen* und *Tanz* die Balance aus Entgrenzung und Abgrenzung zu steuern.

Ein anderer Favorit ist der Delfter Maler Jan Vermeer, dessen Werk *Das Mädchen mit dem Perlenohrring* sie besonders anzieht. »In diesem Bild offenbart sich für mich das Geheimnis der Seele in einem Moment der Entrückung – unnachahmlich sichtbar gemacht im dunklen Glanz der Augen und dem Schimmer der Haut.« Bei Chaim Soutine dagegen fasziniert sie seine »fulminante, saftige, bis zur Groteske expressive Malerei« und bei Francis Bacon, dass es ihm, wie er selbst es einmal formulierte, so perfekt gelang, »die Vitalität des Zufalls zu bewahren und dennoch eine Kontinuität zu erhalten«.

Wie der Jahrhundertkünstler beschäftigt sich auch Katharina von Werz intensiv mit der Rolle des Zufalls für ihre Arbeit: »Besser als Bacon selbst kann ich es nicht sagen«, meint sie, »deshalb zitiere ich ihn hier: ›In meinem Fall ist die gesamte Malerei – und je älter ich werde, desto mehr wird das so – Zufall. So sehe ich sie im Geiste voraus, ich sehe sie voraus, und dennoch führe ich sie kaum jemals so aus, wie ich sie voraussehe. Sie verändert sich selbst durch die tatsächliche Farbe. Ich verwende sehr große Pinsel, und durch die Art und Weise, wie ich arbeite, weiß ich in der Tat sehr oft nicht, was die Farbe tun wird, und sie tut vieles, was sehr viel besser ist als das, wozu ich sie bringen könnte‹«.

Auch wenn ihre Pinsel feiner sind und die Formate in der Regel kleiner, überlässt sich die Künstlerin soweit wie möglich der Regie der Farben, die Formen zerfließen, manchmal sogar explodieren lassen, ohne sie dabei zu zerstören. Sie geraten im Gegenteil in vielperspektivische Bewegungsstrudel, wie sie die großen Meister des Barock so virtuos zu handhaben wussten, allen voran der Antwerpener Peter Paul Rubens.

"I was painting the woman in me."
Willem de Kooning

The words of the genius of Abstract Expressionism appeal to Katharina von Werz. As with all artists, she too moves within the canon of art history and its masters, both classical and modern. She discovers kindred spirits, "elective affinities," primarily in painters who adopt a deconstructivist approach to exploring form and the body—painters who essentially break the body down into rhythms of movement, transforming and therefore reinventing it. Her pantheon of heroes spans from Giorgione and includes Titian, Peter Paul Rubens, and Eugène Delacroix and extends to Leon Kossoff and Alfred Kubin. It would appear, however, that she admires de Kooning most of all. "I love this painter and most especially his Woman Series," she says, "not only because, like me, he is of Dutch stock. But because, I think the fluid rhythms of his brushstrokes are utterly unique. His practiced, sympathetic eye is nourished by his exceptional skill, his fund of experience as a painter that is stored up inside him."

Katharina von Werz also has faith in her "fundament of artistic training," which is embedded deep in her consciousness. De Kooning's "wonderful freedom that borrows from nothing but itself" may sometimes seem inimitable and elusive, but time and again she demonstrates that she too can effortlessly steer between clear delineation and dissolution of form in such series as *Schöne Frauen (Beautiful Women)* and *Tanz (Dance)*.

Another one of her favorites is the painter from Delft, Jan Vermeer, whose *Girl with a Pearl Earring* she finds especially captivating. "In this picture," she says, "I catch a glimpse of the secret of the soul, revealed in a moment of rapture. It is rendered visible here, quite inimitably, in the dark shine of her eyes and the shimmer of her skin." Chaim Soutine, by contrast, is a fascinating painter for her, because of his "utterly brilliant, expressive painting, so luscious it verges on the grotesque." Francis Bacon, on the other hand, inspires her because, as he himself once said, he managed so perfectly to "keep the vitality of the accident[al] and yet preserve its continuity."

In a manner somewhat akin to this giant of 20th-century art, Katharina von Werz also explores the role of chance in her work. She says: "I cannot put it better than Bacon himself did, so I'll quote him directly. He said: 'You know in my case all painting—and the older I get, the more it becomes so—is accident. So I foresee it in my mind, so I foresee it, and yet I hardly ever carry it out as I foresee it. It transforms itself by the actual paint. I use very large brushes, and in the way I work I don't in fact know very often what the paint will do, and it does many things which are very much better than I could make it do.'"

Even though she uses finer brushes and her canvases tend to be smaller, the artist surrenders herself to what the colors dictate as they melt the forms, sometimes even exploding them, but all without actually destroying them in the process. In fact, far from being destroyed, they flow into a multiperspectival stream of movement, of a kind the great masters of the Baroque knew how to handle so deftly, most of all Peter Paul Rubens.

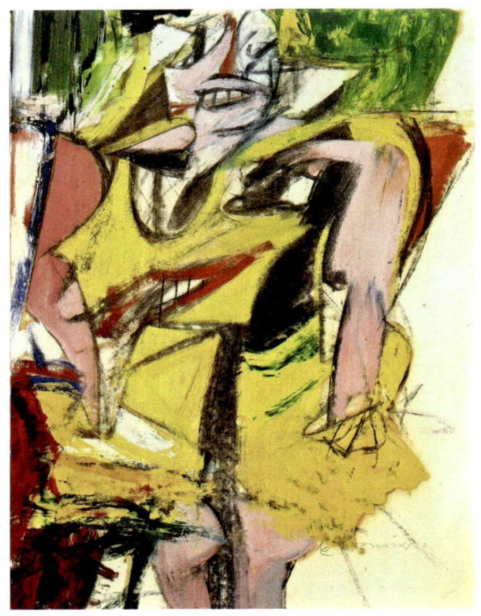

Willem de Kooning
Woman, 1953

Jan Steen
Die verkehrte Welt/Luxury Beware,
um/c. 1663

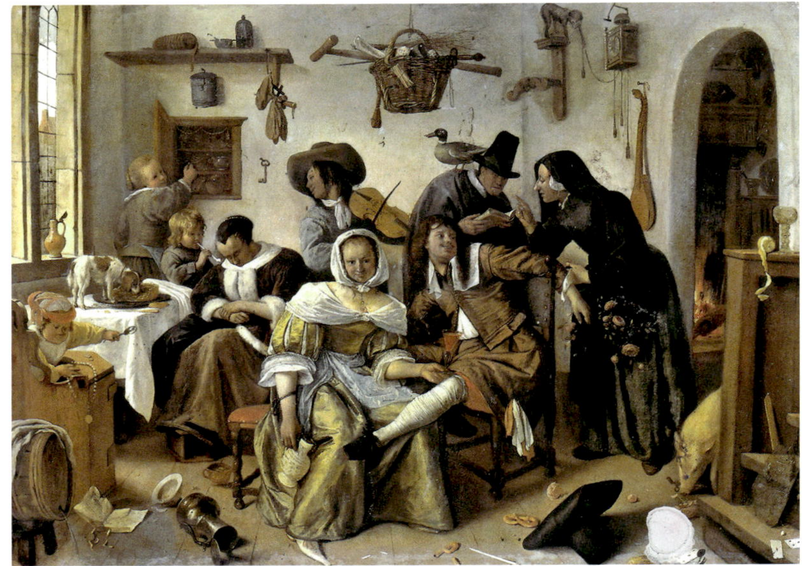

Aus seinem um 1638 entstandenen Gemälde *Schäferszene,* das in der Münchner Alten Pinakothek hängt, entlehnte die Künstlerin bestimmte kompositorische »Gesten der Zuwendung und Hingabe«. Im Arbeitsprozess verfremdete und verdichtete sie sie weiter und band sie in einen völlig anderen atmosphärischen Rahmen ein, einen fernen Horizont aus blauem Himmel und verstreuten Häusersilhouetten (Abb. S. 196, 198, 201).

Ein weiteres Rubens-Motiv, das 1617 entstandene *Der Raub der Töchter des Leukippos,* ebenfalls im Besitz der Alten Pinakothek, taucht in *Entführung,* einem anderen Werk der Künstlerin, auf (Abb. S. 194). Hier extrahiert und kondensiert sie die Allüre entfesselter Leiblichkeit und fügt mit dem tizianrot konturierten Pferdekopf als liebevoll karikierendem Zitat eine subtil ironische Note hinzu.

Auch Jan Steens Genrebild *Die verkehrte Welt*, das der holländische Meister um 1663 malte, wurde Katharina von Werz zum »Vorwand für Variationen zu den Dramen und Komödien der Paarung«. In Gemälden wie *Verkehrte Welt* (Abb. S. 110), *Paar* (Abb. S. 82, 114) *Lustiges Paar* (Abb. S. 116) und *Vergnügtes Paar* (Abb. S. 108) stilisiert sie die Dynamik zwischen der männlichen und weiblichen Figur zu delikat rosé-nude-farben erotischen Wolke Sieben-Schaumgebilden oder verfremdet sie zu farbglühenden Bällen aus türkisen, gelben und orangeroten Funken.

Bei Tizians *Venus und Adonis* aus dem Jahr 1554 wiederum forderte sie die Sinnlichkeit der Szene sogar zu rund zwölf Adaptationen heraus, entstanden zwischen 2008 und 2010 (Abb. S. 184–192). Sichtbar wird eine immer radikalere Abstraktion. »Je besser ich die Komposition kennenlernte, desto besser konnte ich mich lösen«, erklärt die Künstlerin, »desto mehr Nuancen für Leib und Haut fand ich«.

Sind diese »all over« die gesamte Leinwand überflutenden Tableaus Meditationen über Verlangen und Leidenschaft, so war das sich im Louvre befindliche *Concert Champêtre* (Ländliches Konzert) des Renaissancemalers Giorgione, das heute allerdings mehrheitlich Tizian zugesprochen wird, Anregung für eine Reihe von Konzerten und Picknickszenen (Abb. S. 154–159). In ihren Versionen verschmilzt Katharina von Werz Figur und Landschaft untrennbar miteinander zu einer farbsatten Hommage – nicht nur an das Vorbild, sondern auch an die Jahrhunderte überdauernden, unstillbaren Träume von Idylle und Paradies.

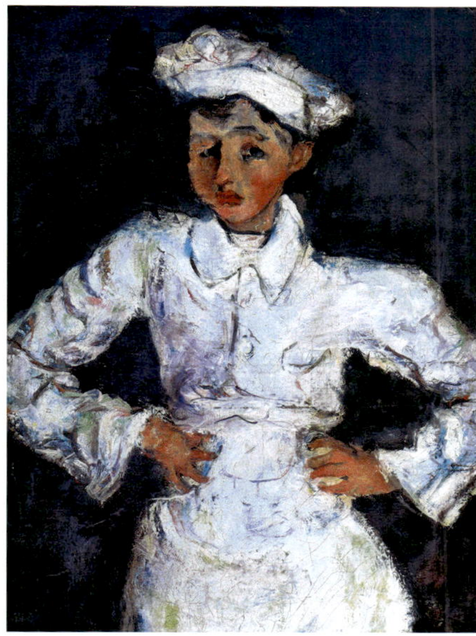

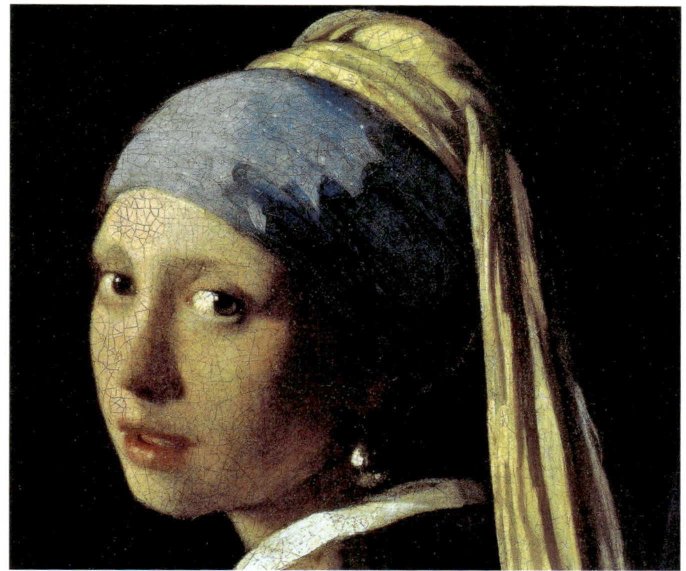

Chaim Soutine
Konditor/The Little Pastry Chef, 1927

Jan Vermeer
Das Mädchen mit dem Perlenohrring/
The Girl with a Pearl Earring (Detail),
um/c. 1665

From his 1638 pastoral scene of a *Shepard and Shepherdess*, a version of which now hangs in the Alte Pinakothek in Munich, von Werz has borrowed certain compositional "gestures of devotion and surrender." In the studio she abstracted and condensed them further and bound them in a completely different atmospheric setting, a distant horizon of blue sky dotted with the silhouettes of buildings (fig. pp. 196, 198, 201).

Another Rubens subject, the *Rape of the Daughters of Leucippus,* a canvas from 1617 also in the Alte Pinakothek, resurfaces in von Werz's *Entführung* (fig. p. 194). In this work she abstracts and distills the allure of unleashed corporeality and adds a subtly ironic twist in the horse's head, contoured in a Titian-like red, which serves as a fondly caricaturing reference.

Jan Steen's genre painting *Luxury Beware,* painted by the Dutch master around 1663, becomes in Katharina von Werz's eyes a "pretext for the many variations on the dramas and comedies of finding a mate." In paintings such as *Verkehrte Welt* (fig. p. 110), *Paar* (fig. pp. 82, 114) *Lustiges Paar* (fig. p. 116), and *Vergnügtes Paar* (fig. p. 108), she stylizes the dynamic between the male and female figure in delicately pinkish, flesh-tones, erotic "Cloud Nine" nebulous forms, or alienates them by turning them into radiant balls of turquoise, yellow, and orange-red sparks.

In Titian's *Venus and Adonis* from 1554, she draws out the composition's sensuality and channels it into twelve adaptations of the scene, produced between 2008 and 2010 (fig. pp. 184–192). Each version reveals a radical abstraction. "The more I got to know the composition, the more I was able to break away," says the artist, "and the more nuances for body and skin I was able to find."

If these "all-over" paintings, these tableaus that saturate the entire canvas, are meditations on desire and passion, then Giorgione's *Concert Champêtre*, on display in the Louvre and now widely attributed by the majority of scholars to Titian, provides the inspiration for a whole series of scenes featuring concerts and picnics (fig. pp. 154–159). In her versions, Katharina von Werz fuses figure and landscape to create a richly colored homage that pays tribute not just to the older painting, but also to the insatiable dreams of idyll and paradise that have endured over the course of centuries.

II

SCHÖNE FRAUEN
BEAUTIFUL WOMEN

Jede möchte – heimlich und Emanzipation hin oder her – eine Traumfrau sein. Prinzessin, Dornröschen, Schneewittchen, Aphrodite, und seit Madonna am liebsten alles je nach Laune und (meist) männlichem Begehren. Mit Haar wahlweise wie Ebenholz und Feuer, Haut wie Seide und Samt, Augen wie Smaragd, Lapislazuli oder Palisander, Beine lang, Hüften rund, Brüste üppig.

Noch immer gilt: Schönheit ist weiblich. Und: Schönheit entsteht im Auge des – männlichen – Betrachters. Wie aber sieht Venus im Urteil des Paris heute aus? Erstaunlich ist, wie zeitlos die allseits begehrten Ikonen der Attraktivität geblieben sind, allem modischen Wandel zum Trotz. In den Hitlisten der Idole tauchen, Jahrtausende umspannend, stets dieselben Namen auf: Nofretete und der David von Michelangelo, Grace Kelly und Cary Grant, Julia Roberts und George Clooney.

Mit solchen medialen Idealkonstruktionen haben die Frauen von Katharina von Werz nicht das Geringste gemeinsam. Jenseits von symmetrischem Ebenmaß, makelloser Marmormaske, glatter Reglosigkeit und statuarischer Perfektion entfaltet sich ihre Schönheit als Anmut der Bewegungen und Mimik des Flirts. Sie sind ganz Sinnlichkeit, Gefühl und Empfindung: Motion und E-motion, die sich in den Wirbeln der Farbe und der Pinselrhythmen herauskristallisieren.

Deep down and irrespective of emancipation, everyone wants to be a dream woman. Princess, Sleeping Beauty, Snow White, Aphrodite—ever since Madonna, women want to be them at whim, pleasing (mostly) male desire. With a choice of hair anywhere between ebony and fiery red, skin like silk and velvet, eyes the color of emeralds, lapis lazuli, or rosewood, with long legs, round hips, and voluminous breasts.

Beauty is still very much feminine. And what's more: beauty arises in the eye of the—*male*—beholder. But what does Venus look like in today's Judgment of Paris? What is astonishing is how timeless the icons of attractiveness, desired on all sides, have remained over time, despite all changes in fashion.

In the hit lists of the idols that span centuries and centuries, the same names crop up again and again: Nefertiti and Michelangelo's David, Grace Kelly and Cary Grant, Julia Roberts and George Clooney. Katharina von Werz's women do not have the slightest thing in common with such medial constructions of beauty. Far beyond the symmetry, immaculate marbled masks, smooth inertia, and statuary perfection, her vision of beauty unfolds as the charm of movements and the mimicry of flirtation. It is full of sensibility, feeling, and sensation: motion and e-motion, which crystalize in the flurry of color and rhythmic brushwork.

Serafina, 2010
Acryl auf Pappe
Acrylic on cardboard
41 × 36 cm
Privatbesitz, München
Privately owned, Munich

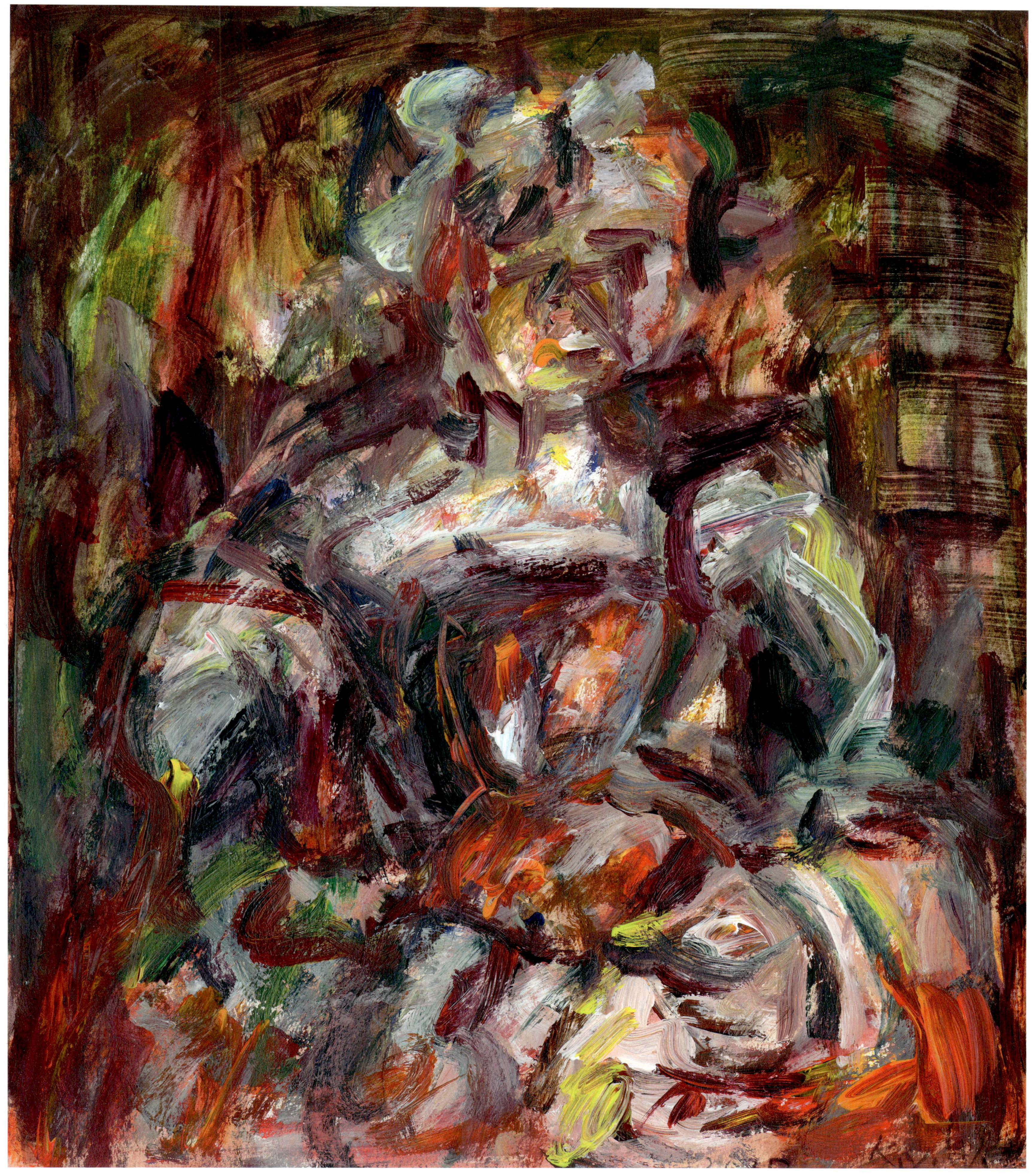

Dame in Gelb I, 2010
Acryl auf Pappe
Acrylic on cardboard
56 × 42 cm

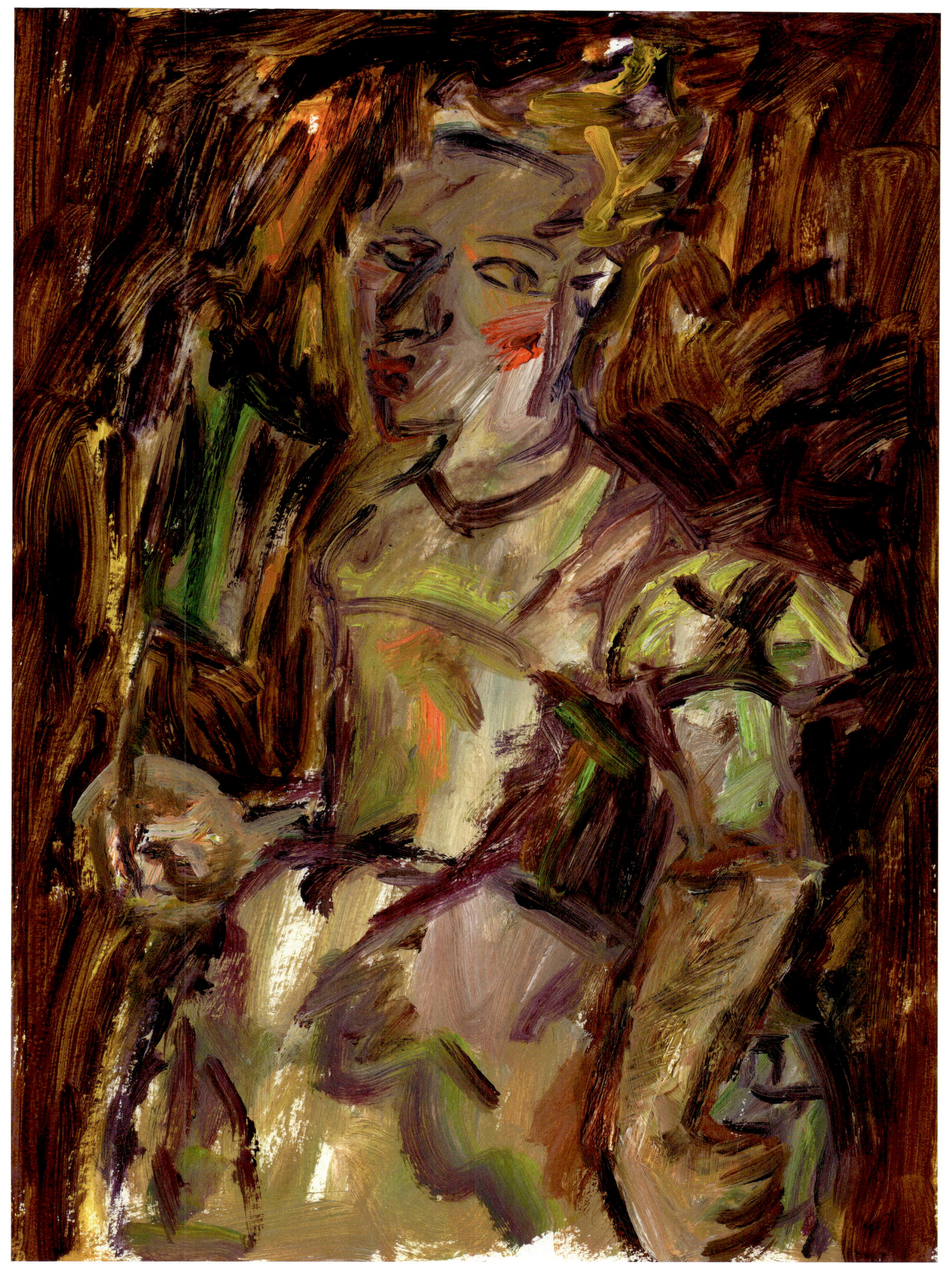

Dame in Gelb II, 2010
Acryl auf Pappe
Acrylic on cardboard
56 × 42 cm

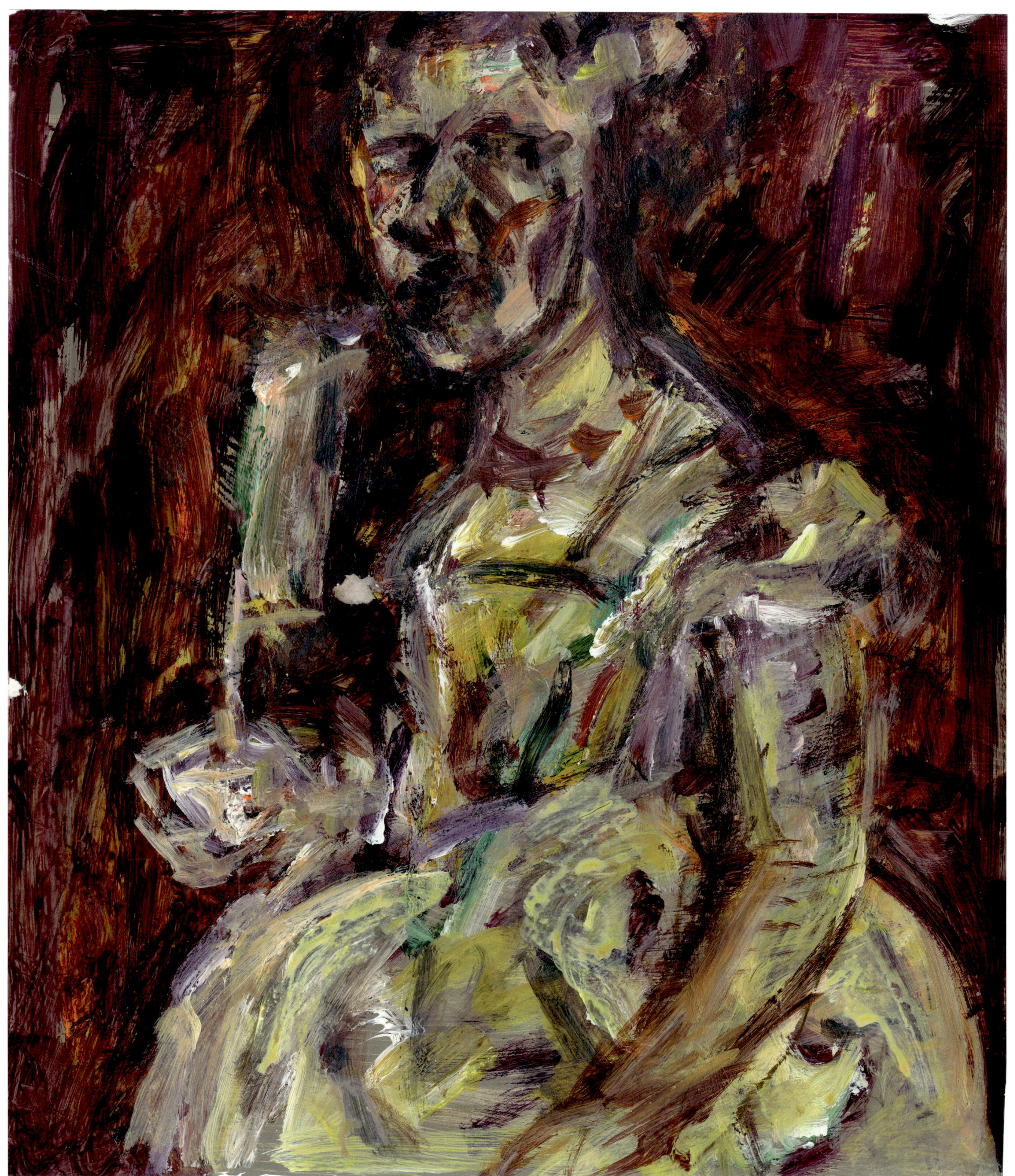

Afghanistans Frauen, 2009
Acryl auf Papier
Acrylic on paper
56 × 40,5 cm

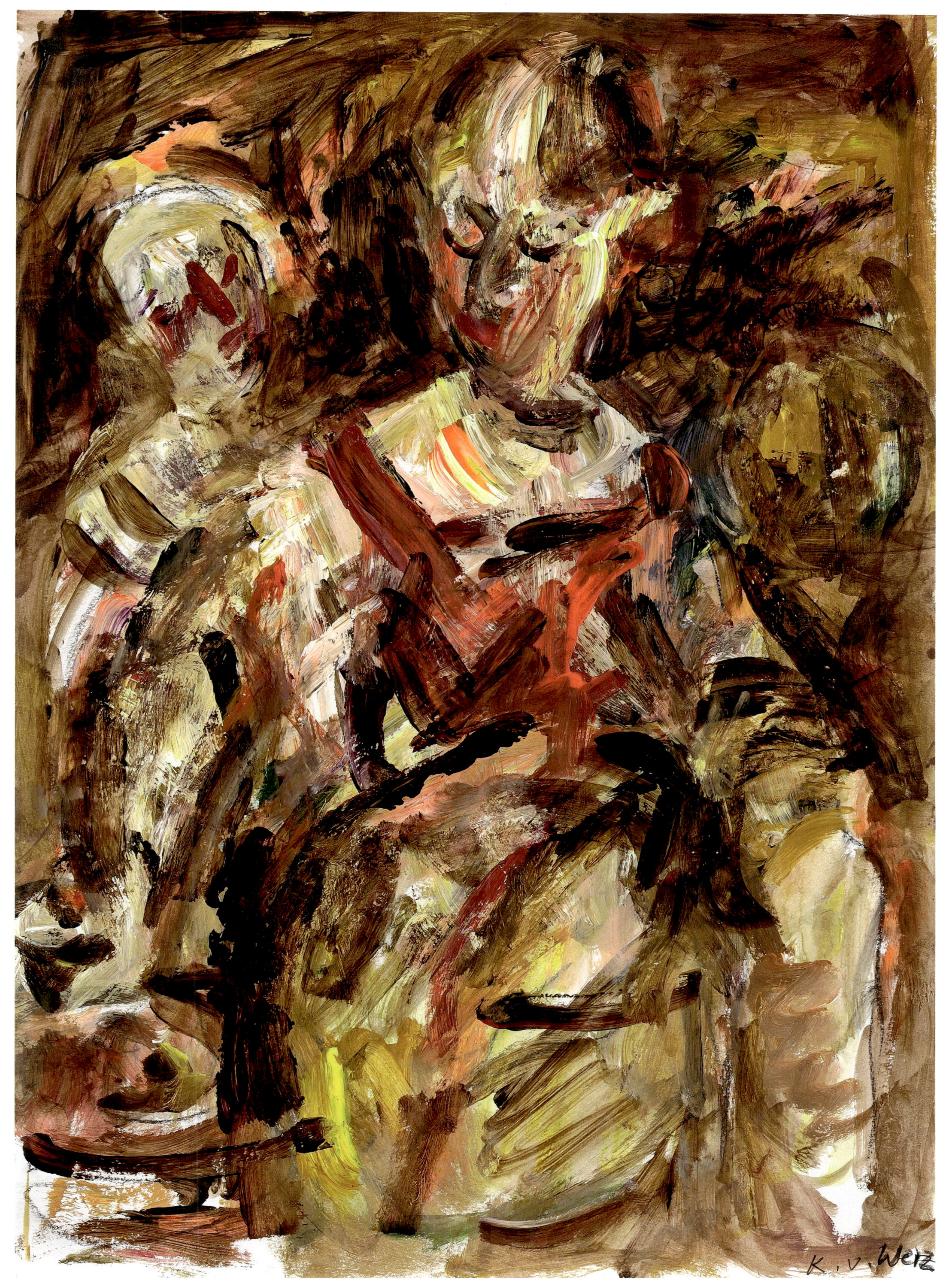
K. v. Werz

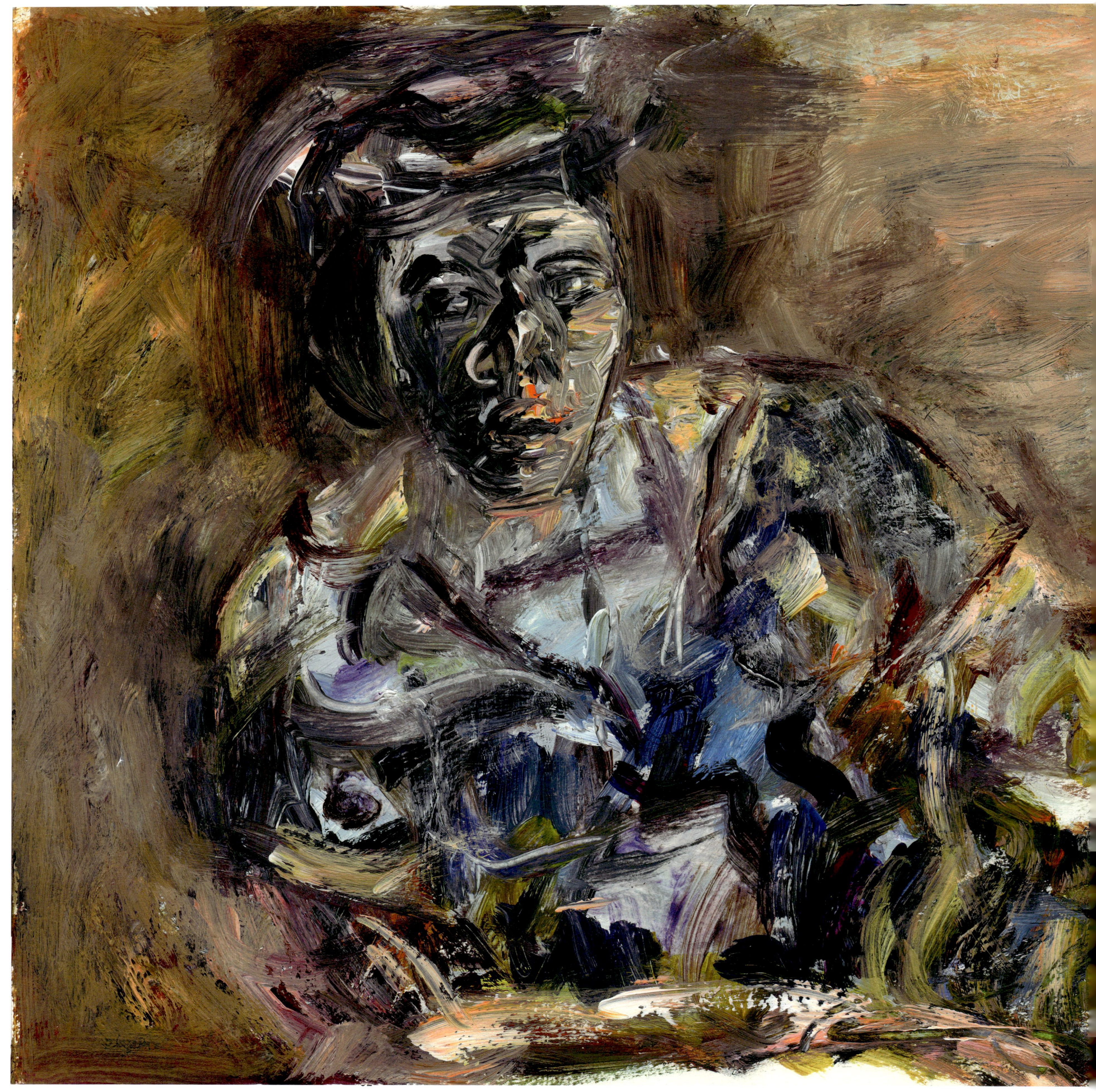

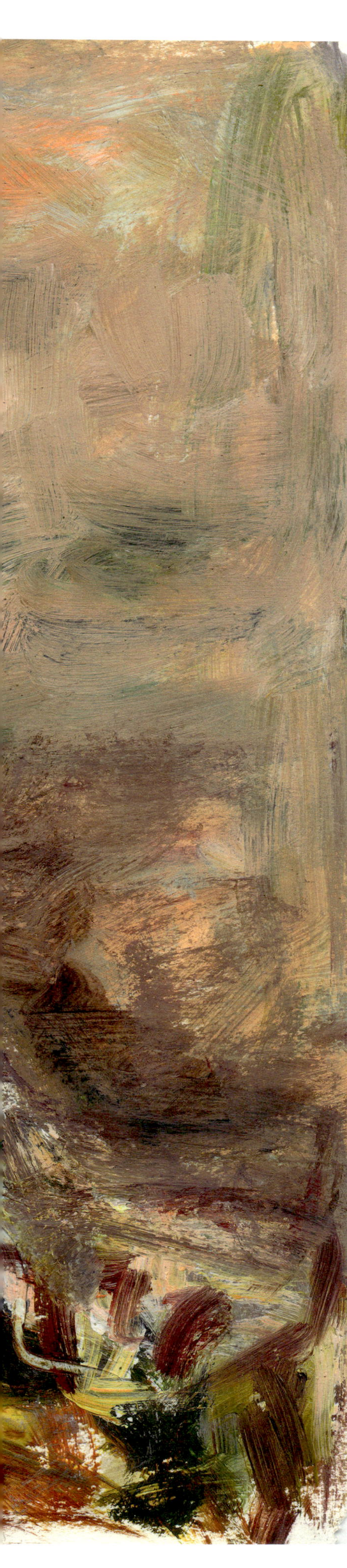

Betrachtung, 2009
Acryl auf Papier
Acrylic on paper
40 × 65 cm

Dame mit Hündchen, 2009
Acryl auf Papier
Acrylic on paper
36 × 33 cm
Bayerische Staatsgemäldesammlungen,
München/Munich

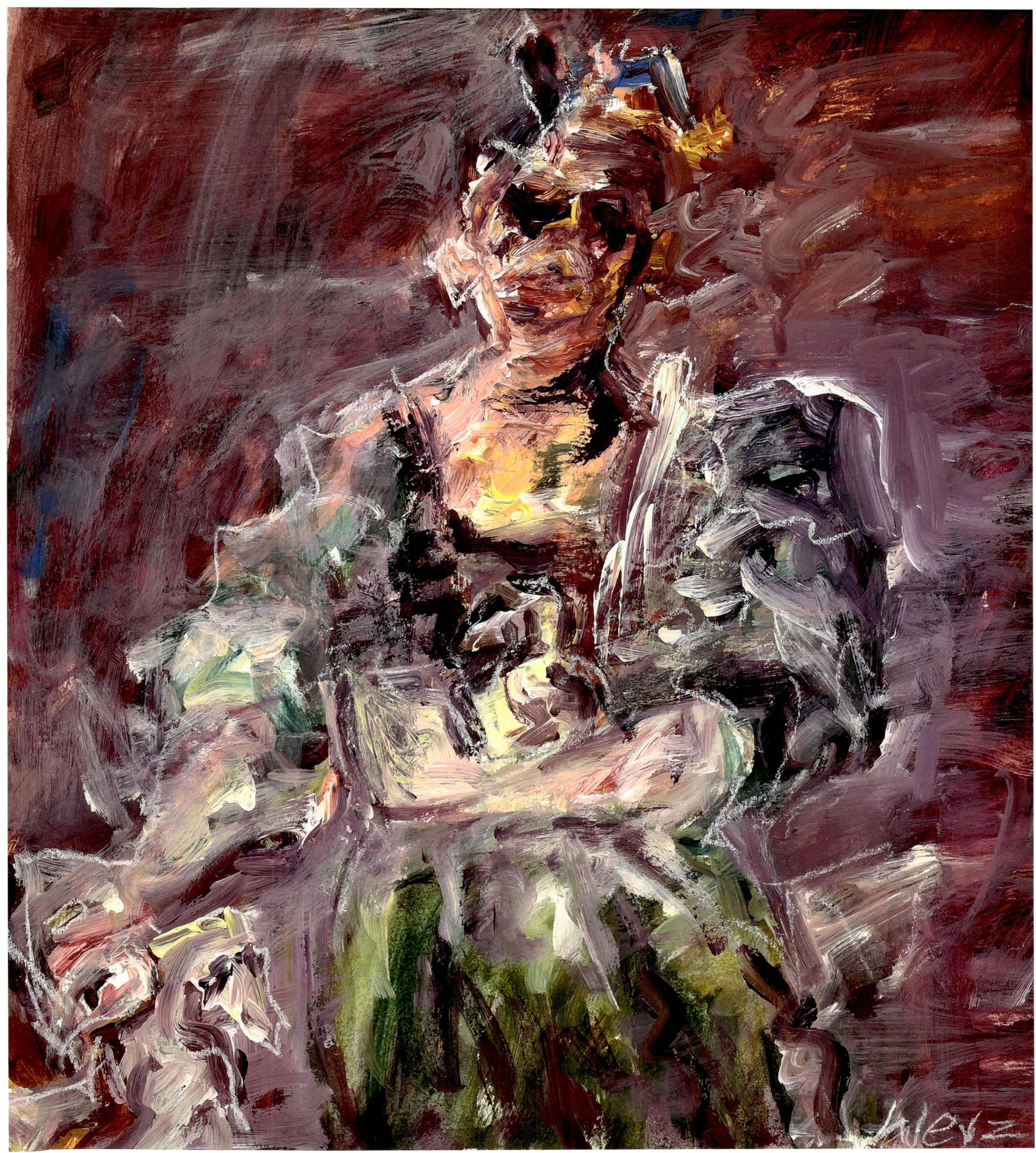

Freundin, 2010
Acryl auf Pappe
Acrylic on cardboard
48 × 41 cm
Privatbesitz, München
Privately owned, Munich

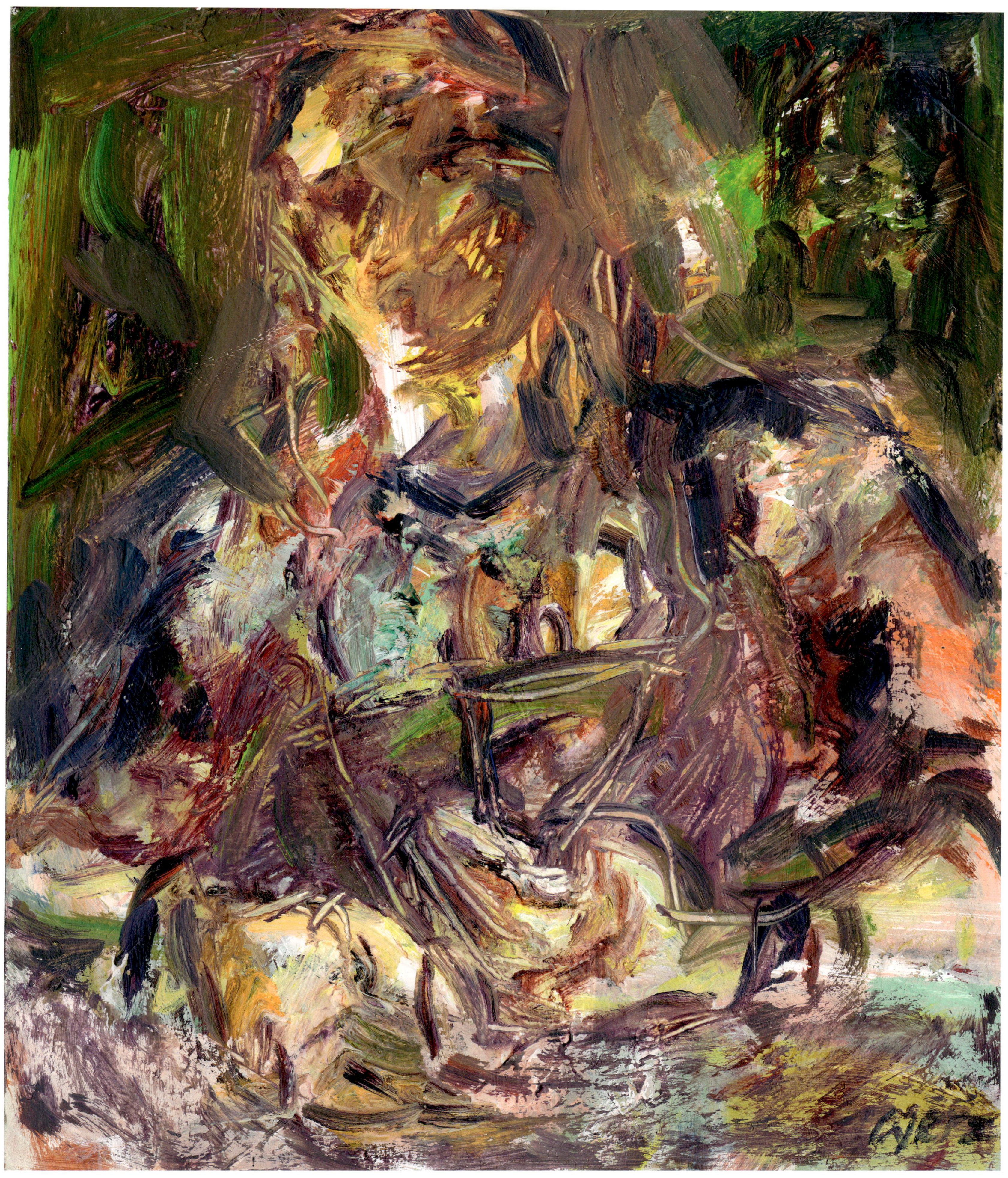

o. T., 2009
Acryl auf Papier
Acrylic on paper
36 × 33 cm
Staatliche Graphische Sammlung,
München/Munich

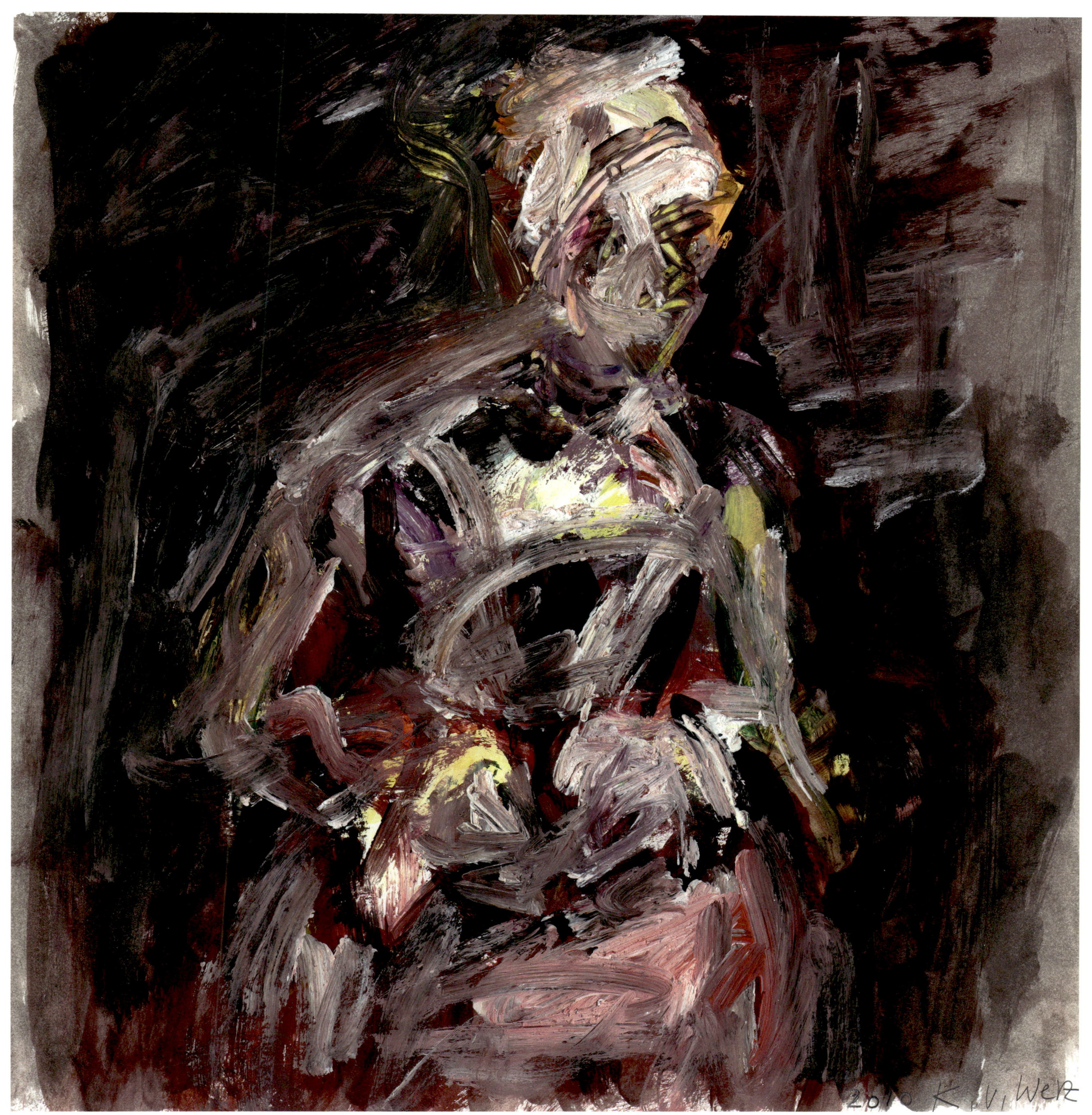

2010 K.H. Werz

Die Goldschmiedin, 2009
Acryl auf Papier
Acrylic on paper
38 × 30 cm

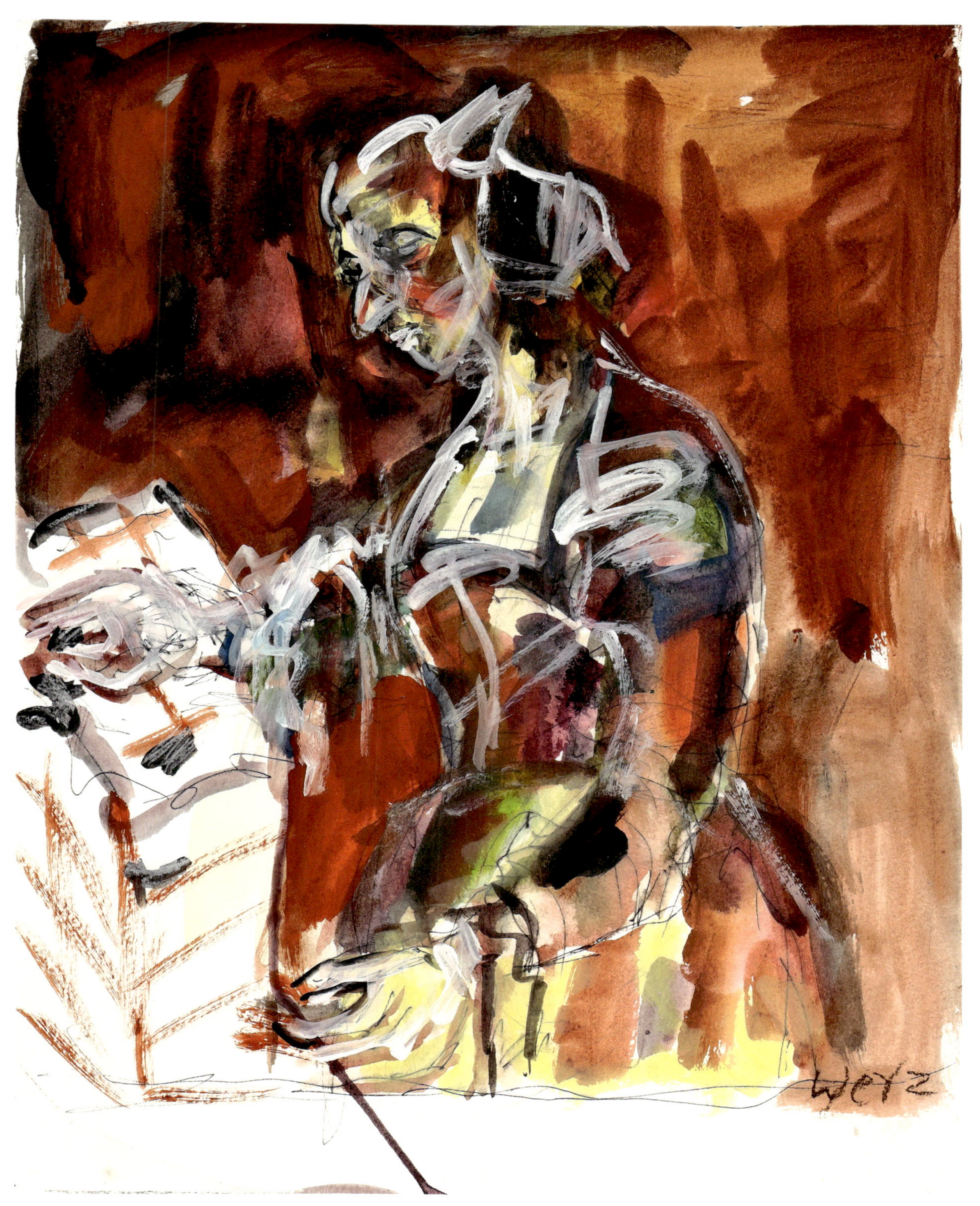

Es hilft, sich Balance nicht als statischen Zustand vorzustellen, sondern als ständige Schwingung, wie Atmen. Katharina von Werz liebt es, zu tanzen: »Die universellste und elementarste Sprache ist die des Körpers.«

In ihren Gemälden beschwört sie diese geballte Urkraft, die Räume so radikal mit Bewegung auffüllt, dass sie zu zerspringen scheinen. Ekstatisch feiern ihre Tänzer weitab von jeder Zivilisation vor hohen Himmeln die eigene Leiblichkeit und laden ihre Umgebung mit ihrer Dynamik auf. Sie huldigen dem Leben und der Natur, sie befinden sich in schwebendem Gleichgewicht zwischen Äußerem und Innerem, Körper, Seele und Geist.

»Es ist einmalig, wie total sich die Seele im Tanz offenbart«, erkennt der weltberühmte belgische Choreograph und Tänzer Sidi Larbi Cherkaoui. Die »Durchlässigkeit von Körper und Seele« zu vermitteln, ist auch das Anliegen der Künstlern, denn »trotz unserer vielen Unterschiede sind wir alle eins«. Viele Körper, verschmolzen zu einem: Katharina von Werz findet berückende Bilder dafür, dass Einfühlung und Liebe die besten Waffen sind gegen die eigenen Angstgrenzen.

It helps to envisage balance not as something static, but as perpetual oscillation, like breathing. Katharina von Werz loves to dance: "The most universal and elemental language," she says, "is that of the body."

In her paintings she evokes this concentrated primal energy, which so radically fills the spaces on the canvas with a sense of movement that they appear on the verge of shattering.

Beyond the clutches of civilization and beneath broad expanses of sky, her dancers make an ecstatic celebration of their own corporeality and give their surroundings a sense of dynamism and vibrancy. They pay tribute to life and nature, suspended in a state of perfect balance between the external and internal, between body, soul, and spirit.

"There is nothing like the way the soul reveals itself in dance," says the world-famous Belgian choreographer and dancer Sidi Larbi Cherkaoui. Katharina von Werz is also concerned with conveying a sense of the "permeability of body and soul", for "despite all our differences, we are all one." Several bodies melted into one: Katharina von Werz creates entrancing images that show that empathy and love are the best weapons against our own constraints.

Tanzendes Paar, 2010
Acryl auf Pappe
Acrylic on cardboard
80 × 100 cm
Staatliche Graphische Sammlung,
München/Munich

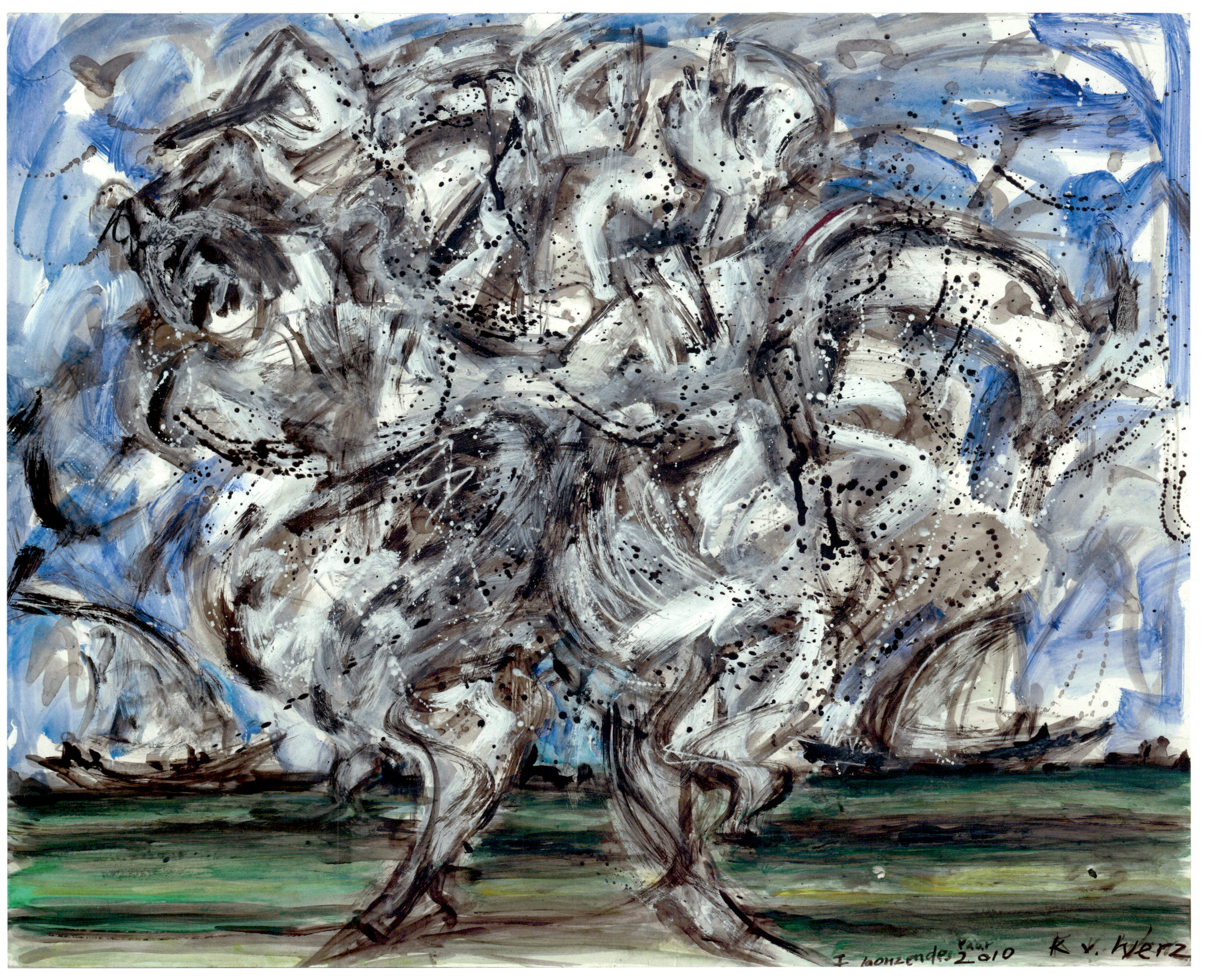
I monzendes Paar 2010 R v. Werz

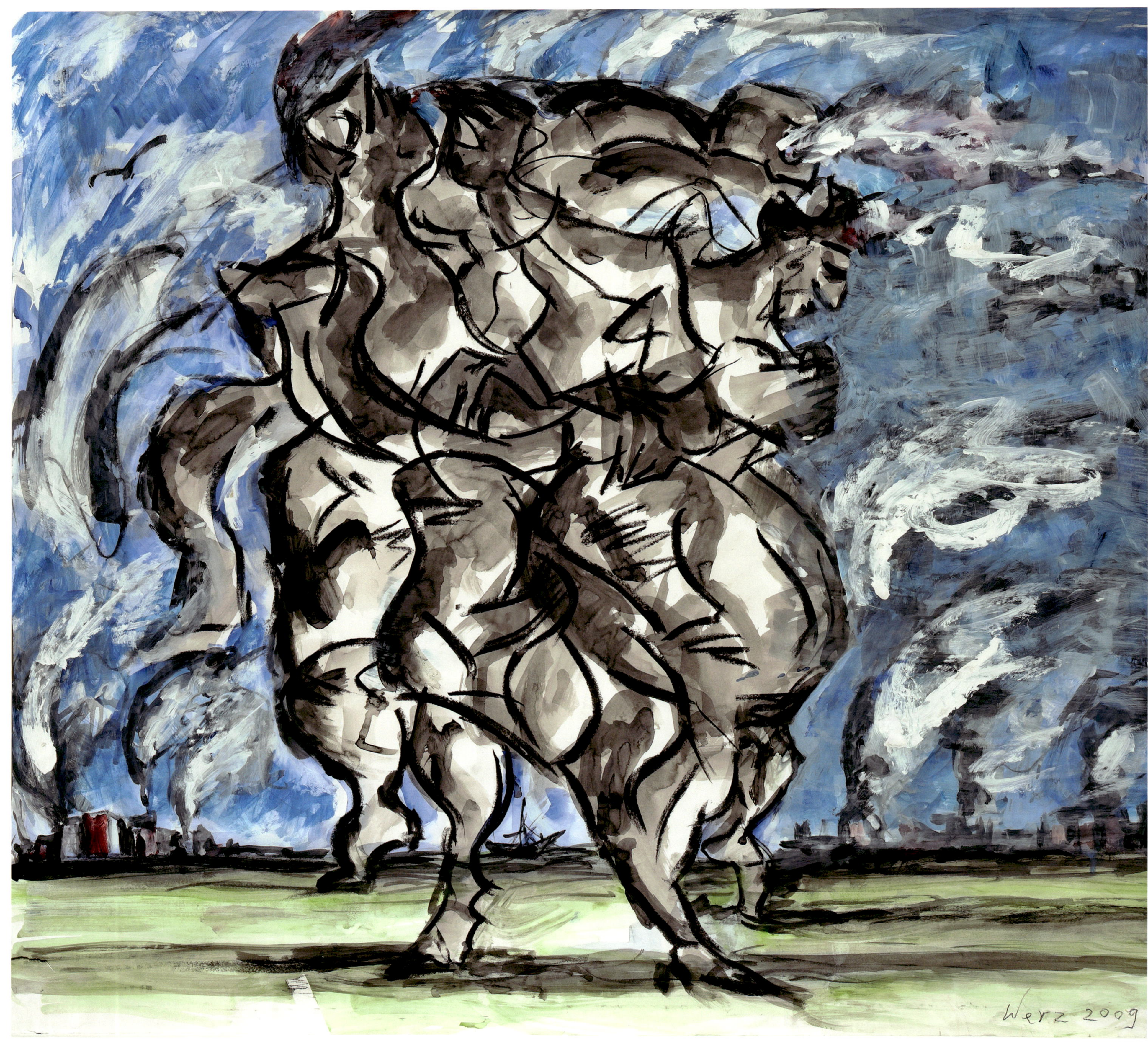
Werz 2009

Tanz vor der Stadt, 2009
Mischtechnik auf Papier
Mixed media on paper
100 × 105 cm

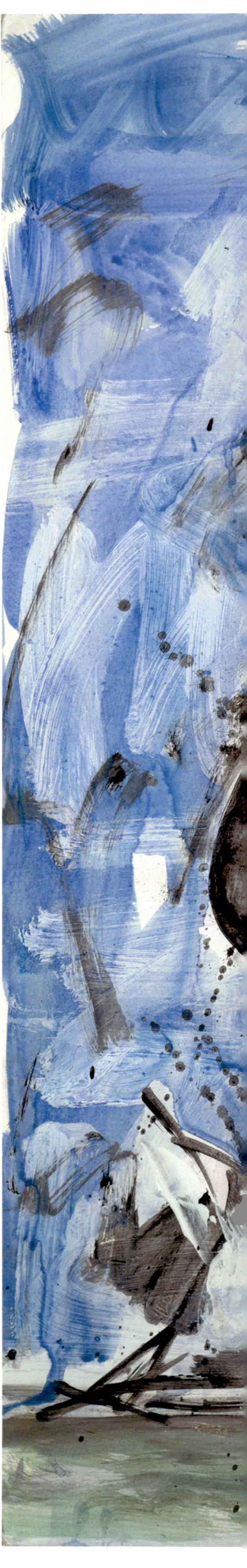

Tanz vor dem Meer, 2010
Acryl auf Pappe
Acrylic on cardboard
80 × 100 cm
Staatliche Graphische Sammlung,
München/Munich

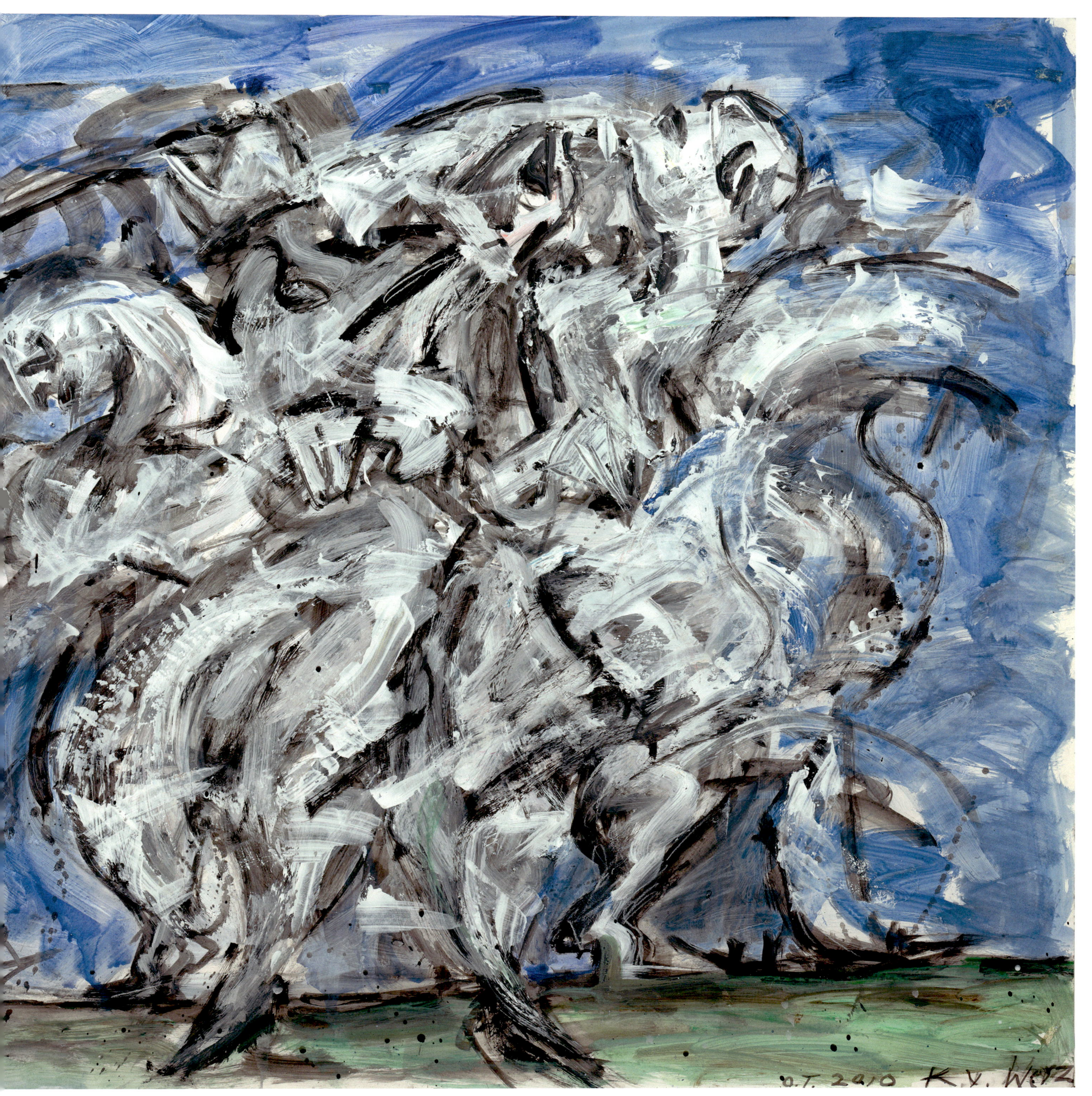

o.T. 2010 K. v. Wer

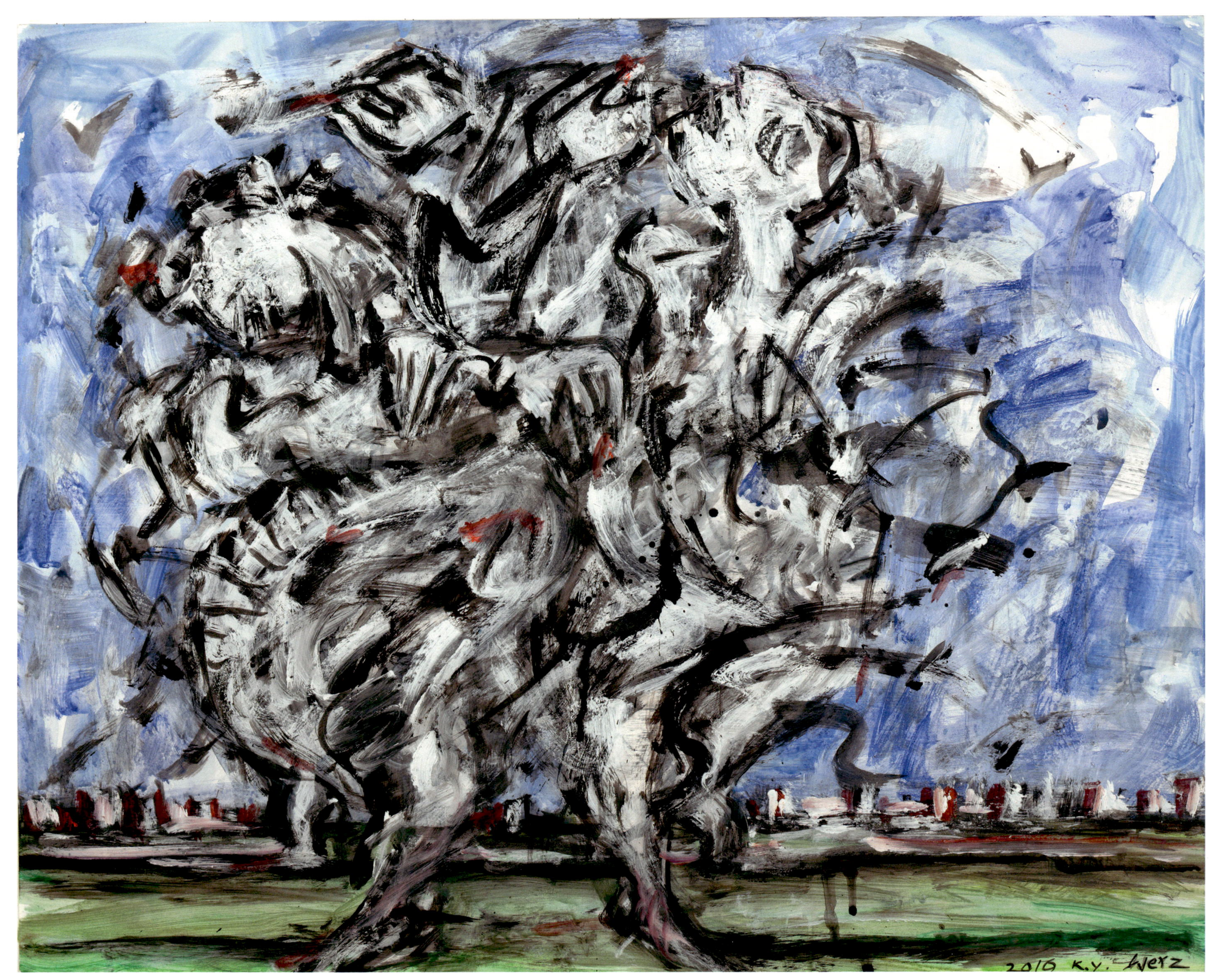

2010 K.Y. Wertz

Tanz vor der Stadt II, 2010
Acryl auf Pappe
Acrylic on cardboard
80 × 100 cm
Bayerische Staatsgemäldesammlungen,
München/Munich

Tanz vor dem Meer II, 2010
Acryl auf Pappe
Acrylic on cardboard
80 × 100 cm
Bayerische Staatsgemäldesammlungen,
München/Munich

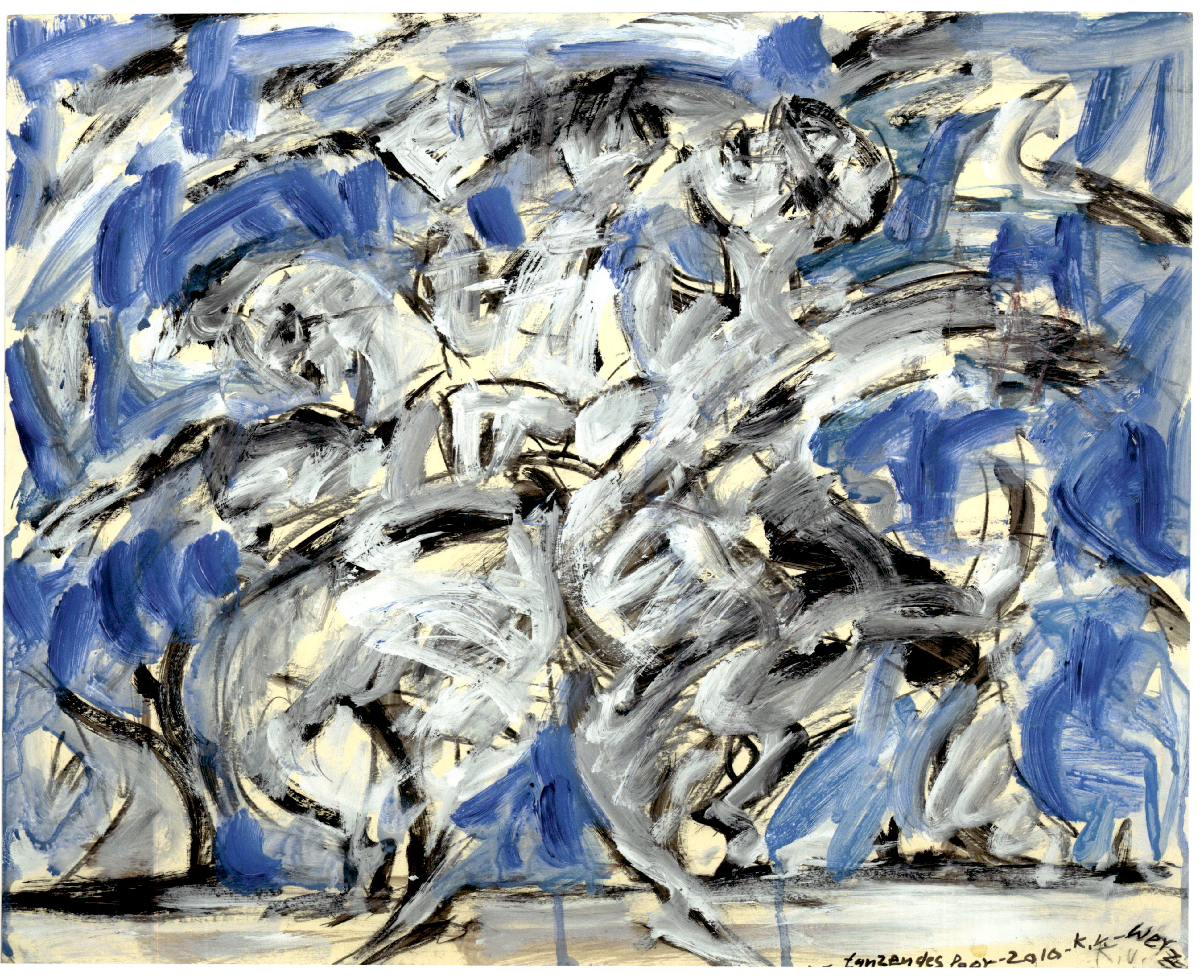
tanzendes Paar - 2010 - K.K.-Weyz

Paar, 2005
Mischtechnik auf Papier
Mixed media on paper
45 × 55 cm
Privatbesitz, München
Privately owned, Munich

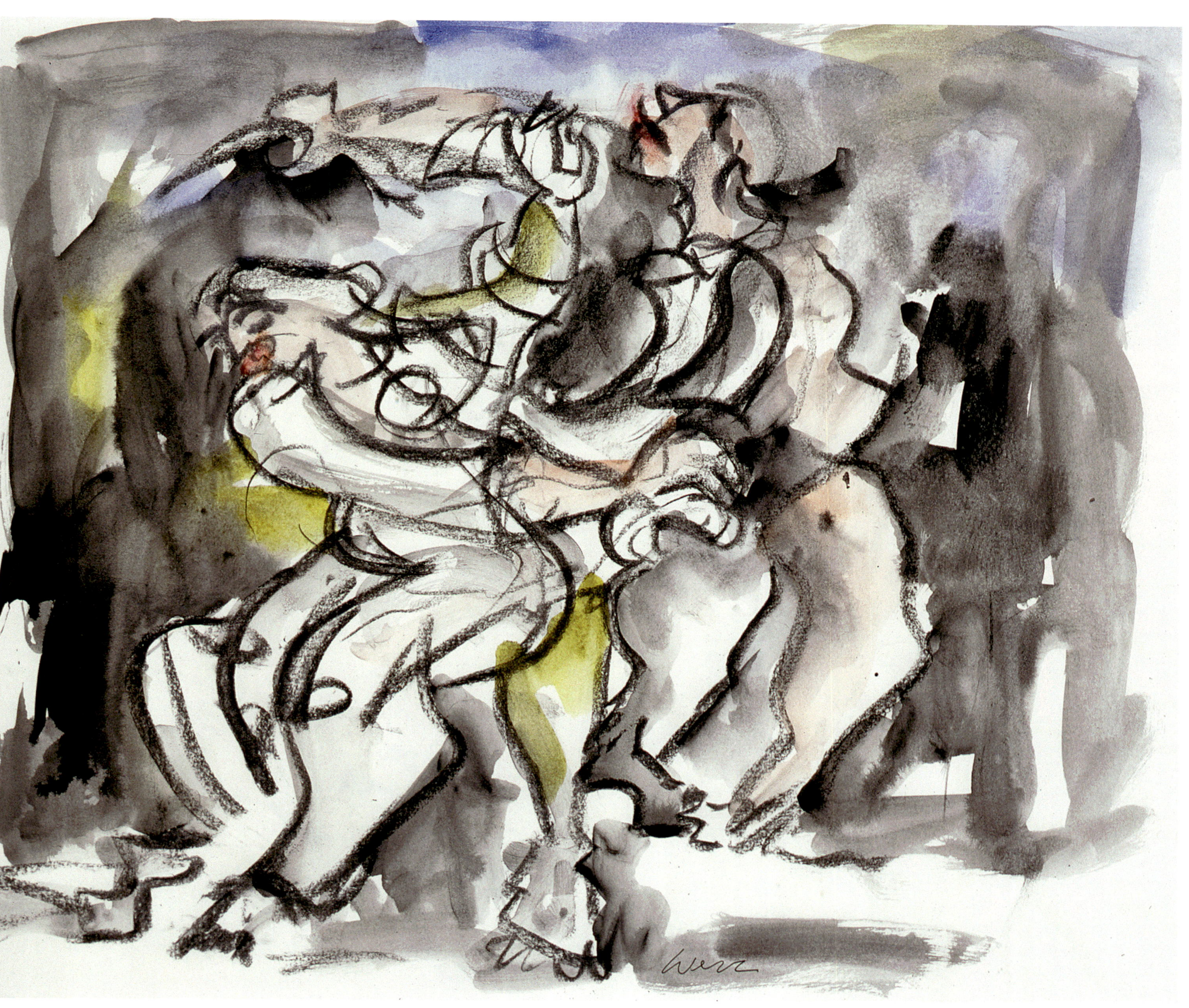

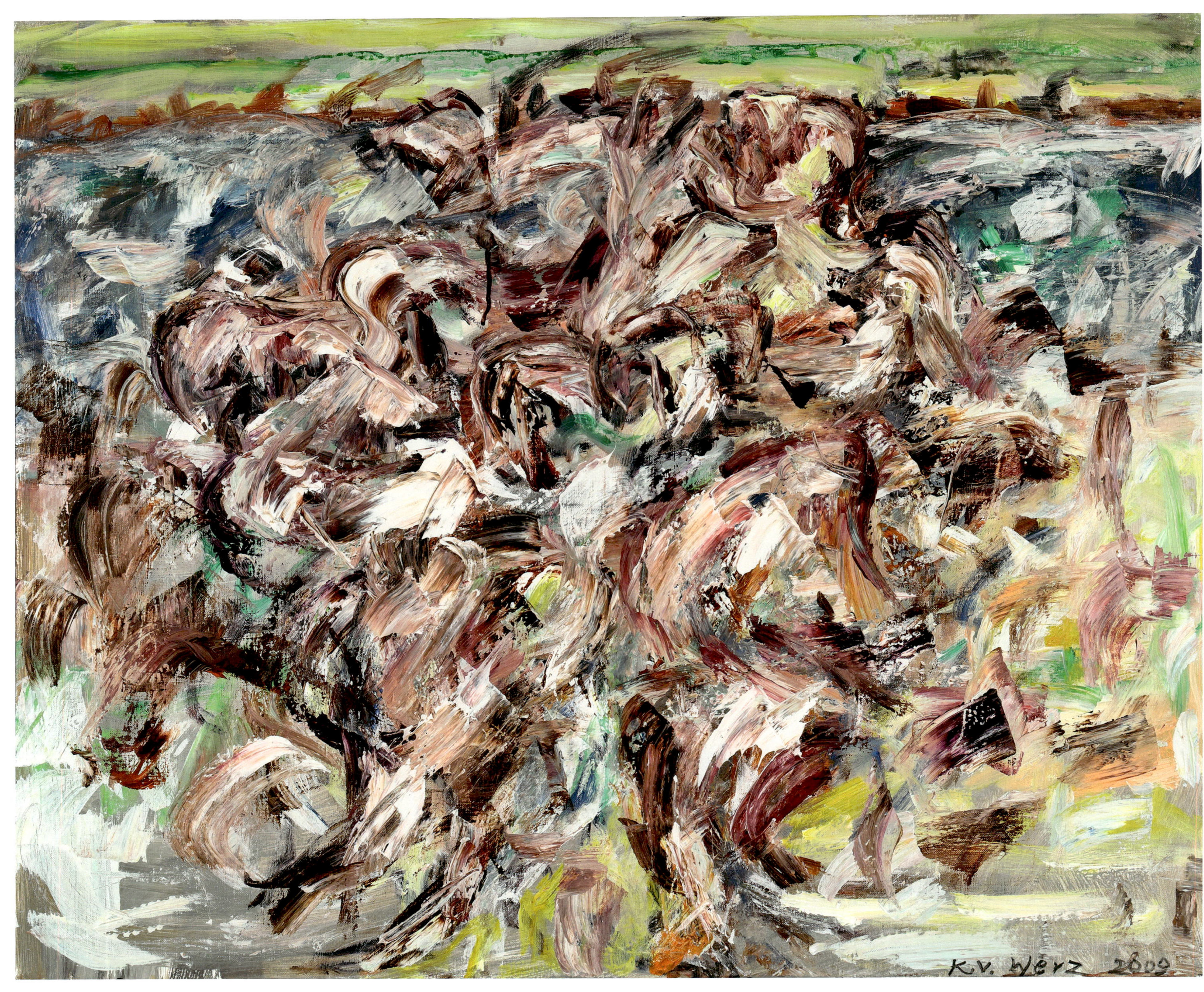

K.v. Werz 2009

Paar vor dem Meer, 2009
Acryl auf Leinwand
Acrylic on canvas
80 × 100 cm

Tanz, 2009
Acryl auf Leinwand
Acrylic on canvas
80 × 100 cm

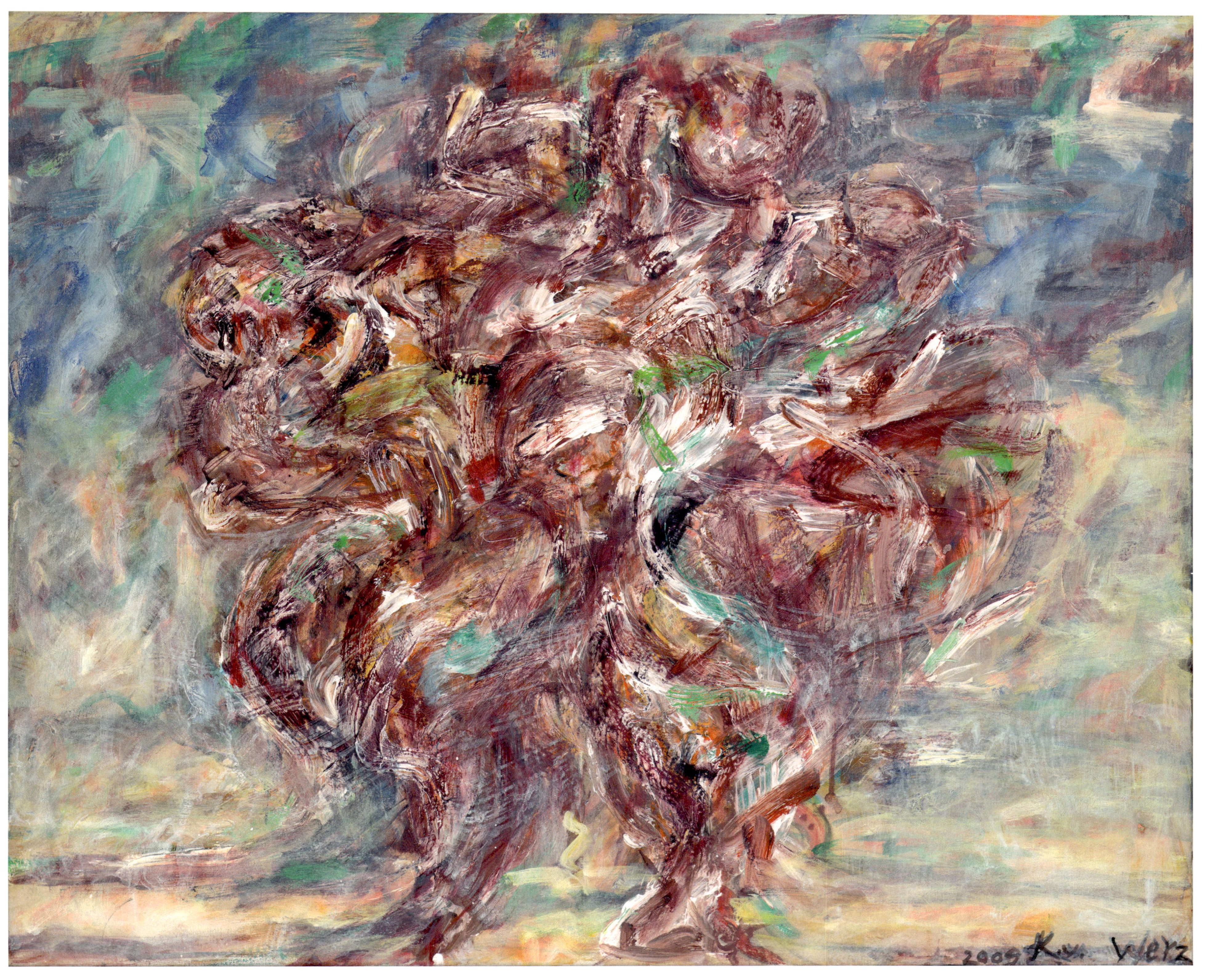

2009 Ku Werz

Im Werk der Künstlerin sind sie eine Randerscheinung – ein weiteres Indiz dafür, wie sehr ihr jede Art von Statik widerstrebt und Motorik entspricht. Voll und ganz teilt sie die Einsicht des russischen Konstruktivisten El Lissitzky: »Die Vergegenwärtigung der Form als Momentaufnahme eines ständigen Prozesses von Werden und Vergehen ist die eigentliche künstlerische Leistung.« Oder identifiziert sich mit dem österreichischen Maler, Grafiker und Illustrator Alfred Kubin, der notierte: »Mein Weltbild ist nie fertig. Es bleibt ein Bruchstück, denn künftige Erfahrungen könnten es anders formen.«

Während das Genre darauf abzielt, Dinge so täuschend echt wiederzugeben, dass die Grenzen zwischen Realität und Illusion verschwimmen, und den Betrachter optisch zu verführen, sucht Katharina von Werz eine Art stummes Zwiegespräch mit dem Betrachter über seine Assoziationen und Eigenbeobachtungen: »Er müsste seine Aufmerksamkeit auch der eigenen Dunkelkammer träumerischen Bewusstseins zuwenden.« Wieder ein Satz von Kubin, den sie darin bewundert, »dass er mit jedem Bild einen neuen Stil zu schöpfen scheint«.

Still lifes do not figure highly in the artist's work—another indication of her aversion to stasis and the appeal that dynamism has over her. The Russian Constructivist El Lissitzky encapsulates her sentiments when he states: "The illustration of the form as a momentary snapshot of a continual process of becoming and transpiring is what constitutes real artistic achievement." Similarly, she aligns herself with the Austrian painter, graphic artist, and illustrator, Alfred Kubin, who once noted: "My view of the world is never finished. It remains a fragment, as future experiences may shape it differently."

While the genre of still life aims to render things with such beguiling authenticity that the boundaries of reality and illusion merge and so mislead the viewer, Katharina von Werz aims to engage the viewer in a silent dialogue about his own associations, his own observations.

As Kubin states: "He [the viewer] should also turn his attention to the dark chamber of his own dream-like consciousness." Kubin, the artist feels, is worthy of admiration because, he "seems to create a new style with every picture."

Gegenstände am Strand, 2001
Acryl auf Leinwand
Acrylic on canvas
60 × 80 cm

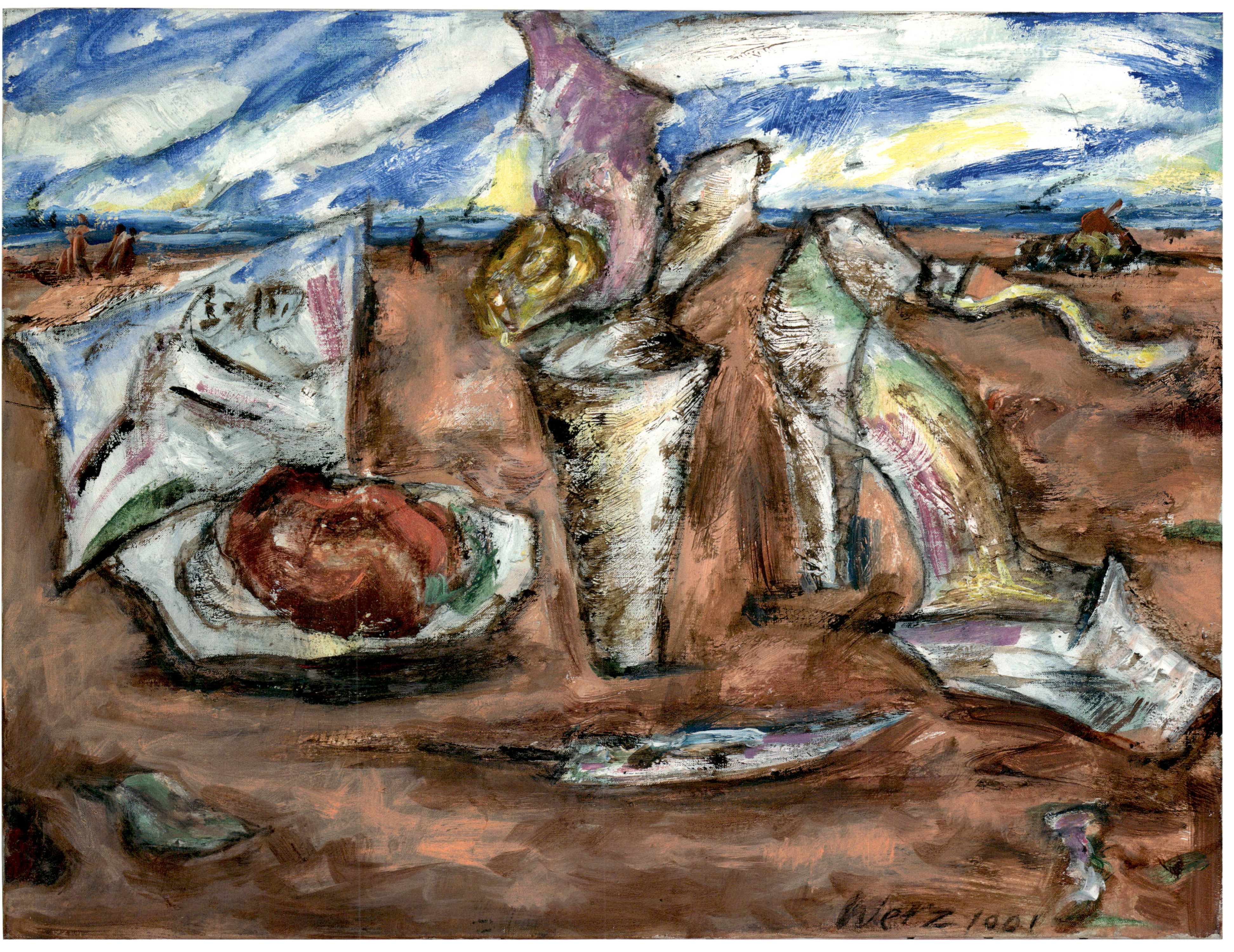
Wetz 1991

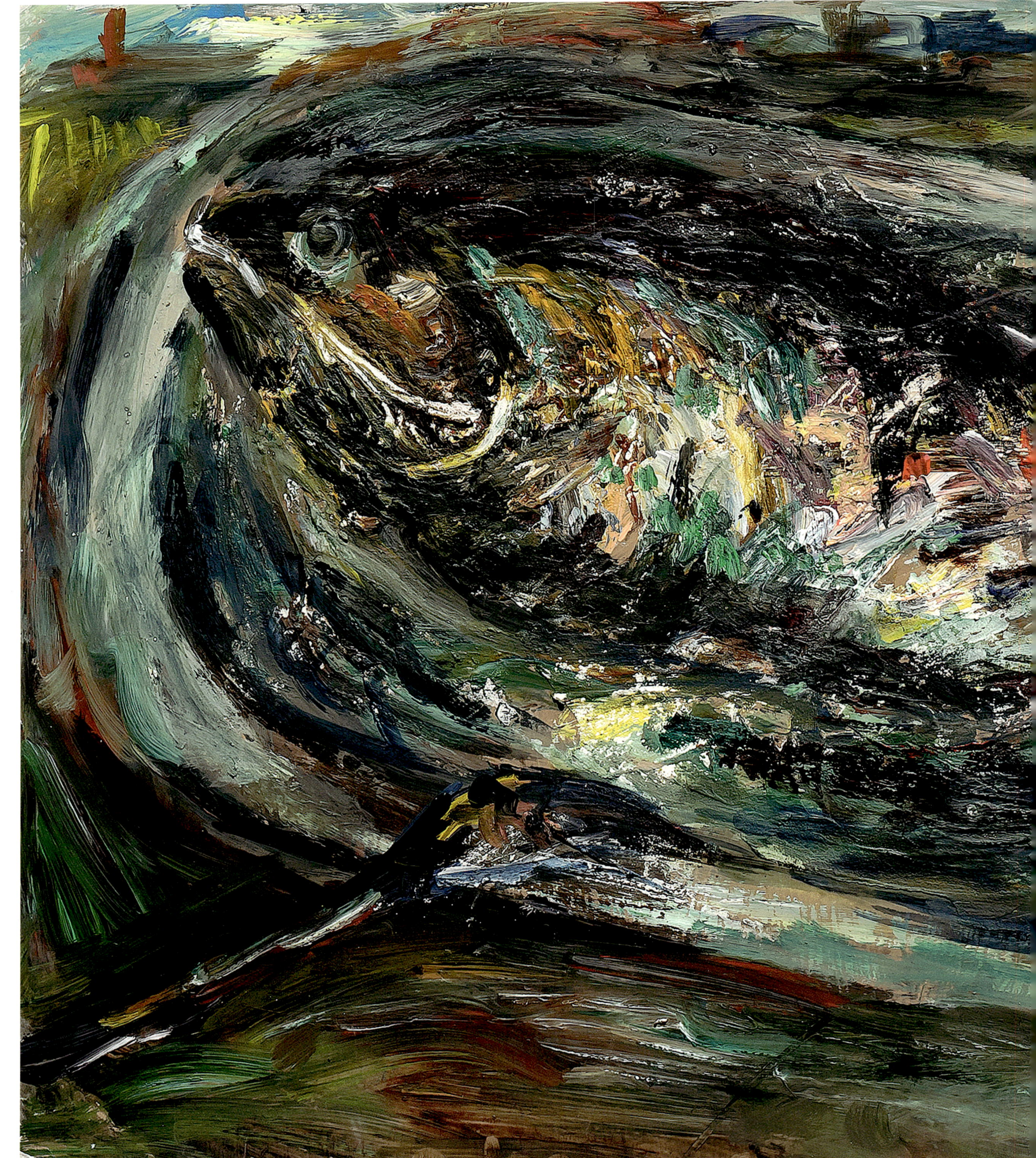

Fisch, 2009
Acryl auf Pappe
Acrylic on cardboard
50 × 81 cm

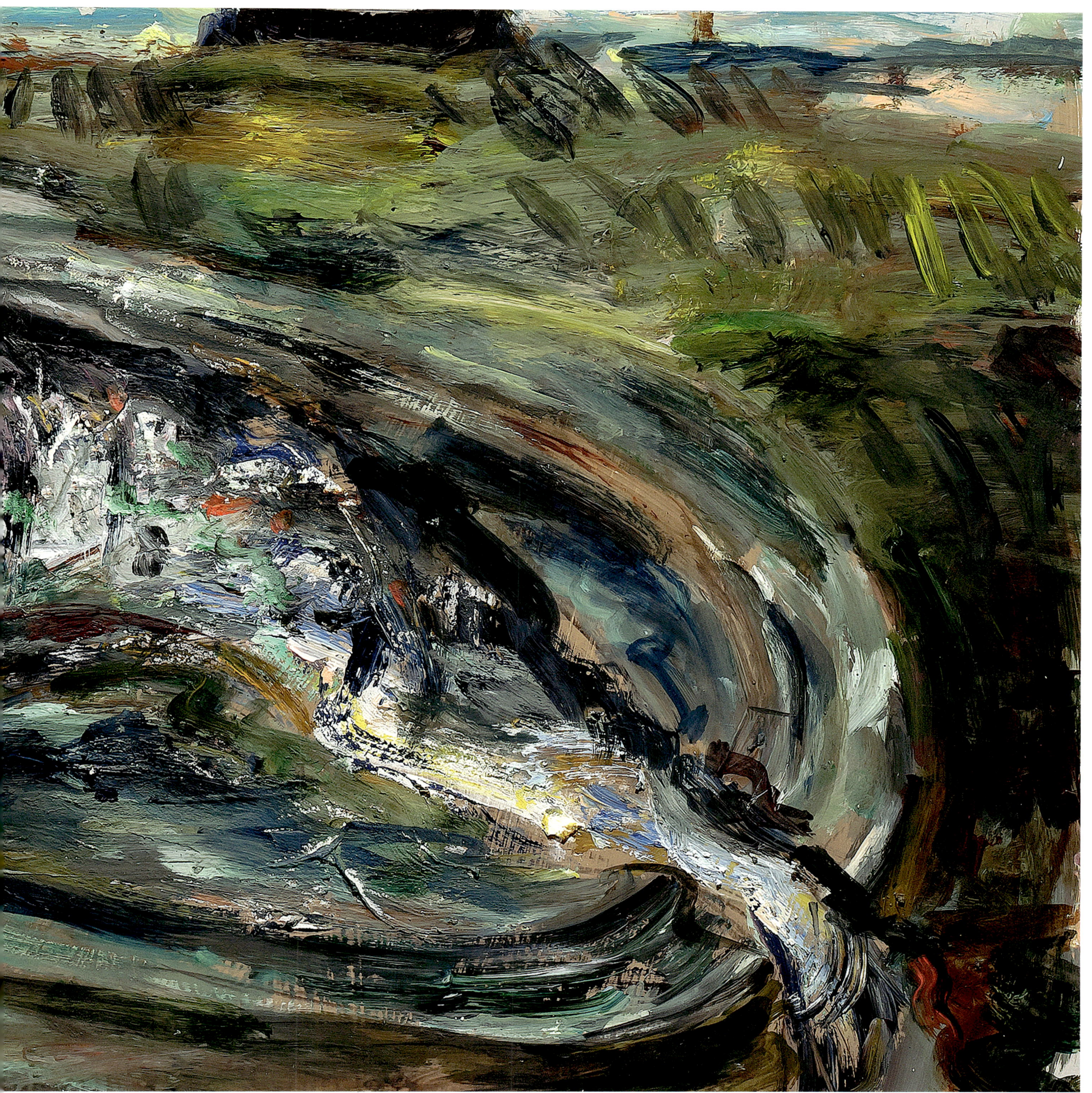

»Figürlich oder abstrakt? Mit Bedacht reizt die Künstlerin diese Grenzen aus. Das Uneindeutige ist ihren Skulpturen zueigen geworden: das Aufscheinende und das sich Verflüchtigende, die Selbstversunkenheit wie die Geste des Augenblicks.«

Was die Münchner Kunstkritikerin Dorothea Baumer im plastischen Werk der Künstlerin entdeckt, bestätigt diese, wenn sie im Interview auf Seite 14 erzählt, wie spielerisch sie mit dem Material Ton umgeht: »Es ist der ideale Stoff für mich, denn ich kann ihn formen und deformieren. Terrakotta ermöglicht mir ein weiches Modellieren, vergleichbar mit dem Malen.«

Katharina von Werz vertraut ihrer haptischen Intelligenz. Sie moduliert Körper und Volumen in einem Wechselspiel von Improvisation und Konstruktion, intuitiv und gleichzeitig analytisch. Ihre Skulpturen, ob figurativ oder abstrakt, schwingen in einem virtuosen Gleichgewicht zwischen Dekoration und Expression, wie es zuletzt das Rokoko zu kultivieren wusste.

"Figurative or abstract? The artist cautiously plies the boundary between the two, pushing it to its limits. Her sculptures appropriate the unclear: moments of appearance and dissipation, the act of being wholly immersed in thought and the gesture of the moment."

What the Munich-based art critic Dorothea Baumer gives voice to here is confirmed when the artist herself relates how much she relishes handling the material of clay: "It really is the ideal material for me, as I can form and deform it. Compared to painting, terracotta allows me to model the figure softly" (see interview, page 14).

Katharina von Werz puts faith in the intelligence of her fingertips. She models, intuitively and at the same time analytically, body and mass through the interaction of improvisation and construction. Her sculptures, be they figurative or abstract, are held in a masterful balance between decoration and expression, in a style that was last systematically cultivated by the artists of the Rococo.

Tanz auf dem Pokal, 2008
Keramik, glasiert
Ceramic, glazed
30 × 20 × 21 cm

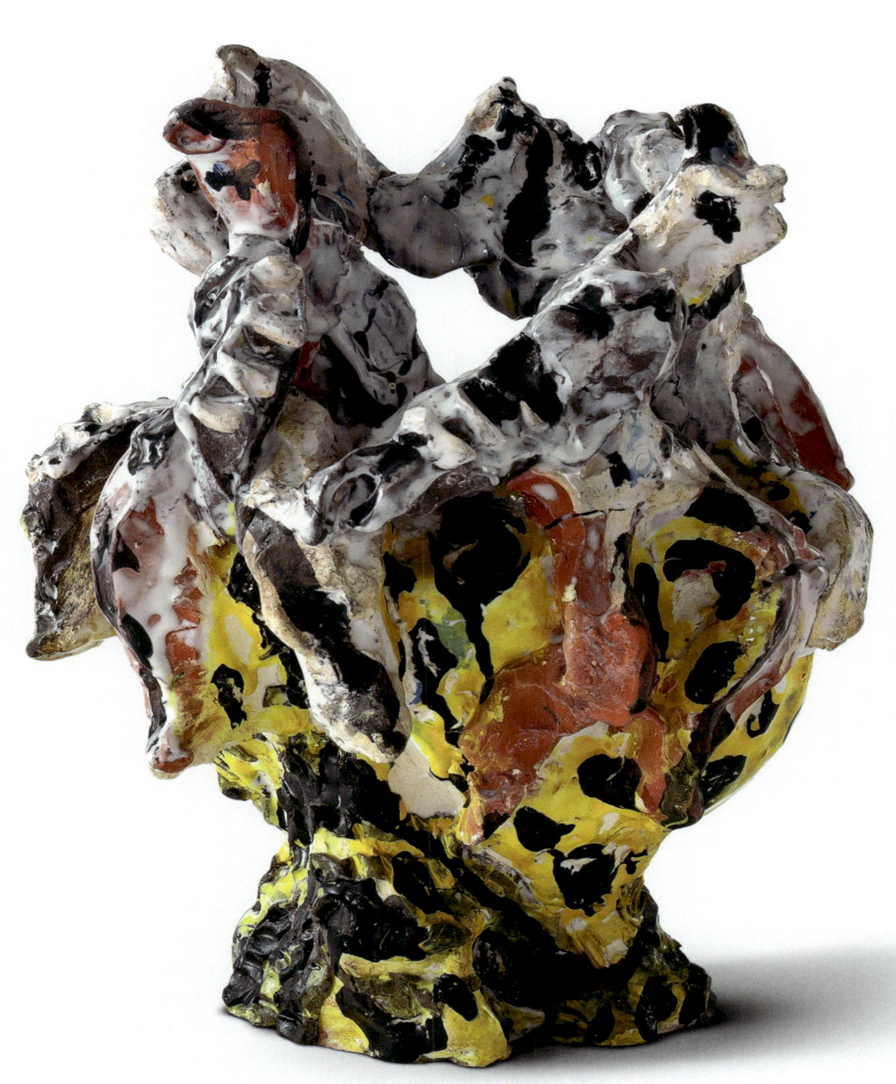

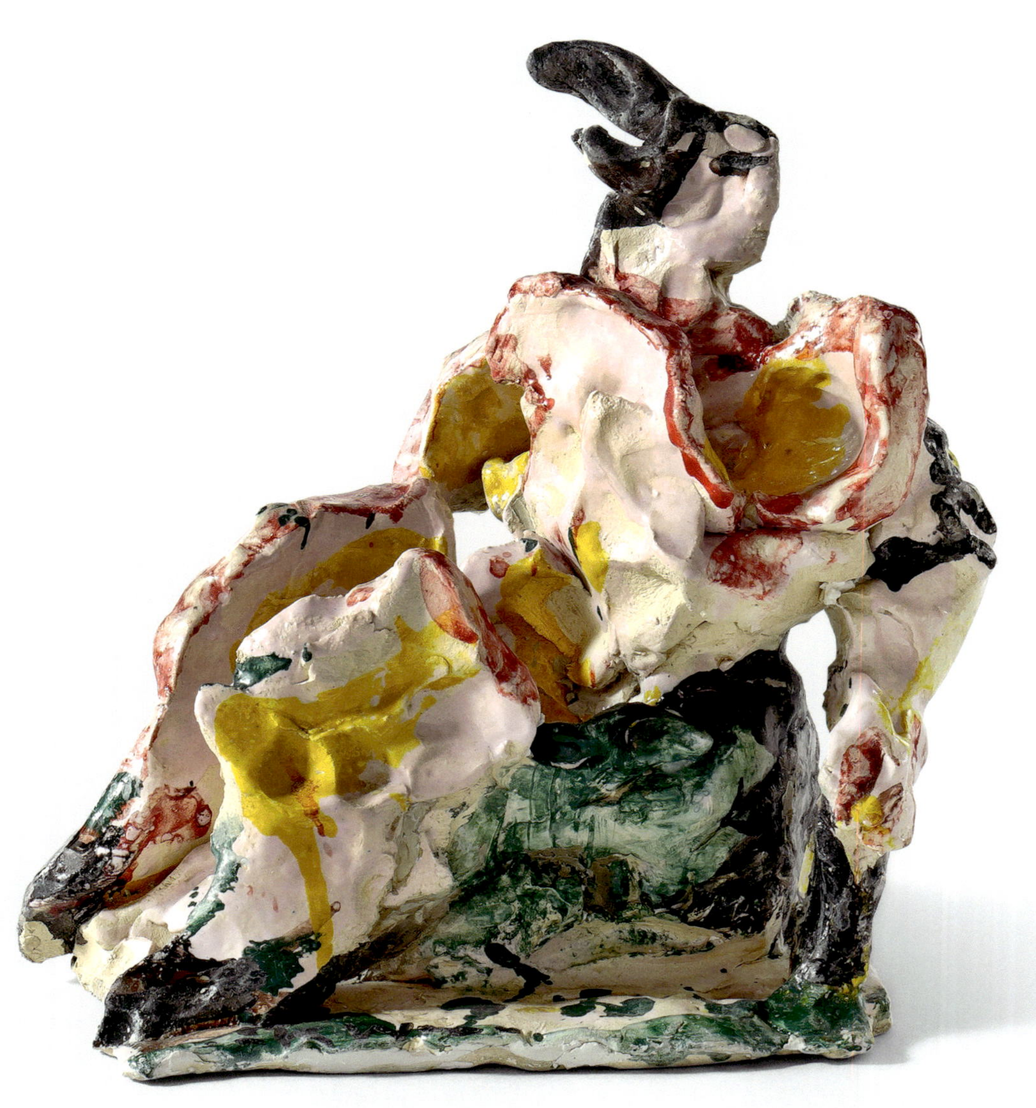

Isabella von Kastilien im neuen Kleid, 2009
Keramik, glasiert
Ceramic, glazed
23 × 18 × 14 cm

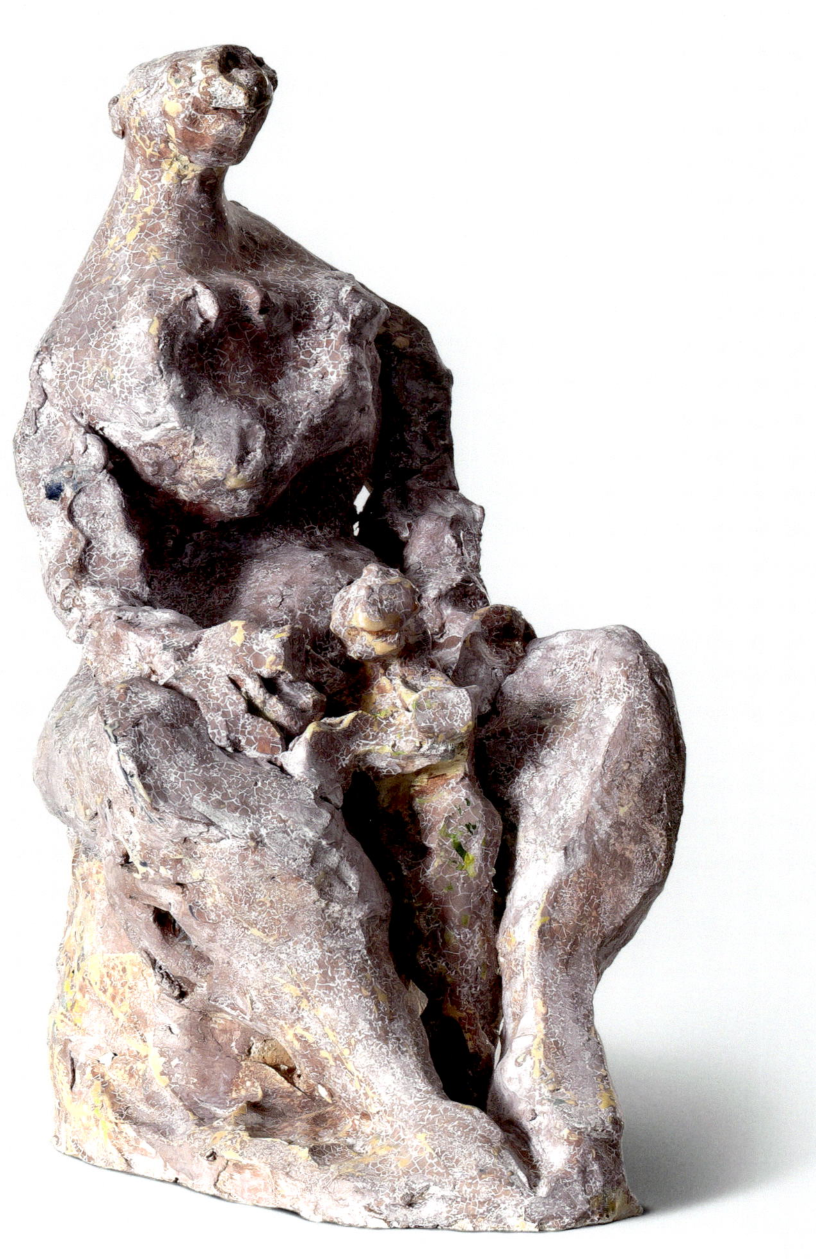

Hendriekje und Titus, 2007
Terrakotta, bemalt
Terracotta, painted
41 × 36 × 19 cm

Maria de Medicis Blick übers Land, 2008
Terrakotta/Terracotta
24 × 17 × 10 cm

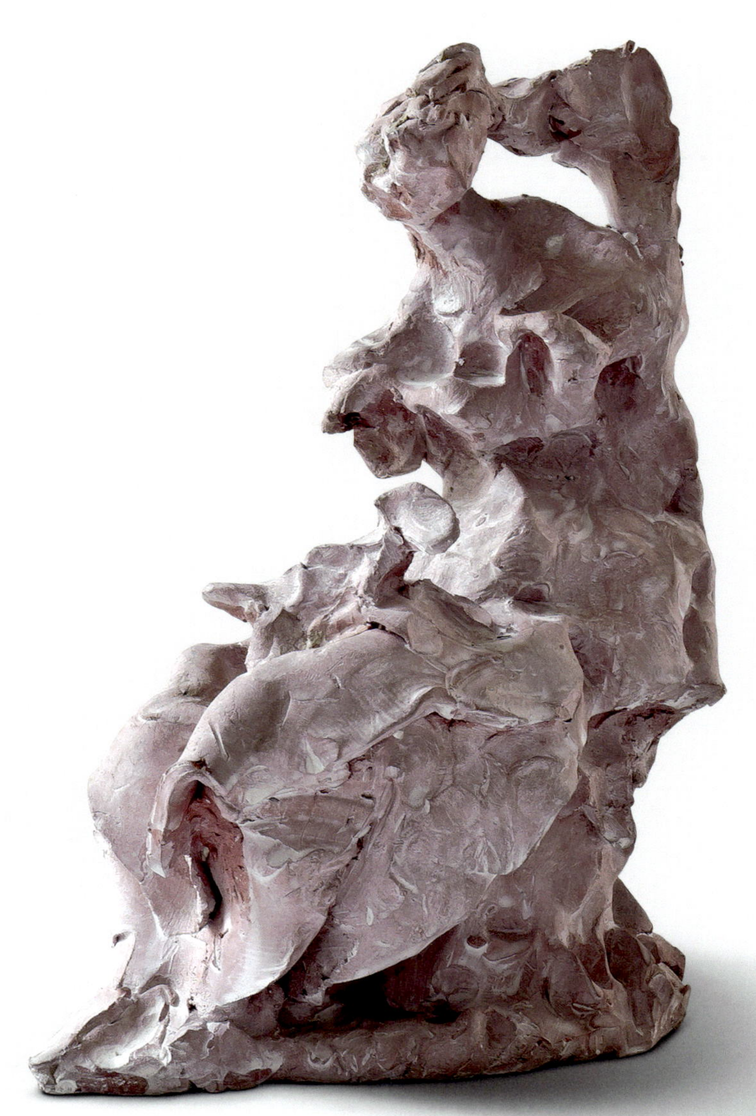

ADAM UND EVA
ADAM AND EVE

Das erste Paar. Sie, die »Mutter aller Lebendigen«, ist die Verführerin mit dem Apfel, er der Herrscher über sie. Auf einem Gemälde der Serie, *Adam und Eva II* (S. 102) windet sich die Schlange als gelbrötlich listiges Biest girlandenförmig am oberen linken Bildrand und scheint das fröhliche Treiben der einander entdeckenden Körper für gut zu befinden.

Denn im irdischen Paradies von Katharina von Werz herrscht Gleichberechtigung – egal, ob es um Abschied oder Vergnügen geht. Wie für so viele Künstler vor ihr ist das Thema auch für sie »Vorwand für kompositorische Variationen zu den Dramen und Komödien der Paarung«. Immer stärker, von Tableau zu Tableau, abstrahiert sie die Konturen der Leiber zu musikalisch schwingend-lodernden, ausschließlich der Eigengesetzlichkeit der Malerei ergebenen Farb- und Formfugen.

Männlicher Geniekult, den die biblische Erzählung im Buch Genesis möglicherweise sogar mitgeprägt hat, sei den Frauen wesensfremd, meint Katharina von Werz: »Mir fällt dazu der Satz von Simone de Beauvoir ein: ›Adam war nichts als ein roher Entwurf, und die Schöpfung des Menschen ist Gott erst gelungen, als er Eva geschaffen hat‹.«

The first couple. She, the "mother of all living men and women" is the temptress with the apple, he her master. In the painting from the series *Adam und Eva II* (p. 102), the serpent, a yellowish red, sly beast, coils itself in garlands in the upper-left corner and appears pleased with the sight of bodies in the joyous act of discovering one another.

For in Katharina von Werz's vision of earthly paradise, gender equality prevails, no matter what the subject: loss or pleasure. Like so many artists before her, for Katharina von Werz the subject of Adam and Eve is also "a pretext for compositional variations on the dramas and comedies of coupling." From tableau to tableau she increasingly abstracts the contours of the bodies until they become musical structures of color and form that vibrate with rhythm and which yield to nothing but the autonomy of painting alone. According to Katharina von Werz, the male cult of genius which perhaps even had a hand in shaping the biblical story in the Book of Genesis is something quite alien to women. "I am reminded," she says, "of Simone de Beauvoir's words: 'Adam was nothing more than a rough draft, and god was only successful at creating humankind once he had created Eve.'"

Faisant la toilette, 2007
Mischtechnik auf Papier
Mixed media on paper
42 × 58 cm
Staatliche Graphische Sammlung,
München/Munich

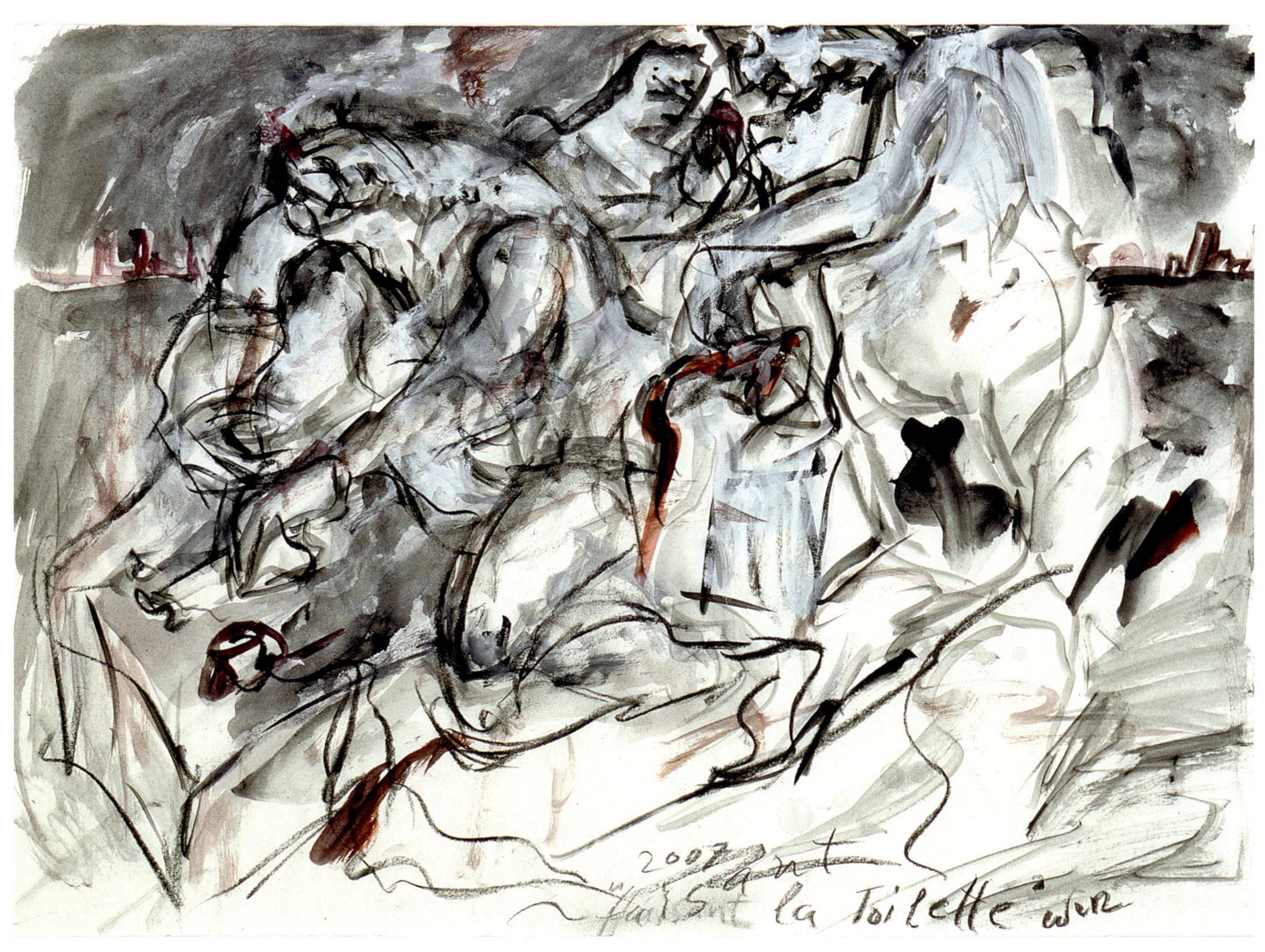

2007
"faisant la Toilette"

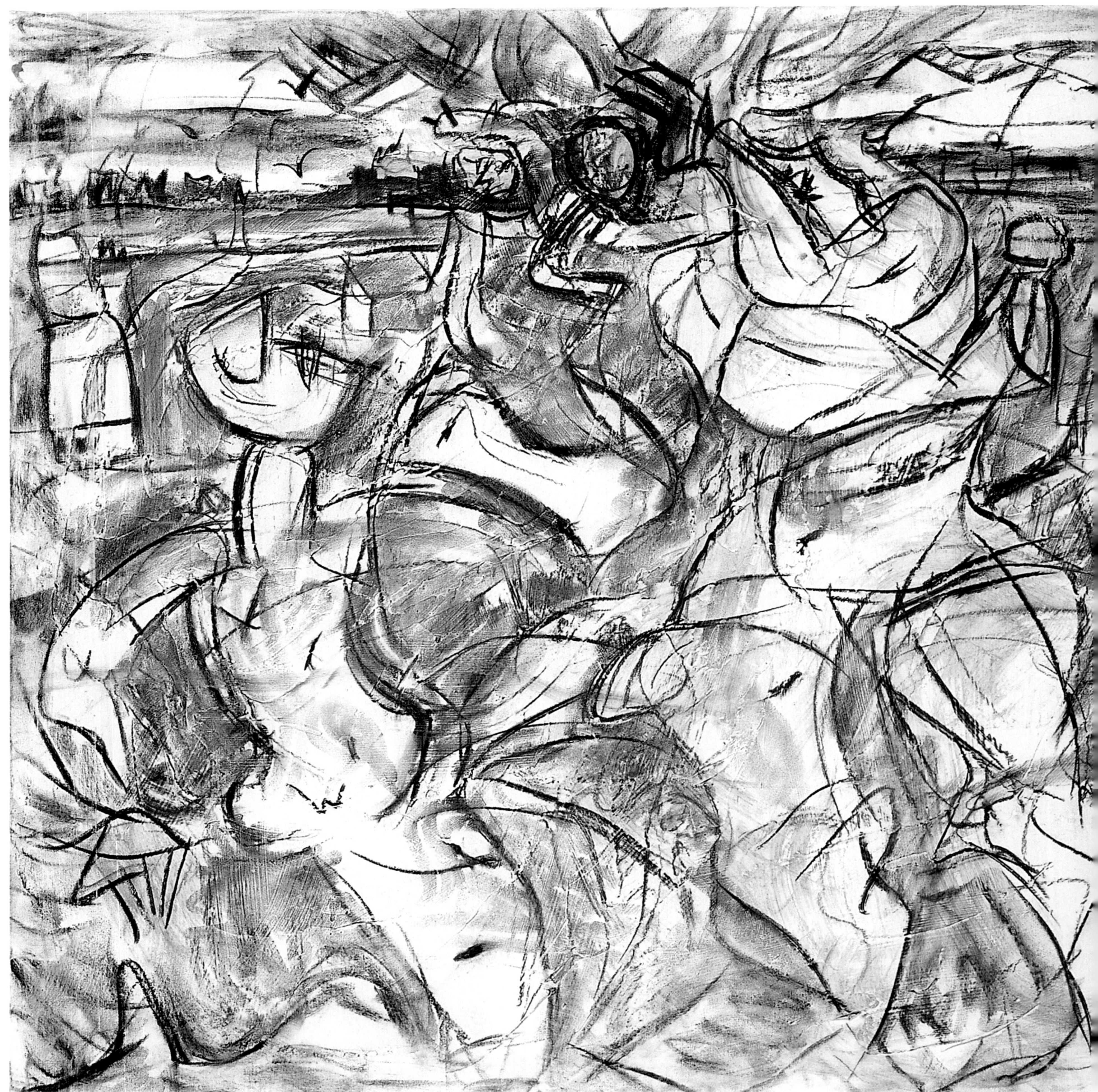

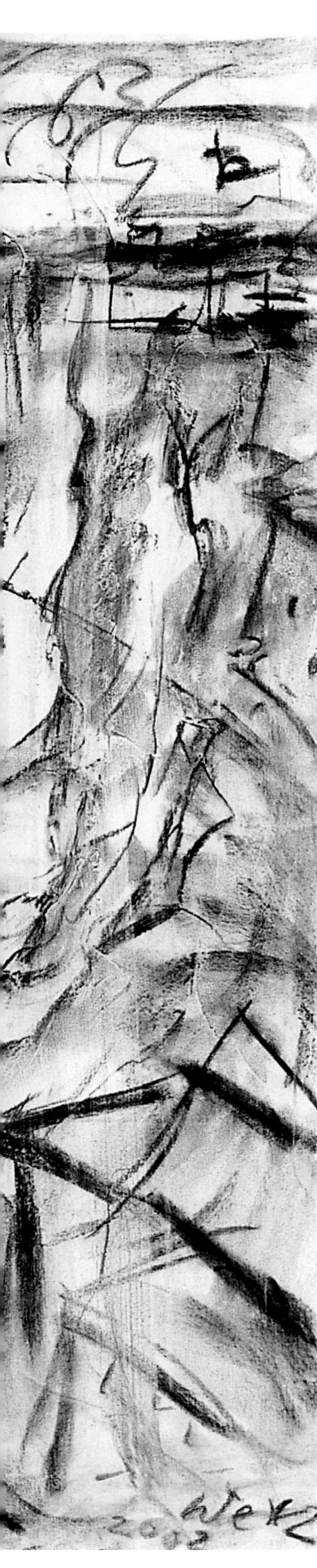

Adam und Eva, 2009
Kohle auf Leinwand
Charcoal on canvas
100 × 130 cm

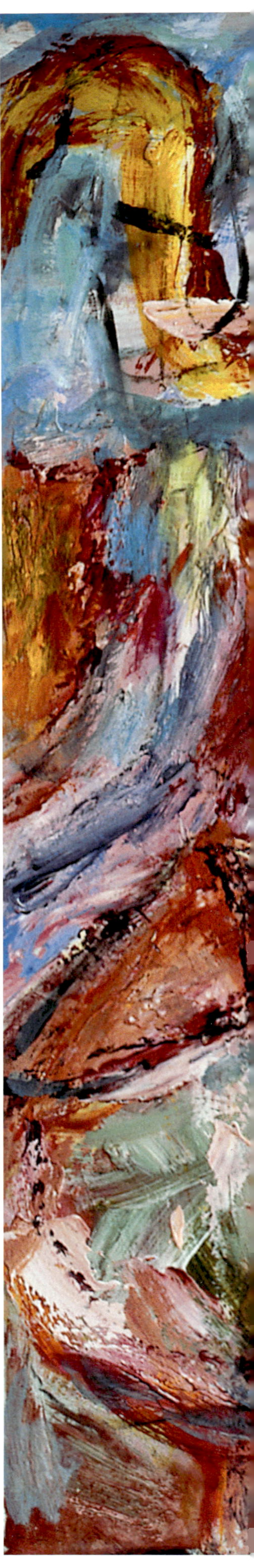

Adam und Eva II, 2002
Acryl auf Pappe
Acrylic on cardboard
80 × 100 cm
Sammlung/Collection Herzog Franz von Bayern,
München/Munich

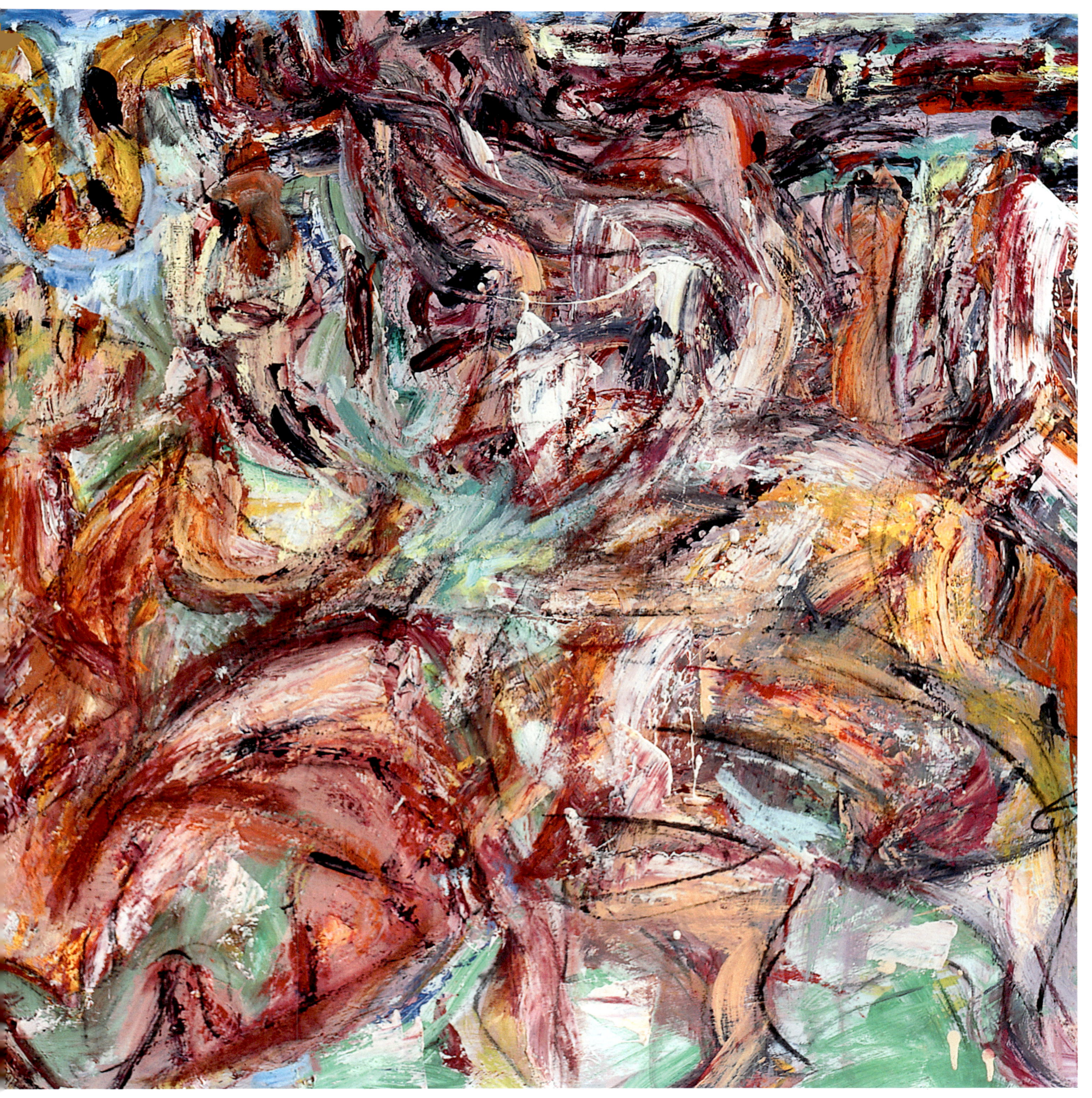

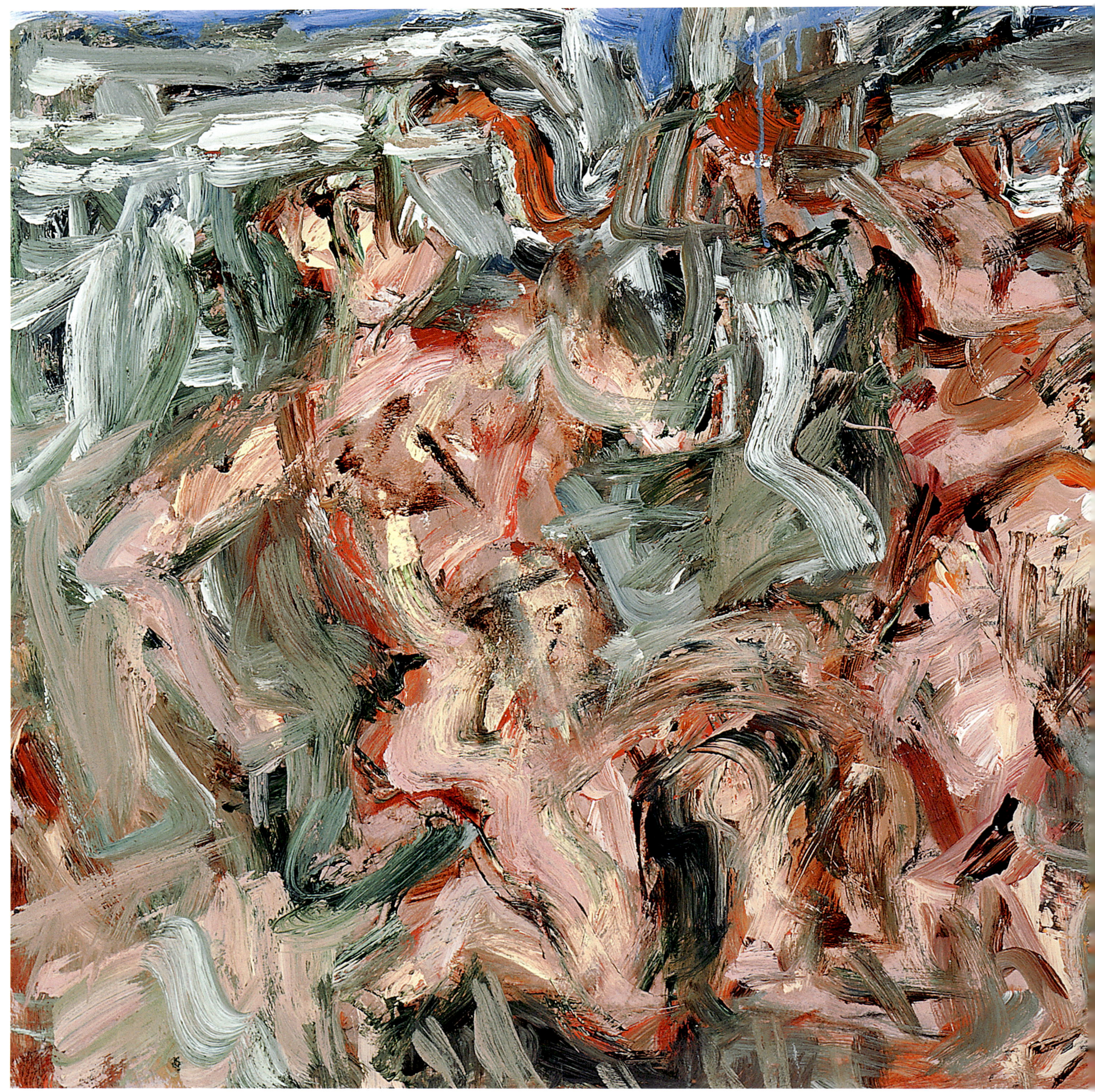

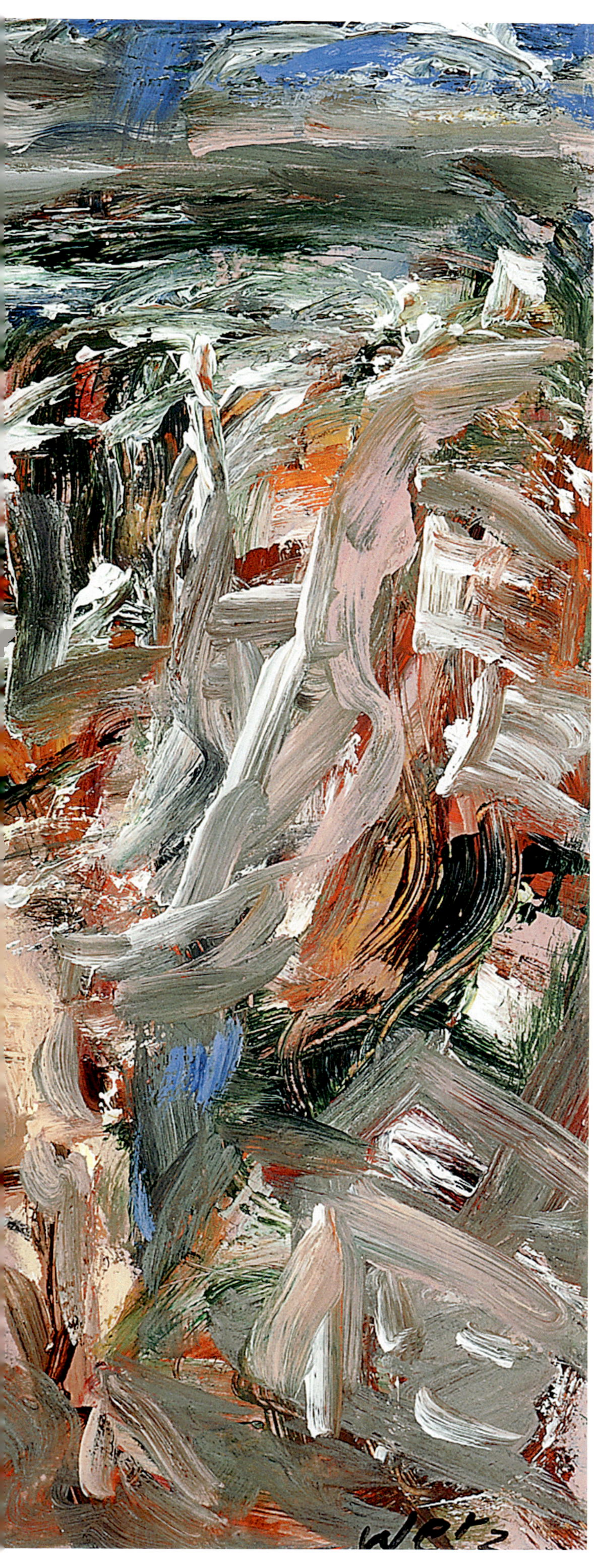

Adam und Eva III, 2001
Acryl auf Pappe
Acrylic on cardboard
80 × 100 cm

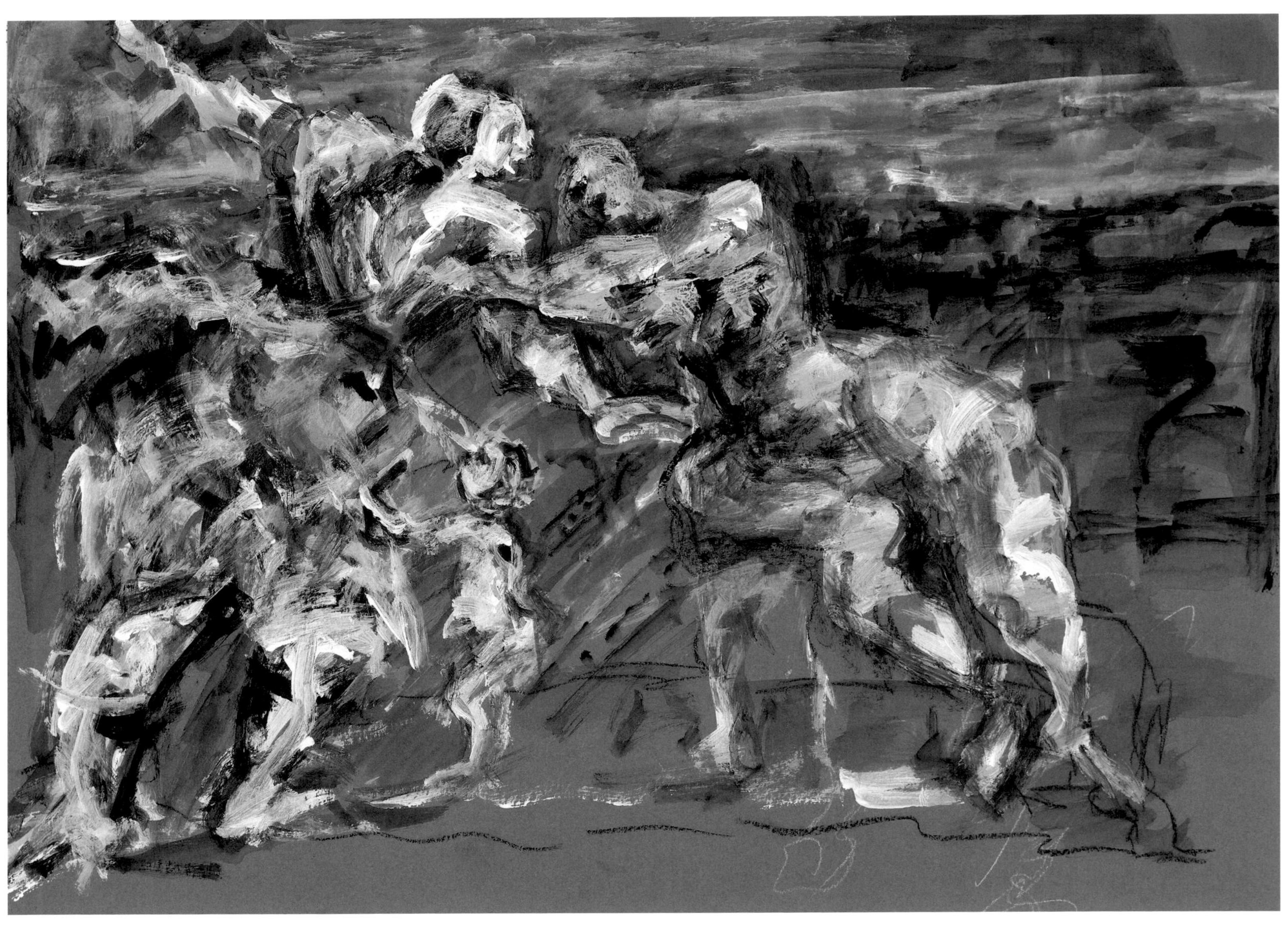

Abschied, 2011
Acryl auf Papier
Acrylic on paper
50 × 70 cm

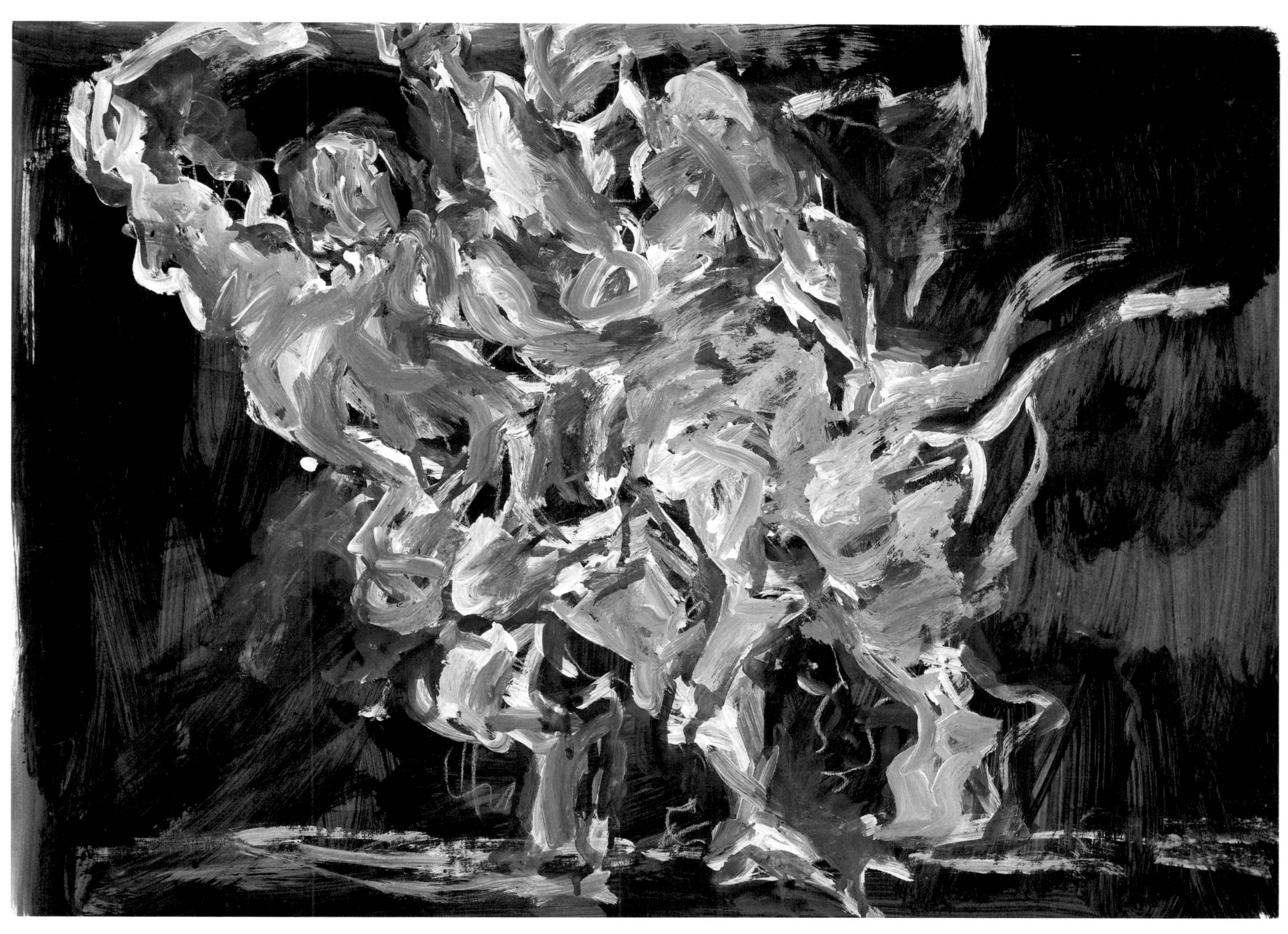

Karneval, 2010
Mischtechnik auf Papier
Mixed media on paper
59 × 84 cm

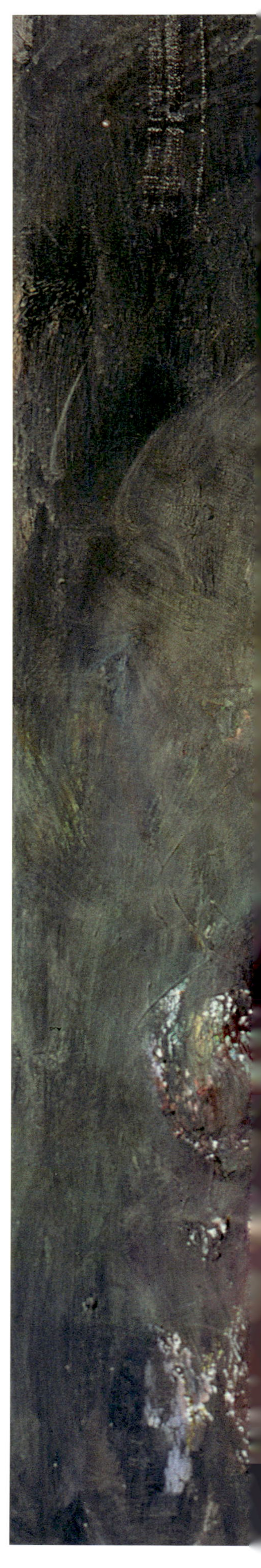

Vergnügtes Paar, 2006
Acryl auf Leinwand
Acrylic on canvas
80 × 100 cm
Privatbesitz, München
Privately owned, Munich

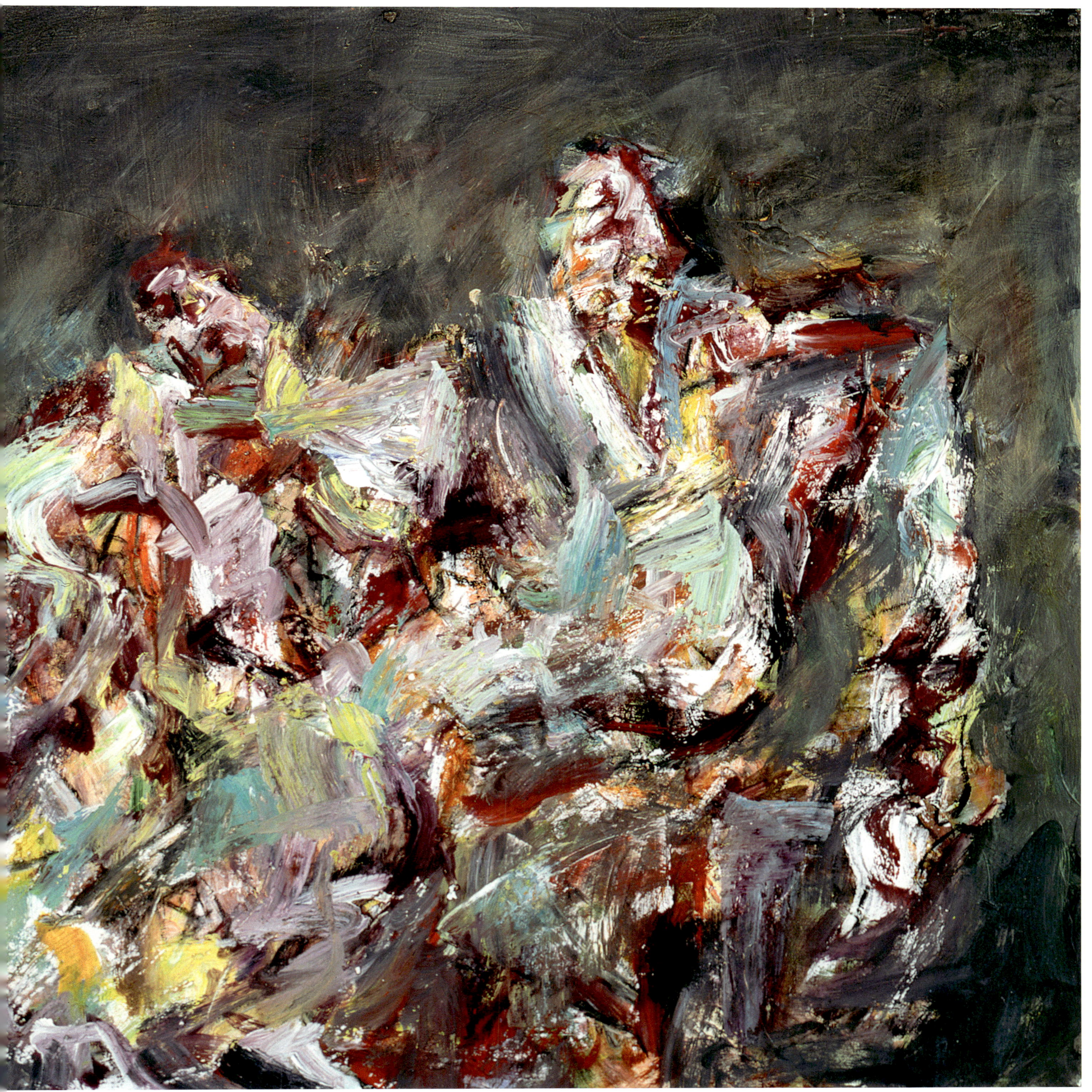

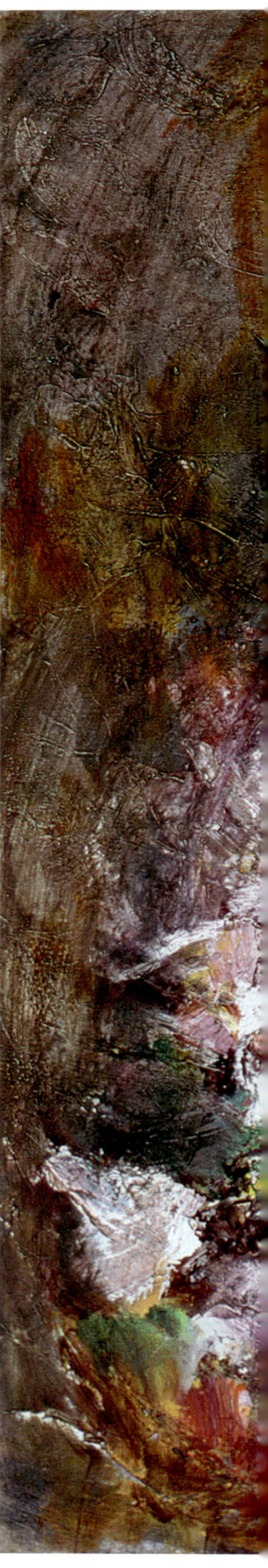

Verkehrte Welt, 2006
Acryl auf Leinwand
Acrylic on canvas
75 × 95 cm
Bayerische Staatsgemäldesammlungen,
München/Munich

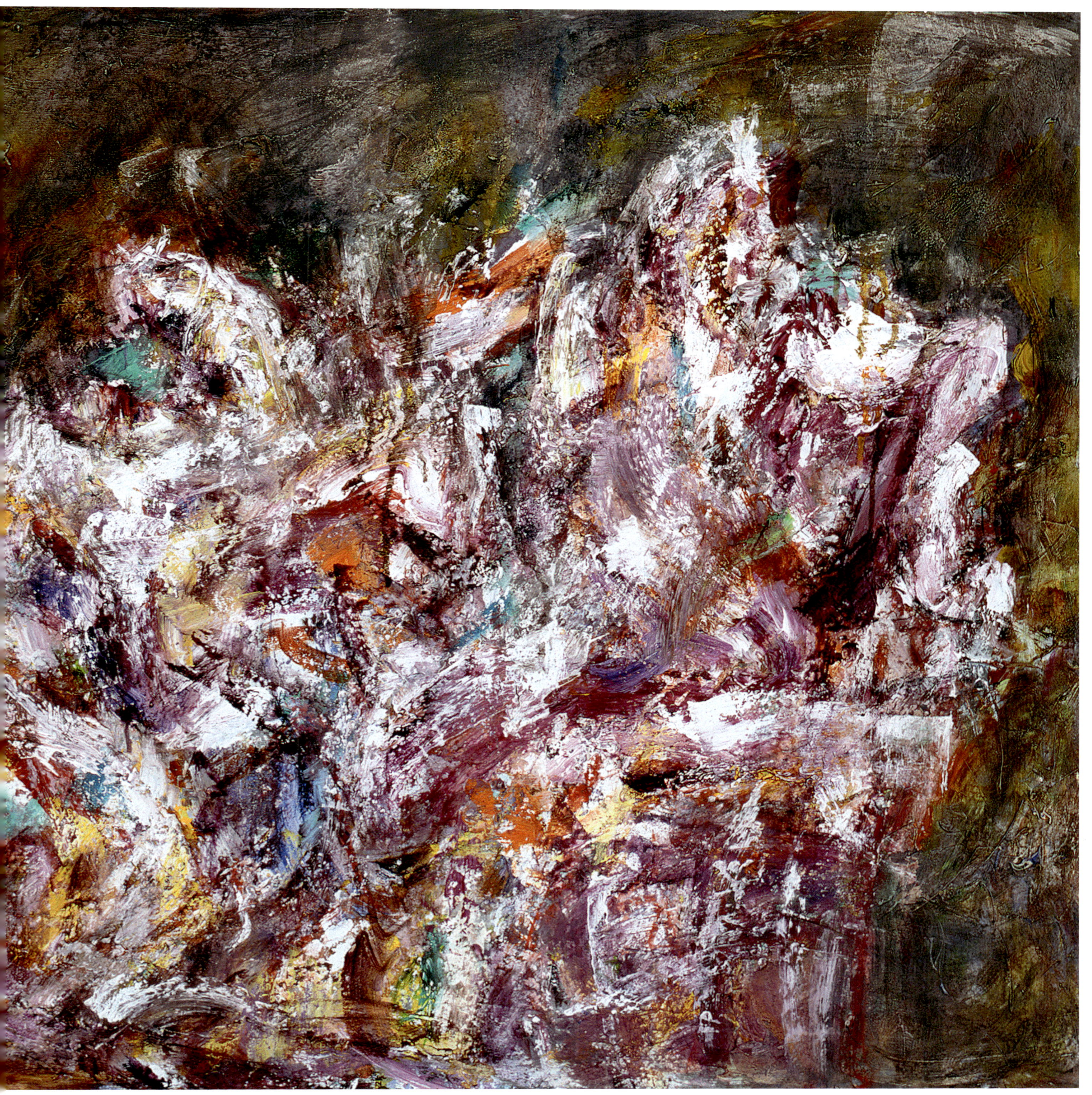

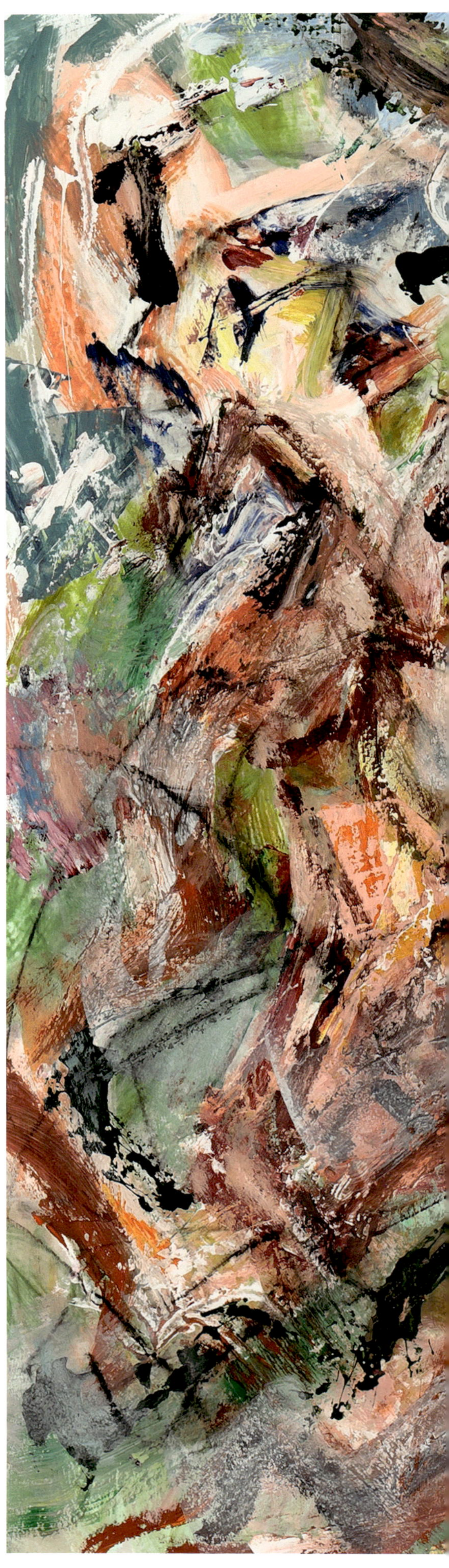

Adam und Eva III, 2012
Acryl auf Pappe
Acrylic on cardboard
95 × 130 cm

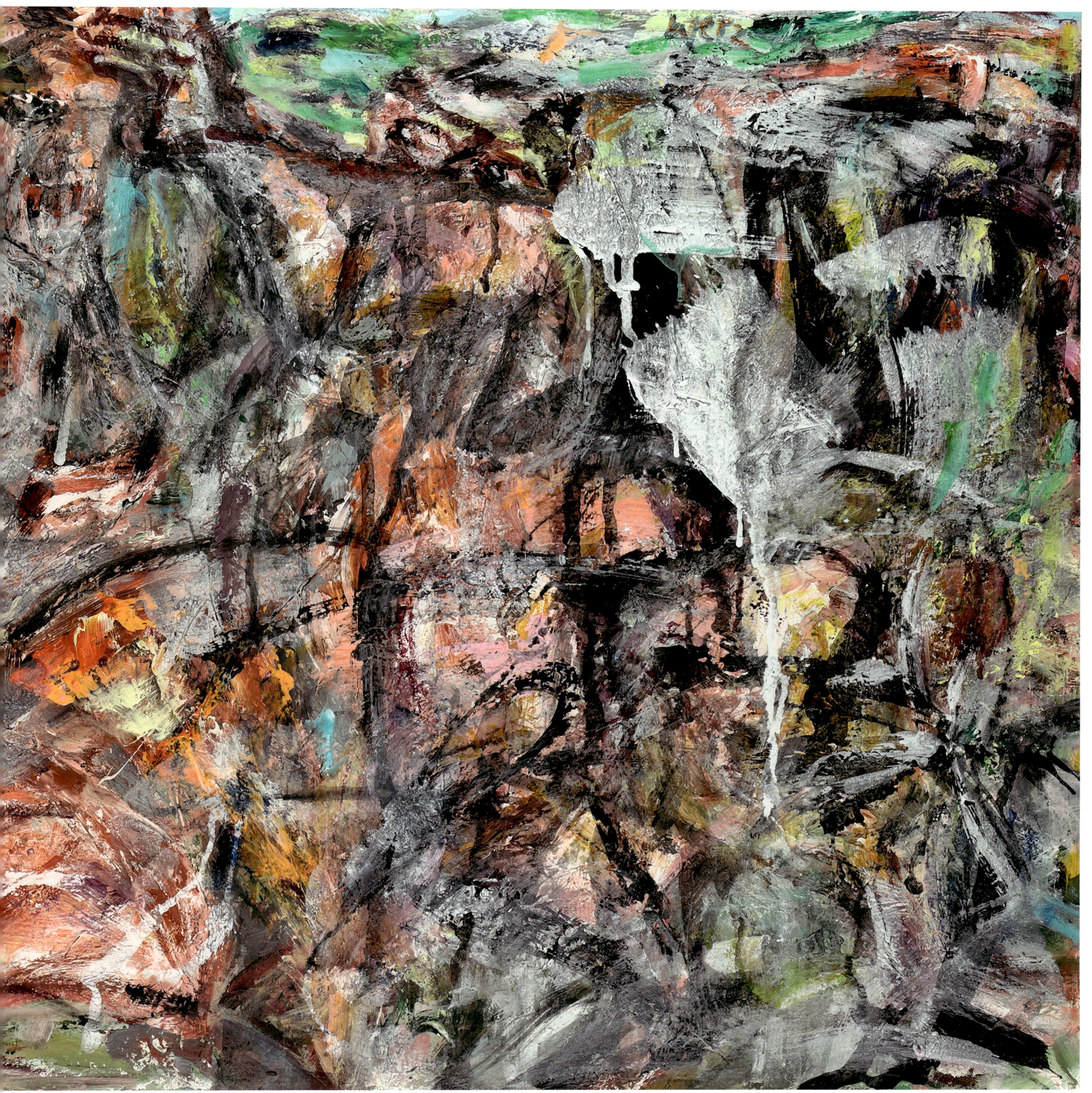

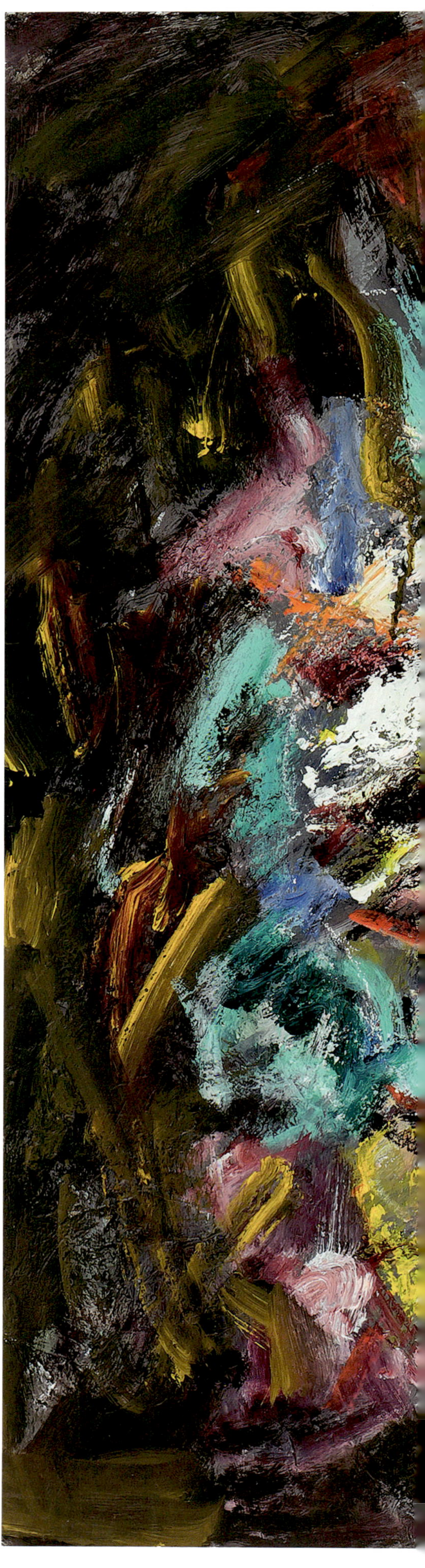

Paar, 2012
Acryl auf Pappe
Acrylic on cardboard
95 × 130 cm
Bayerische Staatsgemäldesammlungen,
München/Munich

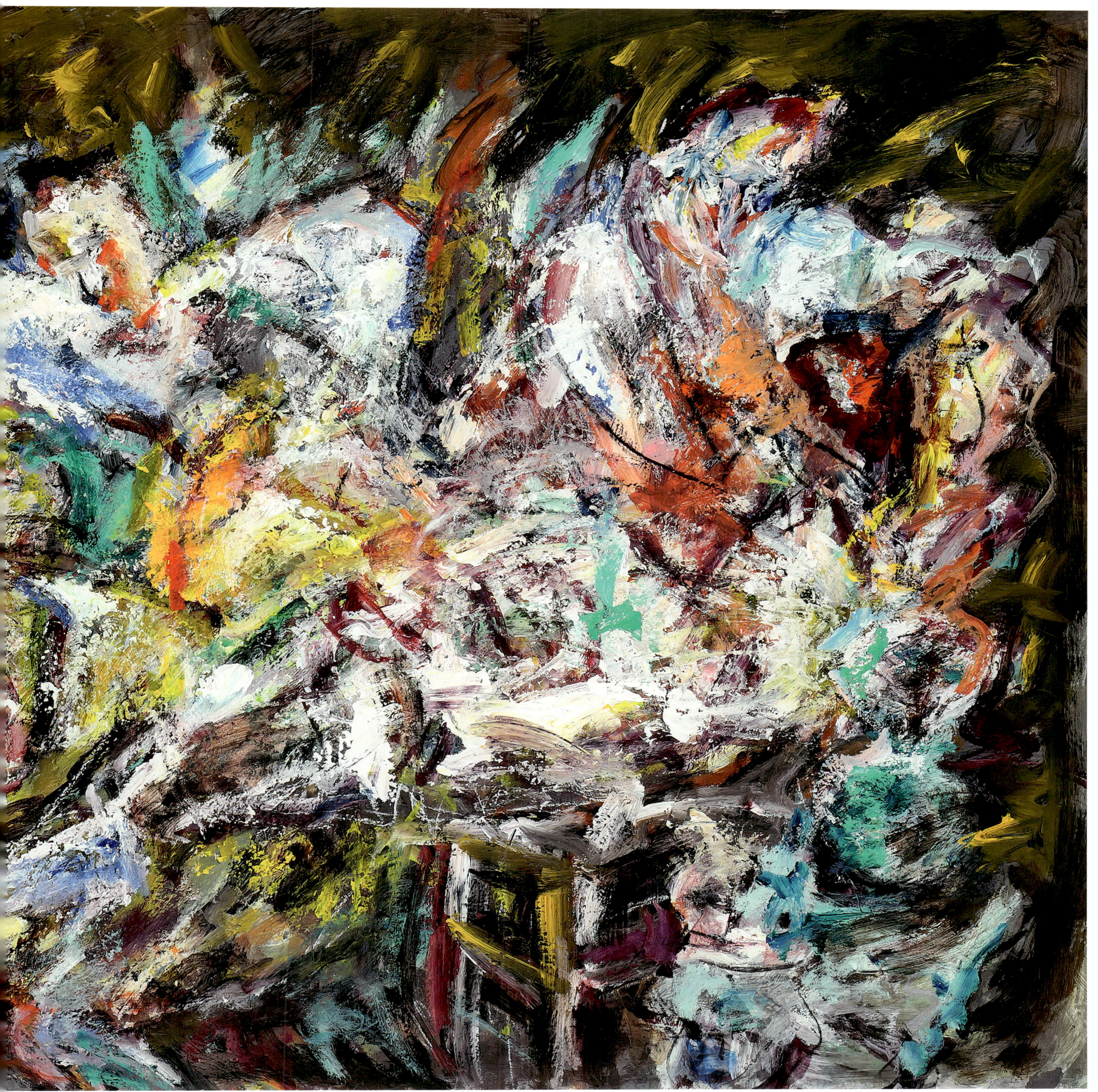

Lustiges Paar, 2012
Acryl auf Leinwand
Acrylic on canvas
105 × 140 cm

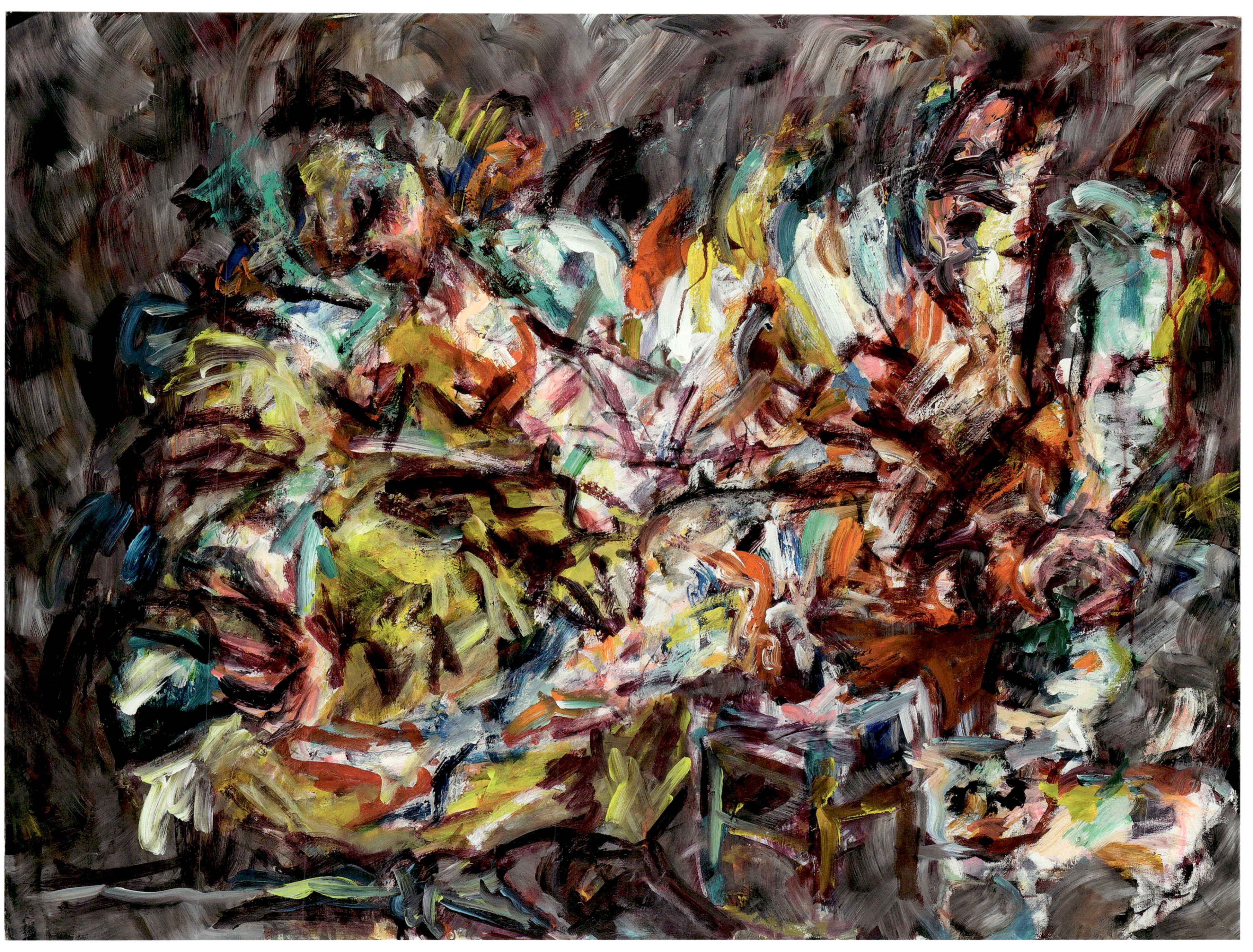

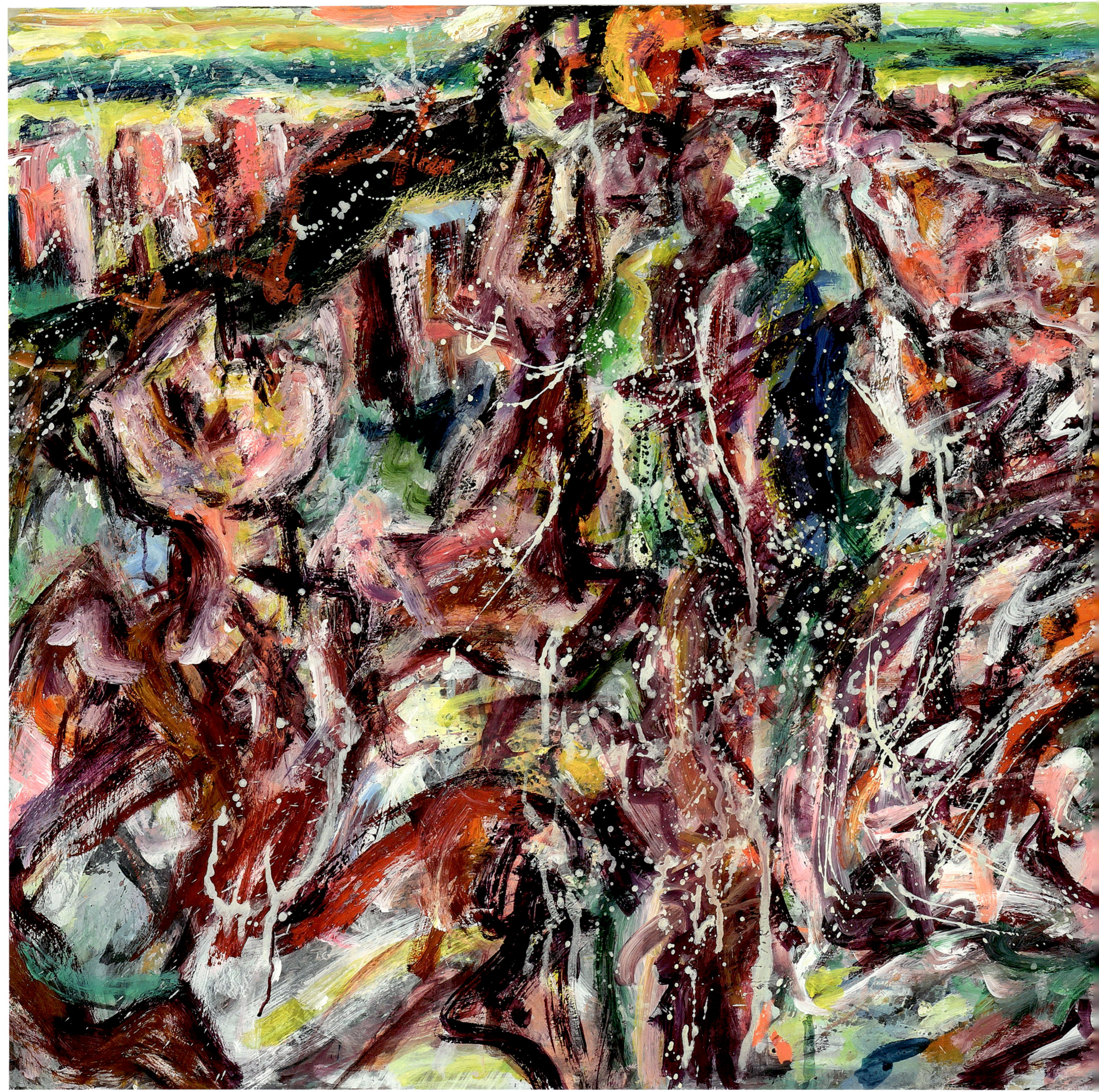

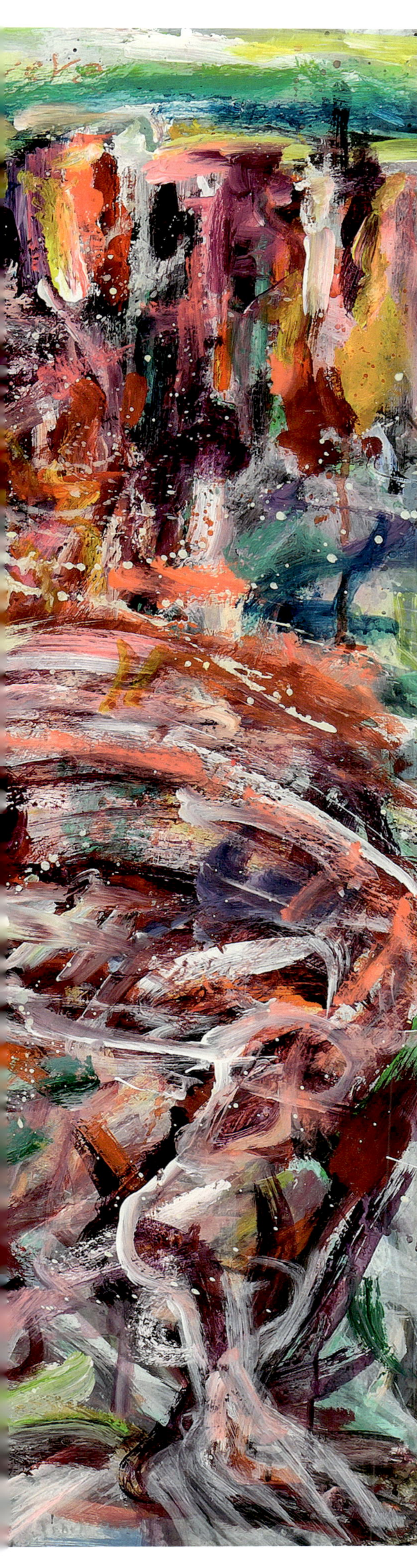

Adam und Eva, 2012
Acryl auf Pappe
Acrylic on cardboard
95 × 130 cm

Vergnügtes Paar II, 2006
Acryl auf Leinwand
Acrylic on canvas
75 × 95 cm

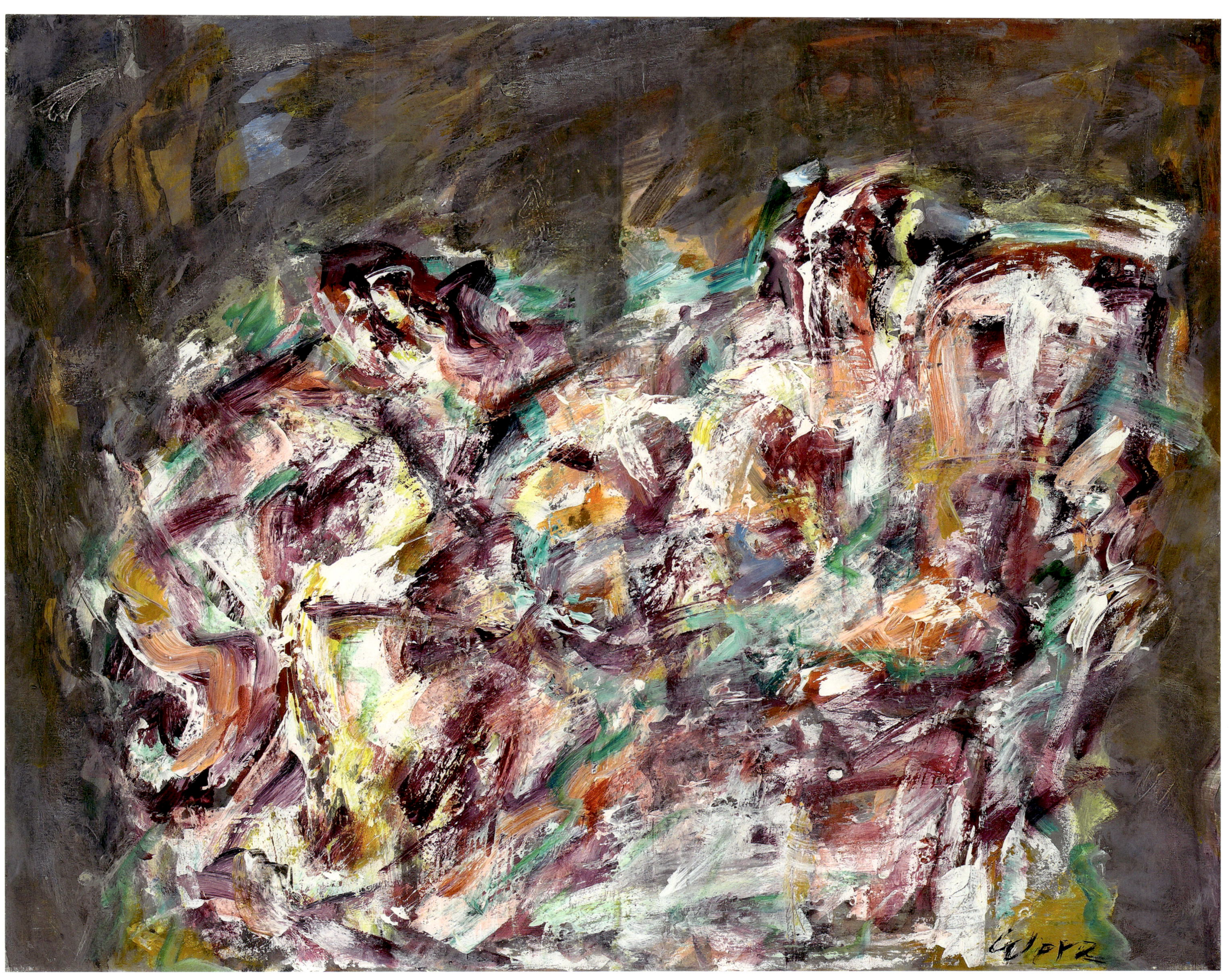

Ihr Blick, schräg auf den Betrachter gerichtet, ist aufmerksam und doch scheu. Diese Perspektive ist typisch für die Künstlerin, wie sie im Interview auf Seite 12 erzählt: »Nach einem Modell zu porträtieren, dazu bin ich zu scheu. Es ist ja eine sehr intime Situation, weil das Innere mitmalt ... Eigentlich ist mein Interesse nicht das Porträt. Es geht mir um eine bestimmte Stimmung, die meine innere Wahrheit spiegelt.«

Insofern stimmt der Satz, jedes künstlerische Werk sei auch irgendwo ein Selbstbildnis. Aber Katharina von Werz erforscht nicht, wie etwa Cindy Sherman, weibliche und indirekt auch männliche Identität als Konstrukt aus individuellen und kollektiven Bildern und Projektionen. Stattdessen findet sie Lebenssinn im kreativen Arbeitsprozess selbst. Mit Alfred Kubin teilt sie die »Gewissheit, dass der Mensch aus einer rätselhaften Verbindung zweier Wesenheiten besteht, dem Chaos und dem Selbst. Es sind die Künstler im weitesten Sinn, die das Chaos des Abgrunds verhüllen, um den Bestand der Welt für sich zu sichern; in Stunden des Schaffens hilft die durchdringende Macht des Selbst auf majestätische Weise, die Welt zu beleben.« Künstler wie Katharina von Werz sind Abenteurer der Unendlichkeit.

Her sideways glance at the viewer is attentive yet shy. This perspective is typical of the artist, as she herself says in the interview (p. 12): "To portray a life model: I was always too shy for that, and I still am. It's a very intimate situation, because the inner you is also present in the act of painting ... But actually my interest lies somewhere other than in the portrait. I am interested in a certain mood that reflects my inner reality." This lends some truth to the idea that every piece of art is also in some way a self-portrait. But Katharina von Werz is not interested in exploring, like Cindy Sherman for example, feminine and thus by extension also masculine identity as constructs, formed from individual and collective images and projections. Instead she derives at meaning in the creative process itself. She shares with Alfred Kubin in the "certainty that humankind consists in a mysterious connection between two beings, chaos and the self. Artists of all kinds dispel chaos so that they can secure the existence of the world for themselves; in the hours of creative energy, the penetrating force of the self is a majestic tool with which to enliven the world." Artists like Katharina von Werz are explorers of infinity.

Figur vor dem Fenster, 1987
Acryl auf Pappe
Acrylic on cardboard
35 × 43 cm

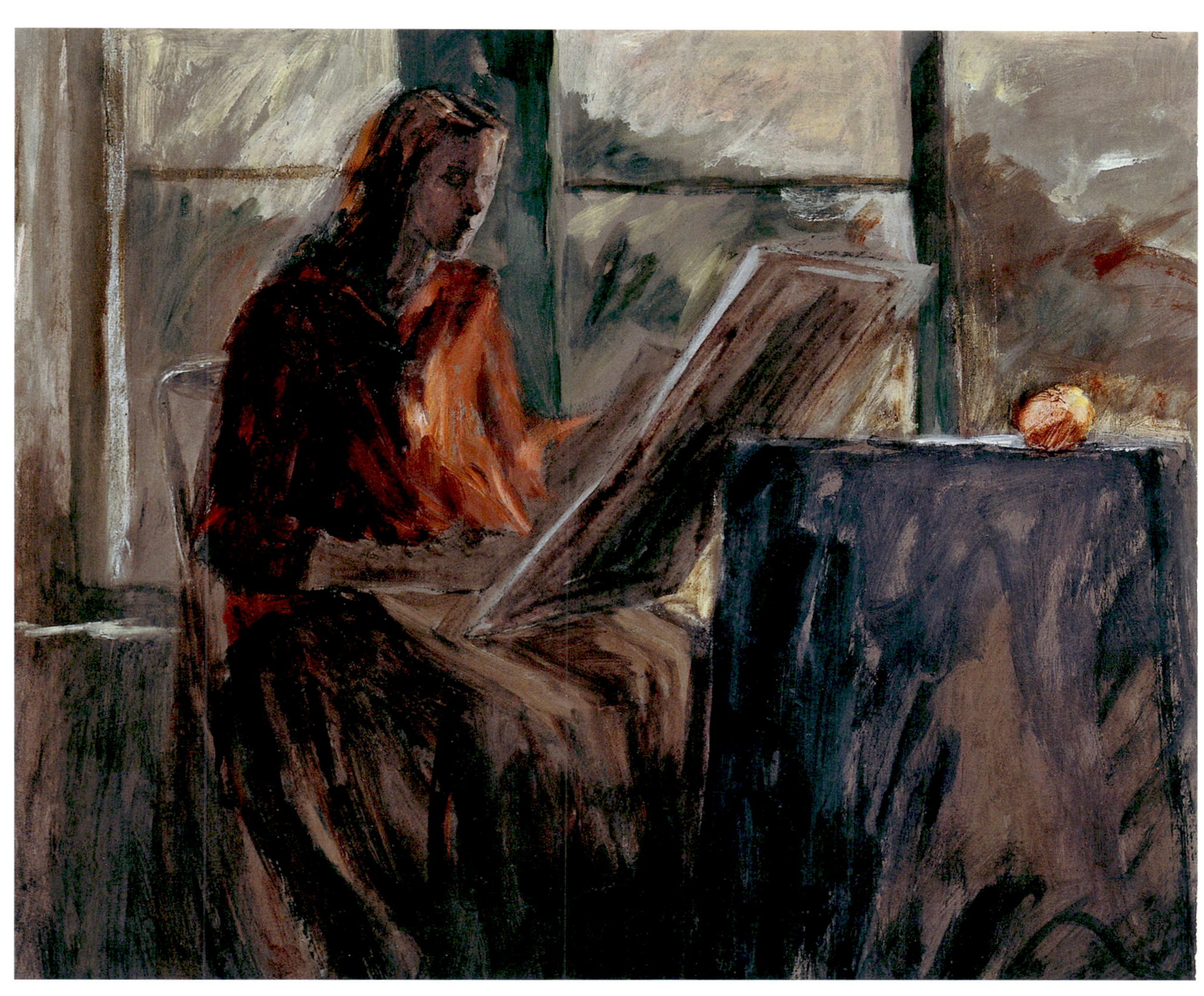

Rosa Jacke, 1983
Aquarell auf Papier
Watercolor on paper
45,5 × 55,5 cm

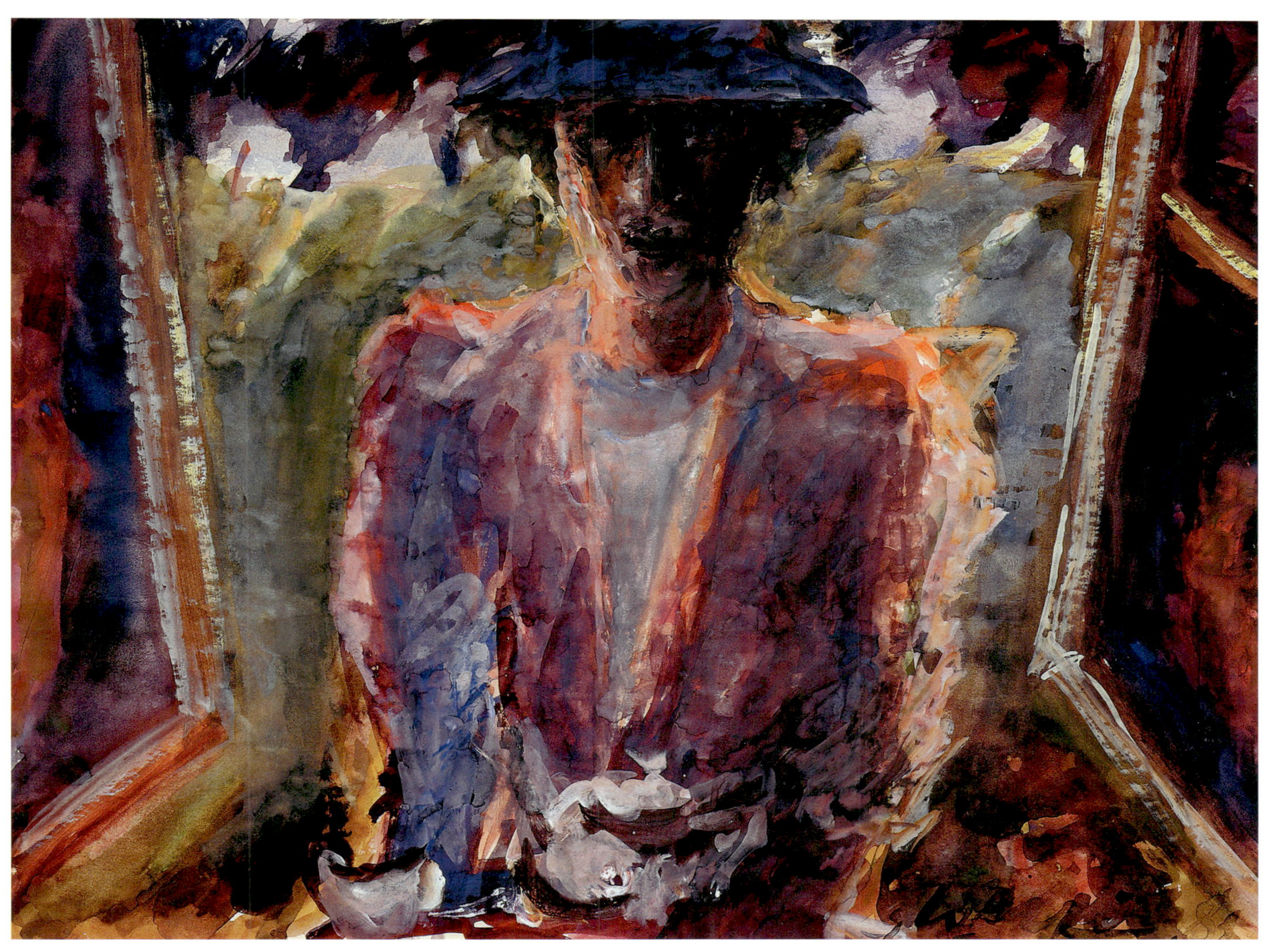

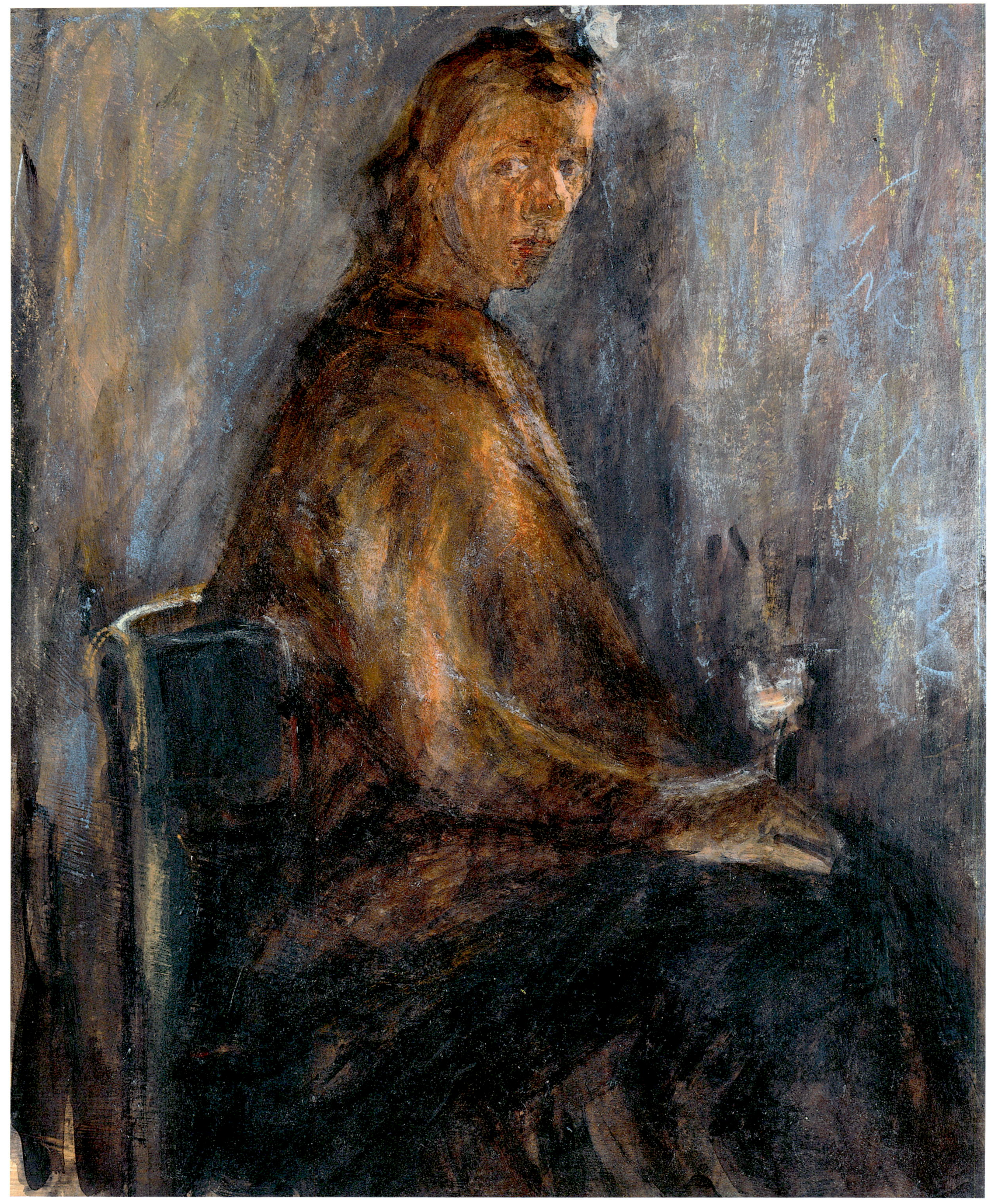

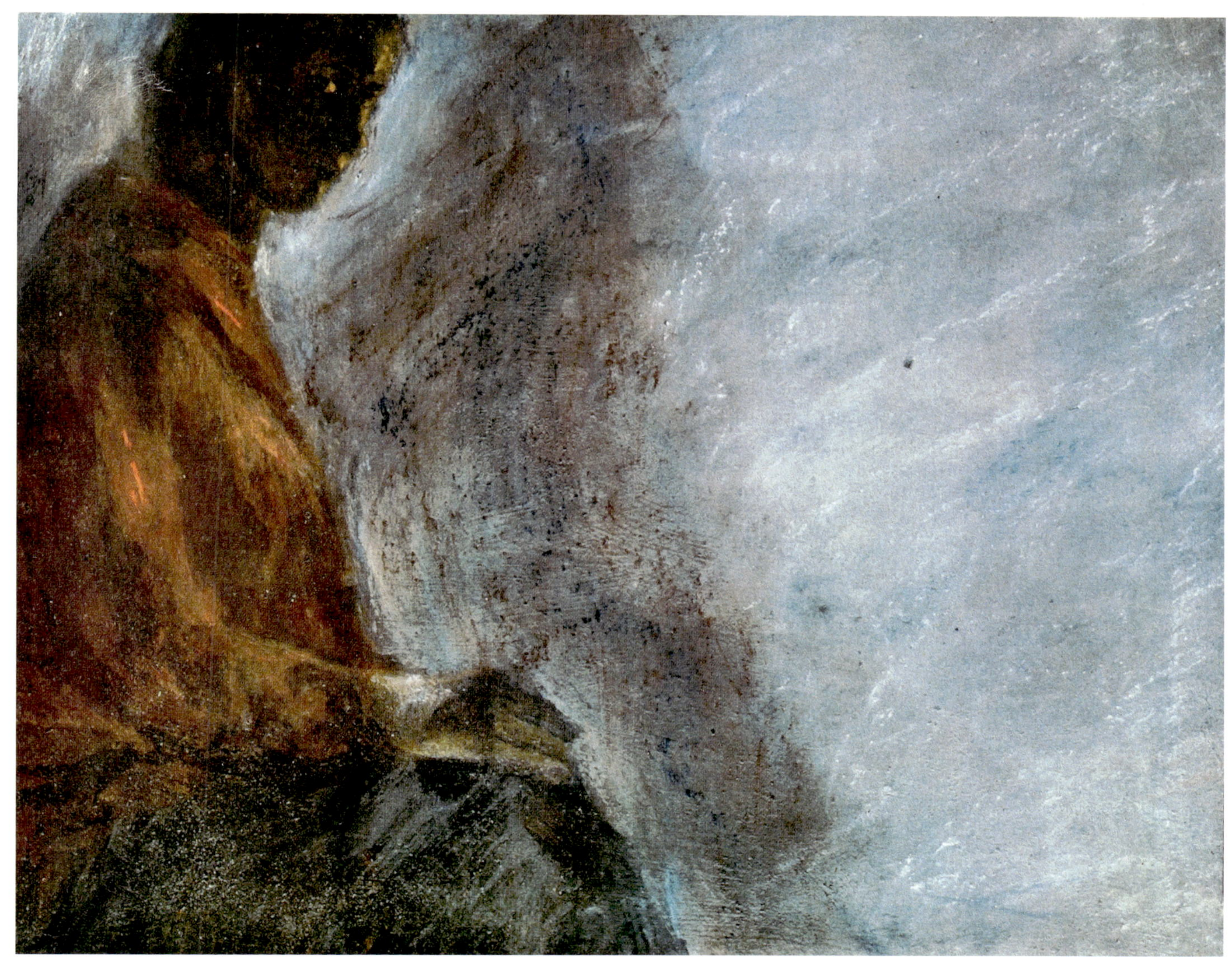

Selbstportrait, 1984
Acryl auf Pappe
Acrylic on cardboard
60 × 50 cm

Selbstportrait, 1983
Acryl auf Leinwand
Acrylic on canvas
45 × 55 cm

Selbstportraits, 1985
Aquarell auf Papier
Watercolor on paper
48 × 58 cm

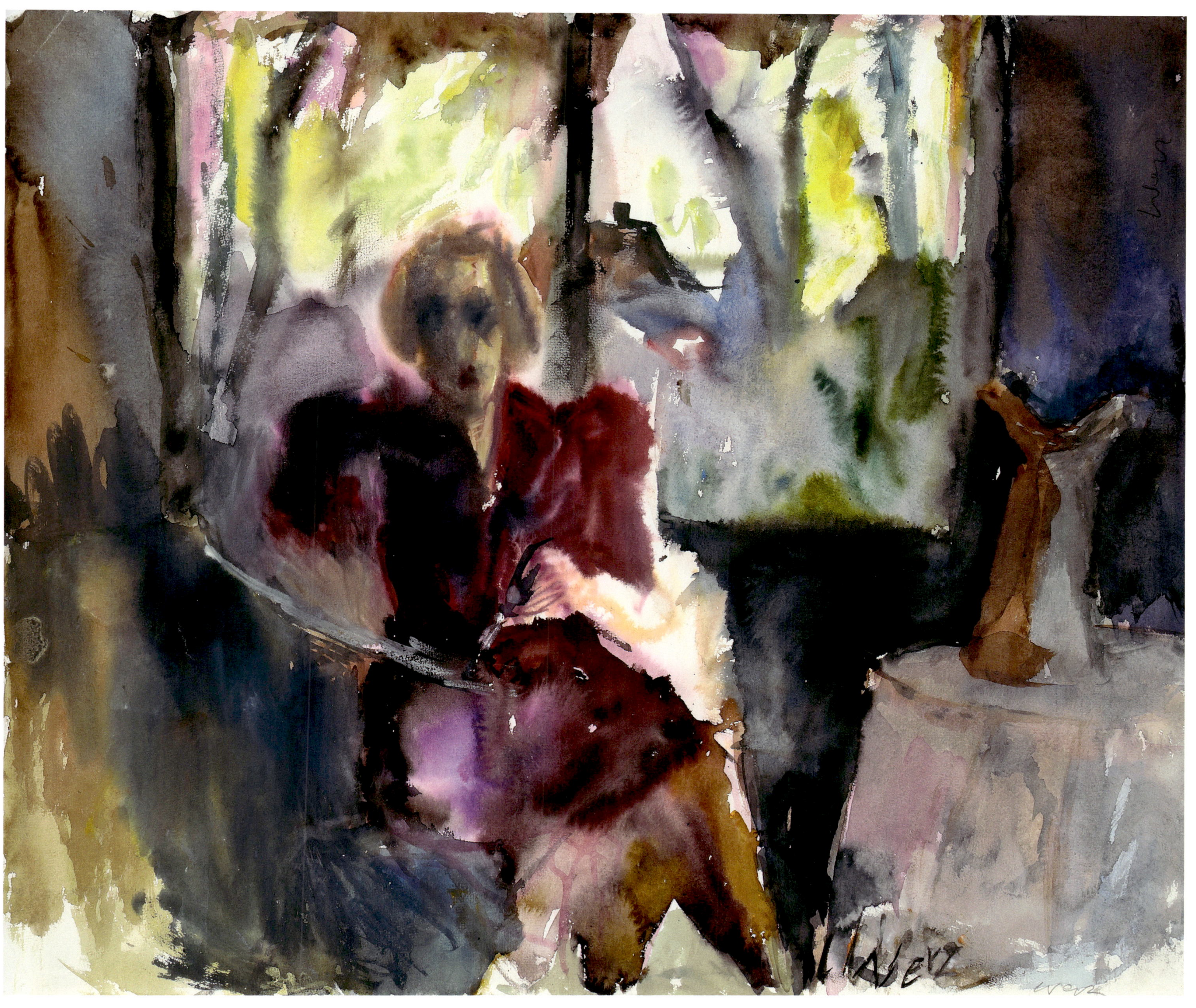

Von ihrer Neigung, am See und am Meer zu zeichnen oder zu skizzieren und den Blick dabei auf den fernen Horizont zu heften, zeugen viele Werke der Künstlerin. Mit Vorliebe malt sie die Grenzlinien zwischen Wasser und Himmel, wie sie ineinander zu zerfließen scheinen, oder zwischen Erde und Firmament, die manchmal wie messerscharf geschieden wirken.

»Der Horizont«, erläutert Carla Schulz-Hoffmann, die ehemalige stellvertretende Generaldirektorin der Bayerischen Staatsgemäldesammlungen, in einem Katalog-Essay, »fixiert eine zwar schwebende, aber dennoch markante Trennung«. Er strukturiert ihre Motive – die Ruderin, eine Liegende oder die Federballspieler – perspektivisch.

»Die Kompositionen«, so Schulz-Hoffmann weiter, »sind ebenso Landschaft wie die Landschaft umgekehrt Figur ist, und beides doch auch wieder nicht. Bewegung, Fluktuation sind entscheidende Merkmale dieser Bilderfahrung, die damit der Momentaufnahme, dem schönen Schein des Impressionismus das Zerfließen in der Zeit hinzufügt«.

Many of the artist's works reflect her fondness for drawing and sketching on the shores of this Bavarian lake, with her view fixed on the distant horizon. She especially likes painting the tentative line between water and sky, how they appear to dissolve into each other, while at other times she depicts the sharp line of the horizon between earth and sky and how it sometimes seems to cut the two apart like a knife.

Carla Schulz-Hoffmann, former deputy director general of the Bayerische Staatsgemäldesammlungen, remarked in a catalogue essay that: "The horizon fixes in place a free-floating, yet striking division." From a perspectival point of view, it structures the artist's subjects: the rower, a reclining figure, or the badminton players.

According to Schulz-Hoffmann, "The [figural] compositions are just as much landscapes as the landscape is a figure, without either being entirely one or another. Movement and fluctuation are decisive characteristics of this visual experience: a visual experience that takes the snapshot of a particular moment—Impressionism's beauty in surface appearance—and adds to it the blurring in time."

>
Ruderin am See, 2010
Acryl auf Pappe
Acrylic on cardboard
130 × 95 cm

>>
Ruderin am Chiemsee, 2009
Acryl auf Pappe
Acrylic on cardboard
130 × 95 cm
Bayerische Staatsgemälde-
sammlungen, München/Munich

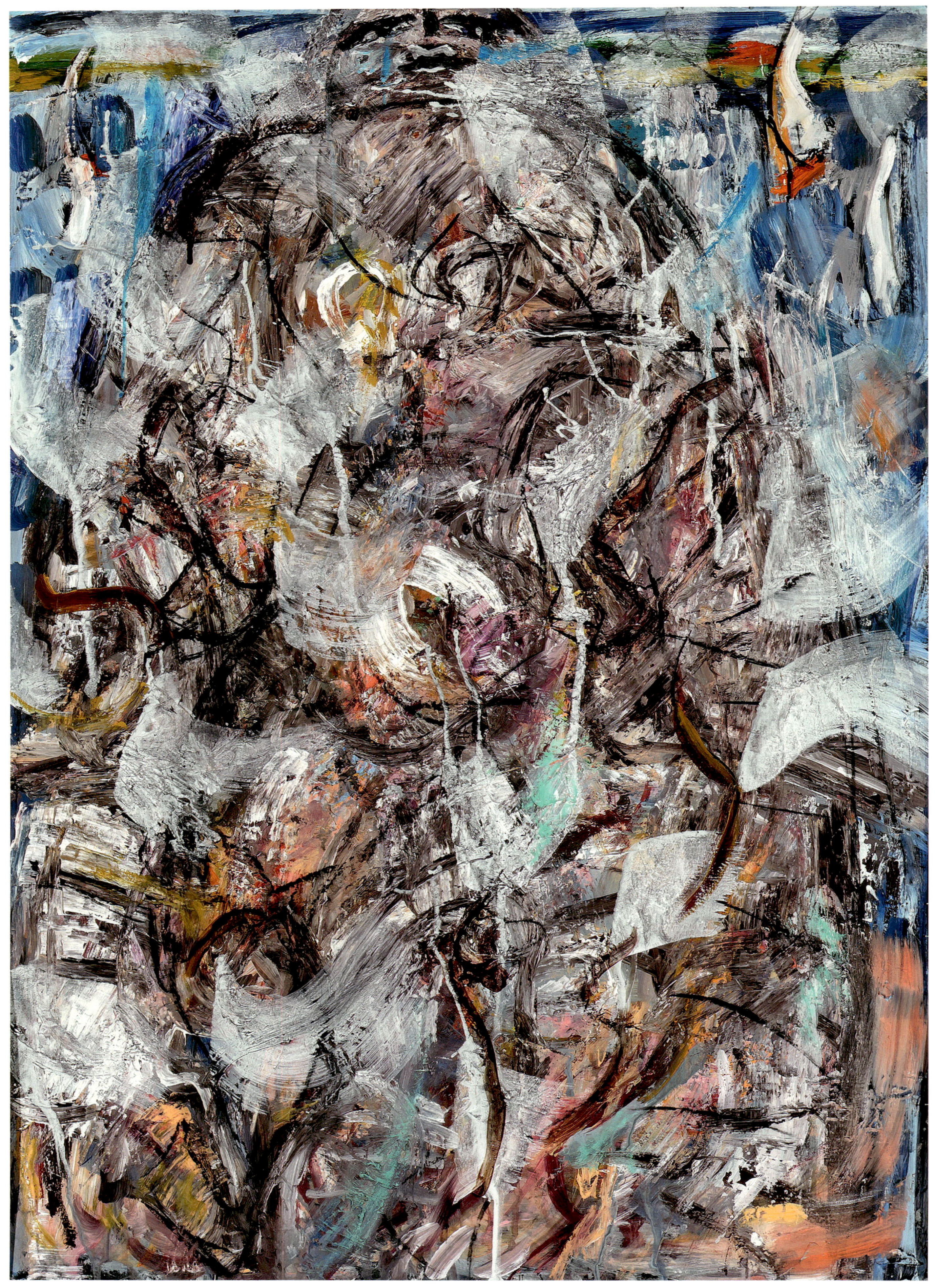

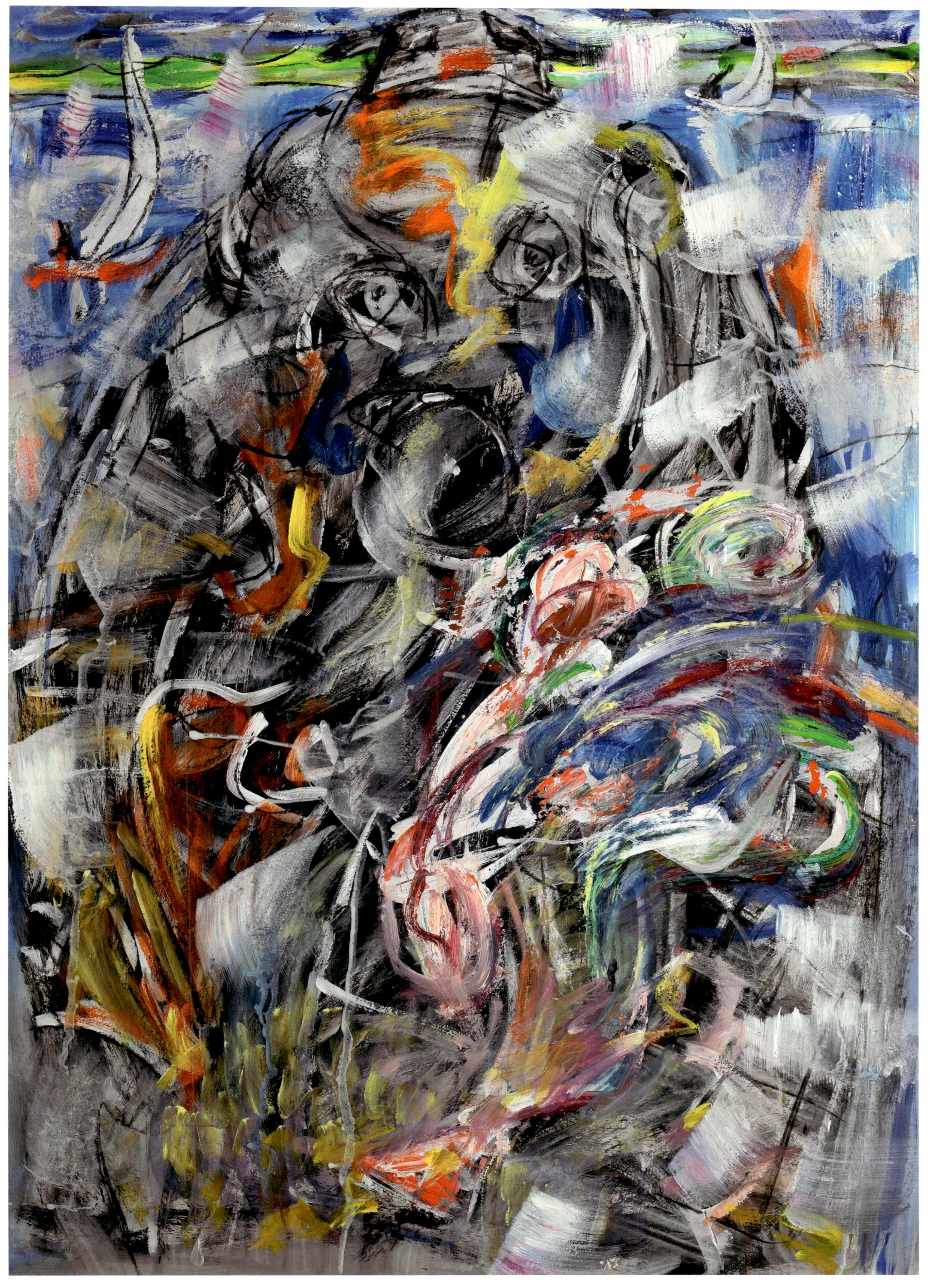

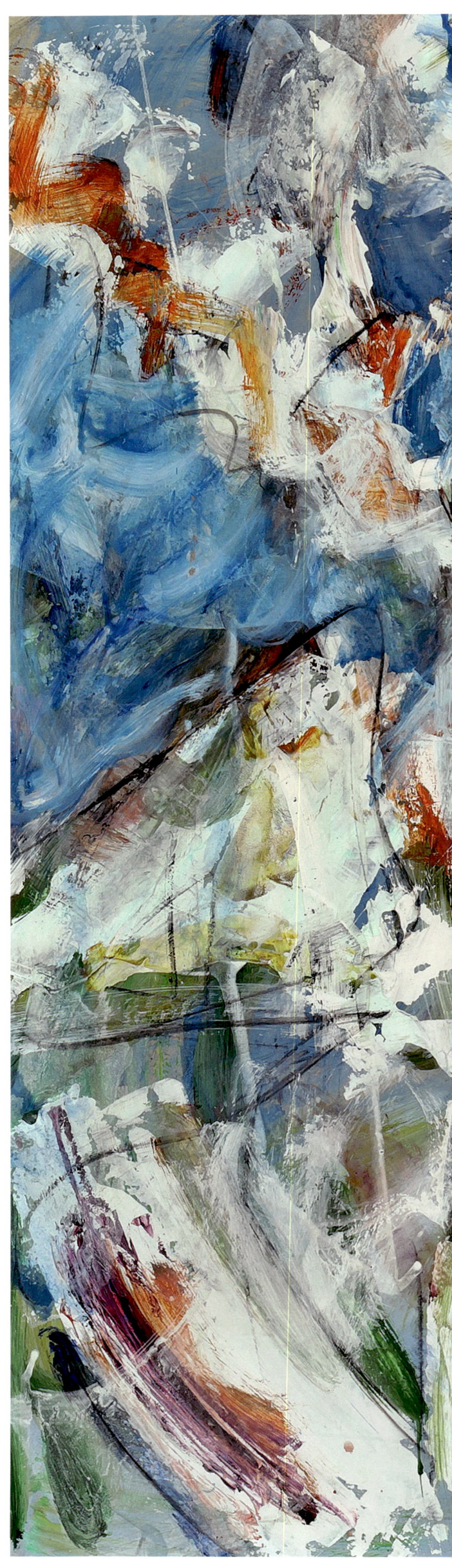

Federballspieler, 2008
Acryl auf Pappe
Acrylic on cardboard
95 × 130 cm
Privatbesitz, München
Privately owned, Munich

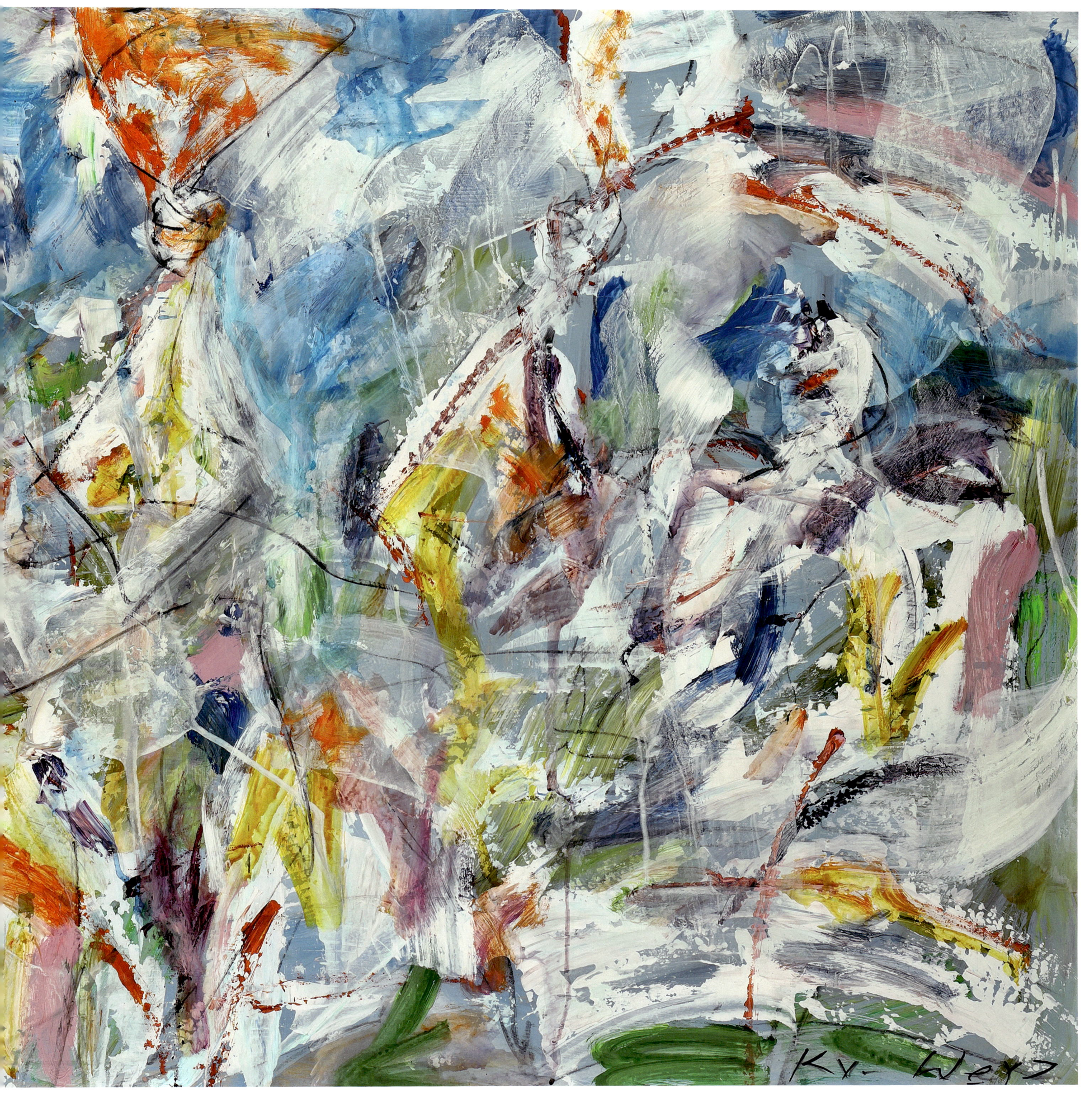
Ky. Wep

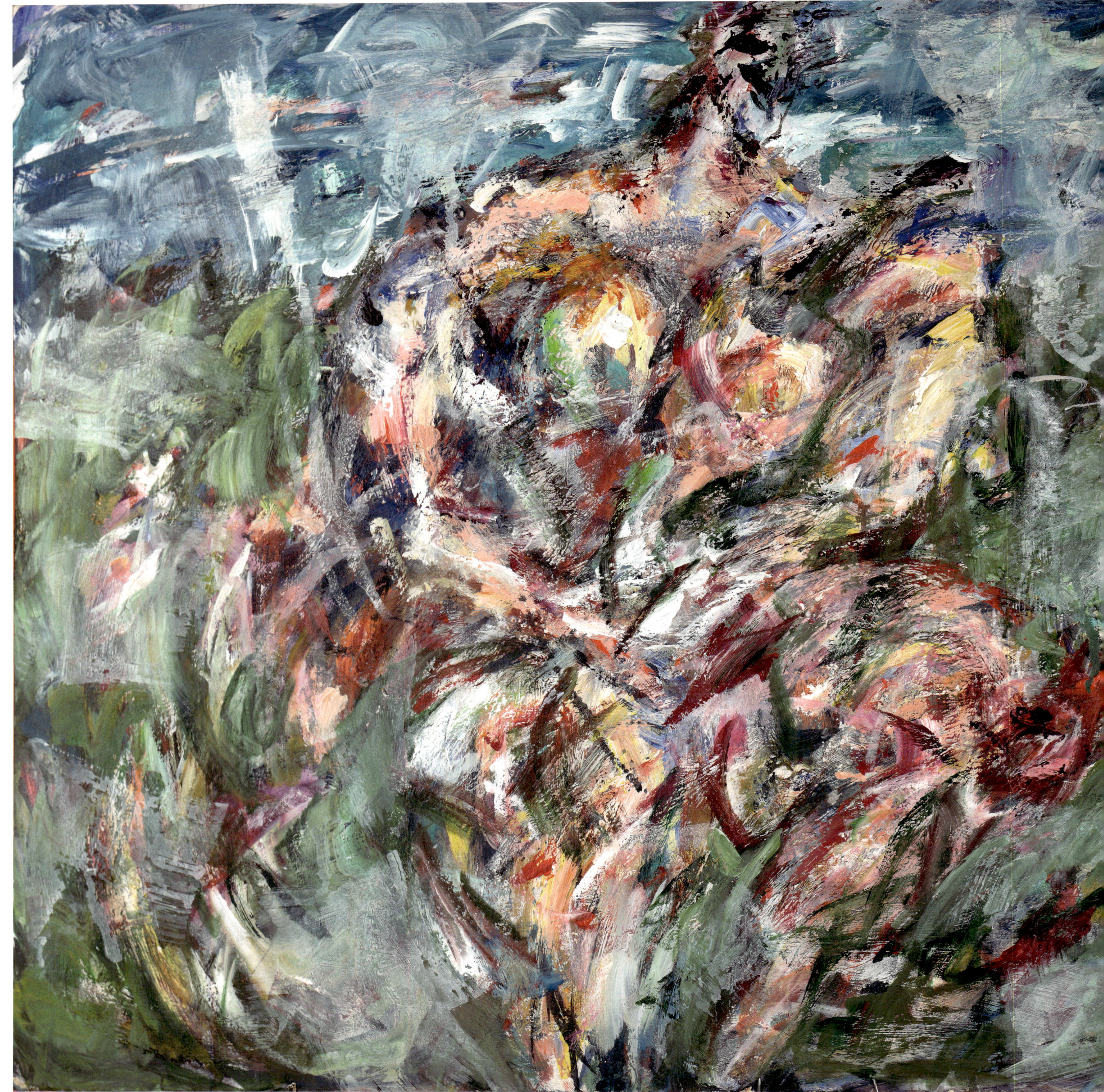

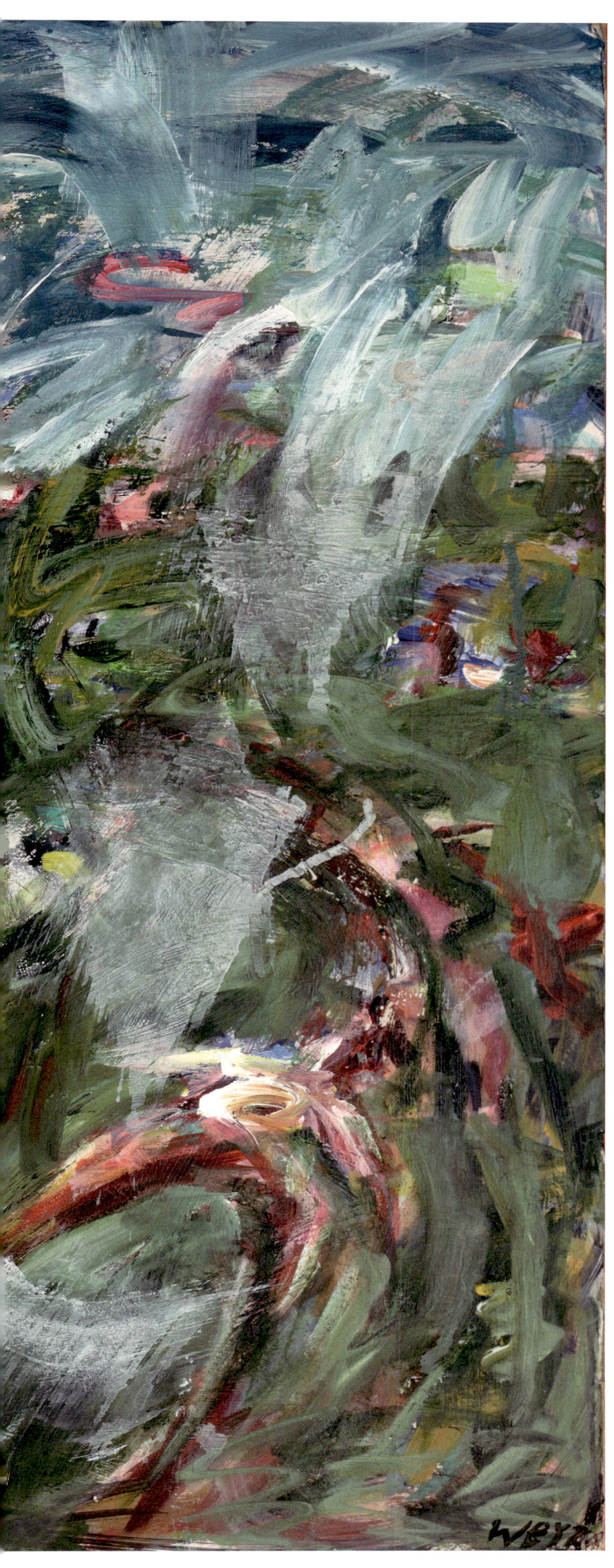

Aurora auf der Wiese, 2010
Acryl auf Pappe
Acrylic on cardboard
100 × 150 cm

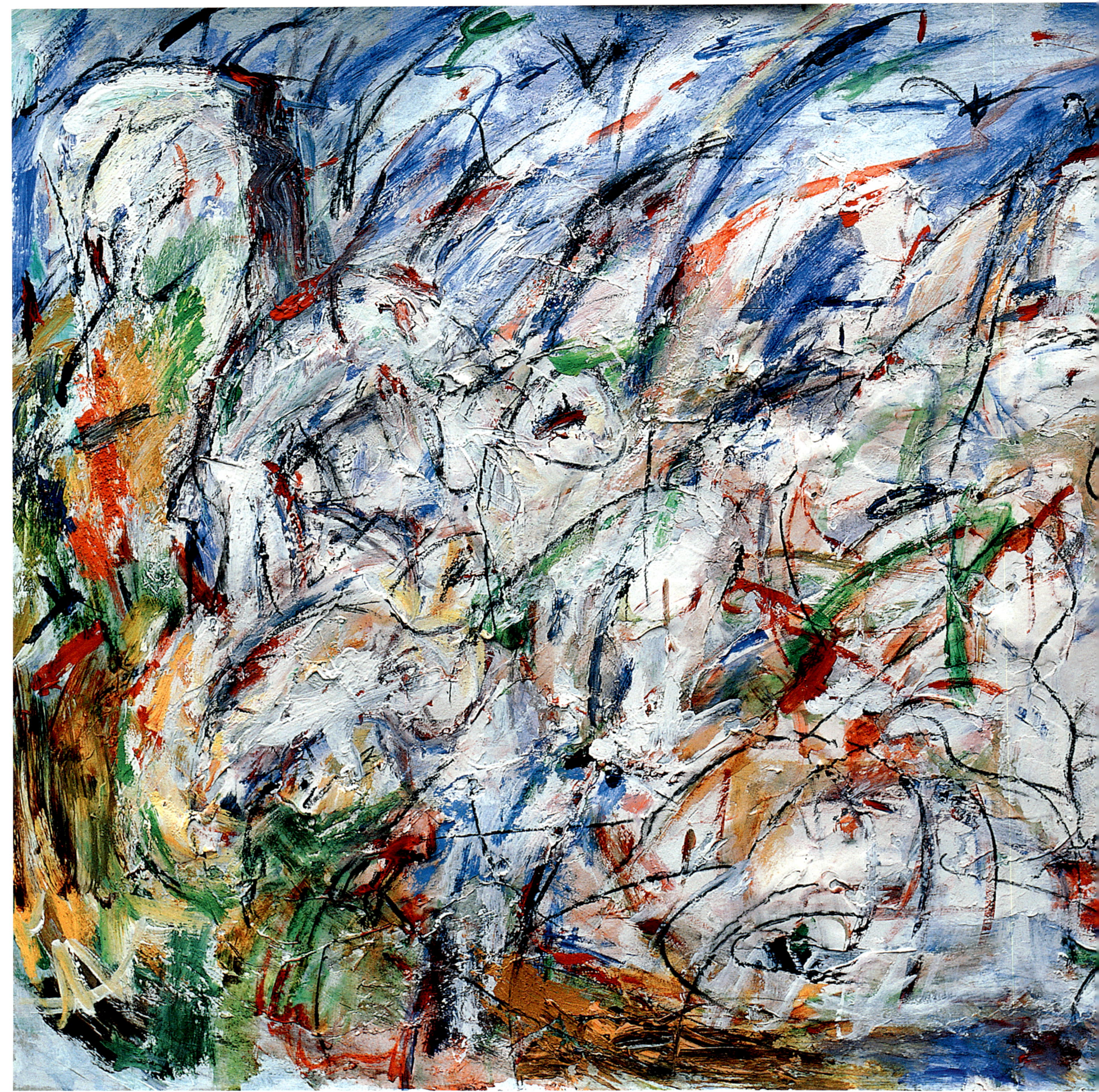

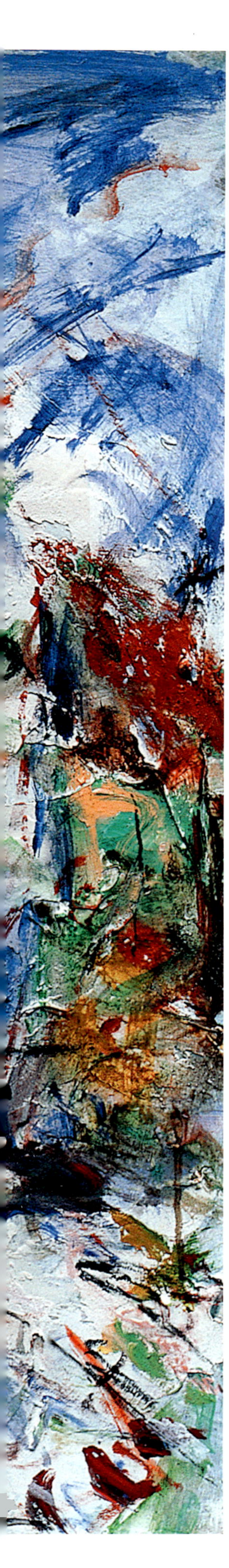

Liegende vor Horizont, 1994
Acryl auf Leinwand
Acrylic on canvas
90 × 110 cm
Privatbesitz, München
Privately owned, Munich

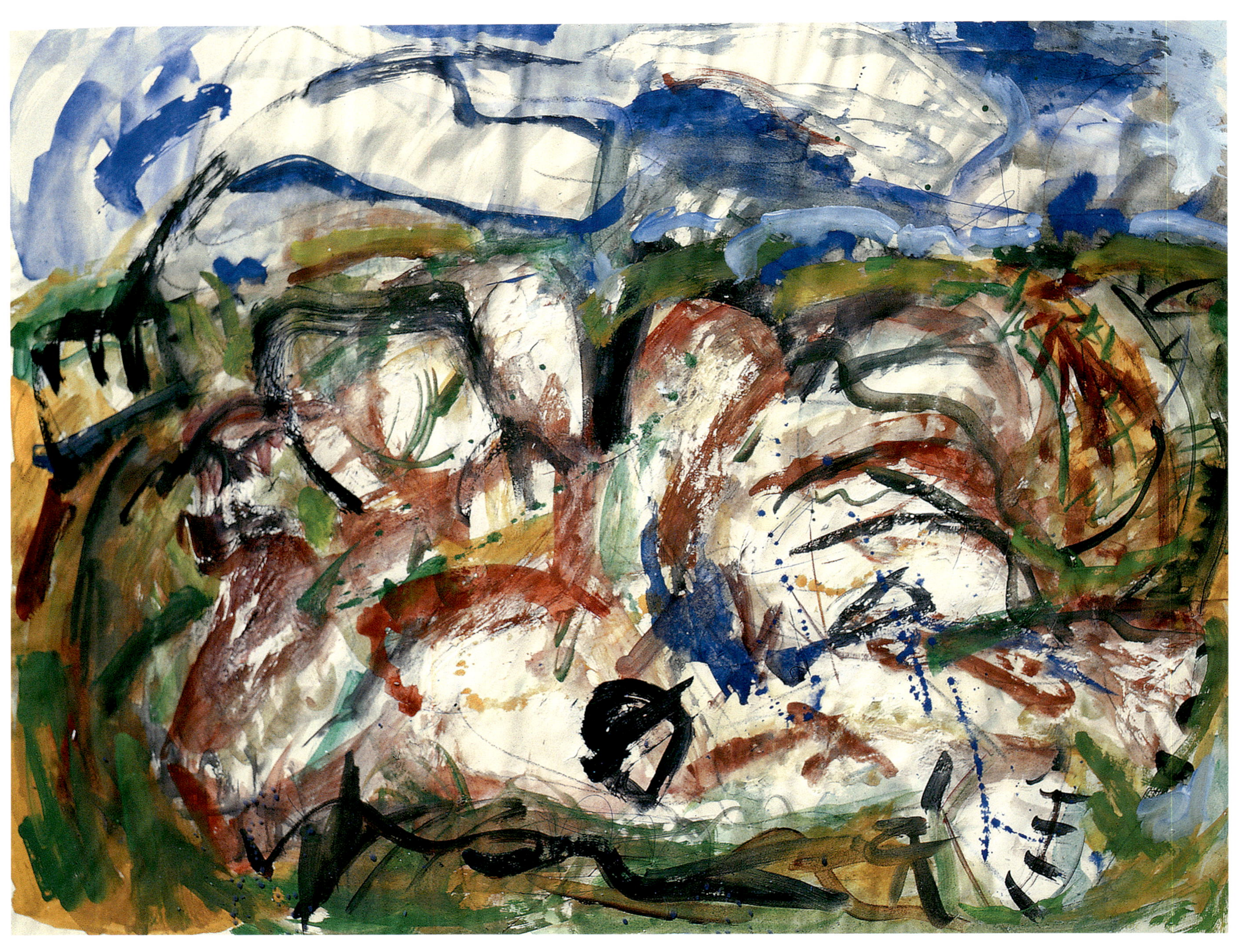

Liegende, 1994
Mischtechnik auf Papier
Mixed media on paper
60 × 80 cm
Staatliche Graphische Sammlung,
München/Munich

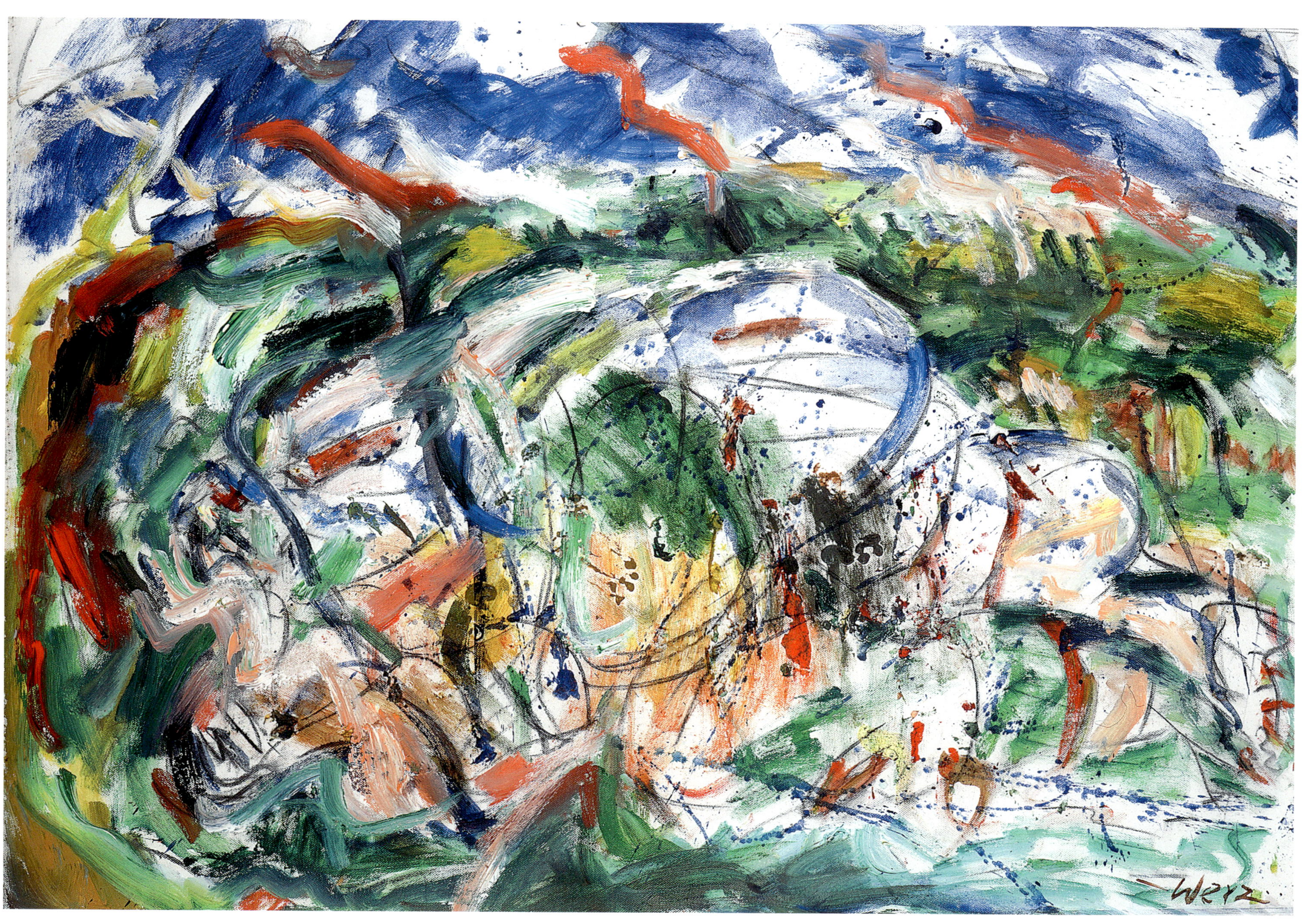

Liegende II, 1994
Acryl auf Leinwand
Acrylic on canvas
70 × 100 cm

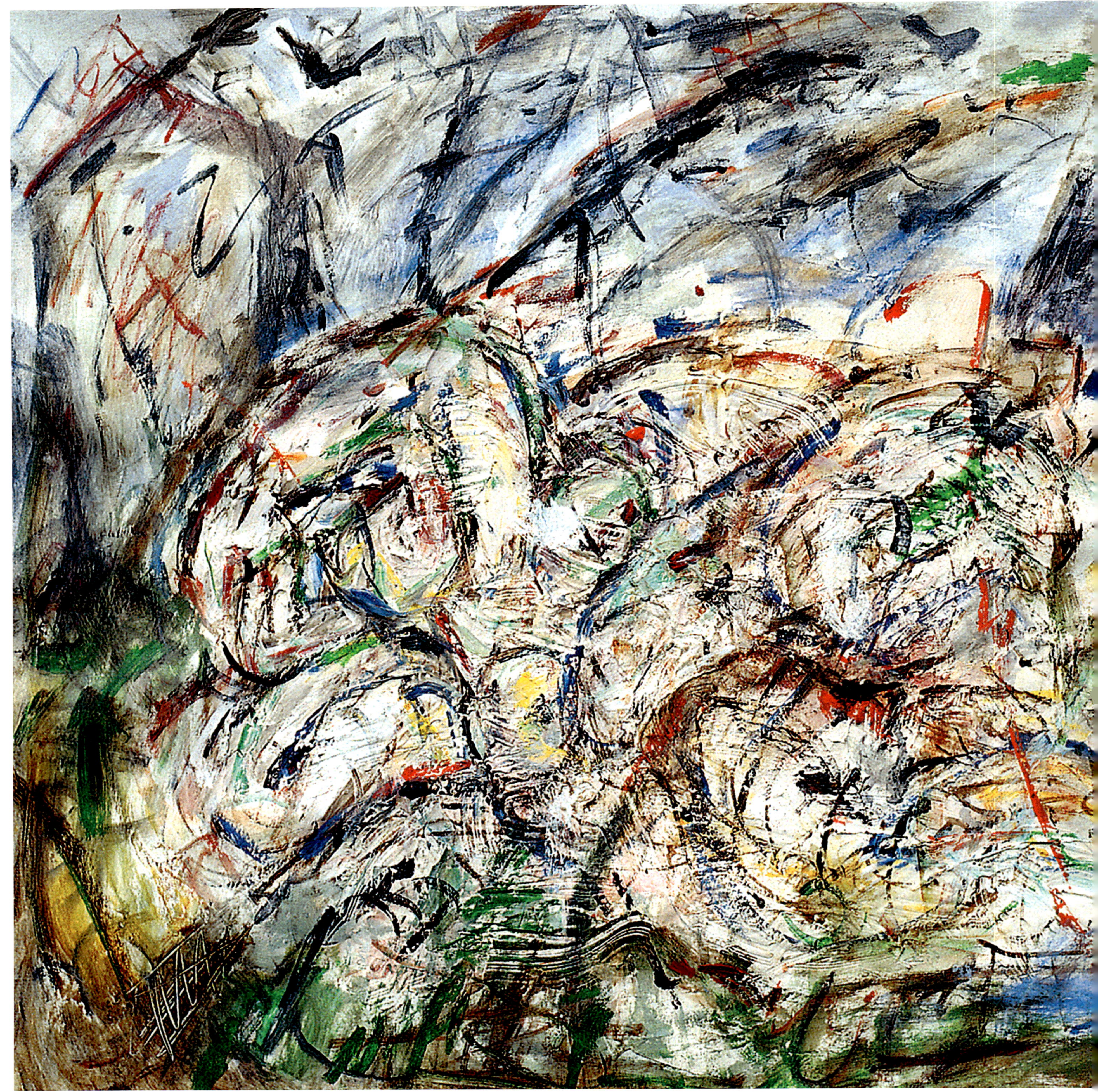

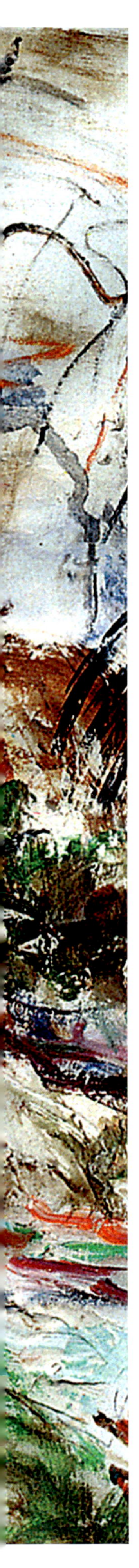

Liegende vor der Stadt, 1994
Acryl auf Pappe
Acrylic on cardboard
80 × 100 cm
Privatbesitz, München
Privately owned, Munich

»Die Skulptur entsteht in einer Umarmung mit zwei
Händen, wie in der Liebe. Sie ist die einfachste, die
ursprünglichste Kunst. Ich muss mich nicht dazu
zwingen, noch mich wirklich hinführen ...«

Max Ernst

"Sculpture arises in a moment of embrace between
two hands, just as love does. It is the easiest, the most
primal art. I don't have to force or guide myself ..."
Max Ernst

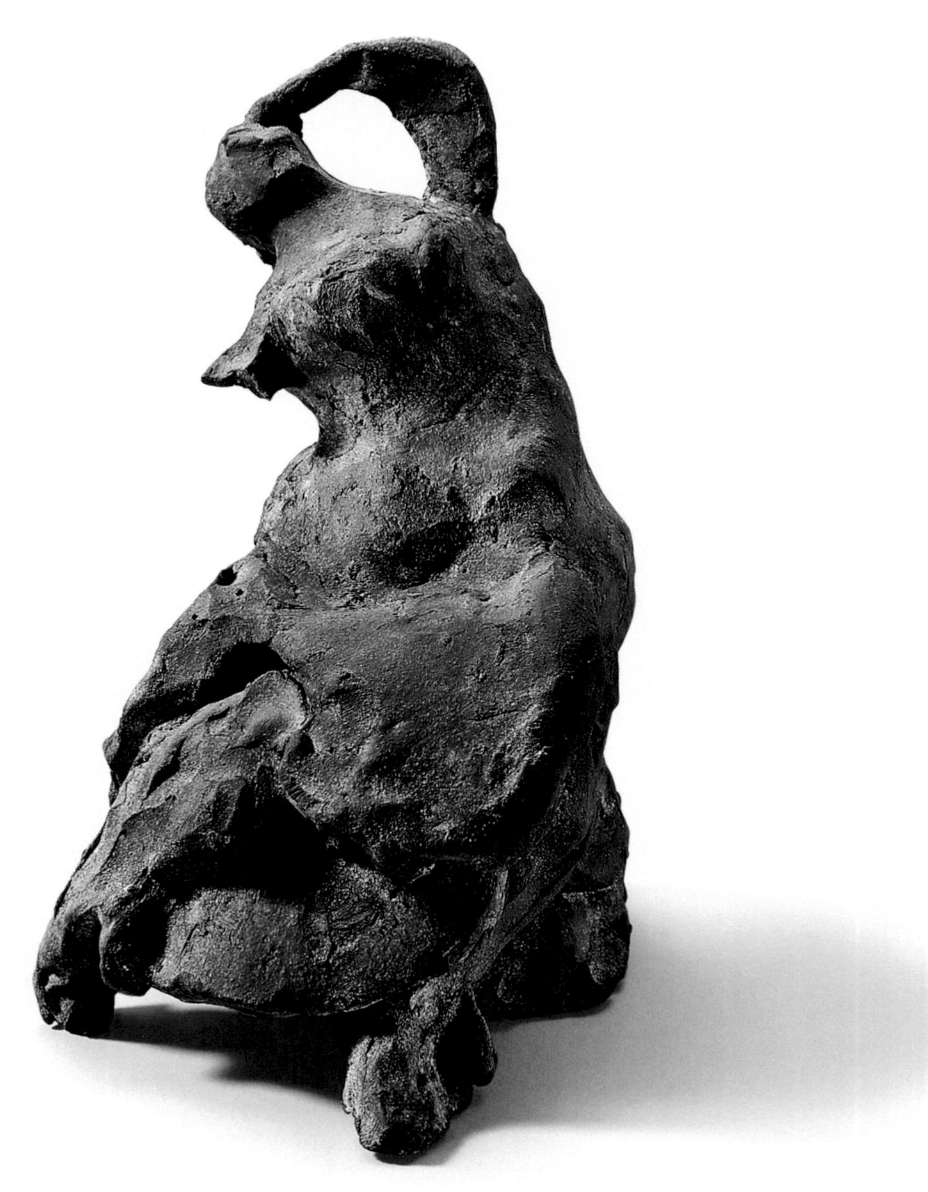

Windsbraut, 2000
Terrakotta/Terracotta
30 × 20 × 17 cm

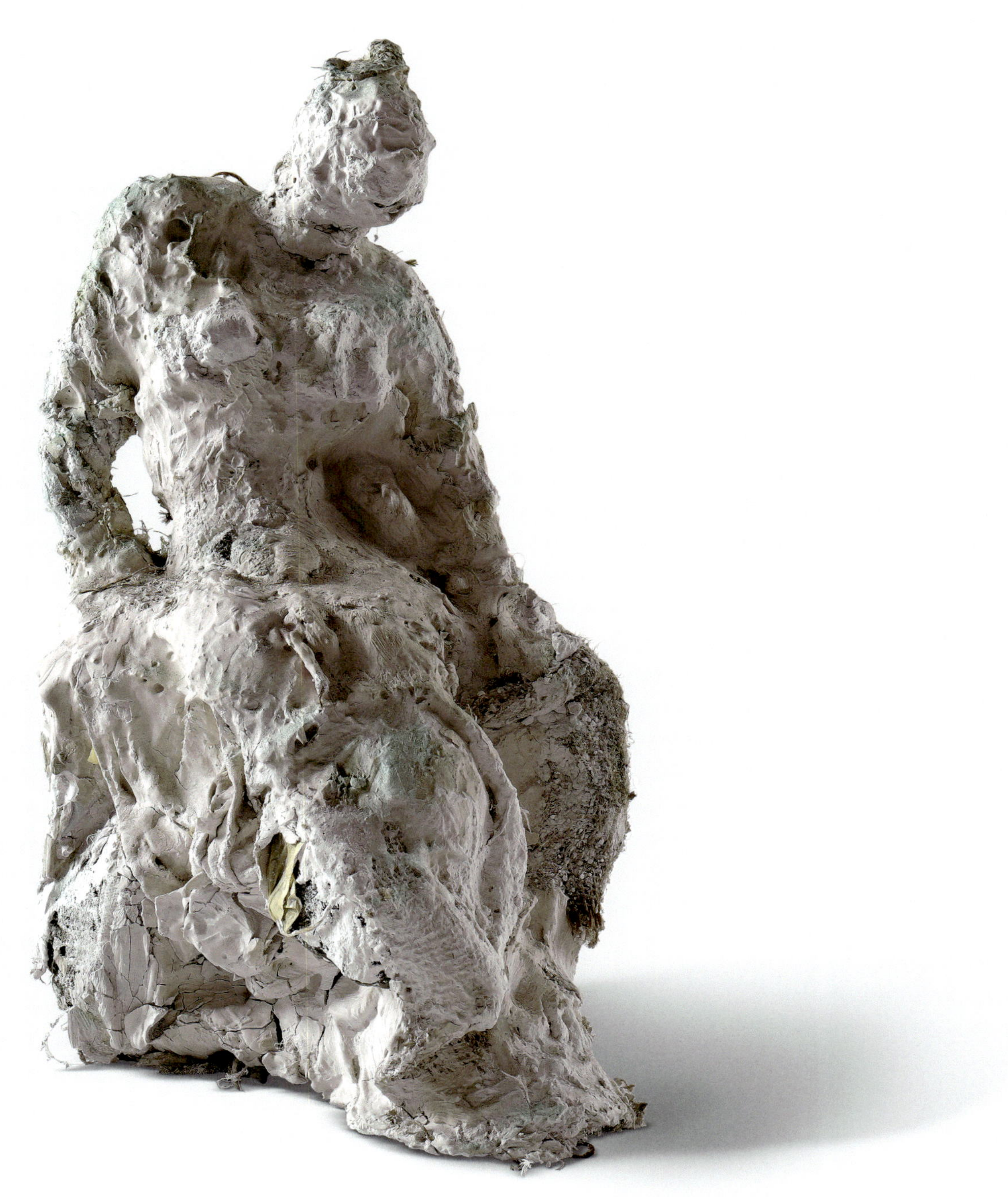

o. T., 2007
Gips und verschiedene Materialien
Plaster and mixed materials
50 × 34 × 25 cm

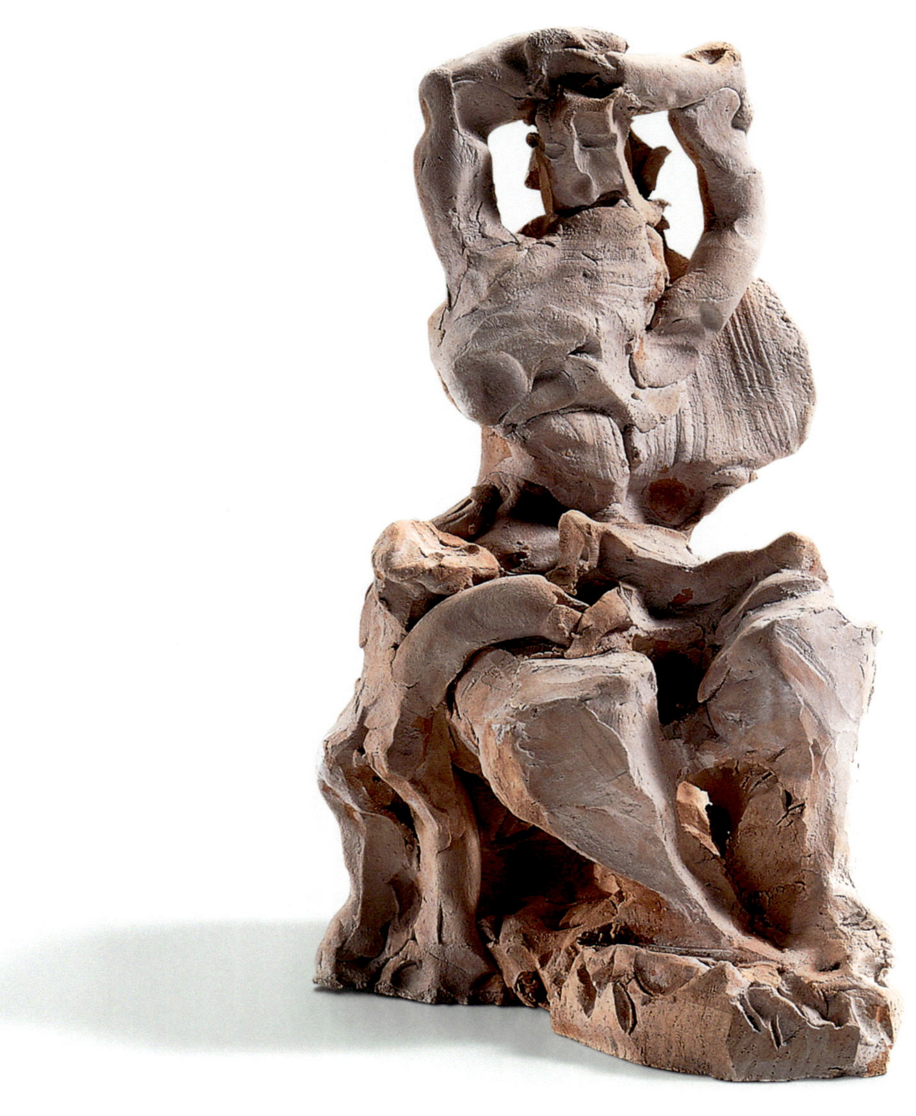

Papagena, 2000
Terrakotta/Terracotta
20 × 15 × 17 cm
Privatbesitz/Privately owned,
Bad Kissingen

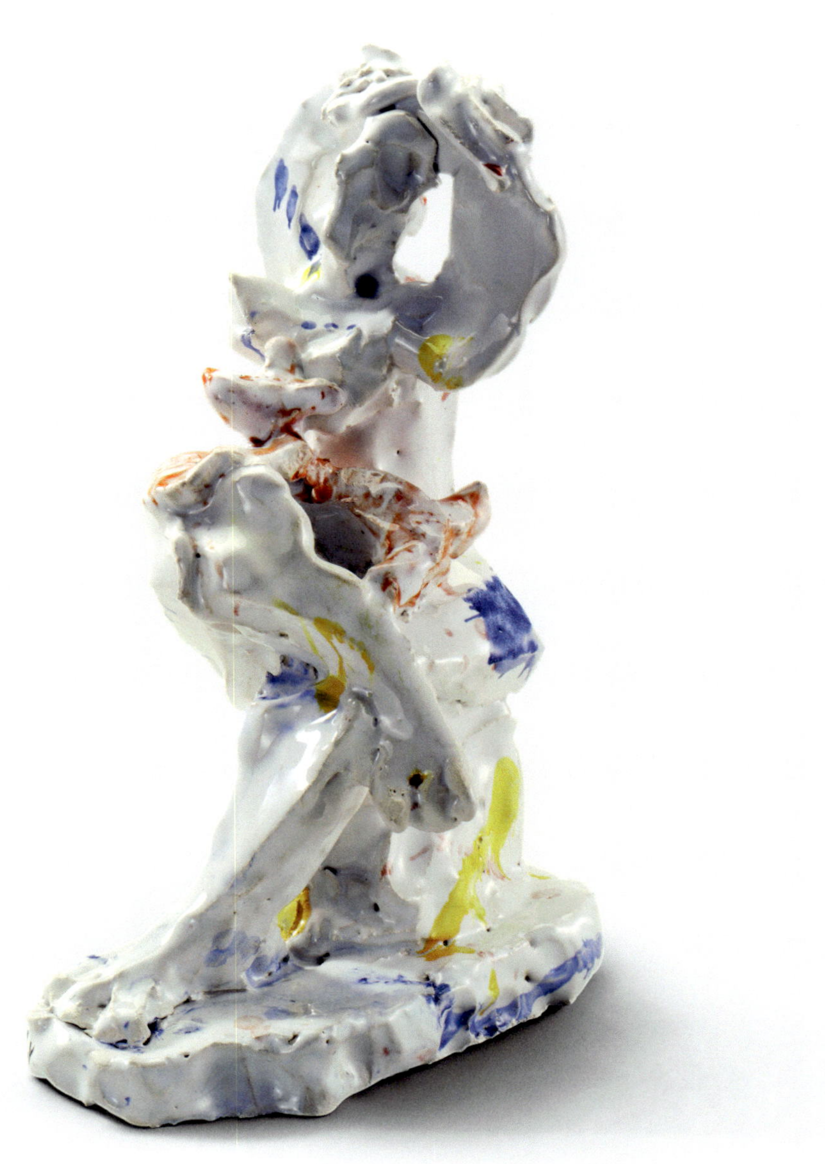

Schneeweißchen, 2000
Terrakotta, glasiert
Terracotta, glazed
20 × 15 × 14 cm

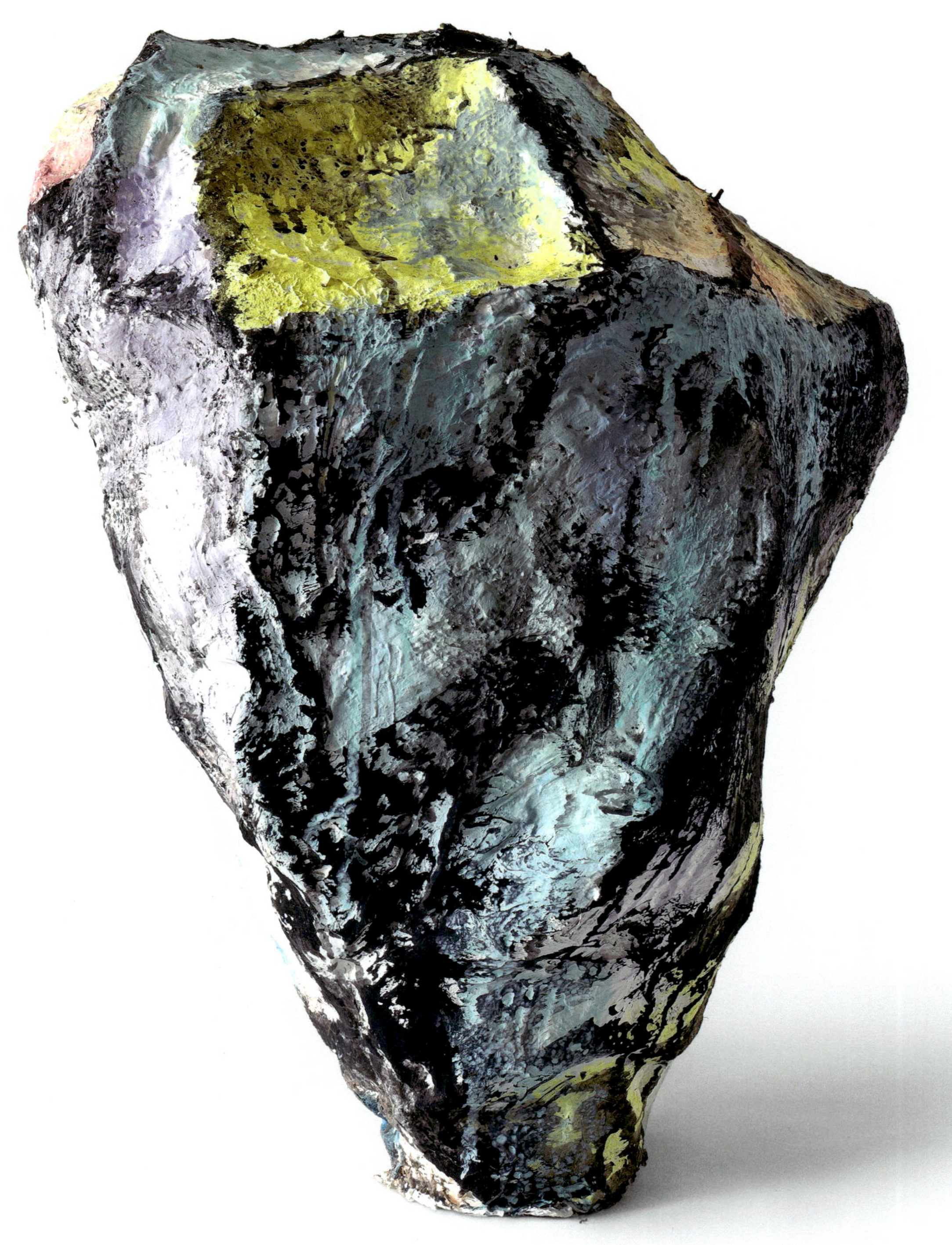

Objekt, 2010
Gips und verschiedene Materialien
Plaster and mixed materials
53 × 47 × 45 cm

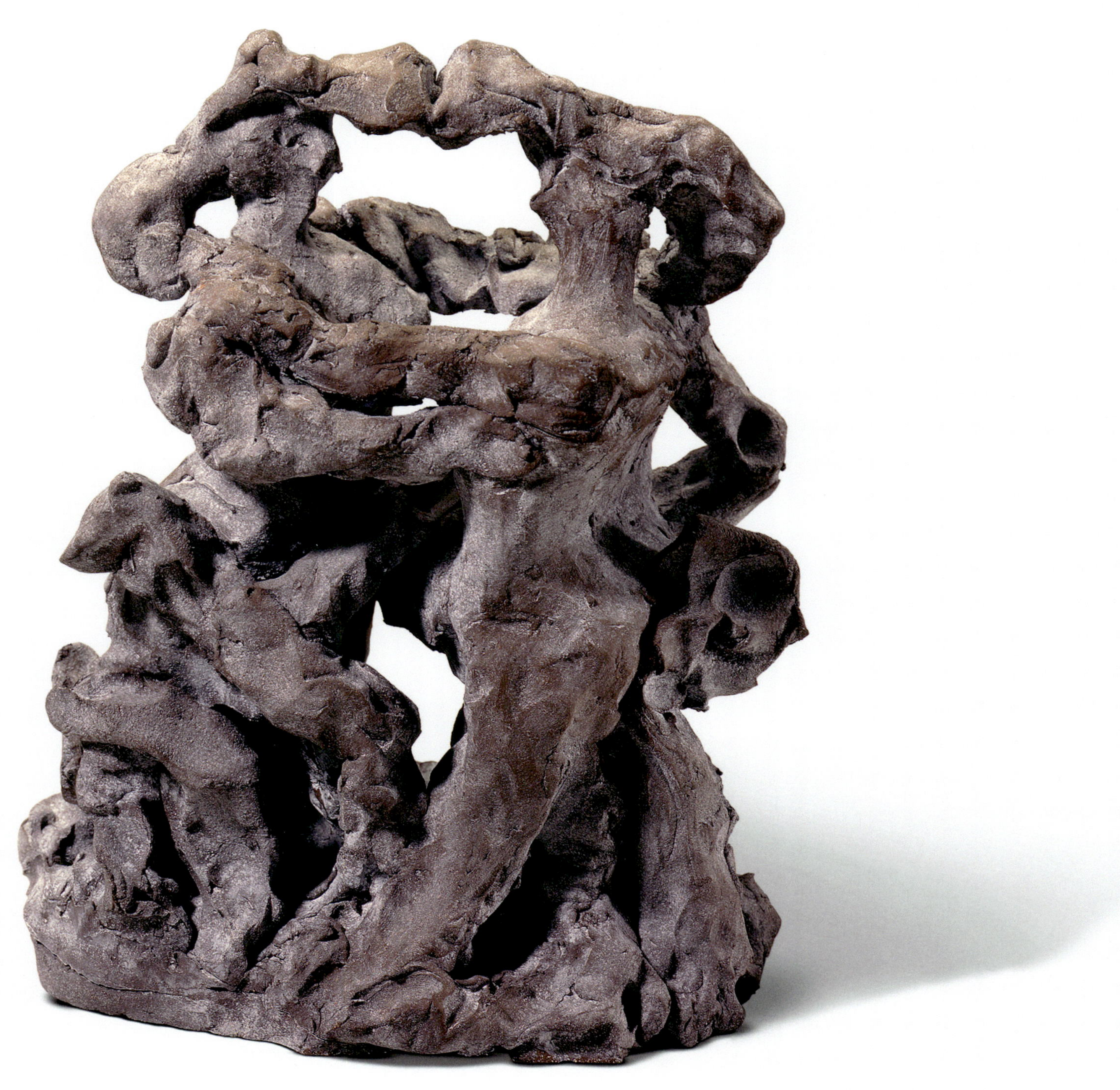

Föhnstürmerinnen, 2000
Terrakotta/Terracotta
30 × 20 × 28 cm

BREAKFAST OUTDOORS

Es war das Skandalbild seiner Zeit. Da sein Gemälde *Le déjeuner sur l'herbe* 1863 auf dem Salon von der Jury abgelehnt wird, stellt Eduard Manet es im Salon des Refusés aus. Die Kritiker heulen auf und begreifen es zu Recht als Generalangriff auf die Malerei. Denn der Künstler zitiert unverfroren Tizians *Konzert im Freien* und Raffaels *Urteil des Paris,* anmaßend mixt er die Genres Stillleben, Landschaft, Porträt, Historienbild und schockiert auch mit seiner Technik, malt etwa Schatten und Licht in starken Kontrasten – und, Gipfel der Obszönität für seine Zeitgenossen: Eine Frau sitzt wie selbstverständlich nackt zwischen zwei Herren in Anzug und Krawatte! Noch schamloser: Sie blickt den Betrachter stolz und selbstbewusst direkt an – und sprengt so die Grenzen zwischen Bild und Außenwelt.

Das ist die eigentliche Revolution Manets. Im Grunde nimmt er die postmoderne Appropriation Art vorweg, die Kunst, sich alle nur verfügbaren Bildquellen und damit auch Stile als Material anzueignen.

Vor diesem Hintergrund setzt auch Katharina von Werz an: »Mir entspricht, was Frank Auerbach zu diesem Thema anmerkte«, meint sie. »Oft zeichne ich von Bildern – Poussin, Rembrandt, etc. –, um mir Qualität in Erinnerung zu rufen. Malen existiert nicht ohne Geschichte«.

It was the most scandalous picture of its age. Because his painting *Le déjeuner sur l'herbe* was turned down by the jury at the Salon in 1863, Eduard Manet exhibited it at the Salon des Refusés. The critics howled with derision and saw it, rightly, as an outright attack on painting. They saw how Manet unabashedly borrowed from Titian's *The Pastoral Concert* and Raphael's *Judgment of Paris*, his arrogant blending of the genres of still life, landscape, portrait, and history painting. They were irritated by his technique of painting light and shade in strong contrast. But most of all, they were outraged by the sight of a woman, sat blithely naked between two men in suit and tie! And to add insult to injury: her gaze, proud and self-confident, is directed squarely at the viewer—thus rupturing the boundary between the picture and the world beyond the frame.

This was the real revolution brought about by Manet. Essentially, he preempts post-modern Appropriation Art, the art that views all available visual sources, and thus all available styles, as material from which to borrow. Katharina von Werz also operates against this backdrop: "I think Frank Auerbach put it best," she says, "when he said: 'I often draw from pictures—Poussin, Rembrandt, etc.—to remind myself of quality.' Painting doesn't exist without the past."

Figurengruppe in Landschaft II, 2006
Acryl auf Leinwand
Acrylic on canvas
65 × 85 cm

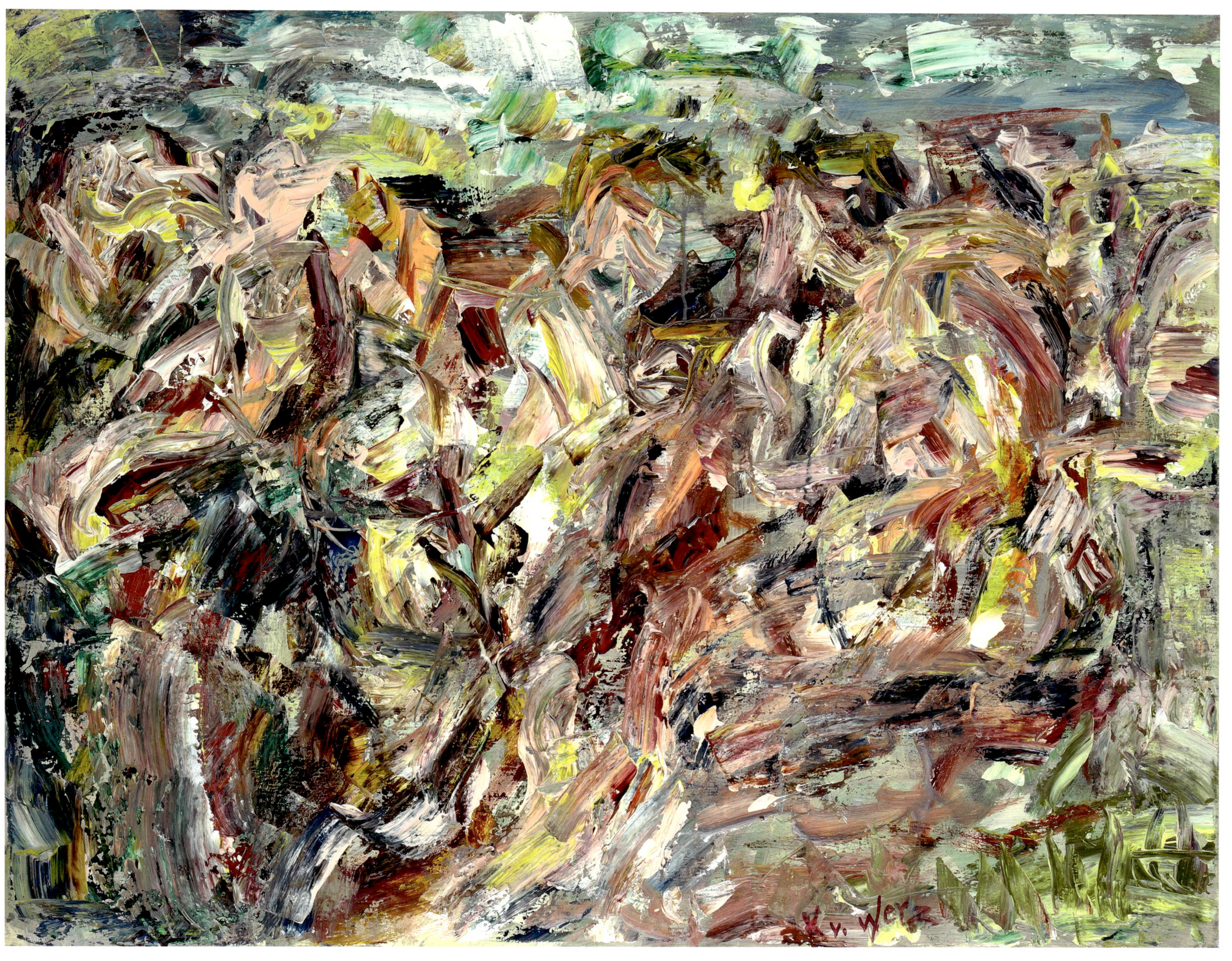
v. Werz

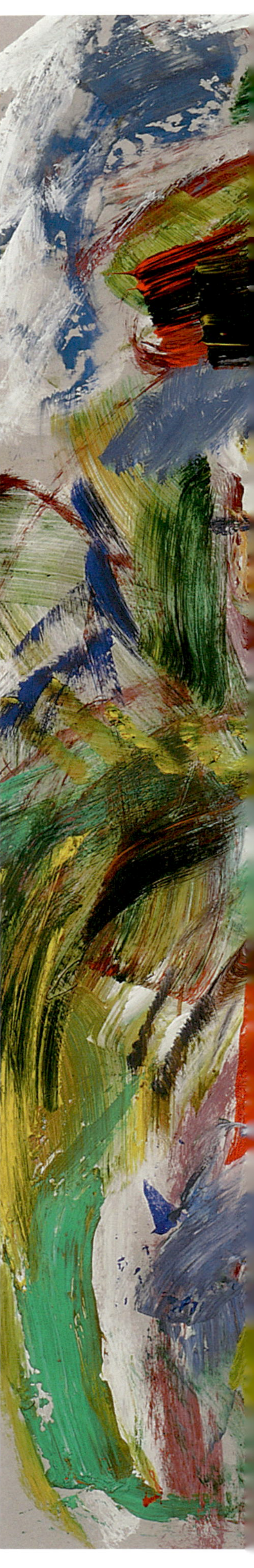

Piquenique bei Sturm, 1997
Acryl auf Pappe
Acrylic on cardboard
80 × 100 cm

154

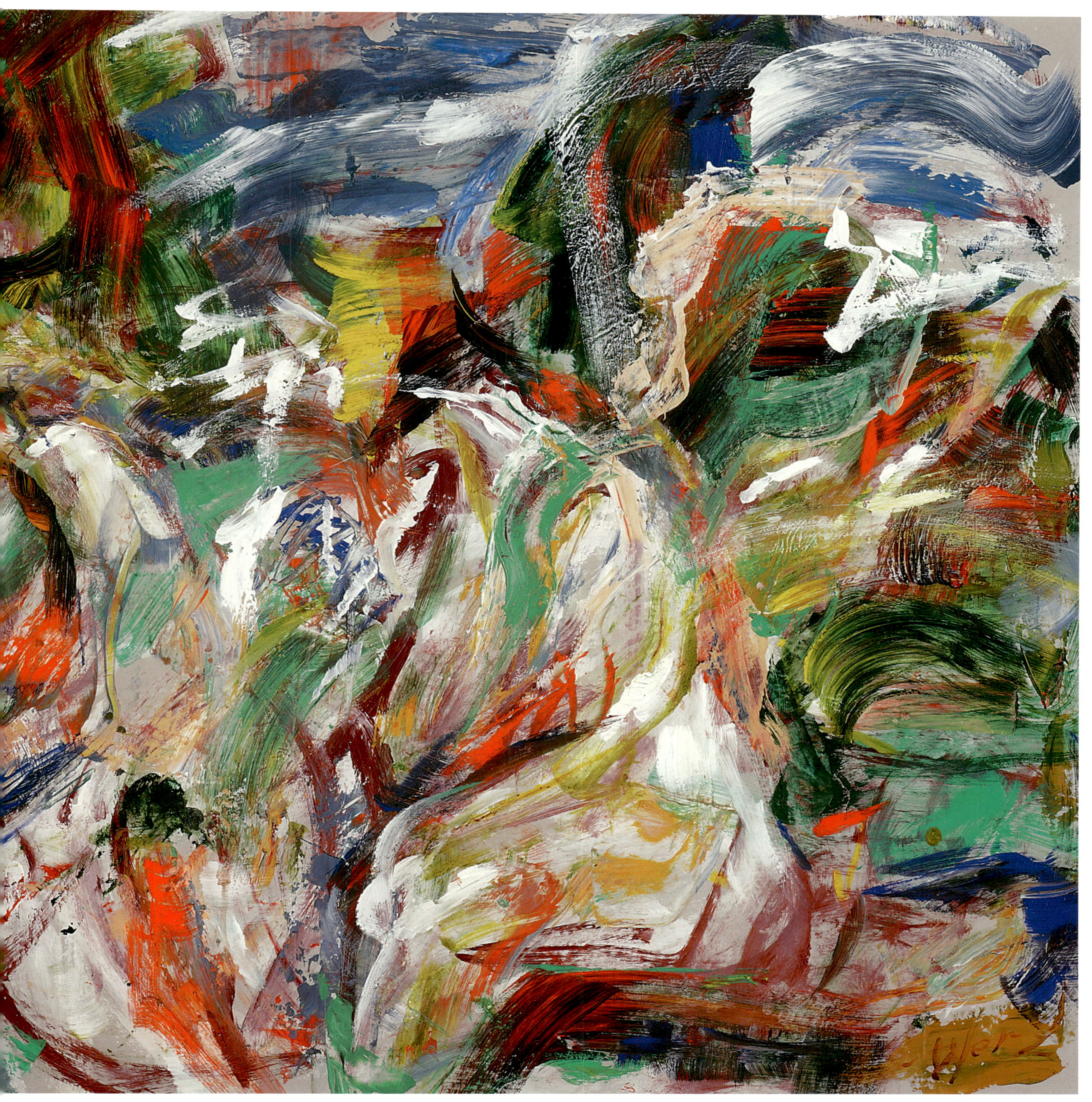

Konzert, 2006
Acryl auf Leinwand
Acrylic on canvas
80 × 100 cm

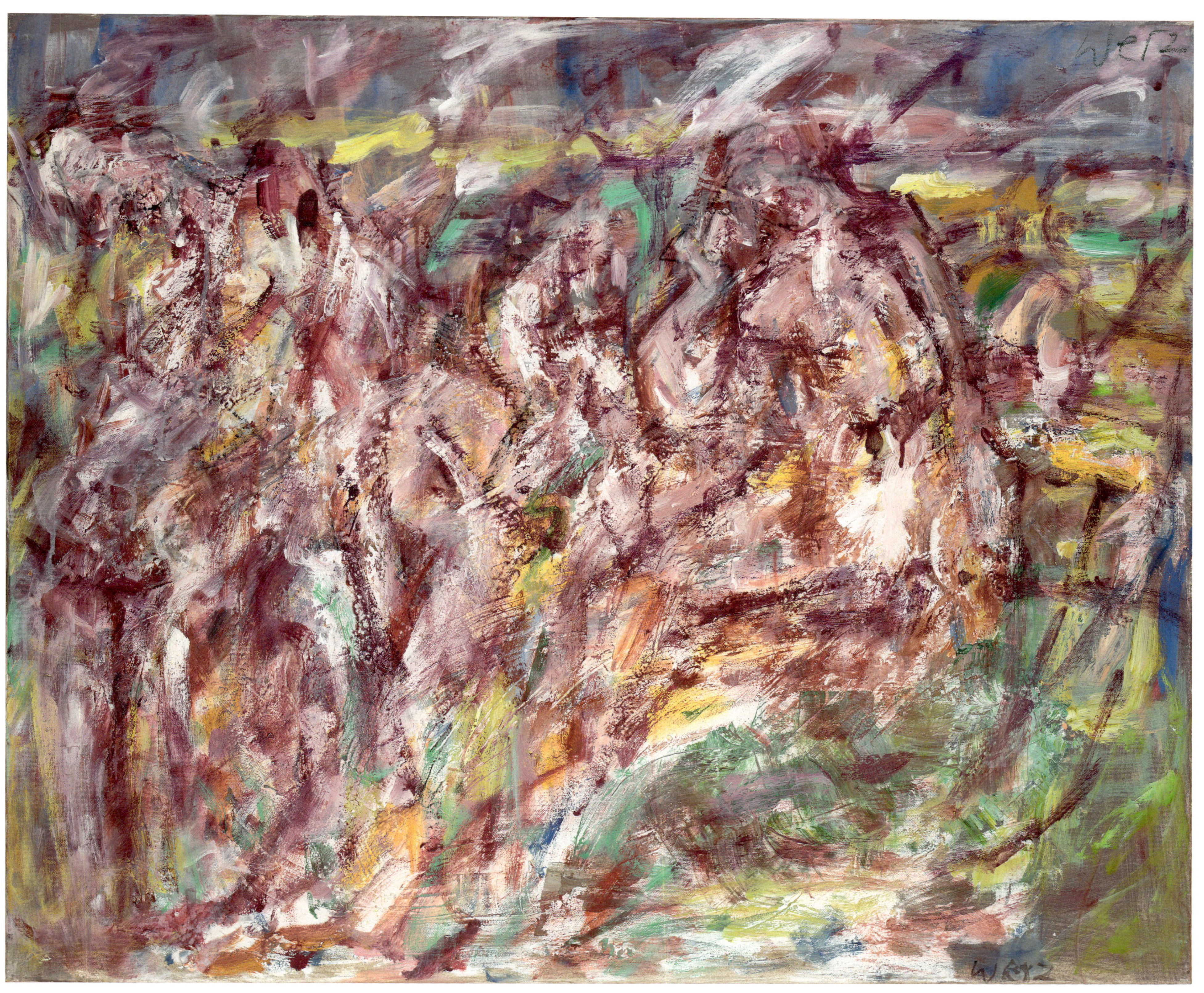

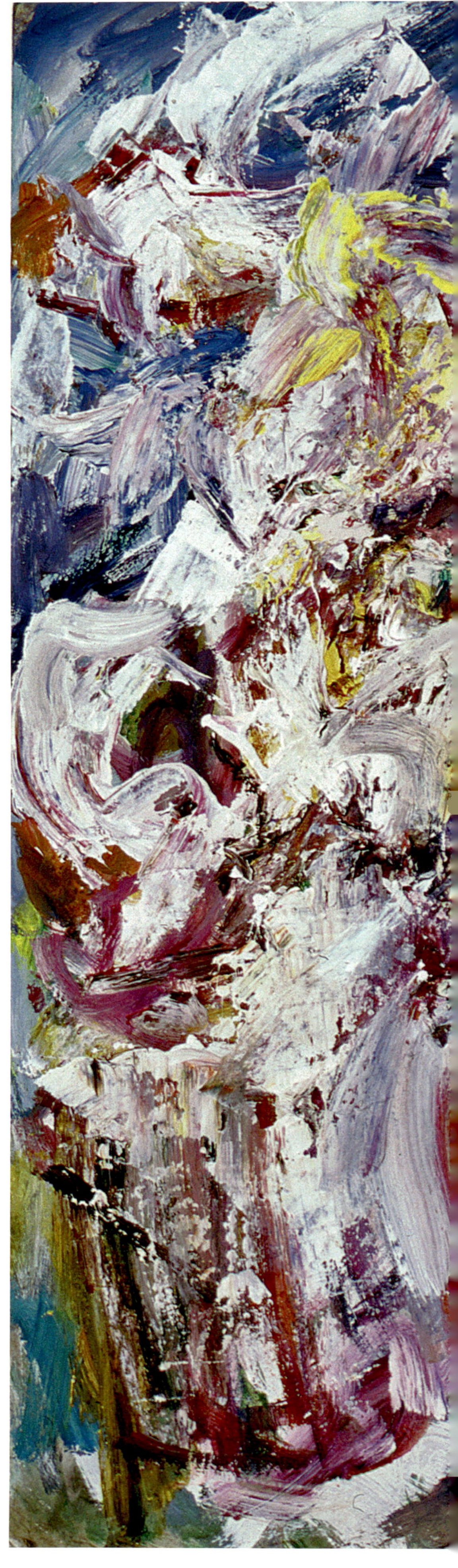

o. T. (Konzert), 2006
Acryl auf Pappe
Acrylic on cardboard
76 × 105 cm

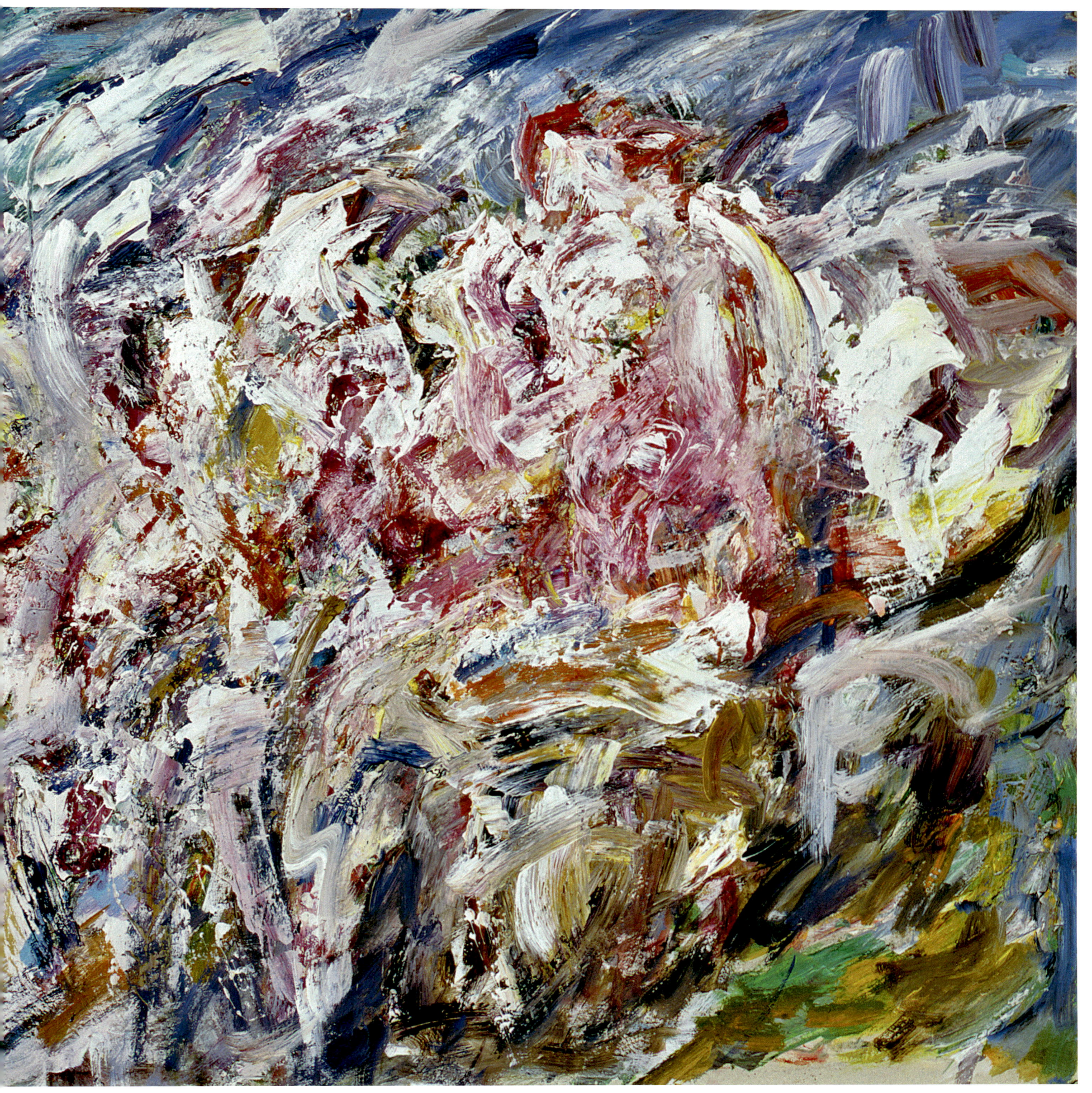

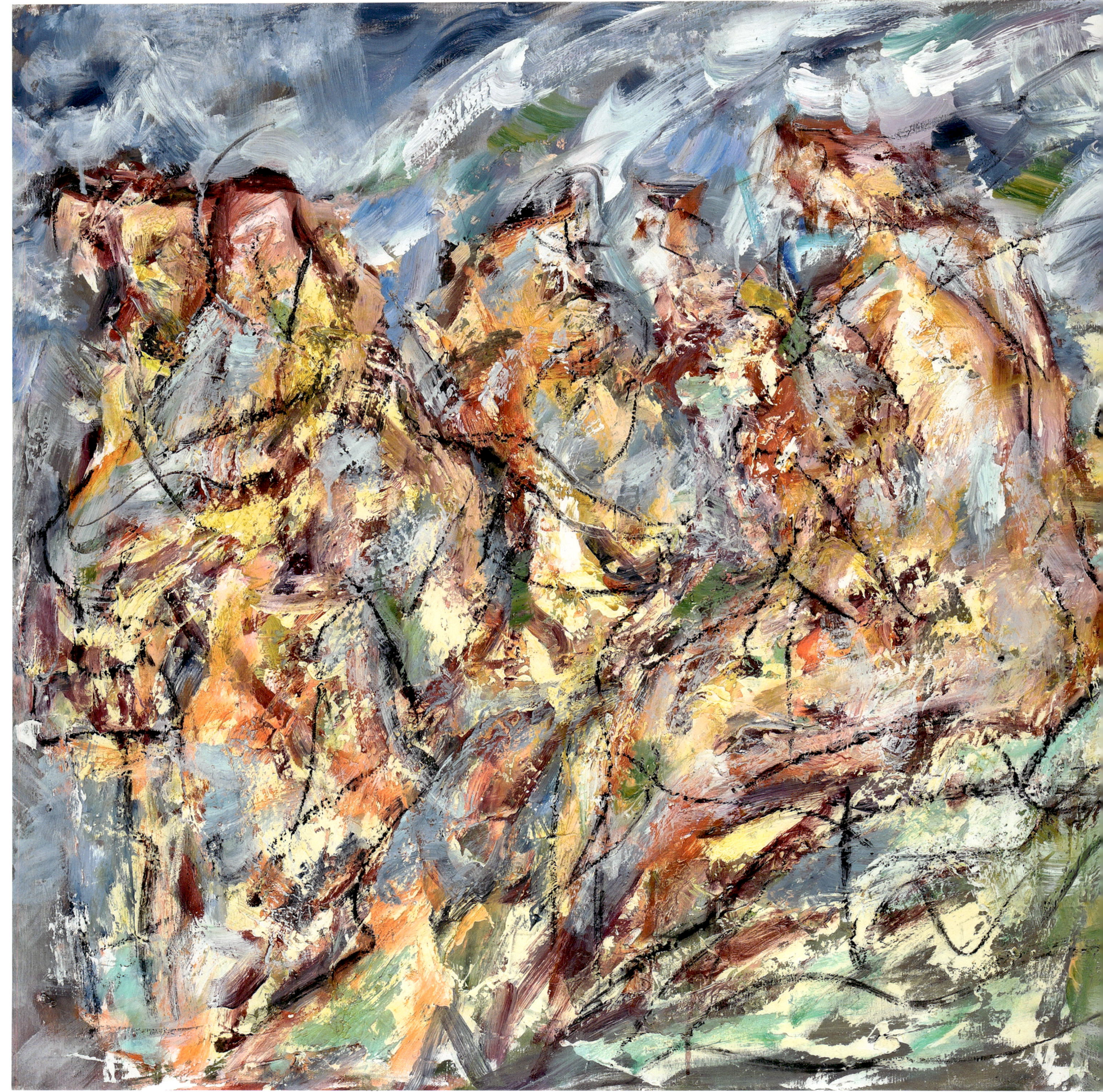

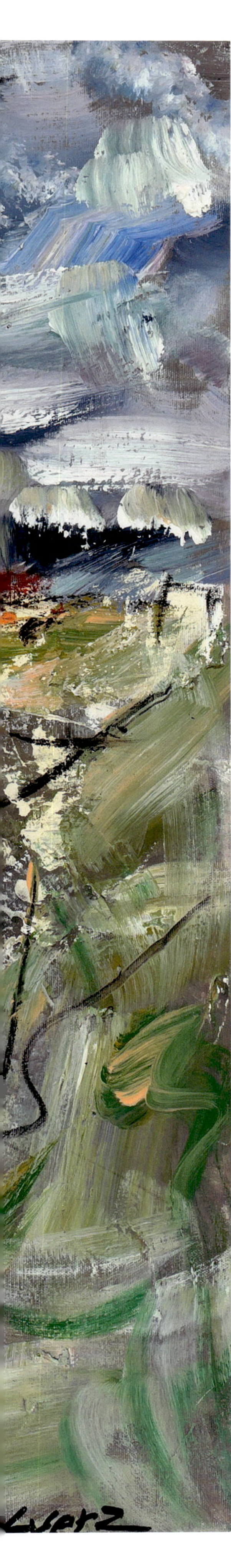

Figurengruppe in Landschaft, 2009
Acryl auf Leinwand
Acrylic on canvas
80 × 100 cm

Wie kommen Herkules und Psyche nach Berlin? Er, der nahezu unverwundbare altgriechische Superheld, und sie, schöner noch als Venus, die nach Irren und Wirren von Amor geheiratet wird und mit ihm die Tochter Voluptas zeugt, die Göttin der Wollust? In der Mythologie wird Herakles, der Halbbruder der eifersüchtigen Venus-Aphrodite aus Versehen von einem Liebespfeil Cupido-Amors getroffen und verliebt sich unsterblich in Psyche.

Eine kleine Skizze von Eugène Delacroix regte die Künstlerin zu ihrer kraftvollen Arbeit an, die das Paar als Giganten zwischen Berliner Gebäuden tanzen lässt und organische mit tektonischen Körpern in elektrisierende Spannung setzt. Auch andere Großstädte wie Hamburg oder München werden zur Folie, um die je nach Wetter und Jahreszeiten wechselnden Stimmungen in Farbatmosphäre zu übersetzen.

Vor allem New York, deren Skyline sie jedes Mal fasziniert, wenn sie sich der Metropole nähert, ist ein Lieblingsmotiv; ideal, um sich mit urbanen im Gegensatz zu natürlichen Landschaften auseinander zu setzen. »In New York habe ich mich von der ersten Sekunde an heimisch gefühlt«, meint Katharina von Werz, »wie schon Truman Capote festgestellt hat, ist sie die einzig echte City-City, die Stadt der Städte«.

How have Hercules and Psyche ended up in Berlin? He, the virtually invulnerable superhero of ancient Greece, and she, more beautiful than Venus herself, who eventually takes Cupid's hand in marriage and gives birth to their daughter Voluptas, goddess of carnal sensuality. In mythology, Hercules, half-brother of jealous Venus/Aphrodite is accidently struck by an arrow from Cupid's bow and falls forever in love with Psyche.

A small sketch by Eugène Delacroix compelled the artist to create this powerful work, which depicts the couple as giants between the buildings of Berlin and pits organic bodies with tectonic ones in a tension that is electrifying. Other cities such as Hamburg and Munich also serve as backdrops that translate the various moods dependent on weather and season into atmospheric color.

Favorite of all backdrops, however, is New York, whose skyline is an endless source of fascination for the artist whenever she approaches the city. It provides her with the perfect urban counterpoint to her landscapes of nature. As Katharina von Werz states: "I felt at home in New York the moment I arrived. As Truman Capote said, it is the only real city-city, the city of all cities."

Herakles und Psyche in Berlin, 2005
Mischtechnik auf Papier
Mixed media on paper
30 × 40 cm
Privatbesitz, München
Privately owned, Munich

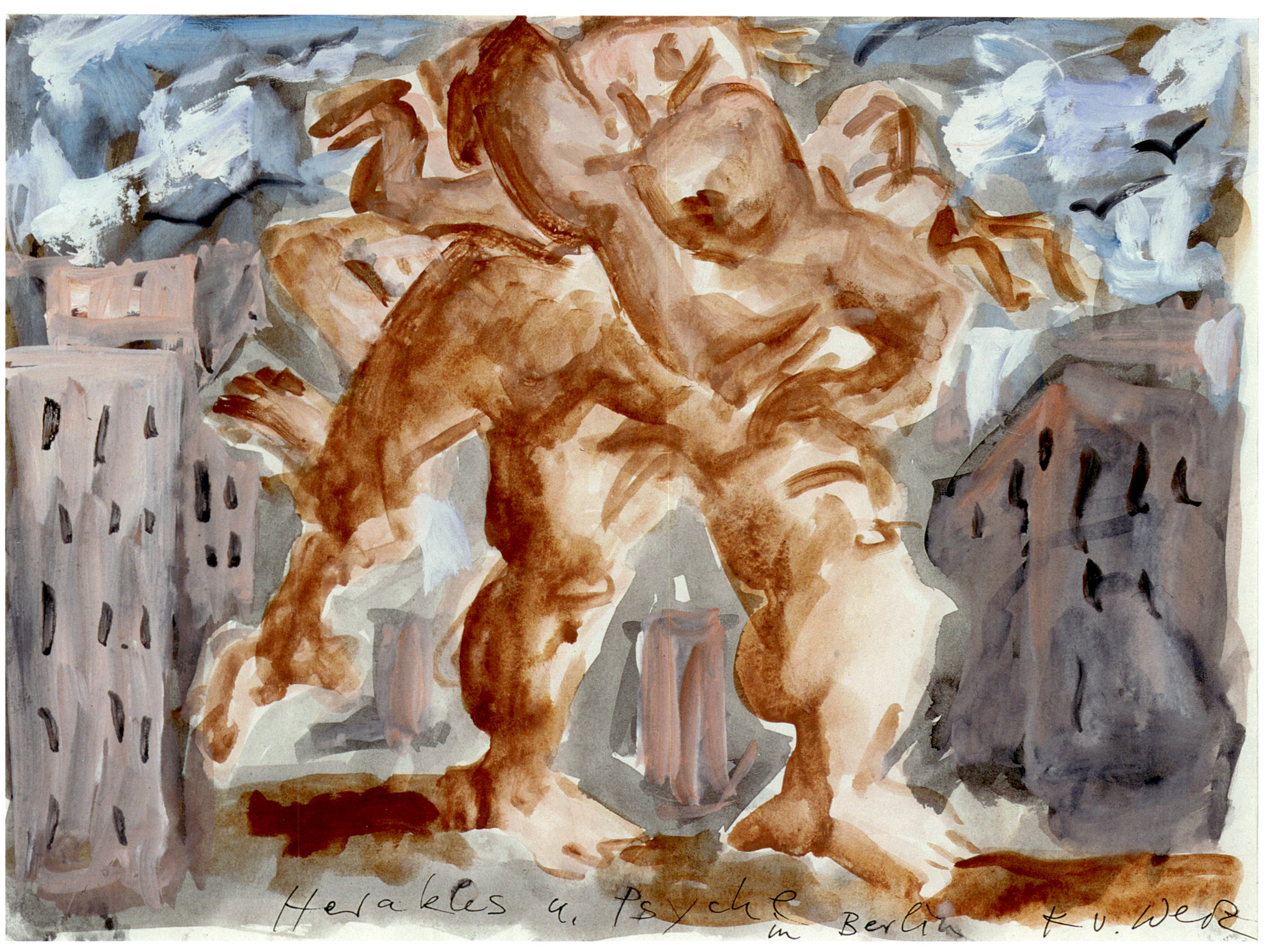

Herakles u. Psyche in Berlin
K. v. We.

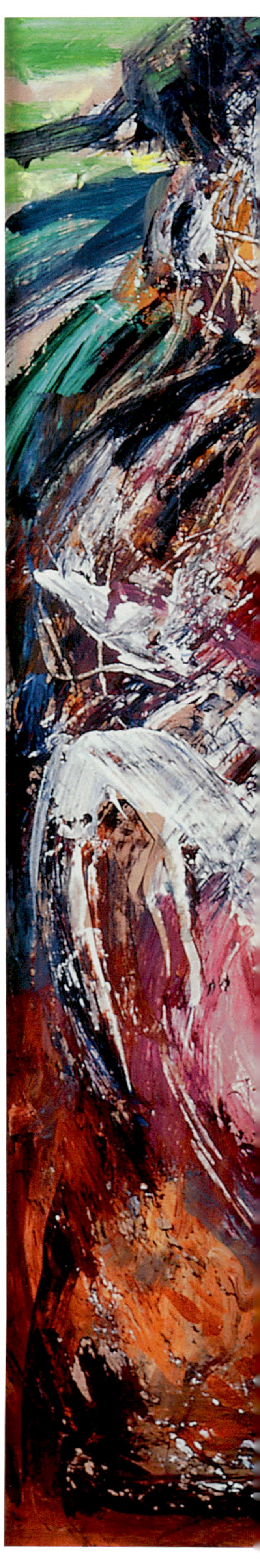

Café an der Alster, 2006
Acryl auf Pappe
Acrylic on cardboard
80 × 100 cm

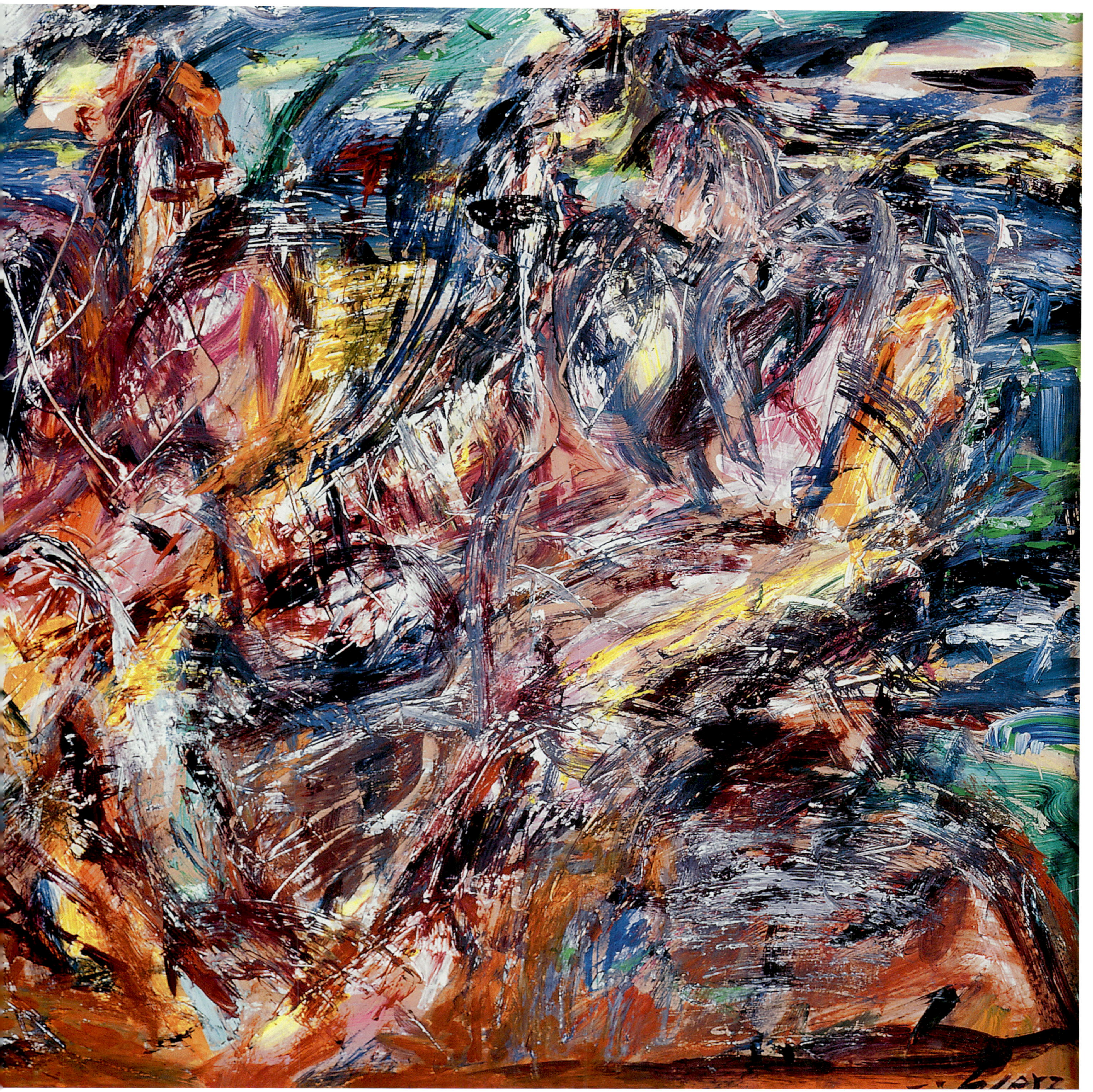

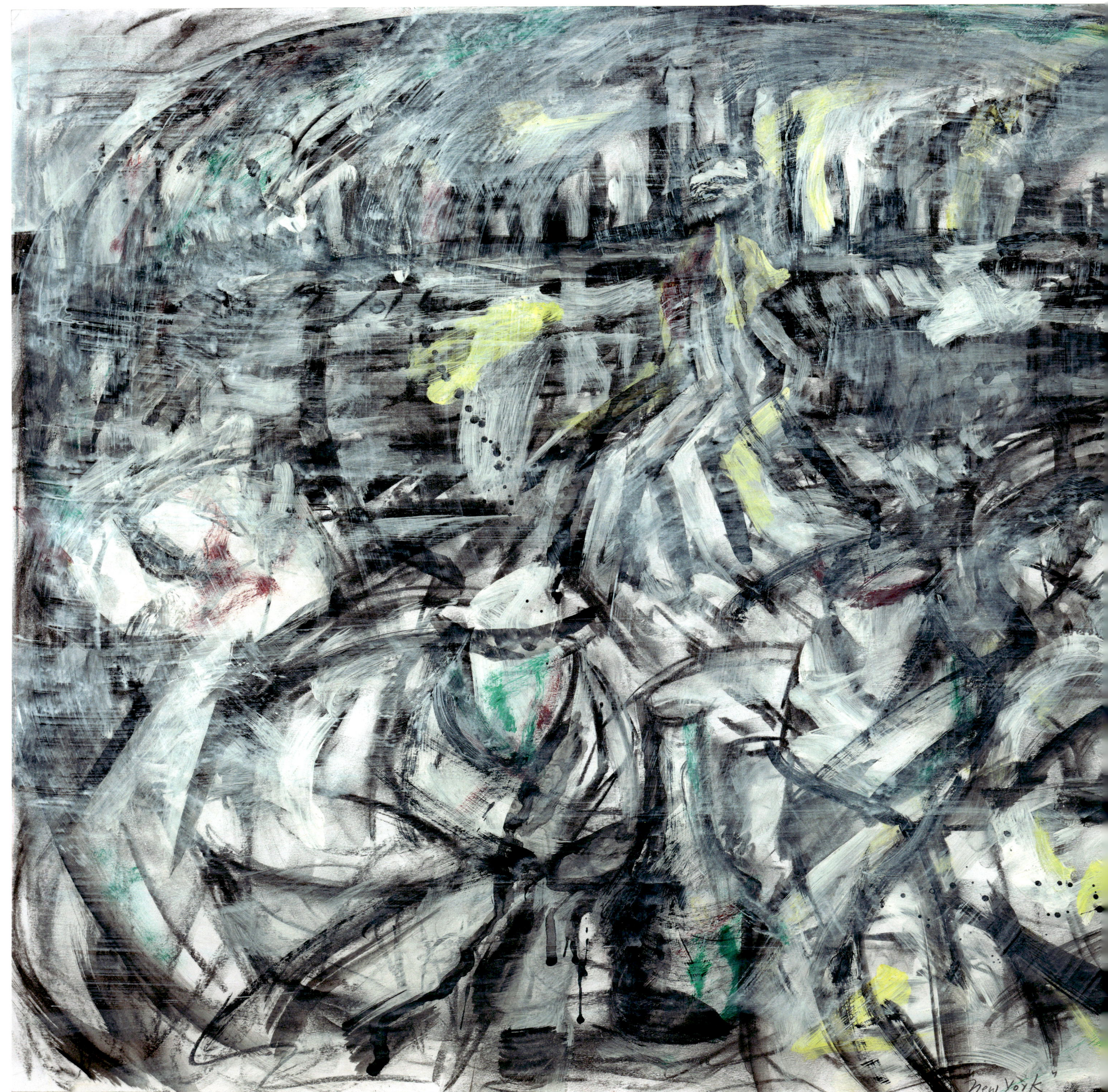
New York

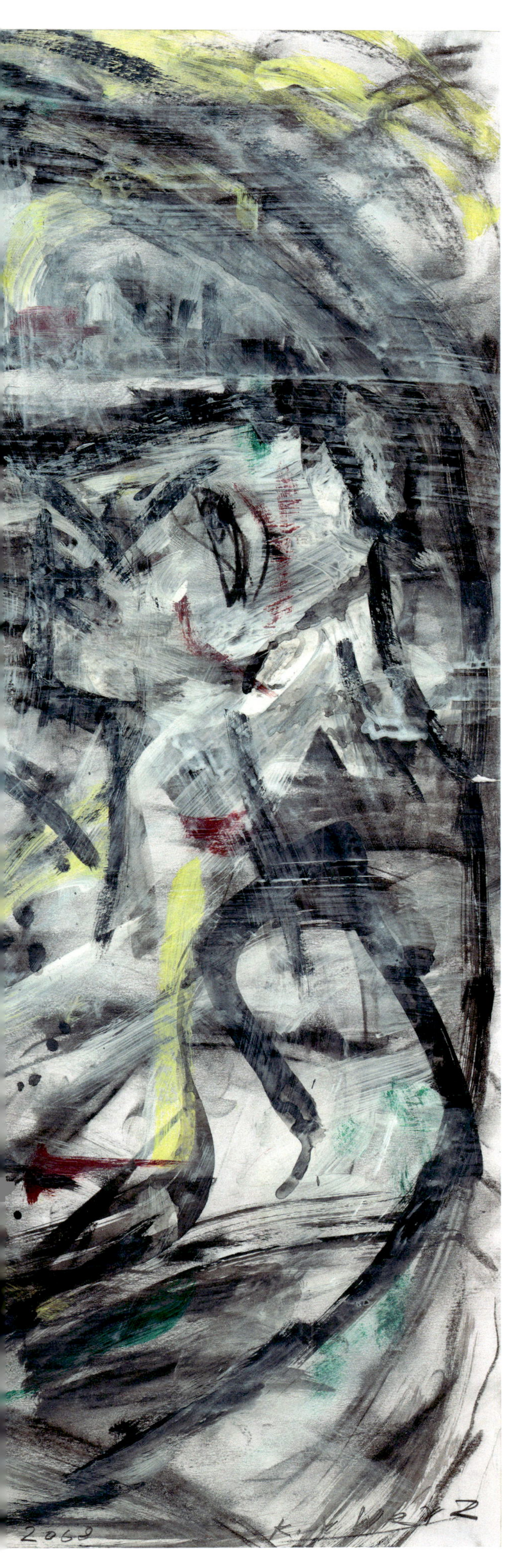

New York, 2002
Acryl auf Papier
Acrylic on paper
70 × 100 cm
Staatliche Graphische Sammlung,
München/Munich

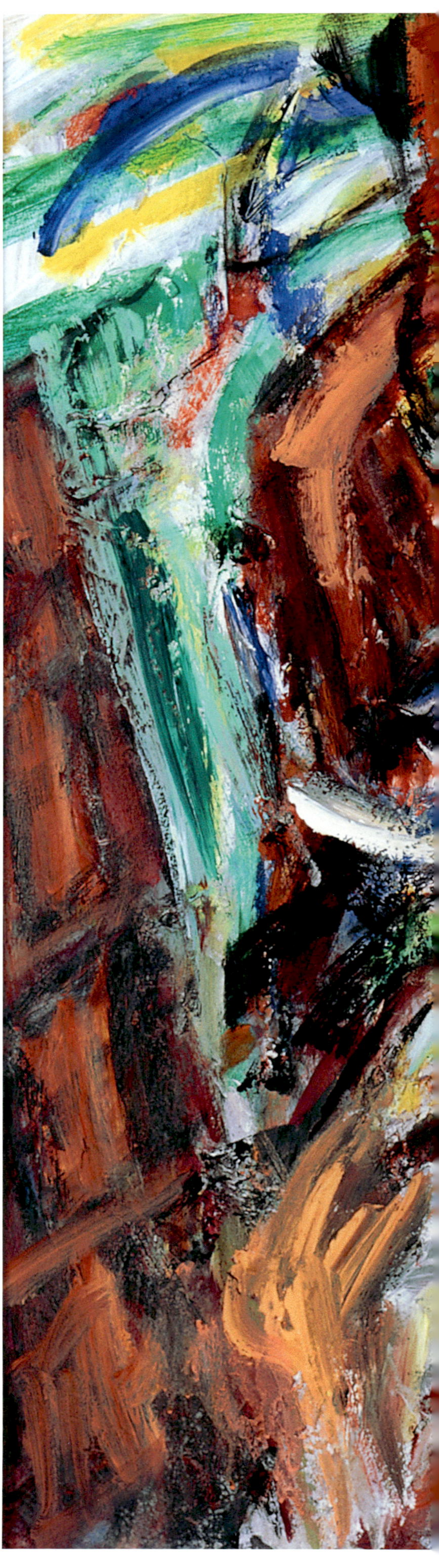

Über den Dächern, 1997
Acryl auf Pappe
Acrylic on cardboard
95 × 130 cm

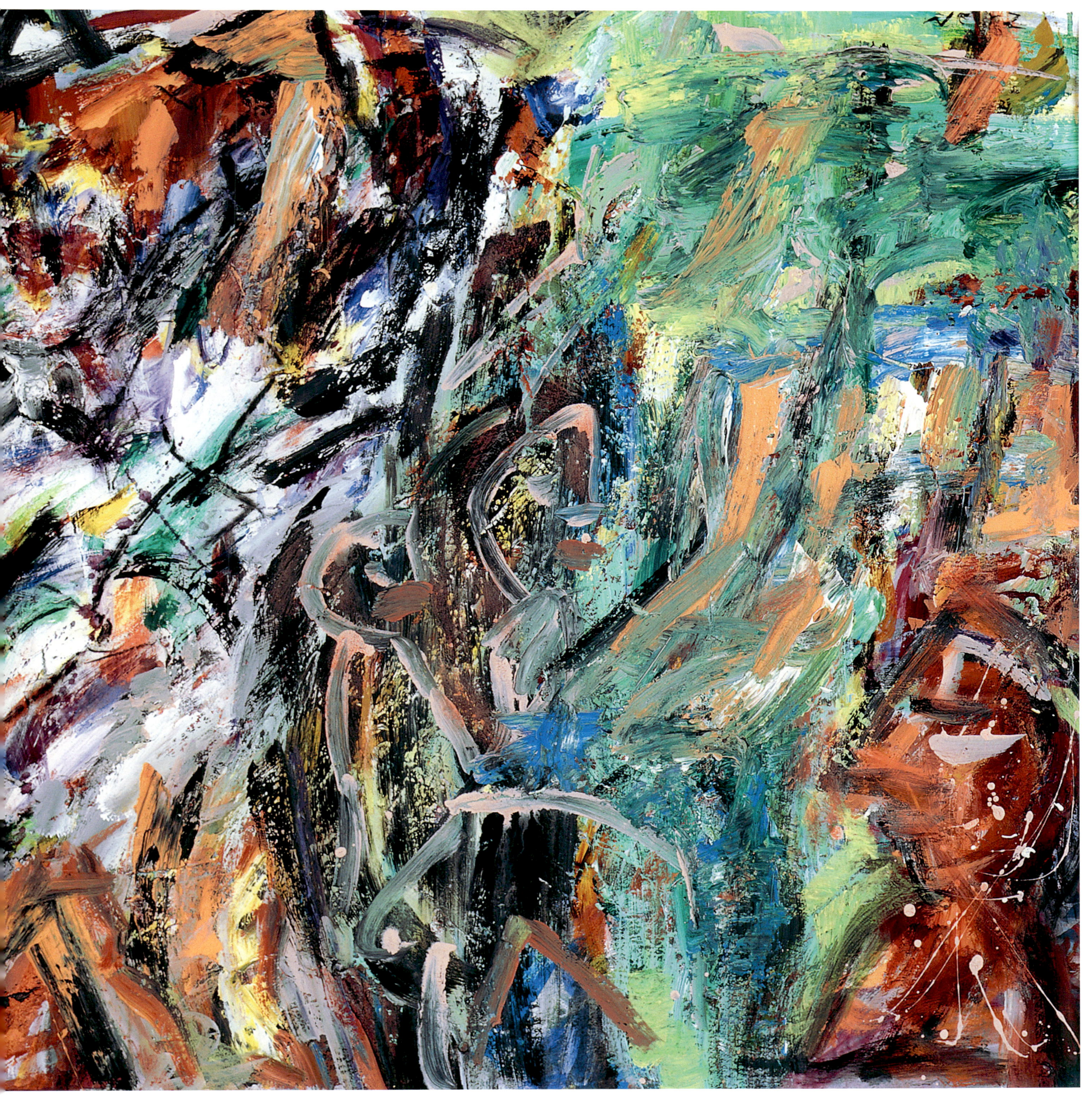

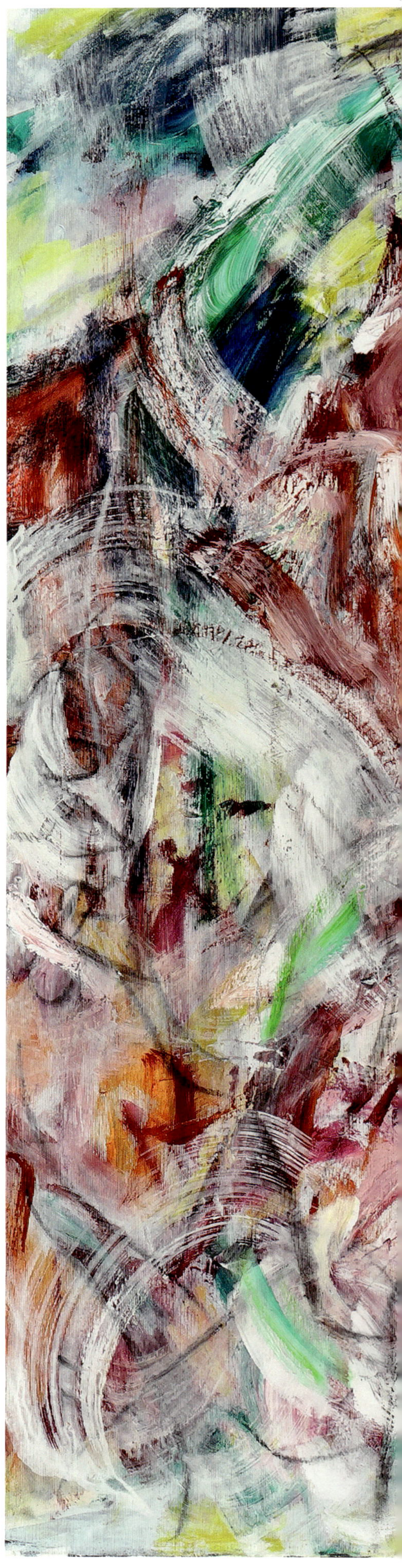

Dachlandschaft New York, 2008
Acryl auf Leinwand
Acrylic on canvas
105 × 140 cm

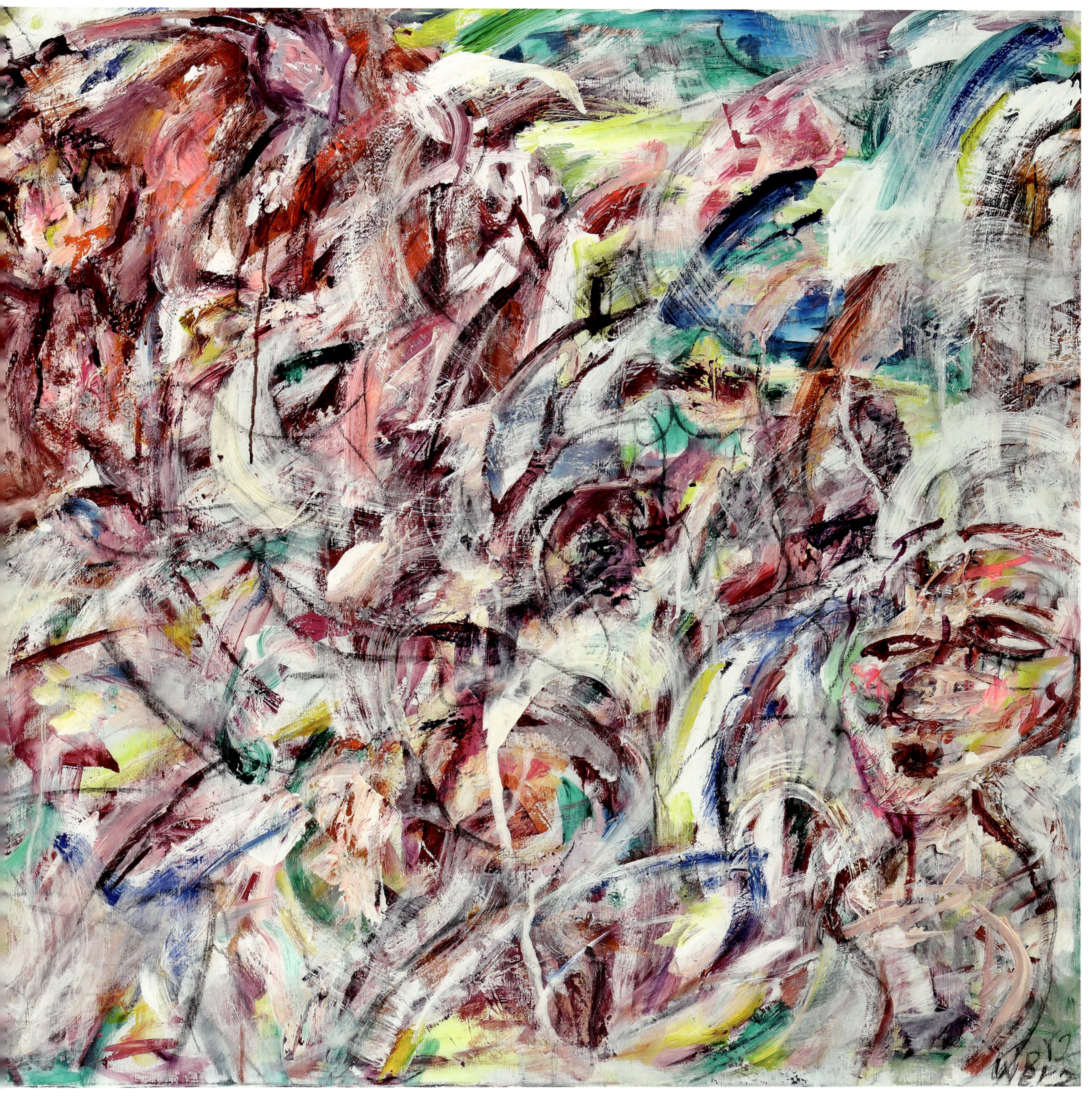

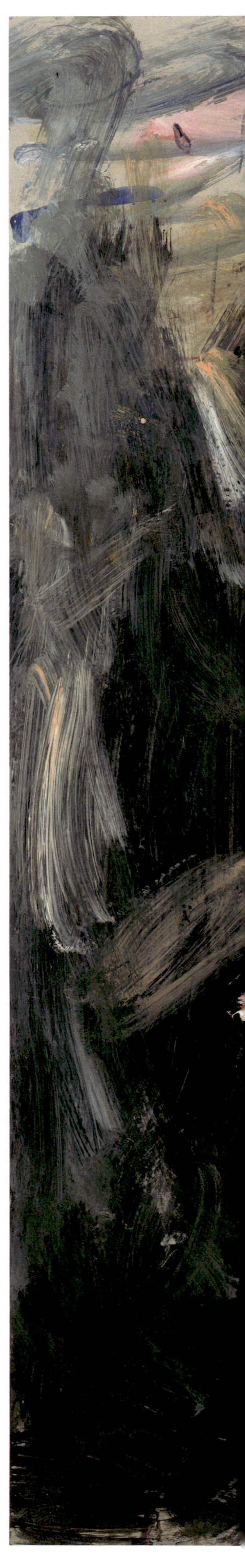

Herbst in der Stadt, 2002
Acryl auf Pappe
Acrylic on cardboard
80 × 100 cm
Staatliche Graphische Sammlung,
München/Munich

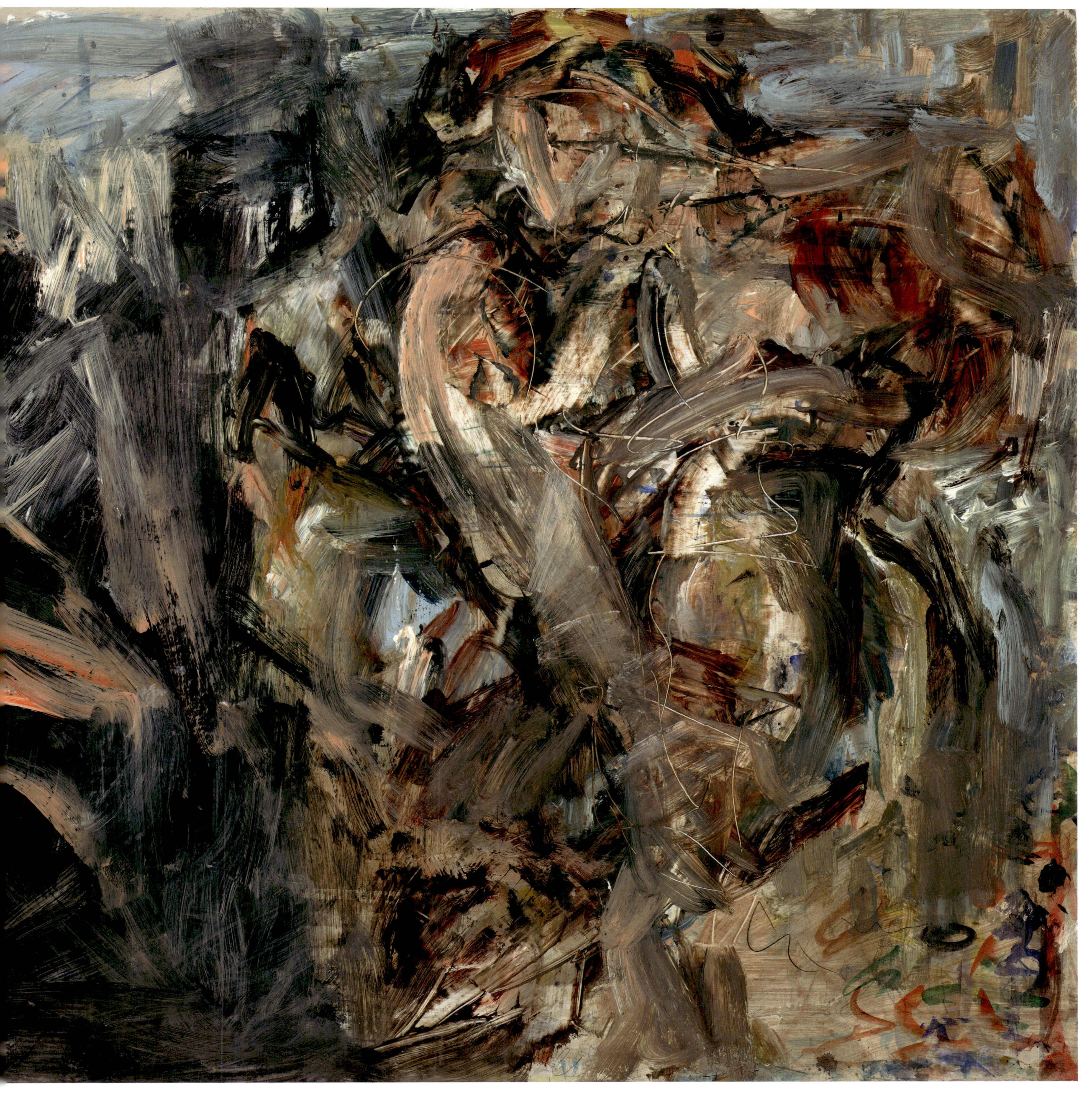

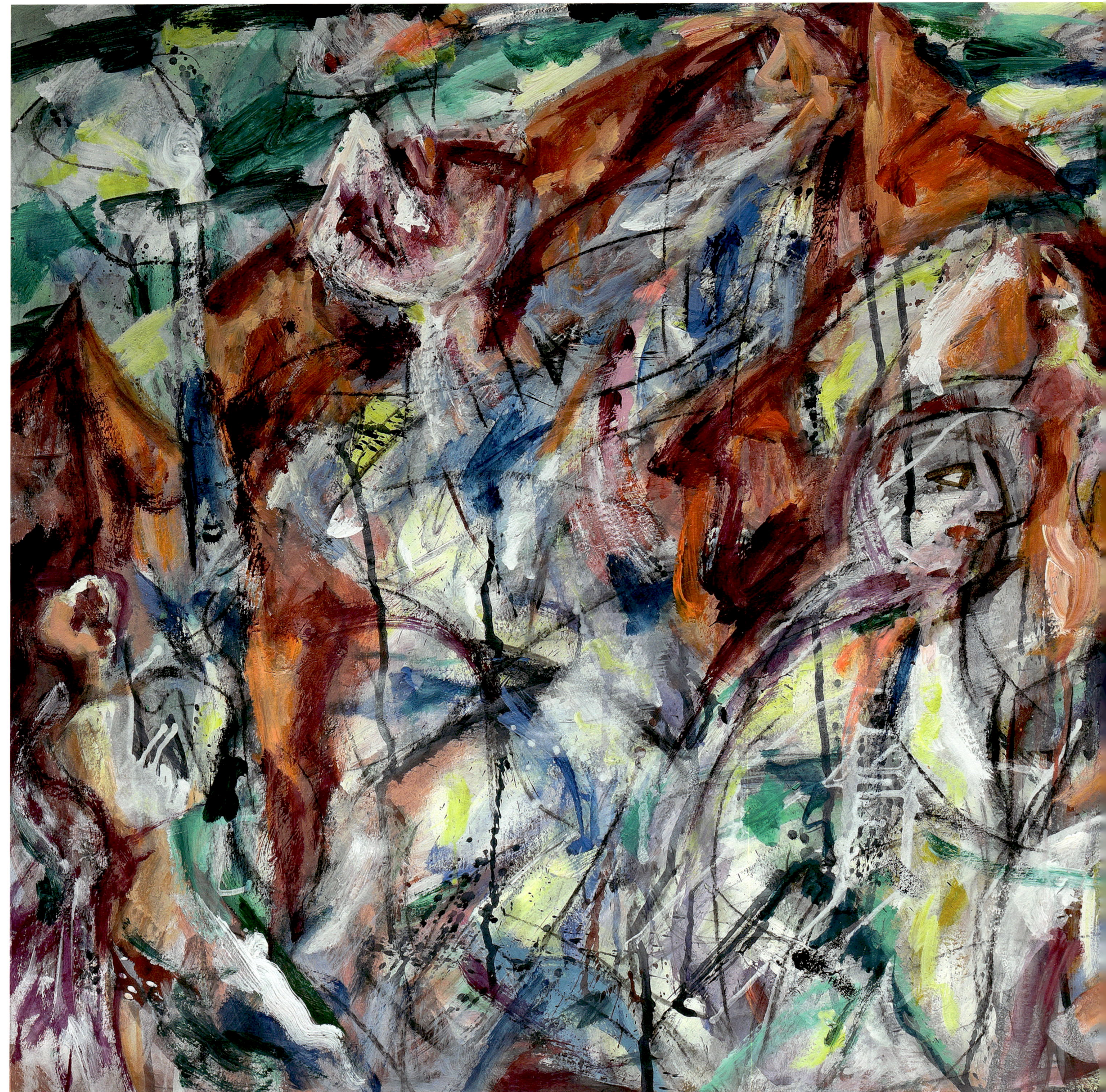

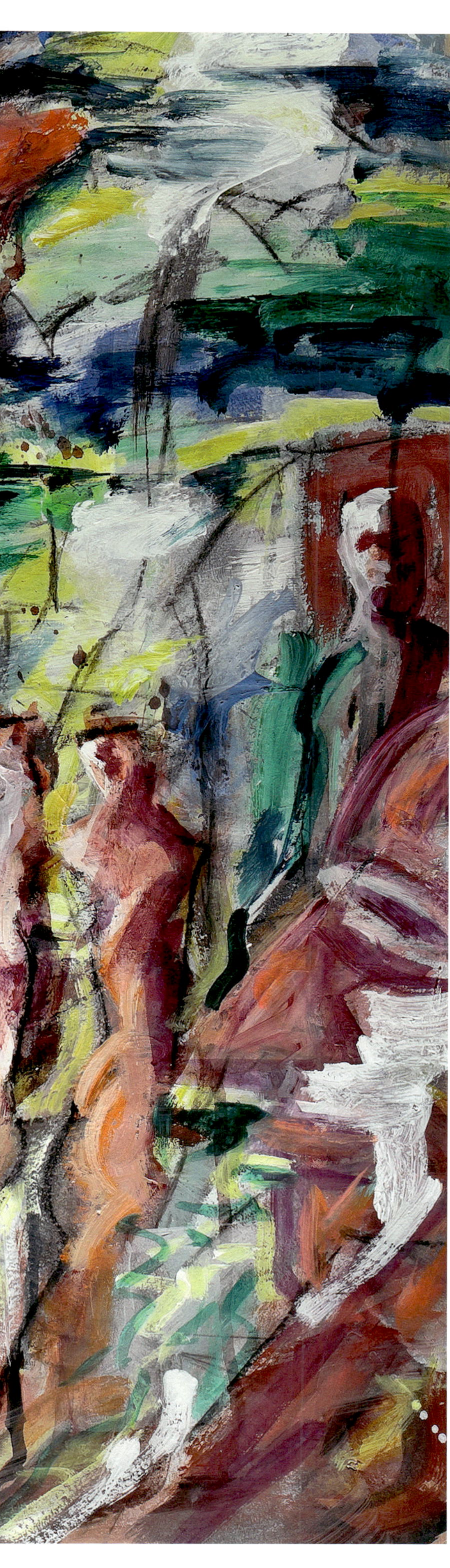

Dachlandschaft New York III, 2006
Acryl auf Pappe
Acrylic on cardboard
95 × 130 cm

München (Johanneskirchen), 2000
Acryl auf Pappe
Acrylic on cardboard
62 × 80 cm

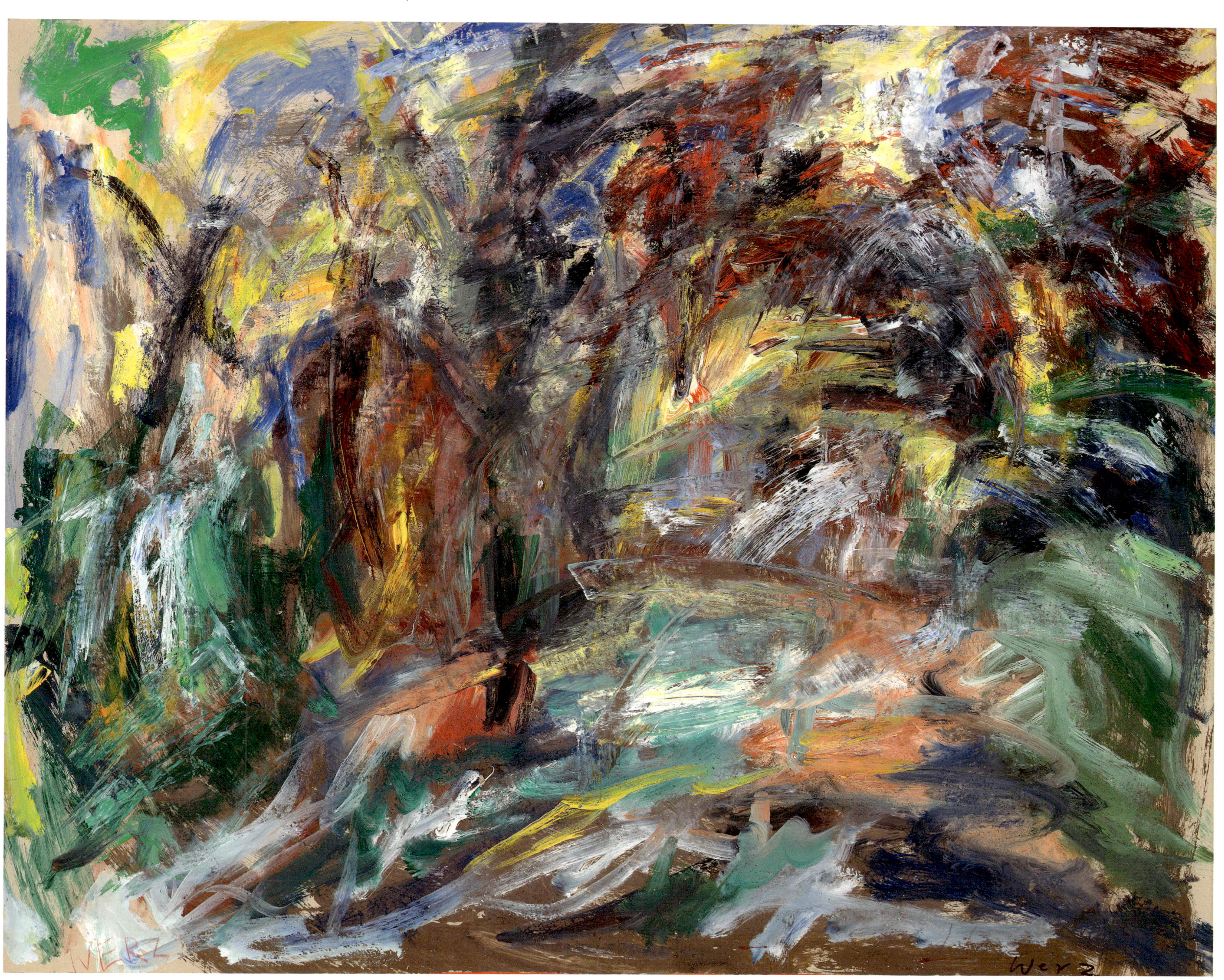

»Die Malerei scheint mir umso besser, je mehr sie der Skulptur ähnelt, und die Skulptur umso schlechter, je mehr sie der Malerei ähnelt. Die Skulptur ist die Fackel der Malerei, und zwischen ihnen besteht der gleiche Unterschied wie zwischen der Sonne und dem Mond.«

Michelangelo Buonarroti

"Painting is at its most beautiful when it succeeds in imitating volume, and sculpture may be deemed bad when it seeks to imitate painting. And yet, it seems to me that sculpture was the torch that illuminated painting, and that between the two arts there is the same relationship as between the sun and the moon."
Michelangelo Buonarroti

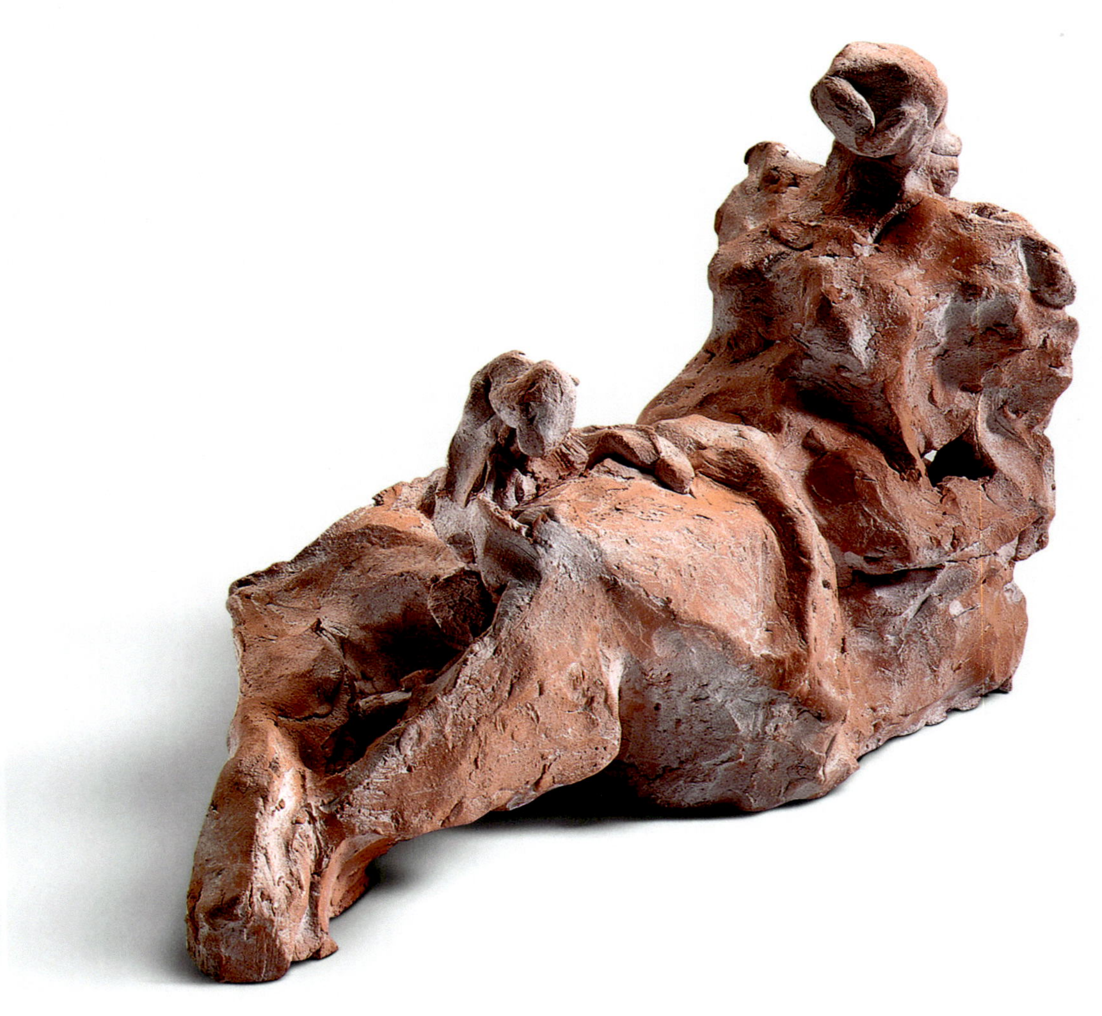

Träumende Rekordläuferin, 2000
Terrakotta/Terracotta
30 × 20 × 50 cm

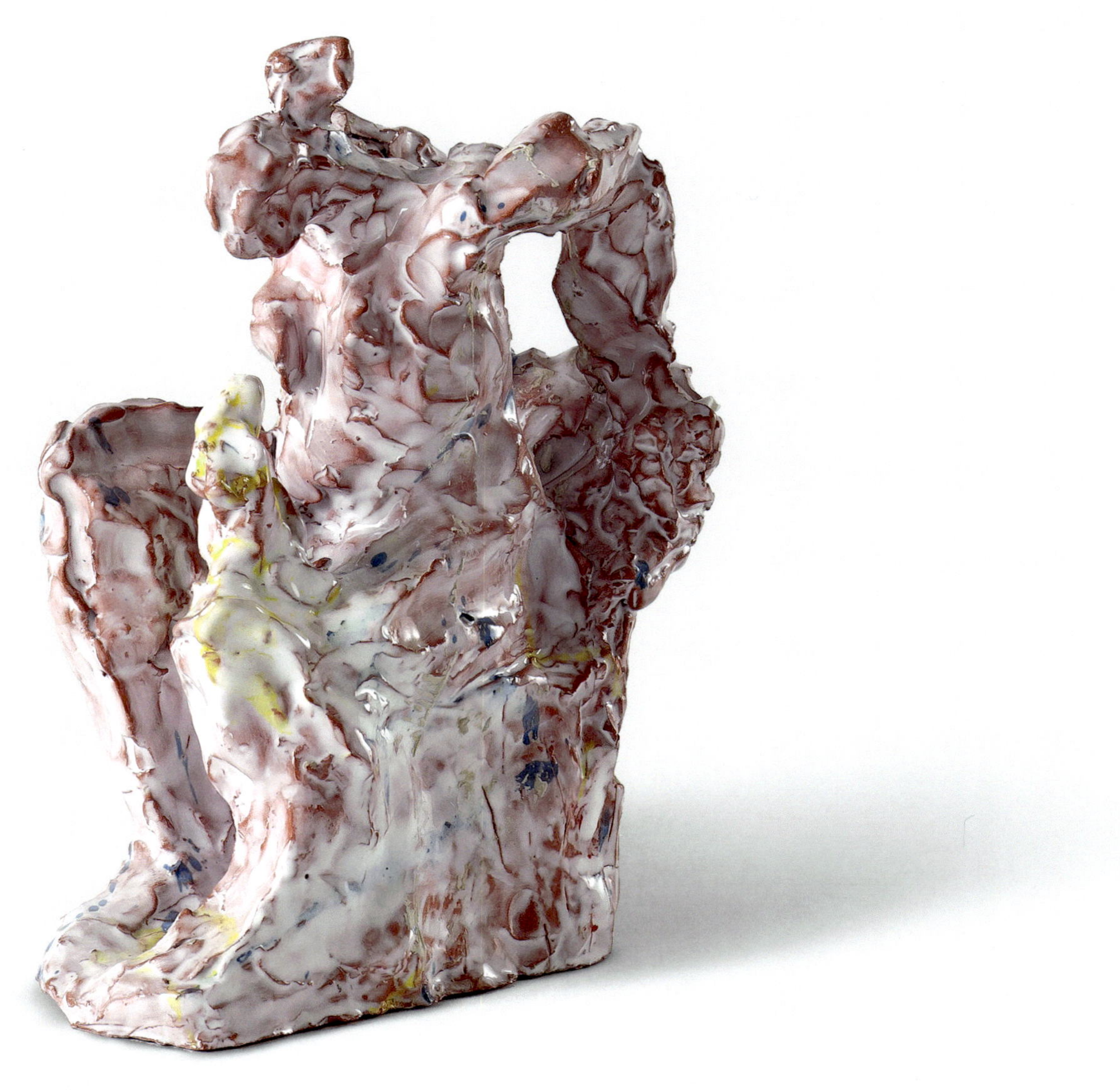

Zeus und Nymphe, 2000
Terrakotta, glasiert
Terracotta, glazed
30 × 20 × 25 cm

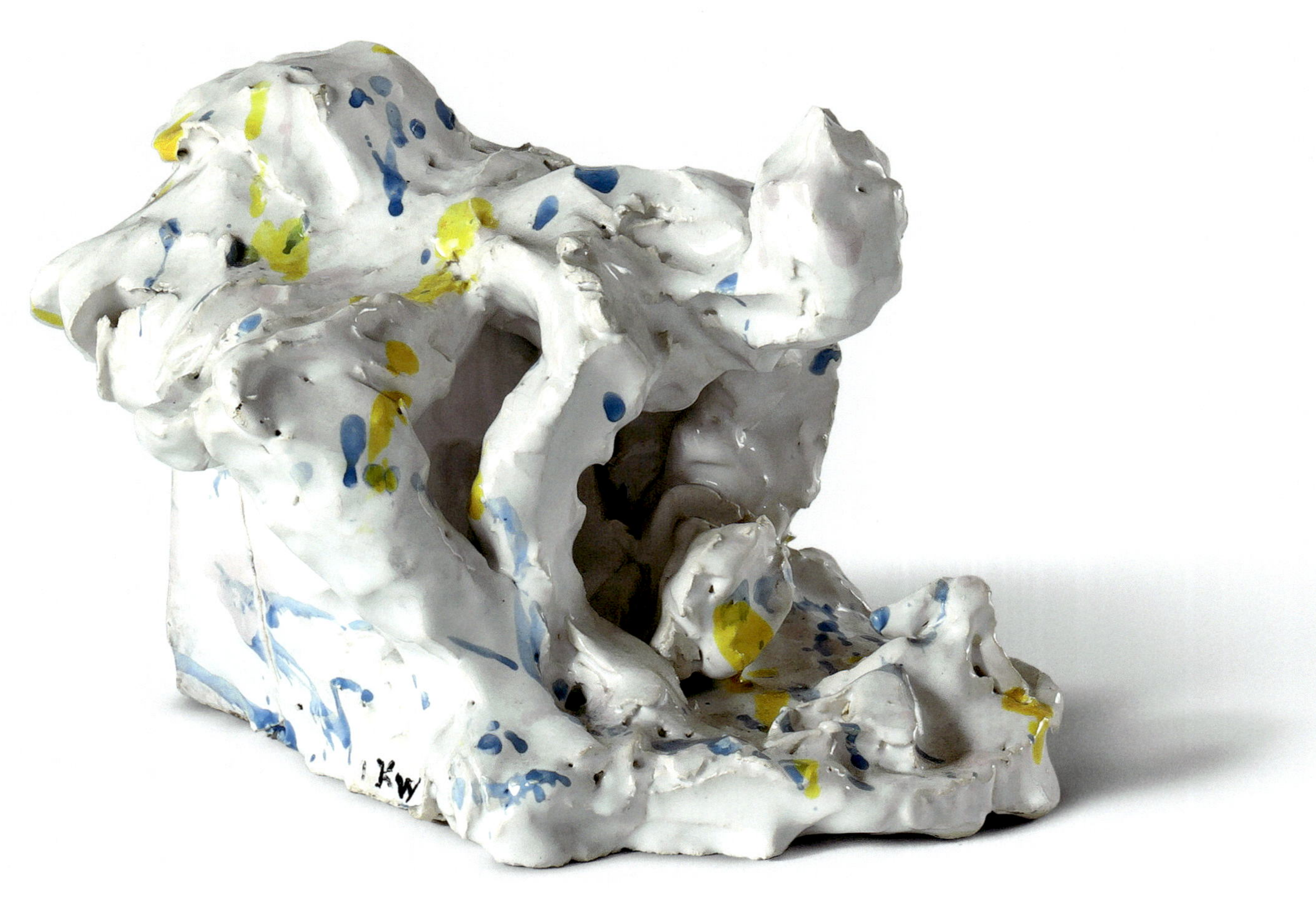

Dame und ihr Hündchen, 2008
Terrakotta, glasiert
Terracotta, glazed
30 × 20 × 22 cm

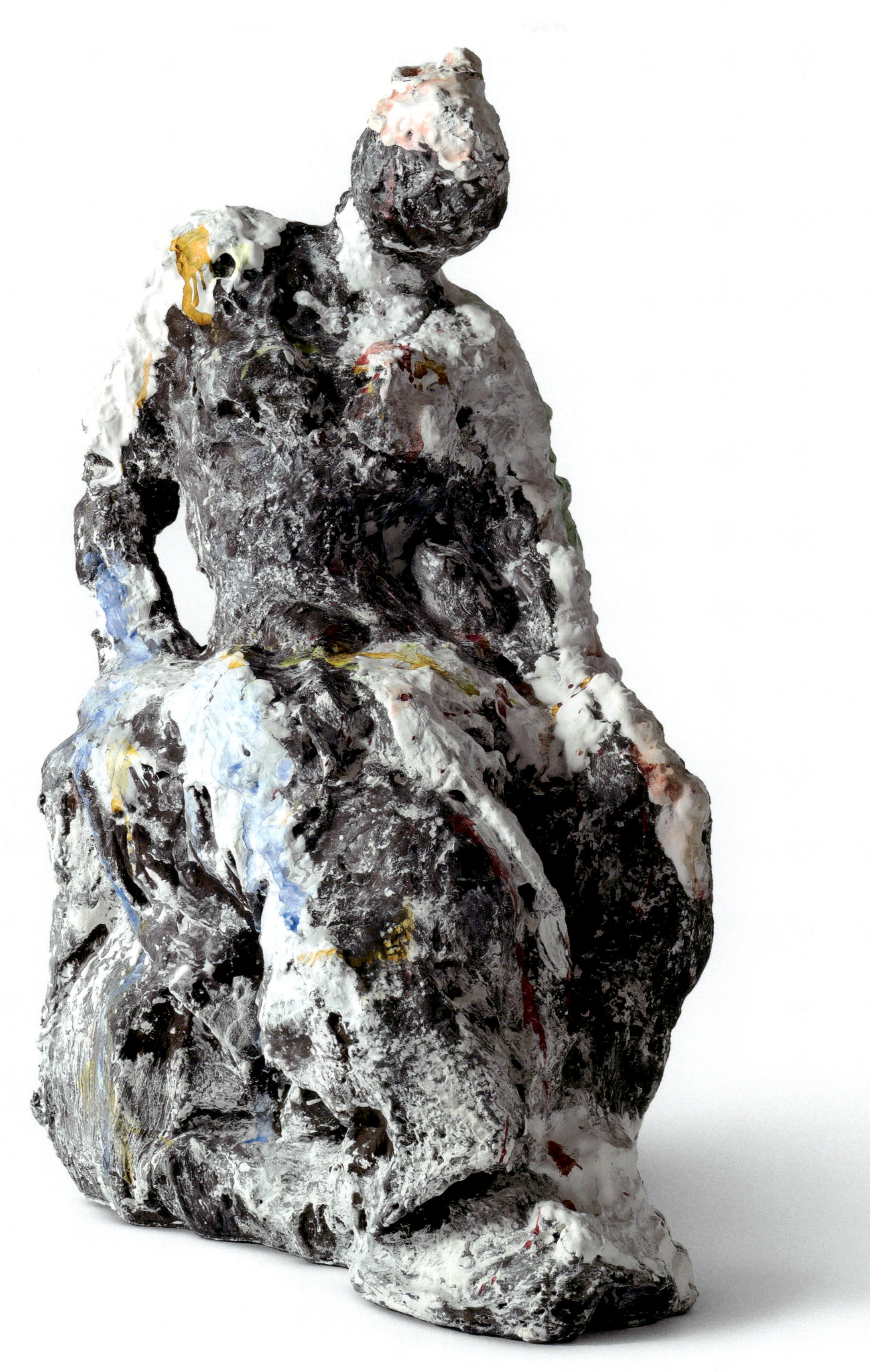

Träumende Europa, 2008
Bronze, bemalt
Bronze, painted
50 × 34 × 25 cm

VENUS AND ADONIS

Die uralte, ewige Geschichte aus Wonne und Leid zwischen zwei Liebenden ist von Ovid über Shakespeare, Rubens und Tizian bis hin zu Hans Werner Henze, der zu den bedeutendsten deutschen Komponisten des 20. Jahrhunderts gehört, ein immer neu faszinierender Stoff für Dichter, Schriftsteller, Komponisten und bildende Künstler. Zur Erinnerung: Der griechischen Mythologie nach sieht Adonis, Gott der Schönheit, noch blendender aus als die muschelgeborene Venus, Göttin der Liebe und Begierde.

Sie schläft mit zahllosen sterblichen und unsterblichen Heroen und verliebt sich eines Tages leidenschaftlich in den jungen Beau Adonis. Nicht ohne dramatische Folgen, rächt sich doch ihr eifersüchtiger langjähriger Geliebter Ares auf tödliche Weise. Verwandelt in einen Eber, tötet der Kriegsgott Adonis auf der Jagd. Venus, untröstlich über seinen Tod, lässt aus Adonis' Blut ein Röschen, nach ihm benannt, sprießen. Fortan darf der Hübsche ein paar Monate im Jahr als Blume unter den Lebenden weilen, den Rest der Zeit muss er in der Unterwelt von Proserpina darben.

Tragödie unstillbarer Lust: Katharina von Werz widmet dem Sujet immer neue Variationen. Eines ihrer Anliegen dabei ist es, Verlangen darzustellen, das sich in die Verschmelzung der Körper steigert. Doch essenziell geht es ihr darum, die Malerei herauszufordern. Wie Alfred Kubin ist sie überzeugt: »Die Kunst wetteifert nicht mit den Erscheinungen in der Natur, sondern schafft Zeichen für diese.«

The timeless story of the pain and ecstasy felt by these two lovers, as variously related by Ovid, Shakespeare, Rubens, and Titian, and, more recently by Hans Werner Henze—one of the most important German composers of the twentieth century—remains a continual source of fascination for poets, writers, composers, and artists. According to Greek mythology, Adonis, god of beauty, is even more beguiling than Venus, goddess of love and desire. Venus sleeps with numerous mortal and immortal heroes and one day falls hopelessly in love with the young and beautiful Adonis. Their love has terrible consequences however, for it spurs her jealous lover, Ares, to seek revenge. Transformed into a boar, Ares, god of war, slays Adonis during a hunt. Venus, inconsolable at his death, transforms him into a flowering anemone, stained red with his blood. Thus, Adonis is allowed to spend a few months each year among the living in the form of a flower, while the rest of the time he must suffer in the underworld.

A tragedy of unquenchable desire: Katharina von Werz approaches the subject in many variations. One of her chief aims in doing so is to depict a form of desire that reaches it apotheosis in the merging of bodies. But in essence, what the artist is really concerned with is testing the transformative powers of the medium of painting. Like Alfred Kubin, she is convinced that "Art does not compete with forms found in nature, but creates signs for them."

Umarmung, 2011
Acryl auf Karton
Acrylic on cardboard
38 × 33 cm

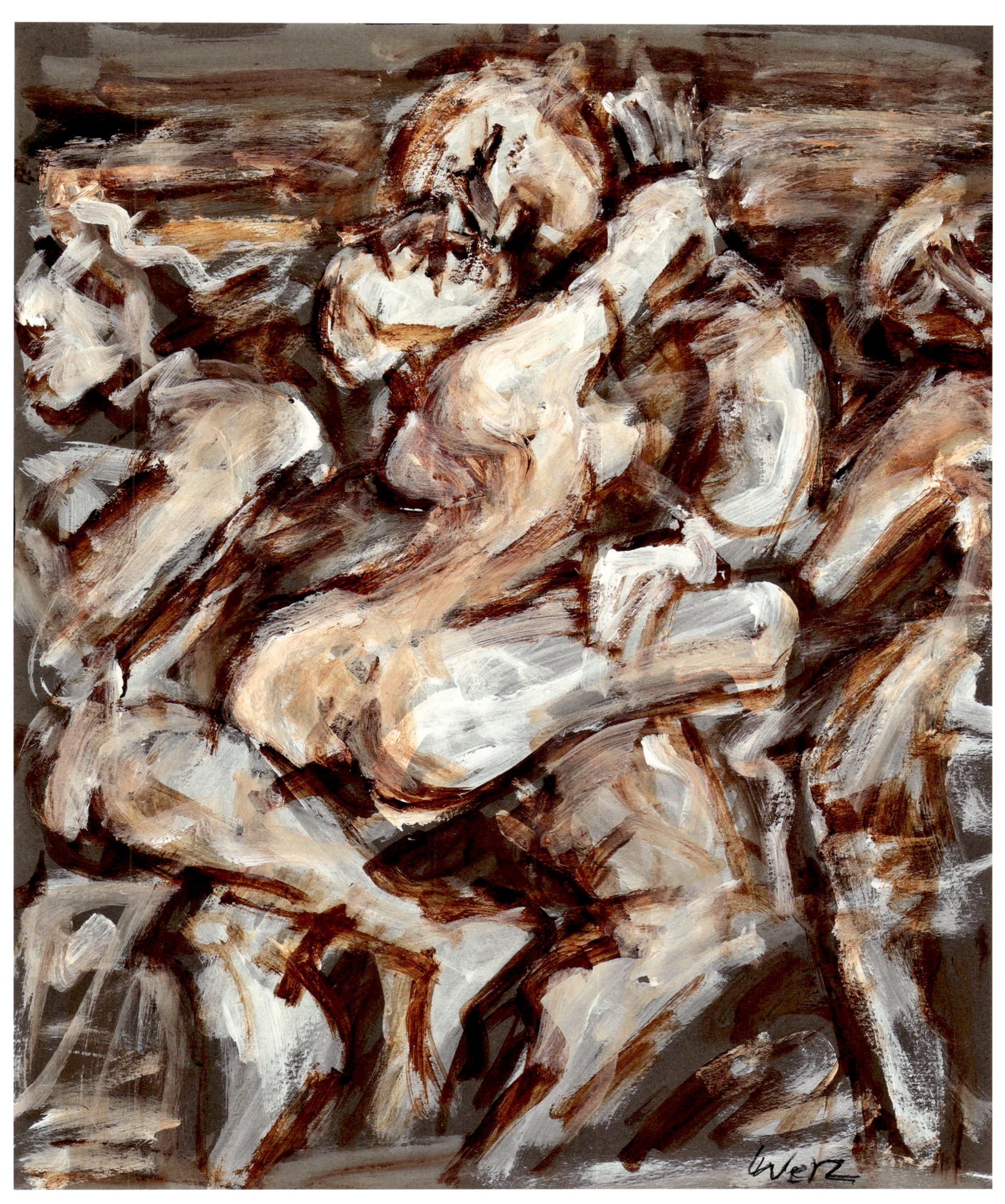
Werz

Umarmung, 2009
Mischtechnik auf Papier
Mixed media on paper
30 × 40 cm

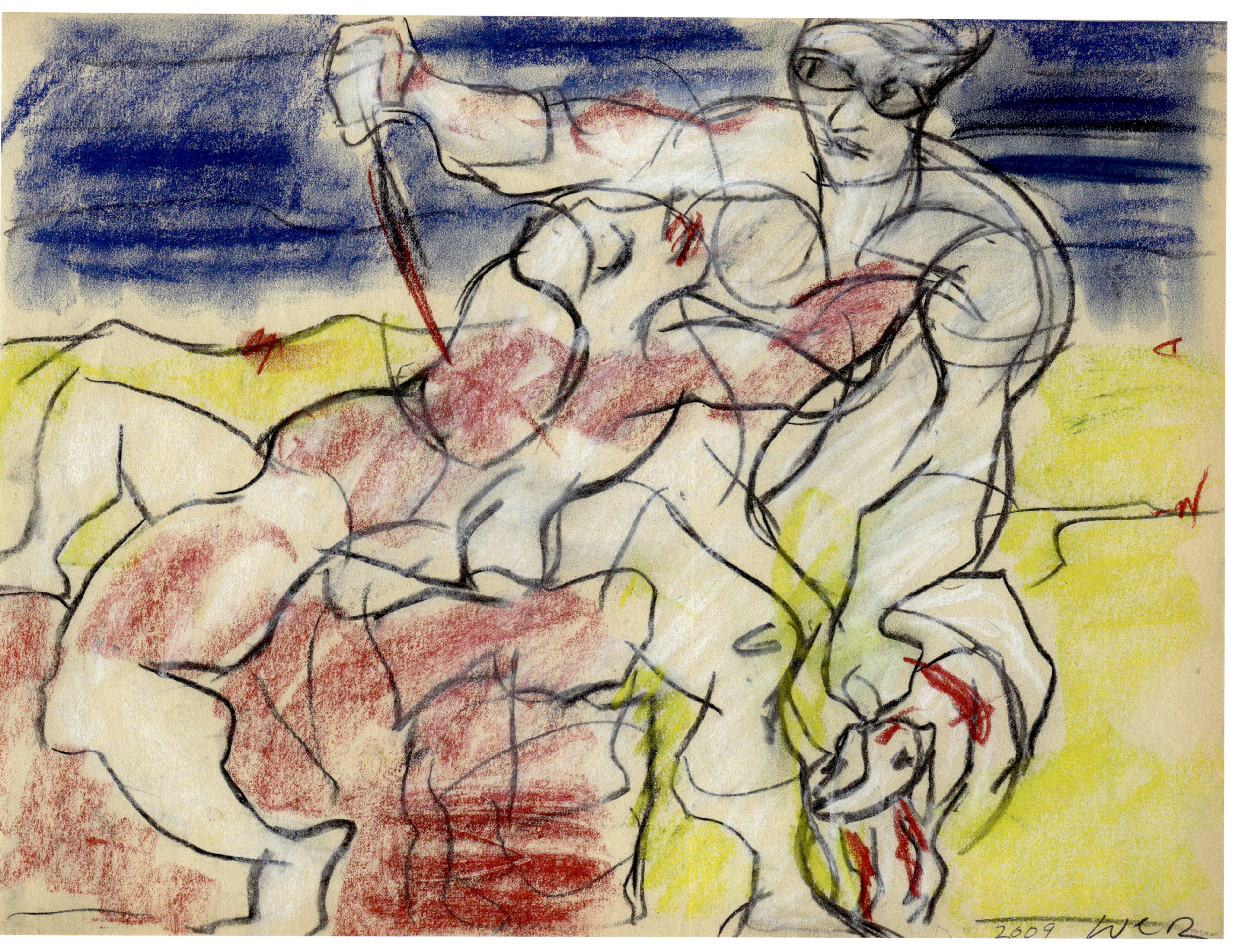
2009 WCR

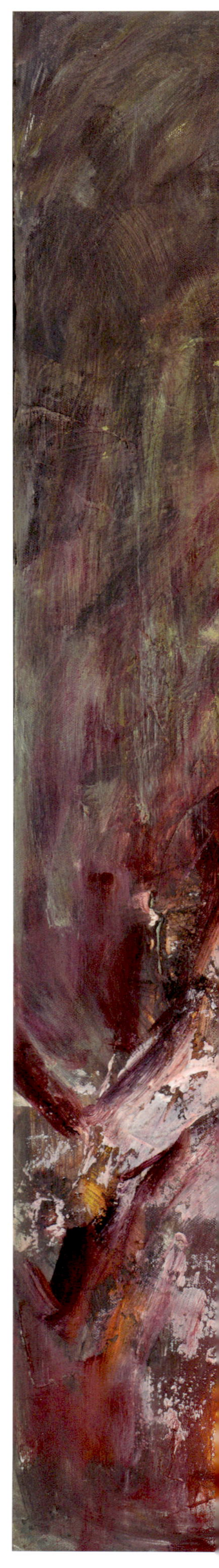

Umarmung II, 2009
Acryl auf Leinwand
Acrylic on canvas
90 × 110 cm

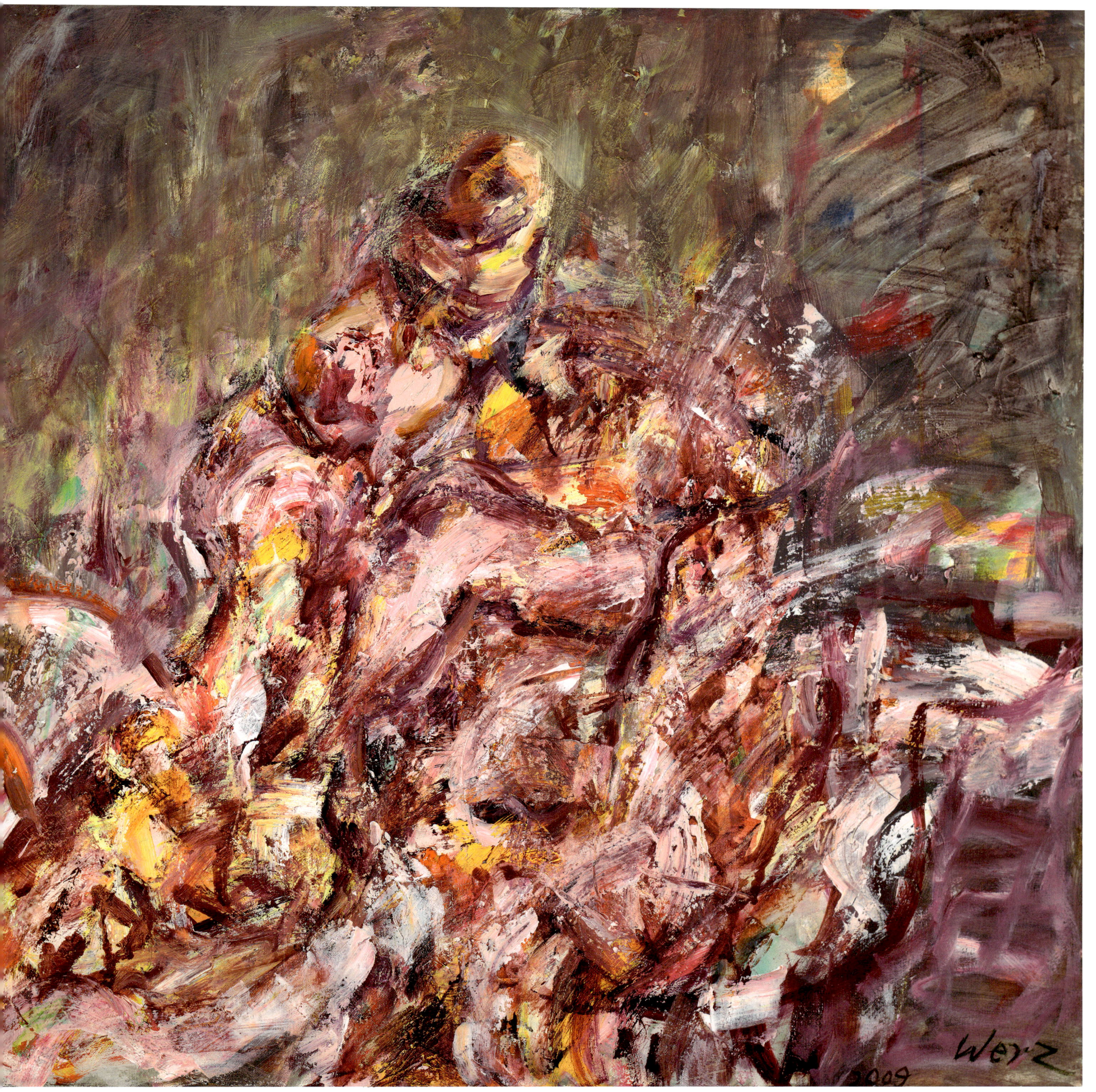

Werz
2009

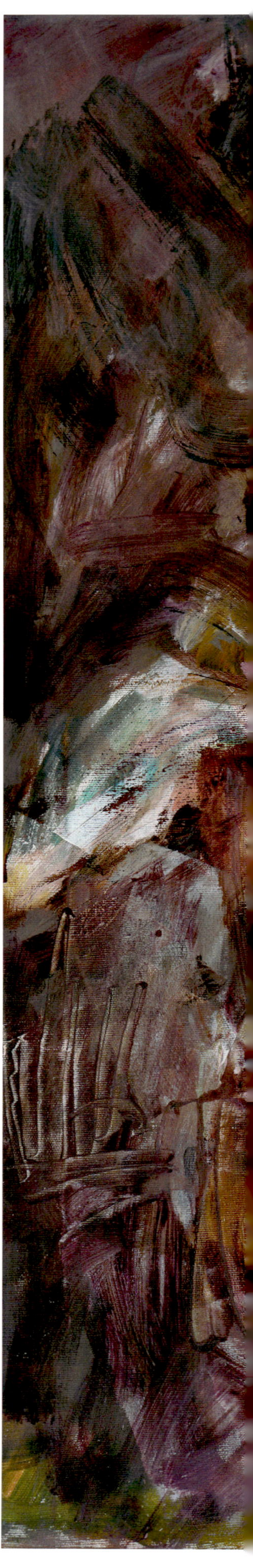

Venus und Adonis, 2009
Acryl auf Leinwand
Acrylic on canvas
80 × 100 cm

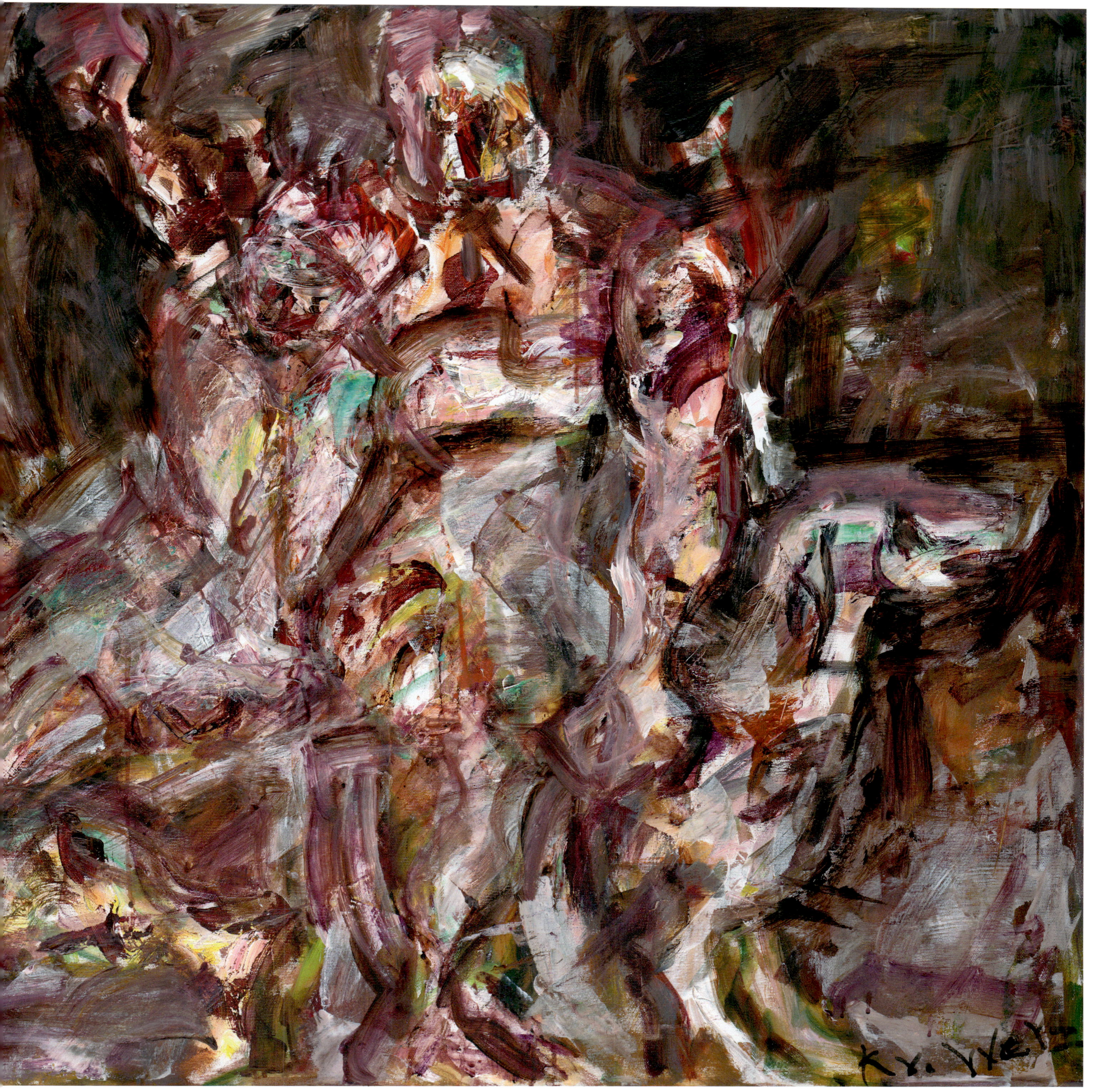
K.v. Wel

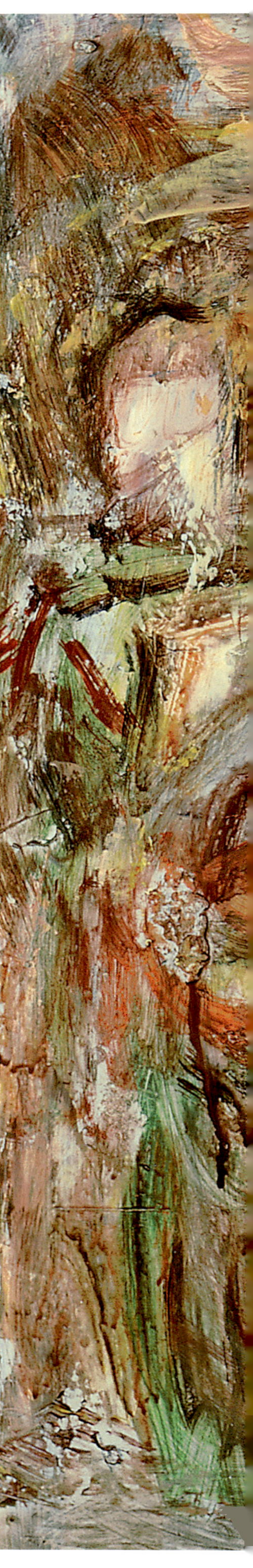

Venus und Adonis II, 2006
Acryl auf Leinwand
Acrylic on canvas
80 × 100 cm

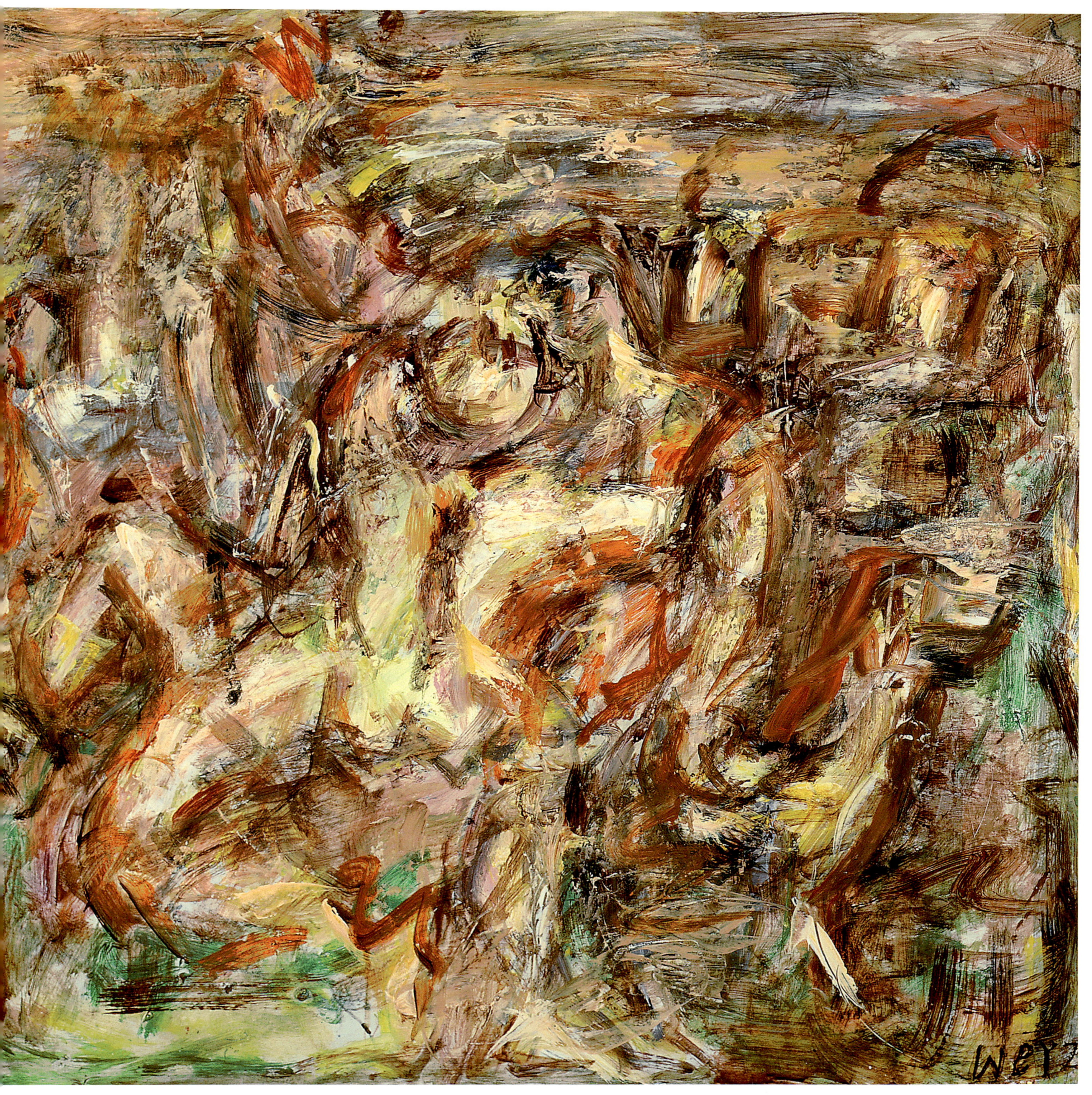

Wetz

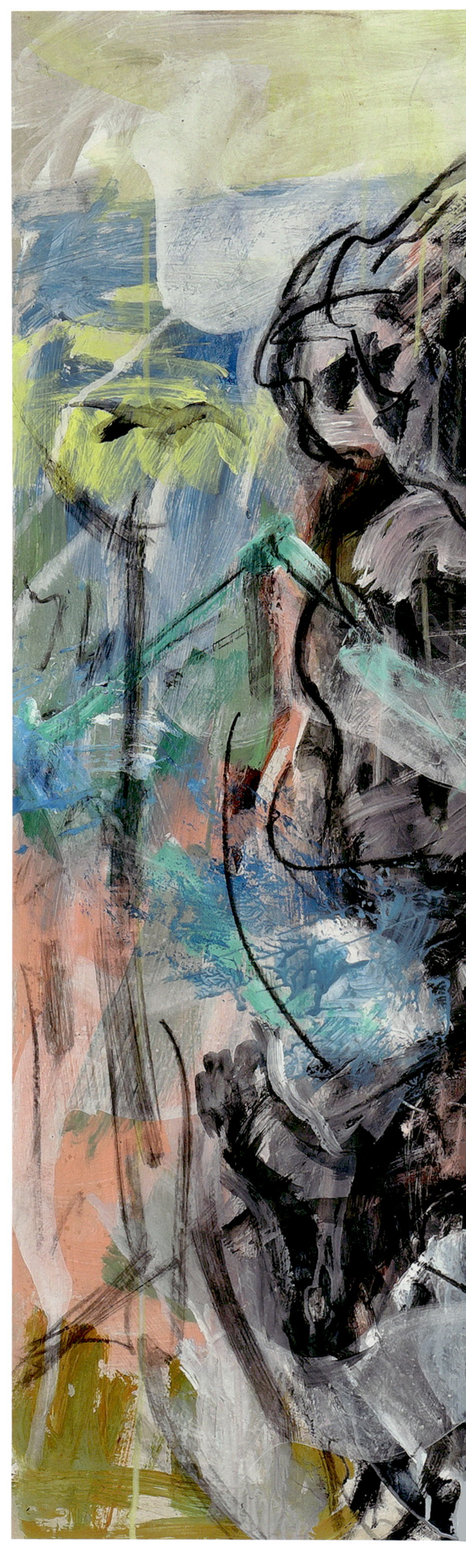

Entführung, 2009
Acryl auf Pappe
Acrylic on cardboard
95 × 130 cm

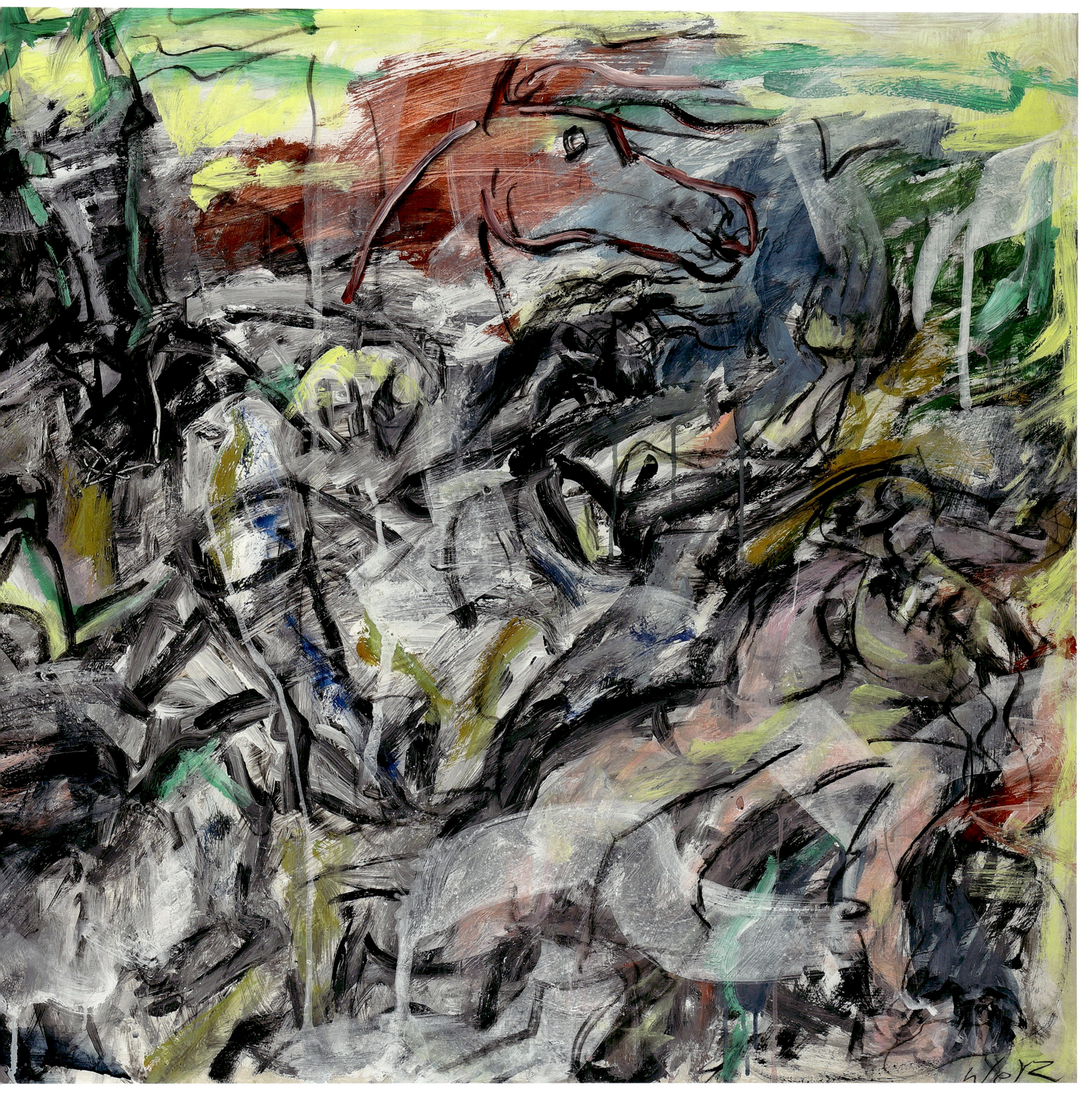

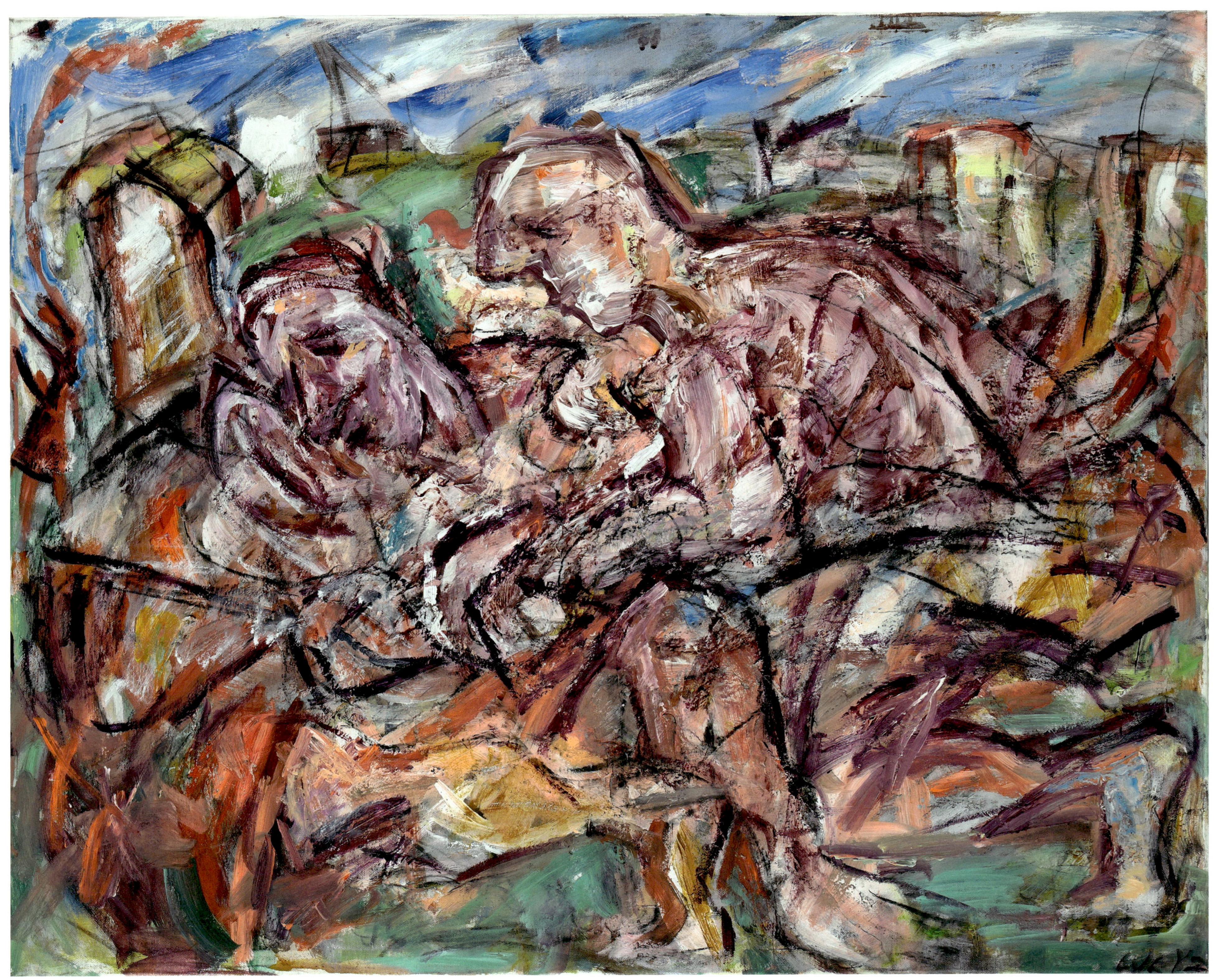

Liebespaar in Landschaft, 2007
Acryl auf Leinwand
Acrylic on canvas
80 × 100 cm

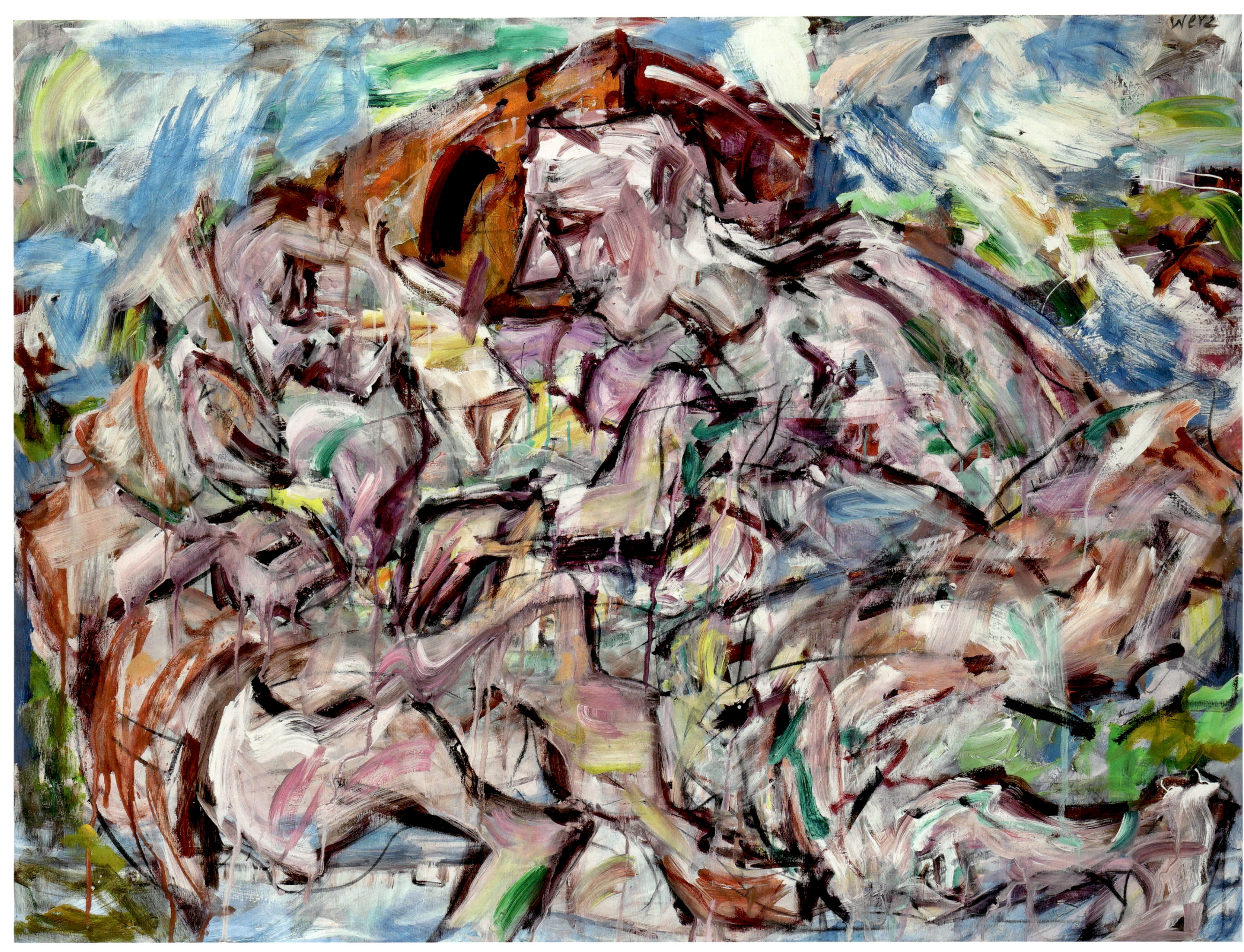

Liebespaar – Hommage à Rubens, 2009
Acryl auf Leinwand
Acrylic on canvas
120 × 160 cm

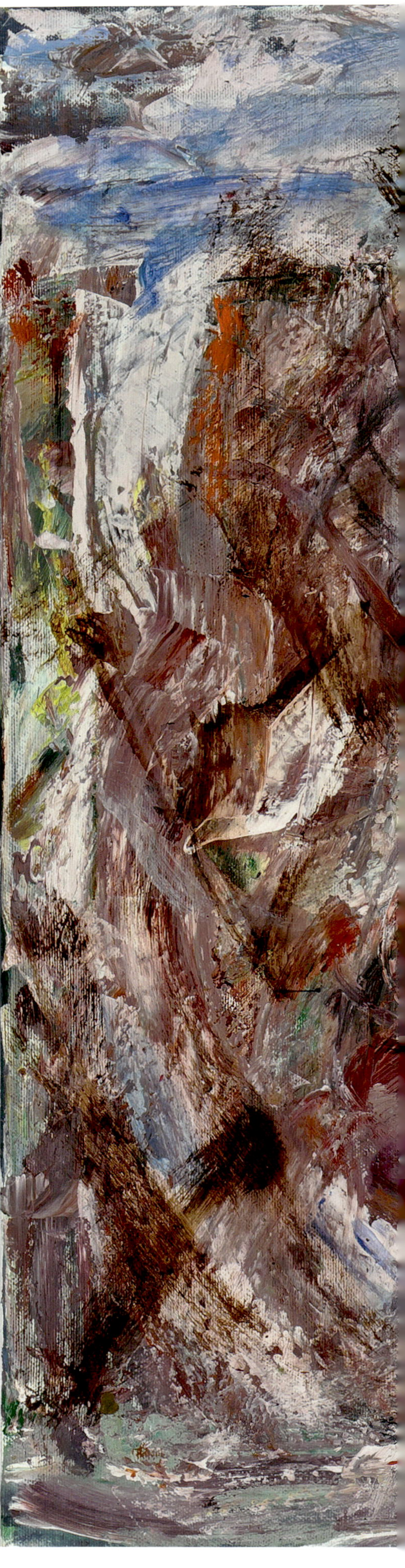

Liebespaar in Landschaft, 2007
Acryl auf Leinwand
Acrylic on canvas
60 × 80 cm

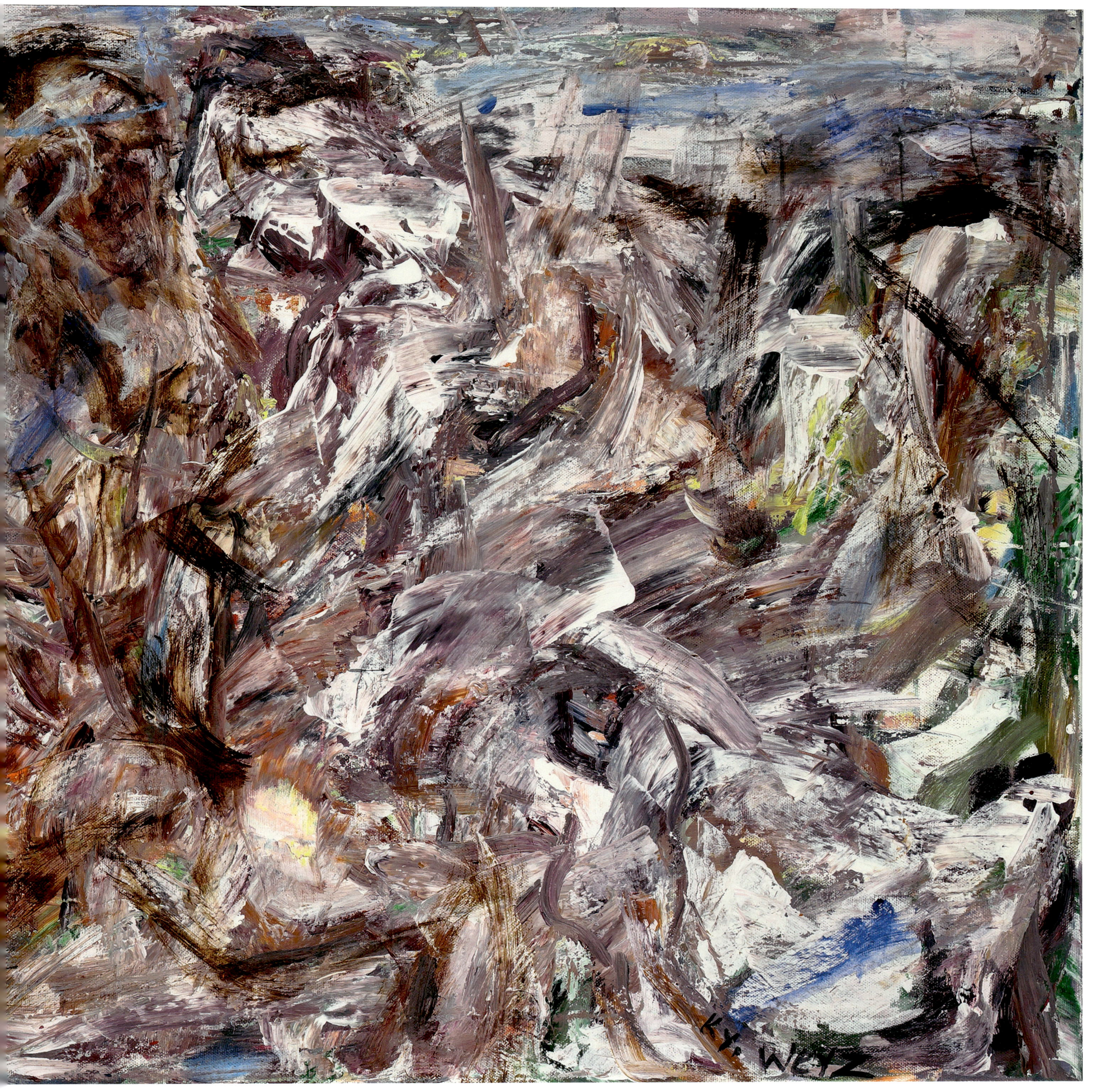

Aphrodite, 2007
Acryl auf Pappe
Acrylic on cardboard
80 × 100 cm

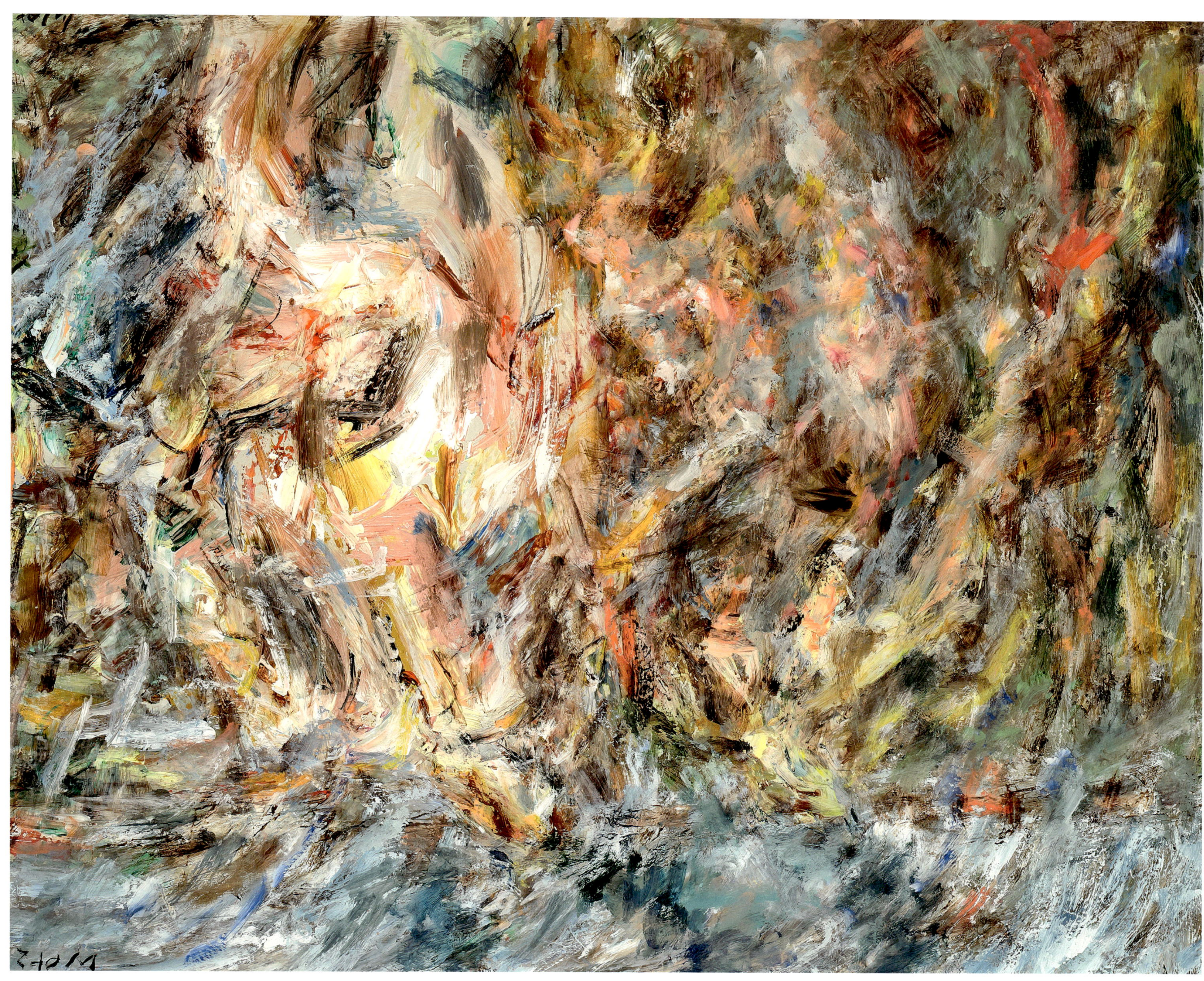

Über Nizza, 1990
Aquarell/Watercolor
40 × 30 cm

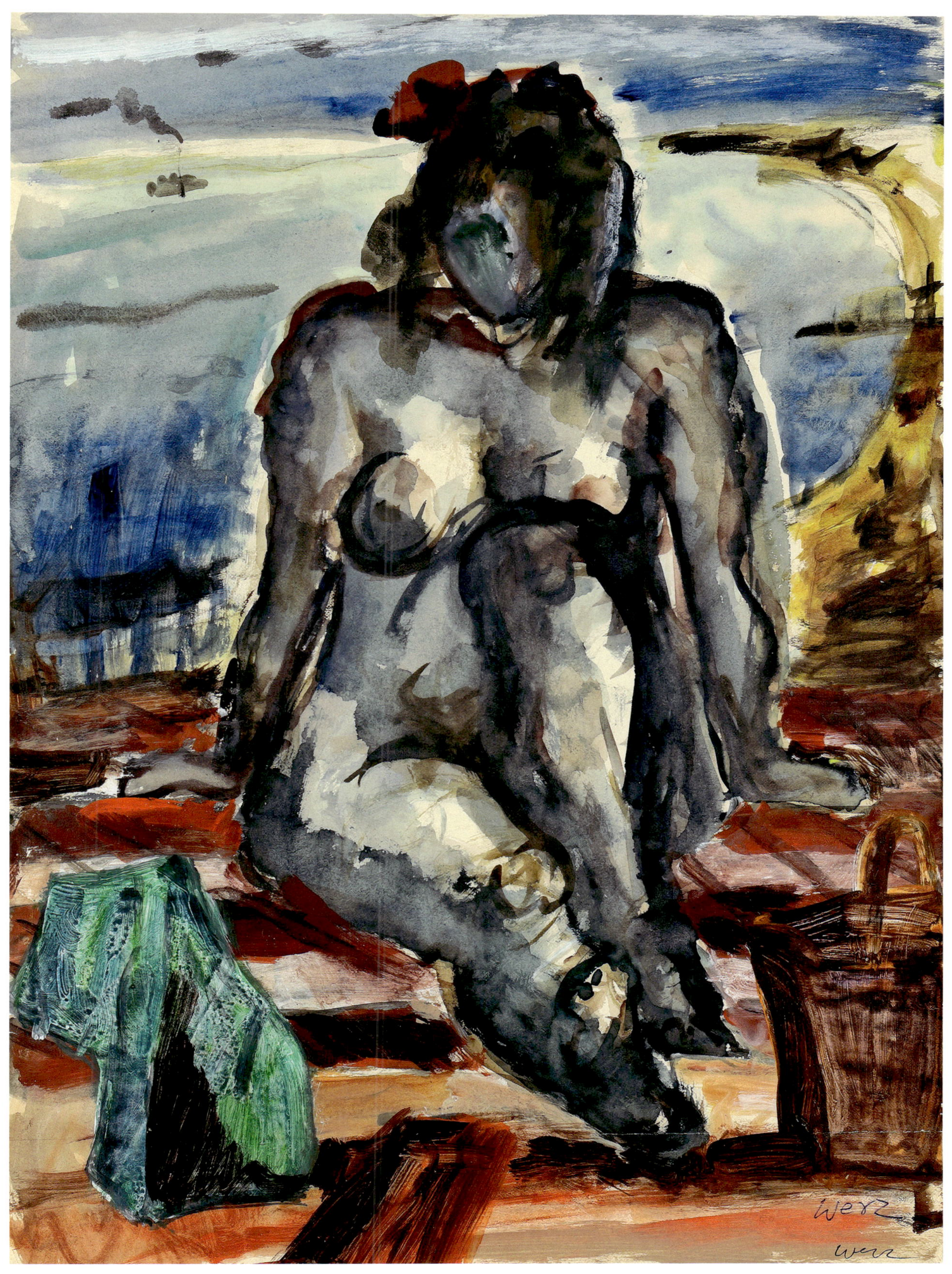

»Im Grunde möchte ich Skulpturen machen, die für eine
neue Art von Erfahrung stehen, die Möglichkeiten von
Skulptur eröffnen, die es so bislang nicht gab.«
Richard Serra

"Basically I would like to make sculptures which
stand for a new kind of experience, which open
up possibilities for sculpture which were simply
not there before."
Richard Serra

Mit gekreuzten Beinen Sitzende, 2000
Terrakotta/Terracotta
30 × 20 × 20 cm

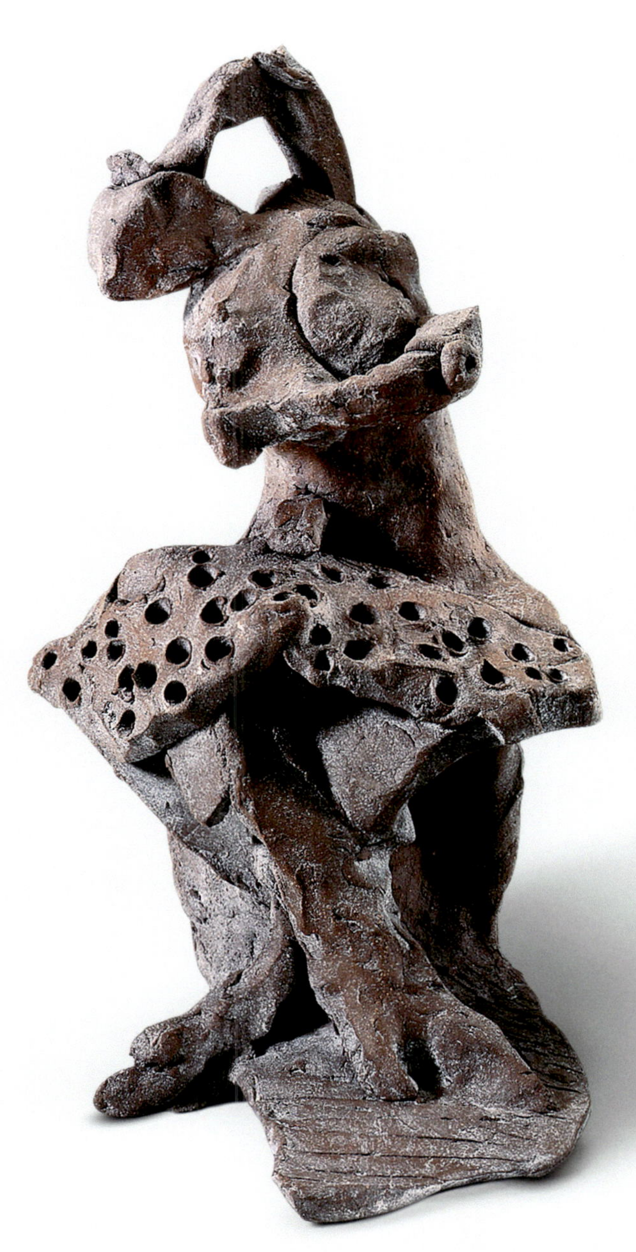

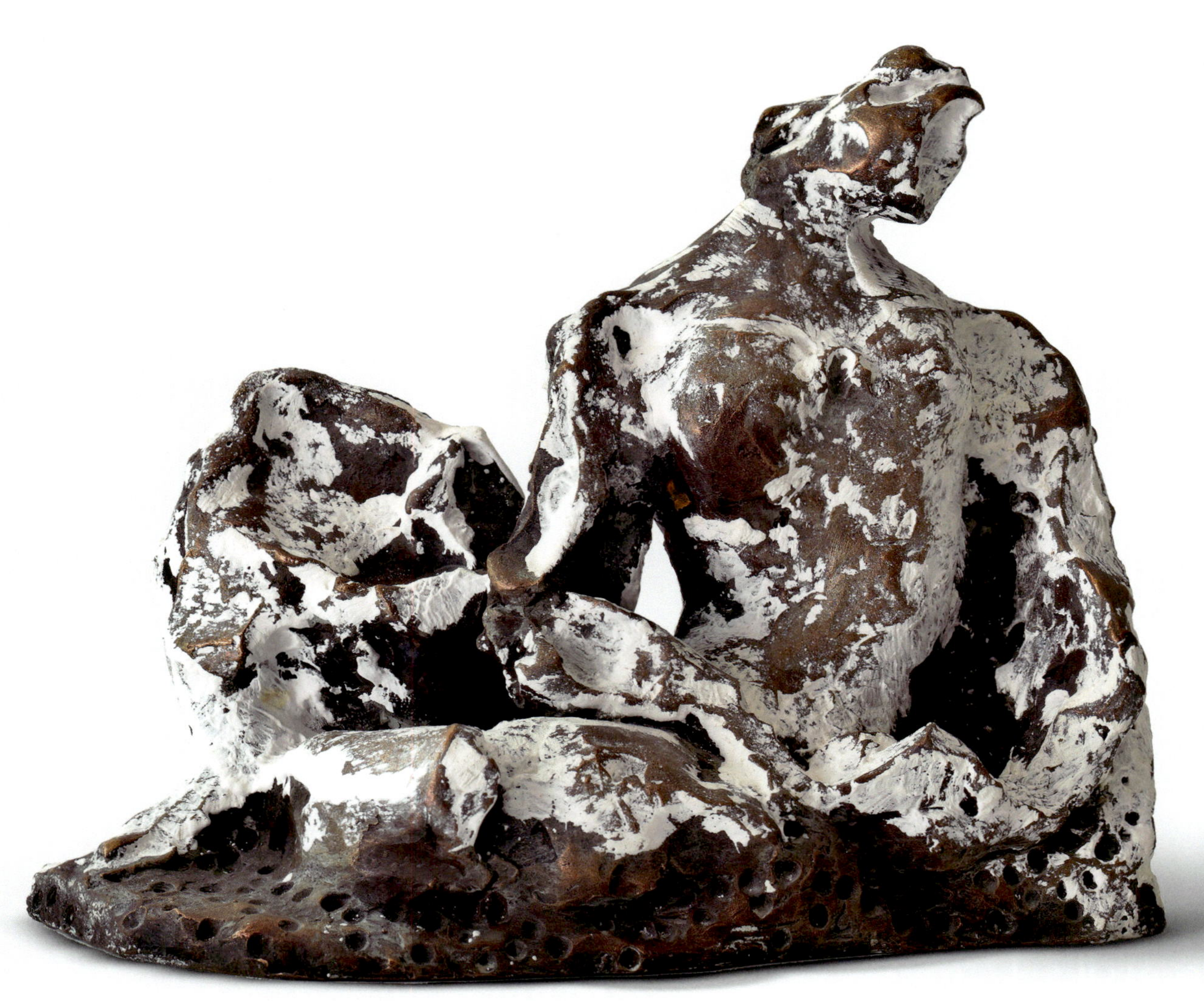

Lola, 2000
Bronze, bemalt
Bronze, painted
30 × 19 × 25 cm

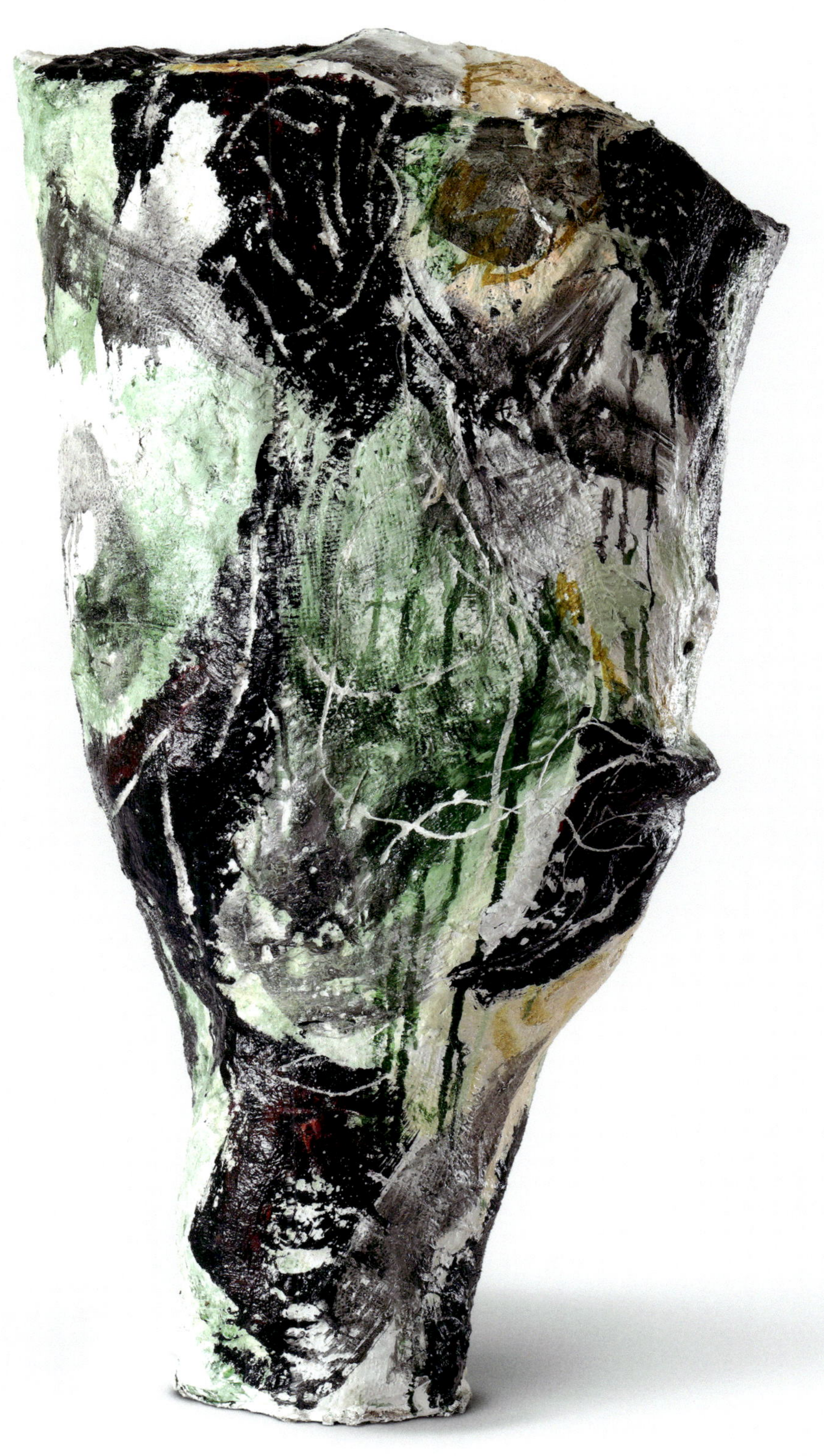

Objekt, 2010
Gips, Kunstharz
Plaster, resin
90 × 45 × 47 cm

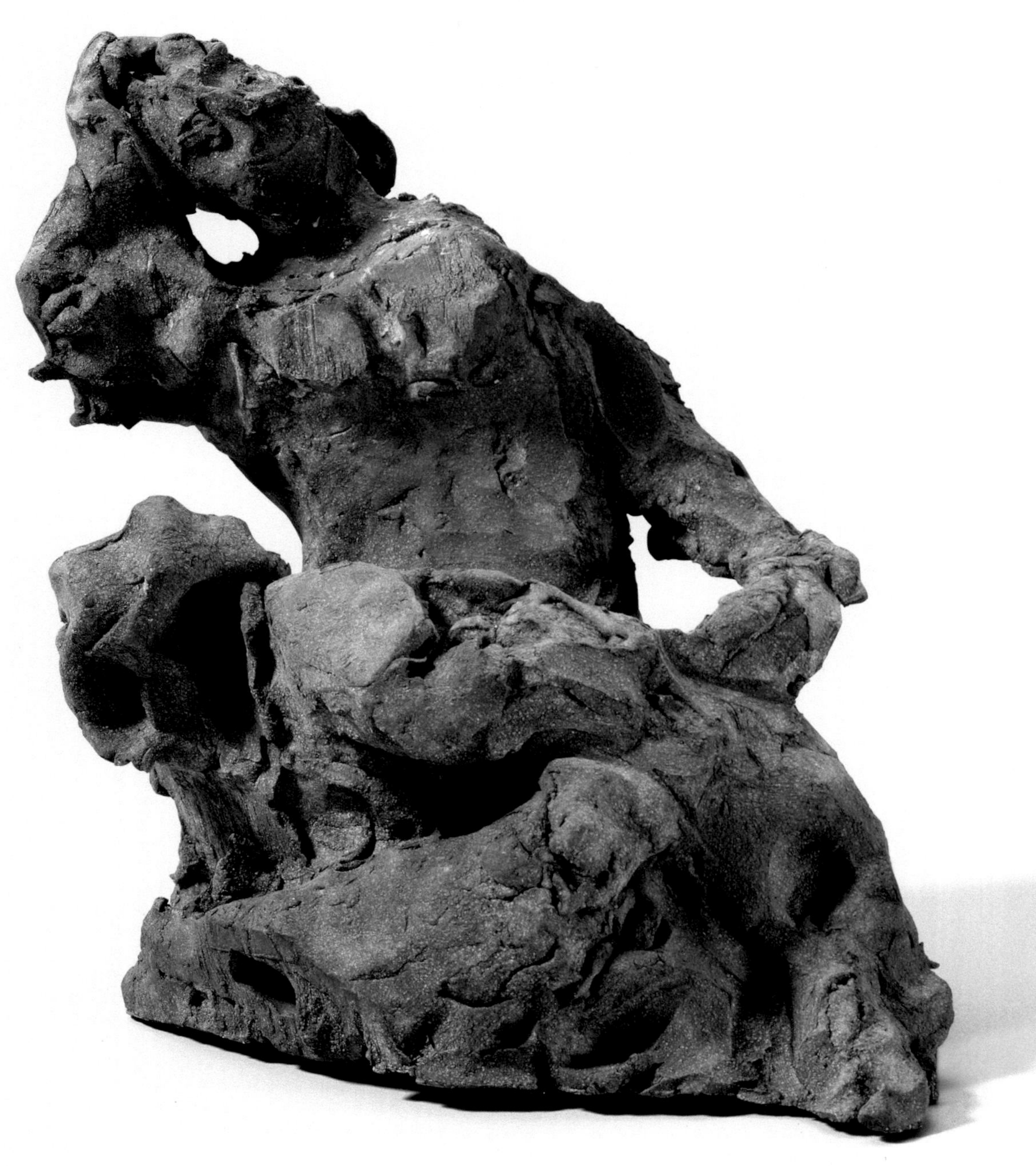

Traumtänzerin, 2000
Terrakotta/Terracotta
20 × 19 × 24 cm

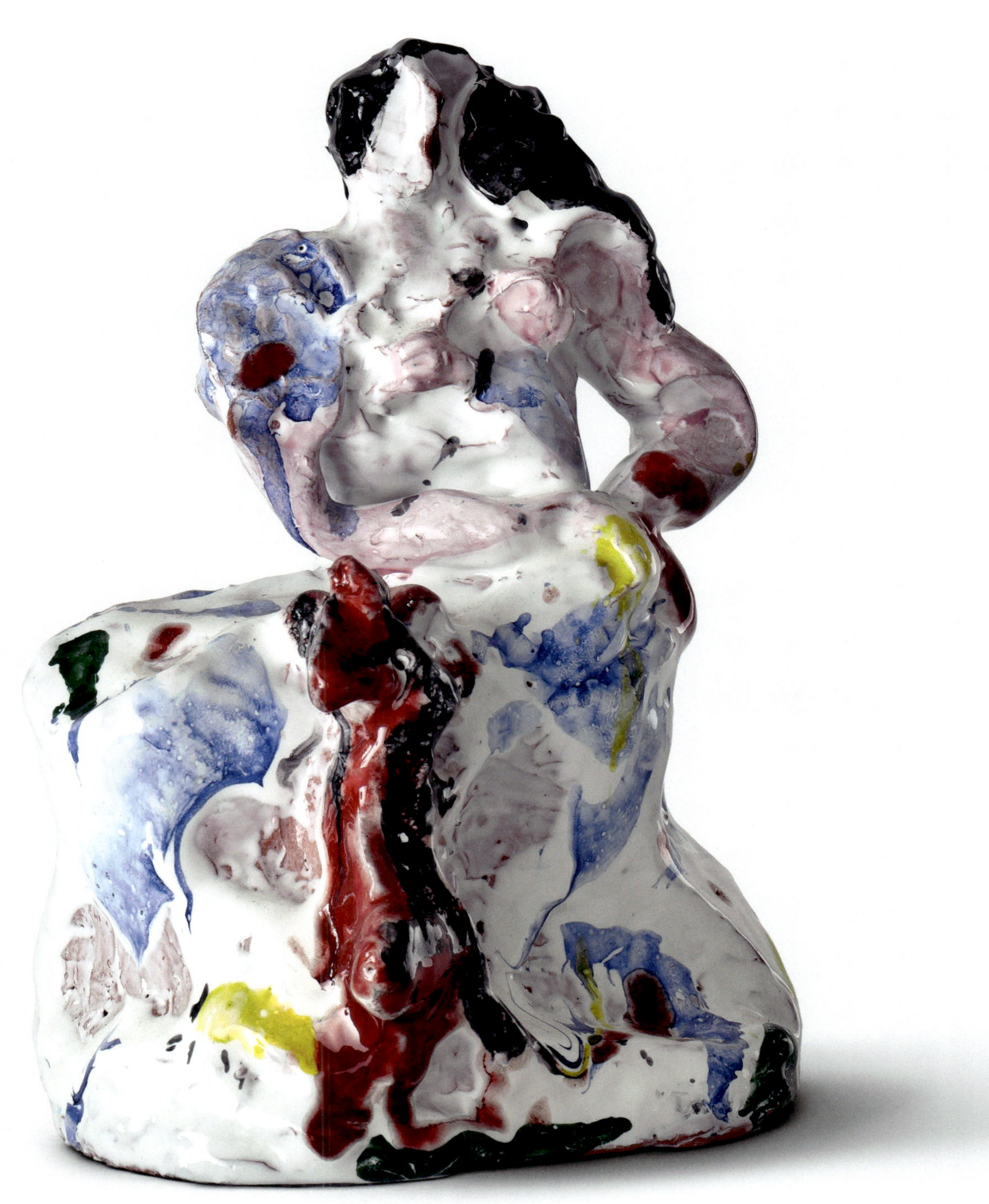

Tango, 2008
Terrakotta, glasiert
Terracotta, glazed
25 × 22 × 19 cm

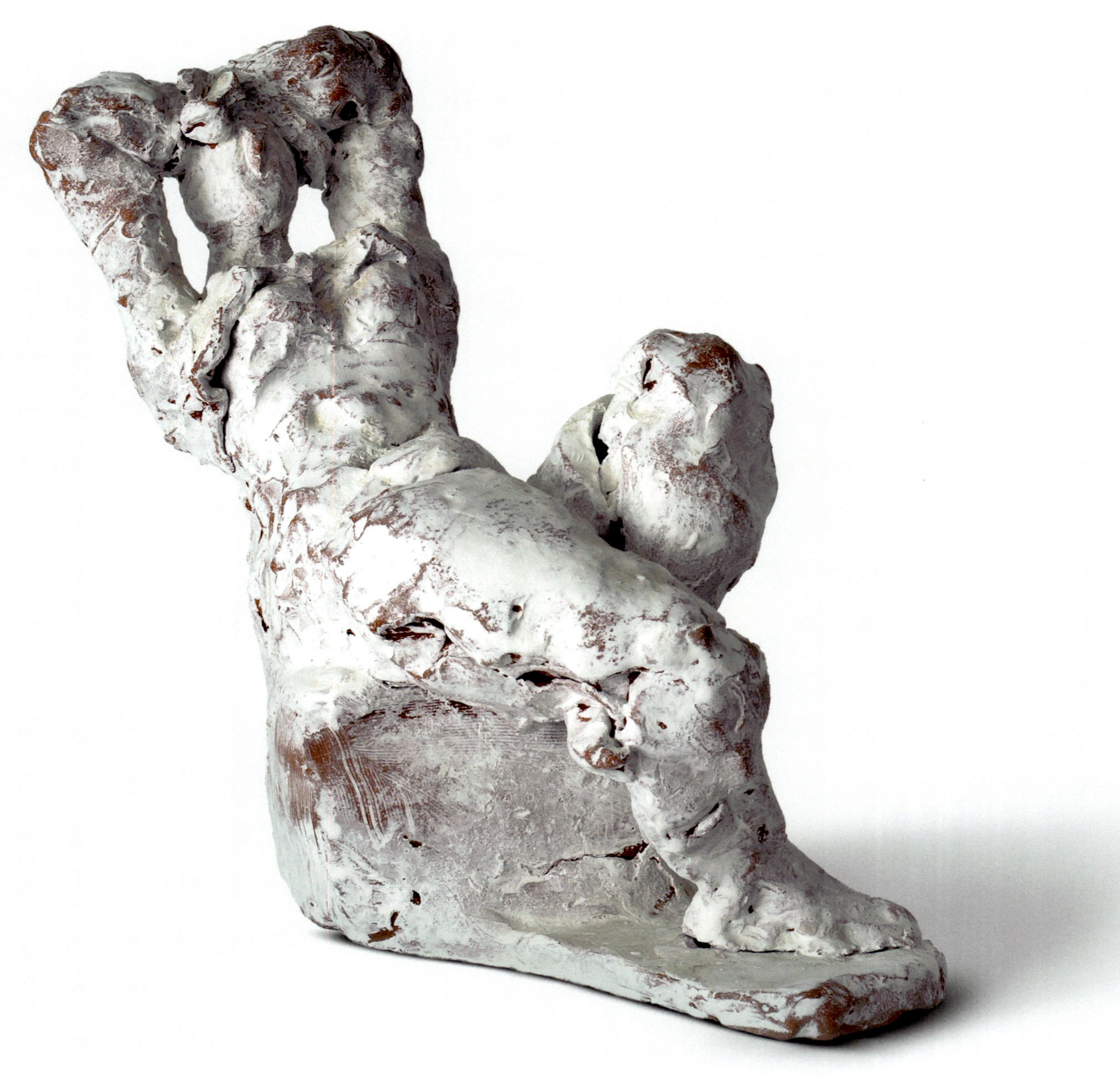

Rigoletta, 2009
Terrakotta, glasiert
Terracotta, glazed
30 × 27 × 25 cm

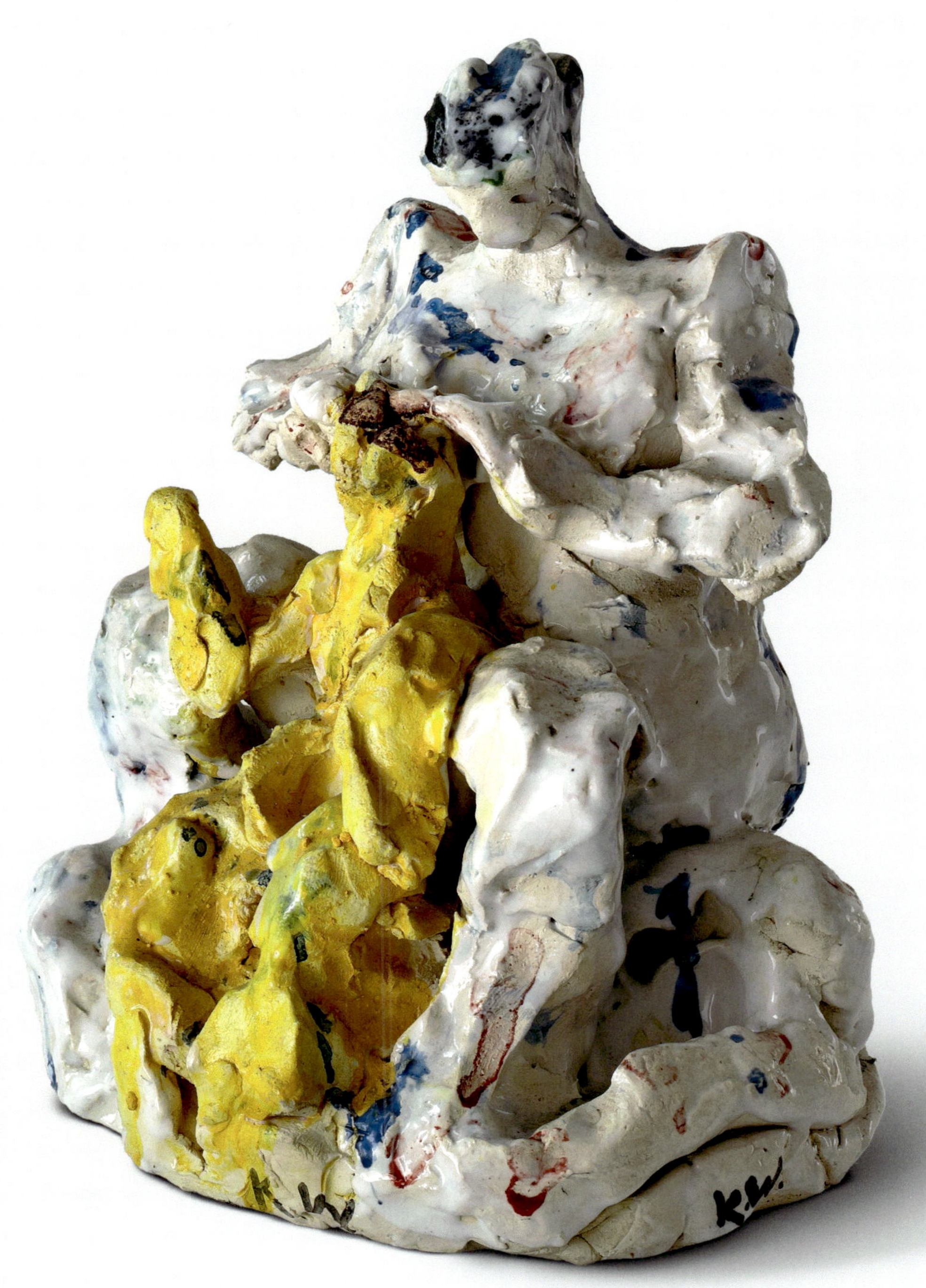

Mutter und Kind, 2007
Terrakotta, glasiert
Terracotta, glazed
30 × 20 × 19 cm

SCHÄUME
FOAMS

Kugeln, Bälle, Seifenblasen, Schäume und Träume. Kunst jongliert mit ihnen, denn sie bewegt sich in sphärischen Endlosräumen und ihre Zeit ist die der Ewigkeit, die kein Metronom mehr braucht. Im letzten Band seiner Sphärentrilogie entwirft der Philosoph Peter Sloterdijk eine »Aphrologie«, (das griechische »Aphros« bedeutet »Schaum«), eine Theorie von Leben und Gesellschaft im 21. Jahrhundert, sie sich »multifokal, multiperspektivisch und heterarchisch entfaltet«, also in simultanen, parallelen, nebeneinander funktionierenden und miteinander verwobenen Netzwerken.

Im »Schaumartigen« erkennt er das »Zukunftsträchtige«, im »Schwebenden«, »Fragilen« und »Unwiederholbaren« das neue Reale. Denn, so Sloterdijk: »Das gegenwärtige Zeitalter erfindet Verfahren, um Unerhörtes ins Register des Realen einzubauen, es schafft die Tasten, die den Benutzern leichten Zugriff auf bisher Unmögliches erlauben.«

Je weiter sich unsere Existenz also einerseits dank immer raffinierterer multidimensionaler Animationen virtualisiert, desto wesentlicher wird es, unsere nach wie vor sterbliche Körperlichkeit mit unseren unzähligen Schaumgeburten zu versöhnen.

Spheres, balls, soap bubbles, froth, and dreams. Art juggles with them, for it moves in spherical, infinite spaces, and its time is eternity, which requires no metronome. In the last volume of his Spheres trilogy, the philosopher Peter Sloterdijk develops an "aphrology" (coined from *aphros*, the Greek for "foam"), a theory of life and society in the 21st century, which "unfurls in a multifocal, multiperspectival, and heterarchical fashion," in effect in simultaneous networks woven together with each functioning in parallel. In the "foam-like" he recognizes the "promise of the future," while in the "floating," the "fragile," and the "unrepeatable" he recognizes the new reality. For, according to Sloterdijk's theory: "The current age invents processes to incorporate unheard things into the register of the real, it creates the keys that grant the user easy access to what was once the impossible." Thus, the more our real existence virtualizes itself thanks, in part, to ever more refined multidimensional animations, then the more essential it becomes to reconcile our corporeality, which remains as mortal as before, with our countless foam "births."

Frühling, 2009
Acryl auf Pappe
Acrylic on cardboard
150 × 109 cm

Sommer, 2009
Acryl auf Leinwand
Acrylic on canvas
150 × 109 cm

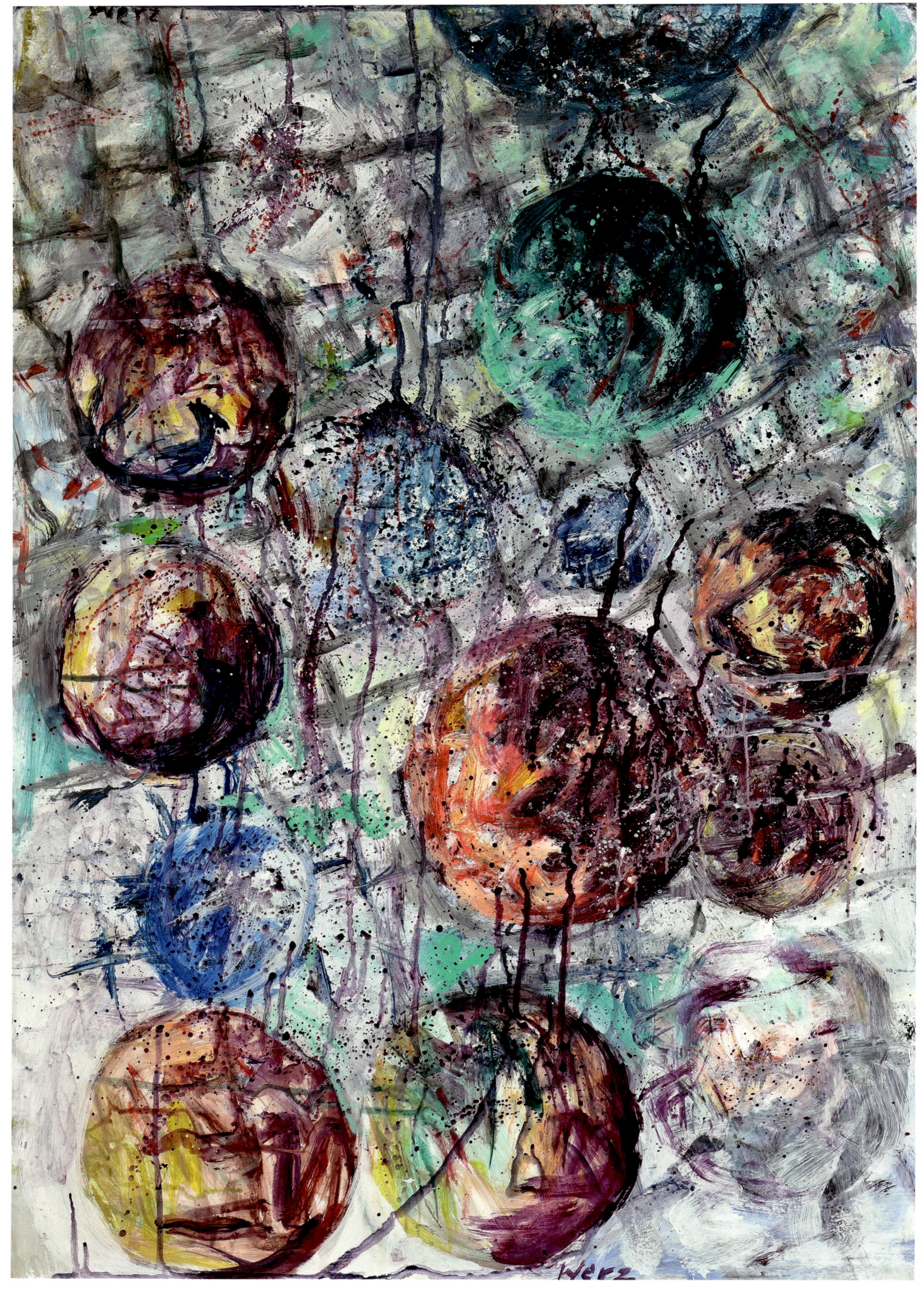
Werz

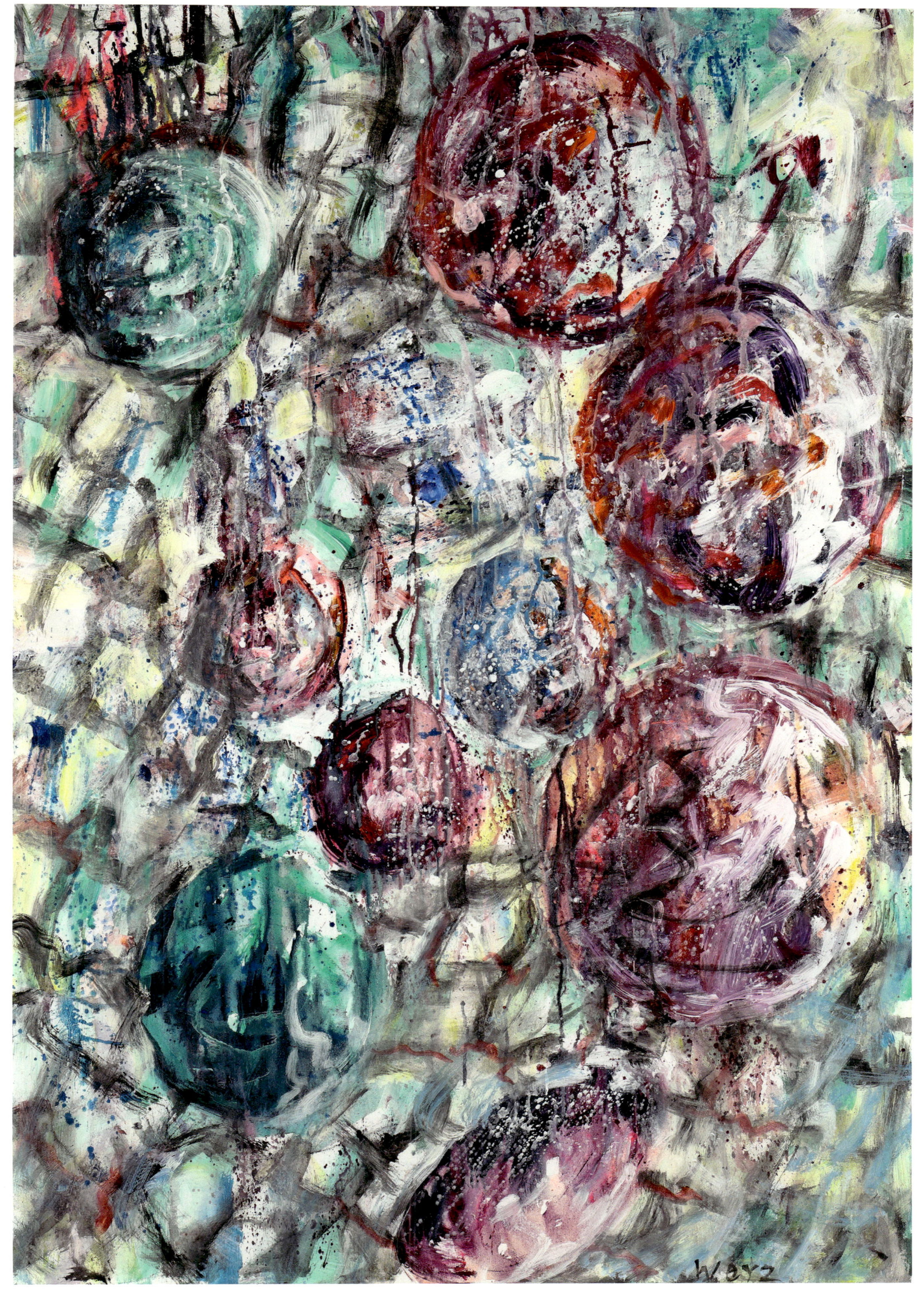
Weyz

1940 geboren/**born** in München/**Munich**
lebt und arbeitet in München/**lives and works in Munich**

1963–1966 Studium der Malerei und Graphik an der/**Studies of painting and graphic design at the**
École des beaux-arts, Genf/**Geneva**
1959–1961 Akademie für das Graphische Gewerbe, München/**Munich**

Einzelausstellungen/**Solo Exhibitions**
2011 Galerie Fred Jahn, München/**Munich**
2004 Rathausgalerie München/**Munich**
2002 Galerie Fred Jahn, München/**Munich**
2000 Galerie Fred Jahn, München/**Munich**
1997 Galerie Schäfer, Berlin
1996 Galerie Klewan, München/**Munich**, mit/**with** H.C. Artmann, Edgar Ende, Johanna Freise
1996 Galerie Klewan, München/**Munich**, mit/**with** Christian Ludwig Attersee und/**and** Johanna Freise
1995 Museum für angewandte Kunst (Muchina), St. Petersburg, mit/**with** Rudi Tröger
1995 Kunstsammlungen der Stadt Limburg, Rathaus/**City Hall**
1984 Galerie Baukunst, Köln/**Cologne**
1983 Galerie XX, Hamburg
1972 Galerie Michael Hasenclever, München/**Munich** und/**and** in 1975, 1978, 1980, 1983, 1984
1972 Galerie Tams, München/**Munich**

Gruppenausstellungen/**Group Exhibitions**
2007 Karl Bohrmann, Heinz Butz, Erwin Pfrang, Friedrich G. Scheuer, Rudi Tröger, Katharina von Werz, Karl & Faber,
     München/**Munich**, in Zusammenarbeit mit/**in collaboration with** Galerie Fred Jahn, München/**Munich**
2002 Sammlung Klewan in der Kestner-Gesellschaft, Hannover/**Hanover**
2002 *Jahresgaben,* Kestner-Gsellschaft, Hannover/**Hanover**
1994 Kunstverein Wasserburg, und/**and** in 1995, 1996, 1997
1993 *Positionen*, Galerie Fred Jahn, München/**Munich**
1973 Kunstverein Rosenheim
1971 *Kunstzone, Erste Freie Produzentenmesse,* St.-Jakobs-Platz, München/**Munich**, mit/**with** Günther Knipp,
     Friedrich G. Scheuer, Karl Bohrmann
1969 *Große Kunstausstellung*, Haus der Kunst, München/**Munich**, und/**and** in 1974, 1988, 1989

BIBLIOGRAFIE
BIBLIOGRAPHY

Kritiken und Berichte/**Reviews and articles**
1995 Peter M. Bode, in: *Münchner Abendzeitung*
1995 Vassilij Kosyrew, in: Ausst.–Kat./**Exh. cat.** Museum für angewandte Kunst (Muchina), St. Petersburg
1995 Dr. Carla Schulz-Hoffmann, in: Ausst.–Kat./**Exh. Cat.** Museum für angewandte Kunst (Muchina),
     St. Petersburg
1995 Dorothea Baumer, in: *Die Süddeutsche Zeitung*
1994 Carin Steinlechner, in: *Die Süddeutsche Zeitung*
1983 H.A., in: *Die Welt*
1975 Wolfgang Wunderlich, in: *Die Kunst*
1972 Dr. Doris Schmidt, in: *Die Süddeutsche Zeitung*

Kataloge/**Catalogues**
2008 *Katharina von Werz. Bilder und Arbeiten auf Papier 2000–2007,* Ausst.–Kat./**Exh. cat.** Galerie Fred Jahn,
     München/**Munich**
2004 *Katharina von Werz. Bilder, Zeichnungen, Skulpturen,* Ausst.–Kat./**Exh. cat.** Rathausgalerie der
     Landeshauptstadt München/**Munich**
1990 *Katharina von Werz. Bilder und Aquarelle,* Ausst.-Kat./**Exh. cat.** Galerie Michael Hasenclver, München/**Munich**
1983, 1980, 1978, 1975, 1972 *Katharina von Werz. Bilder und Zeichnungen,* Ausst.-Kat./**Exh. cat.** Galerie Michael
     Hasenclever, München/**Munich**

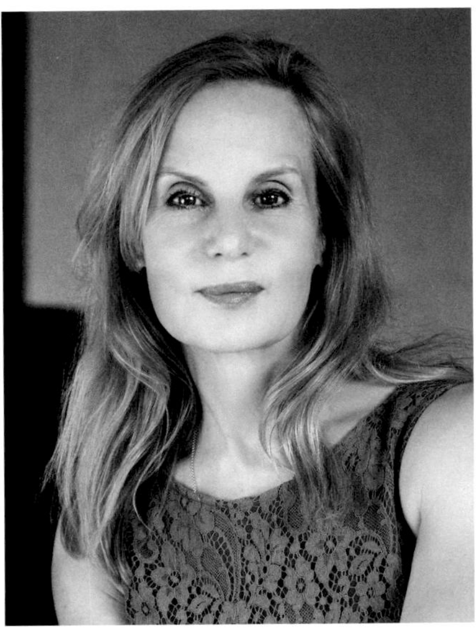

Die Kunsthistorikerin Dr. Eva Karcher (Dissertation über Otto Dix, *Eros und Tod im Werk von Otto Dix*) ist Autorin, Journalistin und Expertin im Bereich der zeitgenössischen Kunst, des Kunstmarkts und des Crossovers von Mode, Design, Lifestyle und Kunst. Seit vielen Jahren arbeitet sie für die Süddeutsche Zeitung und Vogue, außerdem veröffentlicht sie regelmäßig Beiträge in Welt am Sonntag, artinvestor, H.O.M.E, AD, Weltkunst und Monopol. Sie publiziert Bücher, ist an der Konzeptentwicklung von neuen Magazinen und Buchpublikationen beteiligt, kuratiert Ausstellungen und berät als Kunstmarktexpertin Sammler und Unternehmen. Zu ihren Publikationen zählen *Erlkönig/Prototypes* 2009 und *The New New* 2010.

Dr. Eva Karcher (dissertation on Otto Dix, *Eros and Death in the Work of Otto Dix*) is an author, journalist, and expert in the area of contemporary art, the art market, and cross-overs between fashion, design, lifestyle, and art. For many years she has worked for *Die Süddeutsche Zeitung* and *Vogue,* and is a frequent contributor to *Die Welt am Sonntag, artinvestor, H.O.M.E, AD, Weltkunst,* and *Monopol.* She is also the author of several books, is involved in drawing up concept plans for new magazines and book publications, curates exhibitions, and, in her capacity as an expert on the art market, provides a consultancy service to collectors and companies investing in art. Among the publications she has penned are *Erlkönig/Prototypes,* 2009, and *The New New,* 2010.

IMPRESSUM
COLOPHON

Herausgeberin und Autorin
Editor and Author
Eva Karcher

Gestaltung
Design
Bureau Mathias Beyer, Köln/**Cologne**

Redaktion
Editorial Coordination
DISTANZ, Frederik Kugler

Übersetzung
Translation
Lance Anderson

Production Management
Produktion
DISTANZ, Nicole Rankers

Bildbearbeitung
Image Editing
max-color, Berlin

Gesamtherstellung
Production
optimal media GmbH, Röbel/Müritz

Fotonachweis
Photo Credits
Walter Bayer, Elias Hassos, George Meister
sowie Fotos aus dem Privatbesitz der Künstlerin/**as well as photos from the artist's private archive**

© 2013 Katharina von Werz; für das Werk von/**for the work by** Chaim Soutine: VG Bild-Kunst, Bonn;
für das Werk von/**for the work by** Willem de Kooning: The Willem de Kooning Foundation, New York/
VG Bild-Kunst, Bonn; die Autorin/**the author** und/**and** DISTANZ Verlag GmbH, Berlin

Vertrieb
Distribution
GESTALTEN, Berlin
www.gestalten.com

ISBN 978-3-942405-82-9
Printed in Germany

Erschienen im
Published by
DISTANZ Verlag
www.distanz.de